Defend Us in Battle

Catholic Chaplains in the British Military

— JAMES HAGERTY & BARRY HUDD —

Sacristy
Press

Sacristy Press
PO Box 612, Durham, DH1 9HT

www.sacristy.co.uk

First published in 2024 by Sacristy Press, Durham

Sacristy Limited, registered in England & Wales, number 7565667

British Library Cataloguing-in-Publication Data
A catalogue record for the book is available from the British Library

ISBN 978-1-78959-358-7

The publishers gratefully acknowledge the generous support of:

The Roman Catholic Bishopric of the Forces
The Army Roman Catholic Trust
The Royal Air Force Roman Catholic Church Purposes Fund
The Royal Navy (Roman Catholic) Trust

Contents

Acknowledgements

We are particularly grateful to Bishop Paul Mason, Bishop Tom Burns and Bishop Richard Moth, present and past Bishops of the Forces, for their generous encouragement, assistance and support.

The following chaplains, serving and retired, have kindly shared their memories and provided much information and helpful advice: Mgr Stephen Alker, Fr James Allen, Fr Gordon Beattie OSB, Fr Simon Bradbury, Fr Daren Brown, Fr Tim Bywater, Fr Philip Carroll, Fr Mark Cassidy, Fr James Caulfield, Fr David Conroy, Mgr John Daly, Fr Ian Evans, Fr Michael Fava, Fr Bernard Funnell RIP, the Revd Neil Galloway, Fr Nick Gosnell, Fr Paschal Hanrahan, Canon Alfred Hayes, Fr John Humphreys, Mgr Richard Madders, Fr Paul McCourt, Mgr Andrew McFadden, Fr David McLean OP, Fr David Mead, Mgr Noel Mullin, Fr John Nelson, Fr P. J. O'Driscoll, Fr Tony Paris, the Revd John Power, Fr Leonard Purcell, Mgr Phelim Rowland, Fr Stephen Sharkey, the Revd David Skillen, Fr David Smith, Fr Philip Smith, Fr Ian Stevenson, Fr Alex Strachan, Mgr John Walsh, Fr Michael Weymes, Fr David Yates.

The following kindly supplied information, illustrations and advice: Mary Allen and Rebecca Somerset, Archivists, Jesuits in Britain; David Blake, Curator, Museum of the Royal Army Chaplains' Department; Margaret Bluett, Archivist, Spiritans Ireland; Damien Burke, Archivist, Irish Jesuit Archives; Paul Carr, Archivist, Diocese of Salford; Professor Judith Champ and Naomi Johnson, Oscott College, Birmingham; Bernie Deasy, Archivist, Delany Archive Trust, Carlow College; Jenny Delves, Archivist, Archdiocese of Southwark; Noelle Dowling, Archivist, Archdiocese of Dublin; Fr Richard Finn OP, Blackfriars Hall, Oxford; Robert Finnigan, Archivist, Diocese of Leeds; Fr Stewart Forster, Archivist, Diocese of Brentwood; Elena Leith, Archivist, Ushaw and Catholic Collections, Durham University; Jamie McGowan, Glasgow University Catholic Association; Catherine Mullan, Archivist, Oblates of Mary Immaculate, Ireland; Elizabeth Murphy-Sheehan; Dr Linda Parker; Dr Laura Patrick, Regimental Heritage Officer, Royal Irish Regiment Benevolent Fund; Anna Porter, Archivist, St Patrick's College, Maynooth; Michael Rawcliffe; Fr Nicholas Schofield and Judi McGinley, Archivists, Archives of the Archbishops of Westminster; Peter Sims-Coomber, Archivist, Archdiocese of Cardiff; Edward Walsh; Professor Maurice Whitehead, Director of Heritage Collections, Venerable English College, Rome; the Revd Edward Wills RN; Michael Winterbottom, Universe Publications; Miriam van der Molen, Archivist, Vincentians, Ireland. We are also most grateful to Dick Moreland for his technical help with the illustrations and to Diane Restall and Ian Crabtree, RC Pastoral Assistant, Royal Navy, for their assistance and for providing access to the Forces Bishopric's records.

Mgr Noel Mullin, Mgr Stephen Alker, Mgr John Daly and Dominic Crossley kindly read draft copies of this book. We are most grateful to them for their helpful comments. Any mistakes are the fault of the authors.

Finally, we thank Richard Rutherford Hilton and Natalie Watson of Sacristy Press for their professional advice and assistance.

Glossary

AChD   Army Chaplains' Department; Royal Army Chaplains' Department (RAChD) after 1919.

Archbishop   Senior priest responsible for a collection of dioceses, an archdiocese or province.

Bishop   Senior priest responsible for a collection of parishes.

Breviary   Book containing the daily service for the divine office, the official prayer of the Church, which the priest has to recite. It consists of psalms, readings and hymns that are said or sung at stated hours of the day.

Cardinal   A priest of high rank in the Catholic Church. An adviser to the Pope.

CBE   Commander of the British Empire.

CF   Post-nominal: Chaplain to the Forces.

Chaplain   A priest or deacon who serves a community which is not organized as a church. A chaplain may serve a military unit, a ship, a prison, a hospital, or a school.

Chaplain to the Forces   Minister of Religion commissioned by the monarch to provide for the spiritual wellbeing of service personnel and their families.

Chaplaincy   The community of worshippers served by one or more chaplains.

Clergy/clerics   Body of priests/deacons.

CM   Congregation of the Mission (a male religious order). Priests are Vincentians with the post-nominal CM.

CND   Campaign for Nuclear Disarmament.

Cong. Orat.   Congregation of the Oratory (a male religious order). Priests are Oratorians with the post-nominal Cong. Orat.

CSSp   Holy Ghost Fathers (a male religious order). Priests are
                Spiritans with the post-nominal CSSp.

CSsR   Congregation of the Most Holy Redeemer (a male
                religious order). Priests are Redemptorists with the post-
                nominal CSsR.

Deacon   An ordained minister in the Catholic Church.

Diocese   Geographical area of parishes or missions under the
                care of a bishop.

District   A Catholic ecclesiastical area into which England,
                Wales and Scotland were divided, for example London
                District and Highland District. Under the care of a Vicar
                Apostolic.

Episcopal   Relating to the office of a bishop.

Episcopus Castrensis   Bishop responsible for military chaplains
                and the spiritual life of a military community. Appointed
                by the Pope. He is accorded three-star military status.

Fr   Abbreviation of 'Father'; the title accorded to a Catholic
                priest.

Hierarchy   Ecclesiastical organizational structure.

Holy See   Diocese of Rome, whose bishop, the Pope, is head of the
                Church on earth.

In partibus infidelium   Latin term meaning "in the lands of the
                unbelievers". Words added to the name of an extinct
                episcopal see conferred on a non-residential or titular
                bishop.

Mass   The most important celebration in the Catholic Church,
                in which Catholics recall the Last Supper of Christ.
                Gifts of bread and wine, when consecrated by the priest,
                become the Body and Blood of Christ. Also called the
                "Eucharist".

MBE   Member of the British Empire.

Liturgy   A church service. The rites and actions of the priest and
                the responses of the congregation.

Mercenary   A private individual who joins a military conflict for
                personal profit.

Monsignor   An honorific address or title for priests. Abbreviated as "Mgr". Part of the Papal Household.

OBE   Order of the British Empire.

Officiating Chaplain   A civilian priest serving a military unit.

OMI   Oblate of Mary Immaculate (a male religious order). Priests are Oblates with the post-nominal OMI.

OP   Order of Preachers (a male religious order). Priests are Dominicans with the post-nominal OP.

OSB   Order of St Benedict (a religious order). Priests are Benedictines with the post-nominal OSB.

Padre   Popular title given to a forces chaplain.

Pallotine   A member of the Society of the Catholic Apostolate (a male religious order). Priests are sometimes called Pallotines with the post-nominal SCA.

Parish   A geographical division within a diocese.

Pastoral work   Counselling, advising, comforting personnel.

PRCC   Principal Roman Catholic Chaplain.

Priest   Someone ordained (formally appointed) to minister within the Church. His duties are: to proclaim the Word of God, to celebrate Mass, to administer the sacraments, and to exercise a role of leadership.

RAF   Royal Air Force.

Regular priest   A priest of a religious order or a religious institute rather than a diocese.

RM   Royal Marines.

RN   Royal Navy.

Sacraments   The Catholic Church recognizes seven sacraments based on the teachings of Jesus Christ. They are a framework for daily life and important events. The sacraments are the Eucharist (the Mass), Baptism, Confirmation, Marriage, Anointing of the Sick, Reconciliation (or Confession), Holy Orders (Ordination).

Secular priest   A priest of a diocese rather than a religious order.

SM   Society of Mary (a male religious order). Priests are Marists with the post-nominal SM.

Society of Jesus Society of Jesus (a male religious order). Priests are
Jesuits with the post-nominal SJ.

Superior   Senior priest or cleric of a religious order.

Vatican City An independent city state within Rome. The Pope's
residence and ecclesiastical headquarters of the Roman
Catholic Church.

Illustrations

Unless otherwise specified, images are taken from the Archives of the Military Ordinariate.

Every effort has been made to trace appropriate copyright owners. The authors and publishers would be pleased to hear from those who hold copyright where due acknowledgement has not been made.

1. Bishop Paul Mason, Roman Catholic Bishop of the Forces
2. Fr Henry Morse SJ: Chaplain and martyr (Jesuits in Britain Archives)
3. Fr Alexander Cameron SJ before the Battle of Prestonpans
4. Bishop Alexander MacDonell: Fencible chaplain
5. Crimean War medals of Fr Joseph O'Dwyer CF (Royal Army Chaplains' Museum)
6. Bishop Robert Brindle: Padre to Prelate
7. Fr Swarbreck, chaplain during the Boer War (Courtesy of the Trustees of Ushaw College)
8. Fr Peter Grobel: Naval chaplain (Salford Diocesan Archives)
9. Fr William Keatinge CF: Great War chaplain
10. Fr William Finn CF: Gallipoli casualty (Courtesy of the Trustees of Ushaw College)
11. Fr Stewart Phelan OMI: Naval casualty at Jutland (OMI Archives Anglo-Irish Province)
12. Fr William Flynn CF: Chaplain in Africa (Philip Murphy)
13. Mgr Henry Beauchamp RAF: RAF pioneer
14. Mgr John Coghlan (front row, centre) with Senior Catholic Army Chaplains, 1940
15. Fr Thomas Holland RN (right): Naval wartime chaplain (Salford Diocesan Archives)
16. Fr Kevin Whelan CSSp CF: Prisoner of War (Spiritan Archives, Ireland)

List of tables

Foreword

Stories that can so easily remain hidden from our history books and sit outside our collective memory are those of the contribution made by our brave and faithful military chaplains during periods of war.

In this eye-opening and intriguing account, we are given insight into the work and ministry of Catholic chaplains over the past four centuries. Those men and women who place themselves in harm's way for the protection and security of our nation, for the preservation of peace, are owed a special care by the Church. Their experiences can present an existential challenge, put great stress on family life and raise many questions of faith, all in a context of uncertainty. It is into that space that our chaplains have brought hope through Word, Sacrament and through their very presence as they serve those who serve us.

As you read this book, I hope you will feel inspired by the faith and courage of our chaplains and perhaps be encouraged in your own life of faith, which may also be embattled.

Of the many chaplains who made the ultimate sacrifice in carrying out their duty, you can read about Fr Gerry Weston, the last Catholic priest killed in service—by an IRA bomb in Aldershot in 1972. Yet he is but one of 74 Catholic chaplains, 35 of whom were Irish, to have died on active service. Their stories of bravery may well sound like the stuff of a blockbuster movie, but many of us know little about them.

Of note also is the great contribution of Irish priests serving as chaplains in the British military, a fact brought into sharp focus with the case for canonization of Fr Willie Doyle SJ, whose own story is worthy of a book by itself. And even today Irish priests continue to put themselves forward for this ministry, this "calling within a calling", as they support the mission of the Bishopric of the Forces.

I commend this book to you not only as a compelling witness to military history but also as a witness of faith, a witness to the men and women of our Armed Forces by some of the best and bravest Catholic priests and deacons the Church has to offer.

+ Bishop Paul Mason
Bishop of the Forces

Figure 1: Bishop Paul Mason, Roman Catholic Bishop of the Forces

"Defend Us in Battle"

*The origins and development of Catholic
chaplaincy in the British military*

Ministers of religion appointed to care for the religious and spiritual needs of British armed forces personnel are officially termed "chaplains". Service personnel may refer to chaplains as "Sir" or "Padre". The common appellation "padre" derives from its use by British troops in India when referring to Catholic missionaries who acted as their chaplains. In the Royal Navy, chaplains are sometimes referred to as "bish". In this book, "chaplain" and "padre" are interchangeable. For Catholics, the term "padre" equates with "Father", the name traditionally given to all Catholic priests.

Although they concentrate primarily on ministering to the religious and spiritual needs of the armed forces, contemporary chaplains also have other functions in that they contribute to the mental health, moral wellbeing and social welfare of service personnel and their dependants. They may also fulfil an educational and catechetical function with young servicemen and servicewomen and also with service families.

According to one theory, "chaplain" derives from the Latin word *capa* or *capella*, signifying the cloak of the former soldier, St Martin of Tours (316–97). As a soldier, Martin cut his cloak in two so that a beggar might be clothed. Legend had it that the cloak was miraculously restored to its former state and that Martin was baptized as a result of the miracle. After St Martin's death, the restored *capa* was venerated as a relic of the saint and carried into battle by successive Kings of France. In the field, the *capa* was enshrined in a tent and its guardians were named *capellani*. Another theory is that the word *capellani* derives from those who guarded the chapel (*capella*), or tent, erected to cover an altar in the field and before which soldiers would pray and worship.

St Augustine of Hippo (354–430) understood that armed conflict was a manifestation of human behaviour and his theory of the "Just War" related to moral principles which could be applied to judge the legitimacy, or not, of military action. If certain criteria were met, then it was morally justifiable for men to take up arms at the behest of a legitimate authority. St Thomas Aquinas (1225–74) further developed this theory and he also advocated that priests be allowed to provide spiritual and pastoral care to those involved in legitimately waging war. In short, a war must be in a just cause, a last resort, declared by a proper authority, possess a right intention and with the end being proportionate to the means which are used.

From its earliest existence, the Catholic Church has had to consider and judge the legitimate use of force. The Church and Christian states in concert have frequently been associated with war for political and religious motives and together have persuaded men to go into battle. In such cases, the Church has offered combatants the protection afforded by their faith and the efficacy of the sacraments. As Sir John Smyth wrote:

> From time immemorial it has been recognized that religion, and religious faith, was a powerful factor in helping men to fight nobly for their country; it was important that they should believe in the justice of their cause and that they should feel that God was on their side.

The presence of a priest, however, was necessary for sacraments to be dispensed.

The Church built on the Old Testament tradition of invoking God's blessing on a just but warlike cause, especially on those about to fight and die for Israel. The Book of Deuteronomy refers to the conduct of war and the role of the priest invoking God's blessing and protection:

> And when the battle is now at hand, the priest shall stand before the army and shall speak to the people in this manner. Hear, O Israel, you join battle this day against your enemies: let not your

heart be dismayed, be not afraid, do not give back, fear ye them
not: because the Lord your God is in the midst of you, and will
fight for you against your enemies, to deliver you from danger.
(20:2–4, Douay–Rheims)

The Bible refers to battles between the Israelites and their enemies, of
priests blessing men and weapons, and of prayers for victory, but it also
refers to praying for vengeance and the destruction of the foe. There are
also references to soldiers guarding holy places and therein the honour
of God. In Israel's case, war frequently had a religious purpose as well
as being a fight for ethnic survival, and a priestly presence among men
almost perennially under arms was important.

Religion was integral to the life of the Roman army. Altars were
dedicated to pagan deities, sacrifices were offered for protection and
success in battle and shrines were erected in camps and garrisons to
house flags and standards and important military emblems. In various
ways, leaders and men assumed the function of a priest in order to satisfy
the spiritual needs of others. Christian military chaplaincy in the Roman
army, however, can be traced back to the Emperor Constantine, who
took his victory at the Battle of the Milvian Bridge (312) as a sign of
divine favour on his military exploits and was consequently converted to
Christianity. His motto, under a cross on a military banner—*In hoc signo
vinces*—"In this sign you will conquer"—was later adopted as the motto
of the British Army Chaplains' Department. On campaign, Constantine
erected a tent to serve as a chapel and took with him priests and deacons
who were responsible for religious services. Such provision, however, did
not extend to all army units and chaplaincy was certainly not formalized.

In feudal times, when landholding was closely linked to the provision
of military service, churchmen, who were usually aristocrats, powerful
landowners and political figures, often donned armour and led men
in battle. It was an ambiguous position for ecclesiastics as the Church
forbade the carrying of arms and weapons and the shedding of blood by
priests. Yet Anglo-Saxon churchmen were not confined to religious duties
and some actively participated in warfare. St Bede (673–735) wrote of
clergy playing leading parts in battles in the British Isles. The Emperor
Charlemagne (742–814) decreed that before a battle "bishops, counts,

and abbots shall oversee their own men and shall come on the day of the appointed muster and there show how they are prepared". In 1066, King Harold and Duke William of Normandy were served by chaplains at the Battle of Hastings. *The Deeds of King William*, written by the duke's chaplain, William of Poitiers, recounted details of the battle in which Bishop Odo of Bayeux, brother of Duke William, carried a mace so not to transgress papal instructions that priests should not carry swords or shed blood.

When the Scots invaded northern England in 1138, Archbishop Thurstan of York promised English troops that "the priests of his diocese, bearing crosses, should march with them to battle with their parishioners, and that he also, God willing, designed to be present with his men in the engagement". In the English civil war (1135–54) between King Stephen and Empress Matilda, it was reported that some bishops, carrying swords and wearing magnificent suits of armour, rode out in battle and took their share of the spoils. A Synod of Westminster decreed in 1175 that members of the clergy were forbidden to engage in war but, according to Sir John Smyth, up to 1300, "No war was embarked upon, nor was any army raised in England, which had not among its leaders many of the foremost ecclesiastics in the land." During the aftermath of the Peasants' Revolt of 1381, Bishop Henry Despenser of Norwich, "armed as a knight, accoutred with a metal helmet and a strong hauberk impregnable to arrows and wielding a substantial two edged sword", rounded up and dealt with insurgents.

The Crusades, those great military and religious movements of the Middle Ages, were led as much by prelates as by secular nobles and with them went priests to preach and provide sacramental and other liturgical necessities. As the Cross signified Constantine's religious affiliation, so too did the Cross signify the religious nature of the Crusades.

A succession of medieval papal bulls forbade clerics from carrying arms and, as David Bachrach has written, Bishop Ivo of Chartres (1040–1116) clearly defined the priestly rather than military role of chaplains. They were to celebrate Mass for military forces in the field, hear confessions and assign penances, give special care to the wounded and dying through the sacrament of Extreme Unction, and ensure Christian burials for those killed in battle or who died of wounds. Pastoral care was to be exercised among the troops, sacred relics were to be protected and prayers offered for the success of arms, but the chaplain's sacramental role had priority.

When not active in battle, churchmen often used their spiritual authority to preach a cause, raise morale and calm nerves by absolving soldiers from their sins and by the promise of eternal life. At the Battle of Lincoln in 1217, the Papal Legate, Guala of Bicchieri, addressed Earl William Marshal's men "who had undertaken to assist in this war", declaring that

> he, by the power granted to him from the omnipotent God and the apostolic see, granted full pardon for their sins, of which they had made true confession, and as a reward to the just he promised the reward of eternal salvation. Then, after all had received absolution and the blessing of God, they flew to arms, mounted their horses at once and struck their camp rejoicing.

When the battle was over, the Papal Legate proceeded to excommunicate those of Marshal's forces who had looted and ransacked the city.

Priests of lesser ecclesiastical standing often adopted the role of non-combatant army chaplains. Smyth notes that at the Battle of Crécy (1346) in the Hundred Years War there were three classes of paid army chaplains. The first class ministered to the king, and his retinue and household, the second class served the barons and earls and their men, while the third class served the Welsh nobles and their soldiers. Before the Battle of Agincourt (1415), it was recorded that everyone in the English camp who had not "cleansed his conscience" by confession "took on the armour of penitence" and "there was no lack of priests to officiate" and bless the ranks. King Henry V heard Mass, received Holy Communion and invoked the love of Jesus "to maintain the right of England today". Likewise, priests attended to the spiritual needs of the French armies and Joan of Arc had her own personal chaplain. Two priests were present at her execution.

In the European Wars of Religion, military chaplaincy embarked on a new stage of development and it is from this period that this book traces and illustrates its growth. The Jesuits of late-sixteenth- and seventeenth-century Europe provided a ministry to soldiers through the *missio castrensis* (or missions to the camps) of English, Spanish and Irish regiments serving on the continent. Many soldiers were mercenaries and chaplains faced the daunting task of ministering to men of many languages, cultures and religious allegiances. A soldier's life was brutal and, as Hugh Aveling commented, "The military profession seemed to foster a certain indifference to religious niceties."

The Jesuit ministry was characterized by priests praying for protection and the success of arms before a battle, evangelizing men in camps and conducting their sacerdotal duties among soldiers actually engaged in combat. In this book, the ministries of Henry Morse SJ and Peter Wright SJ are cited as examples. The English Civil War, with opposing Parliamentary and Royalist armies, divided the country on confessional as much as on political grounds and chaplains were in the front line of battle for both sides. In the professional army of the Catholic King James II, Catholic priests, nominally under the authority of Fr Edward Cary, conducted a limited and unofficial ministry in the camp and on the battlefield, while in the Jacobite rebellions priests such as Fr Allan MacDonald and his confrères acted as chaplains.

Despite penal legislation designed to eradicate Catholicism, the faith survived and large numbers of Catholics continued to join the British armed forces. The provision of Catholic military chaplains throughout the eighteenth century, however, was deemed unnecessary by the government. Catholics soldiers were compelled to attend compulsory Anglican church services or, as had become the norm by the end of the eighteenth century, were marched by Catholic officers to nearby Catholic chapels. The establishment of the Army Chaplains' Department in 1796, intended to address the poor quality of paid but largely absentee Anglican regimental chaplains, was of no benefit to Catholic soldiers. The new arrangements were reserved for Anglican divines, and the ministry of Fr Sandy MacDonell to the Glengarry Fencibles in the late eighteenth and early nineteenth centuries was all the more unique in its origins, nature and achievements.

Catholic Emancipation enabled Catholics to hold commissions in the British army, but it was the battlefield ministries and deaths of Fr John Wheble and other chaplains in the Crimea and of Fr Patrick Fairhurst and other chaplains in the Indian Mutiny that paved the way for Catholic clergymen to become commissioned army chaplains in 1858. The traditionally large numbers of Irish Catholics in the army also lent weight to calls for Catholic chaplains. But despite persistent agitation and frequent petitions by bishops and English and Irish politicians, Catholics had to wait until 1943 for their priests to be appointed as fully commissioned chaplains to the Royal Navy. The Royal Air Force Chaplaincy Branch, including Catholic padres, was established in 1918 with the formation of the RAF.

Michael Snape writes that irrespective of the Catholic serviceman's personal adherence to the faith and attention to religious duties, there emerged a strong and vigorous Catholic identity and subculture in the British army from the imperial wars of the Victorian era to the two World Wars of the twentieth century. This was manifested in organizations such as the Catholic Soldiers' Association and later in the United Services' Catholic Association. Alongside this there developed a visible Catholic clerical presence in Britain's military forces with the number of serving chaplains depending on the extent of the conflict, the size of military forces and the number of Catholics serving within them.

Fr Robert Brindle and Fr William Keatinge devoted the majority of their priestly lives to the service of Catholic soldiers, while other priests committed a part of their priestly ministry to Catholic men in the army, for example Fr Charles Swarbreck during the Boer War. The two World Wars of the twentieth century also provide many examples of priests who left their normal ministries to work alongside a small cadre of permanent Royal Navy, army and Royal Air Force chaplains. Many gave their lives in the service of their country at war. Thirty-nine army chaplains and two Royal Navy chaplains died in the First World War. In the Second World War, five Royal Navy, 16 army and five RAF chaplains died. Fr William Finn was killed at Gallipoli in 1915, Fr Stewart Phelan was lost at Jutland in 1916 and Fr Bernard Benson died at Arnhem in 1944. Others, such as Fr Eric Green, became prisoners of war. Many were decorated for bravery. All were affected, mentally and physically, by the circumstances of war.

From the mid-twentieth century, the United Kingdom has never been free of some form of conflict or military commitment, whether in Germany, Israel, Korea, Kenya, Aden, Malaya, Borneo, Cyprus or on the streets of Belfast. Catholic chaplains and chaplains of other denominations have served in all of these theatres and later in the Falklands, the Gulf, Iraq, Bosnia, Kosovo, Sierra Leone, Mali and Afghanistan, and also in Poland and the Baltic States.

From Christian Rome to the Crusades and from the post-Reformation wars of fractured Christendom to the present, Catholic military chaplaincy has existed in some form or other and the military careers of the chaplains examined in this book illustrate this development. Unarmed and uniformed Catholic chaplains have voluntarily chosen to serve at sea, on battlefields and on air bases, ministering to those who have fought in wars from a sense of national pride, political sentiment, conscription, a religious impulse or because they were simply caught up in times and circumstances over which they had no control. The scale and technology of war, the organization of military forces and the circumstances of the chaplains' ministry have differed over the centuries, but war is still savage and brutal. Combatants remain in need of spiritual and moral support and the pastoral and sacramental function of chaplains similarly remains unchanged. The modern chaplain, still a volunteer and still unarmed, continues to address and enhance the spiritual experience and religious confidence of those in combat.

With the appointment of military chaplains, states have institutionalized religion within their armed forces and chaplains have continued to be an obvious link between religion and the military. But conflicts and related issues repeatedly challenge the consciences not only of combatants and chaplains but also of civilians who oppose war *per se* or who oppose a particular conflict. If a Christian state is at war with another Christian state, as Great Britain was against Germany in the First World War, the question could be asked: "Whose side is God on?" Alternatively, when emphasizing the need for the provision of spiritual support, others may ask: "Are you on God's side?"

In more recent times, Catholic members of the Campaign for Nuclear Disarmament (CND) opposed the Royal Air Force and Royal Navy carrying nuclear weapons. Aircraft, surface ships and submarines may have been crewed by Catholic personnel and they too may have examined their consciences about their role in the deployment of nuclear force. Some Catholics in the forces, including chaplains, may also have seen the justification of a united Ireland, while in the wider community many Catholics, including priests, publicly opposed the Gulf War. Other Catholics see chaplains in the officer class as paid servants of the state thus acting contrary to their priestly calling to preach Christ's message of peace. This ambiguity remains.

Notwithstanding these objections, St Augustine's theory of a "Just War" helps us to understand that war is sometimes necessary to defeat evil or can simply be an act of self-defence. As Pope Francis said of the war in Ukraine in 2022, the purchase of weapons can be "morally acceptable if done under the conditions of morality". The call of St Thomas Aquinas that priests may be present on the battlefield also recognizes that men and women under fire may be in immediate need of the sacerdotal ministry, the sacraments and pastoral care. In the chaplain, the Church is present where it is needed and its manifestation may be the application of the chaplain's faculties via the sacramental kit in his rucksack. Chaplaincy has been described as "the spiritual dimension of operational capability". As a chaplain conducts his practical and dangerous apostolate in the vagaries of war and the unpredictability of the battlefield, it is more than likely that the theory of a "Just War" and the morality and ethics of conflict are far from his mind whereas the necessity of providing sacramental succour is immediate.

In 1986, *Spirituali militum curae*, the Apostolic Constitution of Pope St John Paul II, stated:

> The Church has always desired to provide with praiseworthy concern, and in a manner suited to the various needs, for the care of military people. They constitute ... a particular social body and because of the special condition of their way of life, whether they belong permanently to the armed forces by virtue of voluntary enrolment, or are called up temporarily by law, they have need of a concrete and specific form of pastoral assistance.

The Church remains committed to the spiritual welfare of Catholics serving in the military and rejects suggestions that it should not be involved.

Catholic military chaplains serve voluntarily because of the privilege of access and service to a talented, professional and predominantly young segment of Catholic society who are exposed to unique challenges, dangers and responsibilities in places and situations where others would not choose to find themselves. The opportunities continue for chaplains to bring the good news of the gospel to such a special community.

Contemporary Catholic military chaplains build on foundations laid by priests, bishops and politicians who ministered and fought for justice when the state refused to acknowledge the religious and spiritual needs of Catholic service personnel. Priests who served, and died in service, were concurrently denied equal recognition with those of the Established Church. When government support was eventually given, it was patchy and parsimonious, especially with regard to Catholic naval chaplains. This book is an attempt to provide a general history of Catholic chaplaincy to the British forces, but the scarcity of sources, a reflection of the value attached to Catholic military chaplaincy, means that it cannot be a comprehensive account.

1

Camp missioners, chaplains and martyrs: The Jesuits and the *missio castrensis*

European Wars of Religion

Warfare in sixteenth- and seventeenth-century western Europe was conducted in a political climate intensified by religious fervour. Calvinists of the Dutch United Provinces fought for independence from the European empire of Catholic Spain and for over a century war raged across Flanders and the Netherlands. The English Civil War (1642–51) led to further bloodshed and combatants in all conflicts fought and died in appalling and brutal circumstances.

Religion was an integral factor in these struggles. Catholic and non-Catholic clergymen moved among opposing armies and as the wars progressed so too did the concept and practice of military chaplaincy.

There were large numbers of English, Scottish and Irish Catholics in the multinational army of Spain and chaplains were drawn from priests working in the continental colleges and exiled English Catholic communities in Europe. Priests ministered in camps, garrison towns and on the battlefield; some devoted their entire ministry to army chaplaincy. They needed to be physically and mentally strong, and proficient in languages to successfully undertake their work among soldiers of many nationalities.

The Jesuits and the *missio castrensis*

The Society of Jesus, organized along military lines, was prominent in the early development of Catholic military chaplaincy. The *missio castrensis*—the mission to the camp—was an apostolate to the military and Jesuits were, as one historian writes, "perhaps the first standing corps of army chaplains". They wrote catechisms and spiritual guides, established confraternities in camps and equated spiritual health with military discipline. Fr James Laynez SJ wrote: "I know that the soldiers will profit from this, for by their peace of mind and confidence in God they will better fulfil their duties in war." The concept of "the Christian soldier", a pious fighting man, as opposed to a faithless and heretical enemy, developed alongside that of the Catholic army chaplain.

Military chaplaincy received papal support. In 1579, the Bishop of Cambrai was appointed Chaplain-General to Spanish forces and the English priest Fr Caesar Clement became Vicar-General for the Spanish Army in Flanders, a position "carrying with it the nomination and jurisdiction" of chaplains. In 1587, the chaplaincy to Spanish troops in Flanders was entrusted to the Belgian Province of the Society of Jesus, who claimed, with papal approval, that no priest could serve English soldiers unless he was under the Society's "approbation". In 1605, this was contested when Fr Augustine Bradshaw OSB was appointed by Lord Arundell as "Chaplain Major" to his English regiment and had the authority to choose chaplains. Fr William Baldwin SJ asserted that only Jesuits had power to select chaplains in accordance with the papal brief. The dispute was short-lived and Bradshaw acknowledged the Jesuits' authority.

The Jesuit military apostolate grew and was refined. In 1585, Fr Thomas Worthington SJ was chaplain to Sir William Stanley's Regiment and in 1592 Fr William Holt SJ was listed as a "military chaplain". In 1623, Fr Edward Dawson SJ "devoted himself to the care of the English and Irish soldiers in camp who were suffering from the plague". In the 1620s, Jesuits from Liège were devoting "their chief care to the sick and wounded English soldiers", while from Ghent they ministered to English and Irish soldiers in military hospitals and camps. The *missio castrensis* bore much fruit in the instruction, conversion and reconciliation of soldiers, but such were the physical demands of the work that "two of the camp missioners overcome by their labours were reduced to a state of hopeless infirmity".

In 1640, it was reported from Ghent that "there was founded this year, and attached to this house, a Camp Mission consisting of four Fathers for the benefit of an English corps on service in the Low Countries". In 1641, Fr James Bettam SJ was listed as "Superior of Army Chaplains" and "head chaplain of the *missio castrensis*" and he was followed in 1643 by Fr John Bluett SJ. In 1642, Fr John Spenser SJ was appointed "superior of the camp mission to the English troops in Belgium" and in 1644 Fr Gerard Gilbert SJ served the military in Ghent, as did Fr William Gilbert in 1646.

Jesuits were active on the battlefield. Henry Foley wrote that the Lancastrian Fr Richard Bradley SJ ministered "amidst the most frequent danger of death". In battle

> he would run through the ranks ... of the entire army, from the rear to the van, undismayed by the shots whizzing around him, armed with the crucifix alone, with which he encouraged the combatants to engage boldly the enemies of the faith, and animated those, who had fallen mortally wounded, to die with fortitude in so good a cause.

English Jesuit chaplains worked alongside English and Irish chaplains who were not of the Society. Among them were Frs Thomas Worthington, John Fenn, Lionel Woodward and John Sherwood, who ministered to Sir William Stanley's Regiment; Frs George Boyce and Francis Martin, who served in Brussels; Fr Thomas Fathers SJ, who served at Aire; Fr George Leyburn, who ministered at Cambrai; and Fr Philip Middleton, who served at Antwerp. Fr James Harding was chaplain to Spanish troops in the Netherlands and an Irish priest, Fr Nicholas Shea, was Senior Chaplain to Dunkirk garrison and Parham's Regiment of English infantry. Irish regiments employed their own chaplains.

Fr Henry Walpole SJ—camp missioner, chaplain and martyr

Fr Henry Walpole was born in 1558. He attended the English College, Rheims and the Venerable English College, Rome (the *Venerabile*). He completed his Jesuit studies at the Scots College in France and was ordained in 1588. Walpole, fluent in Italian, French, Latin, English and Spanish, became a camp missioner and chaplain to English and Irish Catholic soldiers in Sir William Stanley's Regiment in the Netherlands. He was captured and taken to the English fort at Flushing, where he was tortured before being ransomed.

In December 1593, Fr Walpole sailed for the English mission via Scotland but because of stormy seas landed on the Yorkshire coast. He was immediately arrested and from York Castle was transferred to the Tower of London, where he was tortured. He was returned to York, where he was charged with being a Catholic priest. He refused to take the Oath of Supremacy, which acknowledged the Queen's complete authority in religion, and was convicted of high treason. He was found guilty and on 7 April 1595 was hanged, drawn and quartered. Fr Walpole was beatified in 1929 and canonized in 1970.

Fr Henry Morse SJ—camp missioner, chaplain and martyr

Henry Morse was born in 1595 and raised as a Protestant. While studying in London, he travelled to Douai where, in 1618, he was received into the Church. He remained at Douai until 1620 when he entered the *Venerabile*. He was ordained in 1624 and sailed to England but was captured as he landed and spent the next three years incarcerated in York Castle. He was banished from England and having joined the Jesuits in 1625 proceeded to their house at Watten.

Watten was a Spanish base for defending the frontier towns against Dutch forces and there Jesuits ministered to English and Irish Catholic soldiers in Spanish pay. During the winter, they arranged services for soldiers at their church and in the campaigning season they were chaplains to men in battle. It was to this work that Fr Morse was assigned in the autumn of 1630, and throughout the non-campaigning season, he visited English troops billeted in scattered villages, "catechizing them in the faith, giving courses in controversy, ministering the sacraments of the Church". When the fighting season began in spring 1631, he was so exhausted that he was relieved of military duties.

At the end of 1633, Fr Morse was transferred to the Society's house in Liège, where he worked among English refugees and seminarians. In 1636, he returned to England and ministered among the plague victims of London. Under the aliases of Warde and Claxton he tried to evade pursuivants but was captured. He was imprisoned in Newgate, tried and sentenced to death, but the sentence was commuted through the intervention of Queen Henrietta Maria and he was banished in 1641.

On his return to Flanders, Fr Morse was appointed camp missioner to Sir Henry Gage's English Regiment. Gage had been a student for the priesthood but instead decided on a military career and, in 1619, joined the Spanish army. By the 1630s, he was a seasoned campaigner, having served with Parham's English Regiment, but was persuaded to raise his own regiment which duly appeared on the battlefields of Flanders. Foley records that Fr Morse "made another mission amongst the English soldiers of Colonel Gage's regiment, with such diligence and zeal that he deservedly gained the esteem of that great officer, insomuch that he usually called him the *holy father*".

In the winter of 1641–42, Frs Morse, Peter Wright and Edward Mainwaring prepared men for battle by hearing confessions, catechizing and saying Mass in a tent erected for the purpose. Soldiers were given the *Spiritual Exercises* of St Ignatius and such was the success of the camp mission that many soldiers were received into the Church. Fr Morse visited the scattered hospitals, converting and counselling, administering the Last Rites and burying the dead. Foley recorded that he "laboured with much diligence and profit in the camp mission".

Fr Morse and other Jesuits accompanied Gage's regiment on campaign. The fighting was brutal, little quarter was given either to combatants or civilians and victorious troops were especially vicious in their treatment of a defeated enemy. Fr Caraman writes that "Morse would have remembered vividly the scenes of slaughter" for the rest of his life and would no doubt have used such instances of merciless killing to illustrate his sermons. Gage and his chaplains did as much as possible "to make victors humane".

In 1643, Fr Morse returned to England and began a ministry in the north. During the English Civil War (1642–51) Catholic priests were under great pressure from parliamentary spies and in 1644 Fr Morse was arrested in Cumberland on suspicion of being a priest. He was taken to Durham, then to Newcastle-Upon-Tyne, by sea to London and ultimately, in January 1645, to Newgate prison. He was convicted of being a priest and sentenced to death. On 1 February 1645, Fr Morse was taken to Tyburn where he was hanged, drawn and quartered. Fr Morse was beatified in 1929 and canonized in 1970.

Peter Wright SJ—soldier, camp missioner, chaplain and martyr

Peter Wright was born in 1603 and, according to Foley, his "poor but respectable" family were "zealous Catholics". Wright joined the English army in Holland, but this was a short and unpleasant episode in his life. He became appalled at the effects of war and the licentiousness of a soldier's life and realized the error of his decision to enlist. He left the army, or deserted, "running off in the sight of the whole army and amidst a shower of bullets". He reached Brussels and eventually arrived at the Jesuit house in Liège. In 1627, he was sent from Liège to Ghent from where he was expected to proceed to the *Venerabile*, but his wish to join the Society of Jesus convinced him to enrol at the Jesuit house at Watten to begin his Novitiate. He was ordained in 1637.

After a short period in the College at St Omers, Fr Wright embarked on a busy and dangerous mission to the military. It was an appointment he "joyfully undertook" for, as Foley wrote, "a more spacious field . . . for gathering in a rich harvest of souls awaited him in the camp, as missioner or chaplain to the English forces in Belgium". His experience as a soldier had given Fr Wright some understanding of military ways and he seemed to have "a special talent for winning the hearts of soldiers". Foley records:

> He was ever a stout defender of the Catholic cause among all;
> and when in active service, whether on the battlefield or at
> sieges, especially where the struggle was carried on in the cause
> of religion, he refused no labour, and shrank from no danger in
> the exercise of his functions.

In camp or in winter quarters, Fr Wright ministered to the sick, heard confessions and celebrated Mass. He attended to the soldiers' financial affairs, settled disputes, reconciled many to the Catholic faith and endeared himself to officers and men. As Bishop Challoner wrote: "He behaved in such a manner as to gain the esteem and affection of all, and to reclaim great numbers of them from their errors and vices."

In the autumn and winter of 1642, Fr Wright spent nights in the camps by the bedsides of dying soldiers and "on unending journeys from billet to billet in a bare disfigured countryside". He also witnessed the appalling cruelty meted out by the Dutch at the sack of the Brabant village of Tuelmont and the memory of the massacre remained with him throughout his life. He wrote: "What cruelty soever hath been committed by any tyrant, what rape, what beastliness by any savage or brutish man . . . were there also committed" by the Dutch, "the followers of these new Gospellers". Patients had been burned in hospitals and young and old of both sexes had been systematically abused and killed.

Foley wrote that "with unwearied zeal" Fr Wright "served in camp for upwards of seven years, partly in Belgium partly in England". Recruitment for Royalist forces in the English Civil War had weakened English regiments in Flanders and Sir Henry Gage, having worked for the king's cause on the continent, sailed for England. Fr Wright accompanied him as his chaplain and a force under Gage's command was mustered at Oxford.

In late 1644, Gage and a force including Fr Wright went to lift the prolonged siege of Basing House, Hampshire, the seat of the Marquis of Winchester. On 11 January 1645, Gage was wounded and died in the arms of his chaplain, who had administered the Last Rites to him. The Parliamentarians killed six Catholic priests who were caught in the house, but Fr Wright escaped.

After the war, Fr Wright became domestic chaplain to the Marquis of Winchester's family until he was arrested in February 1651. In England or on the continent, priests were hunted by government pursuivants and spies, and the apostate Dominican, Thomas Gage, brother of Sir Henry Gage, eagerly testified against Fr Wright and reported that a chapel had been set up in a tent in a Spanish encampment outside Salle. There, according to Gage, Fr Wright said Mass and heard confessions. At his trial, Wright made no protestation of innocence and was condemned to death for being a Catholic priest.

Fr Wright was taken to Tyburn on 19 May 1651. As he was lifted out of the cart, he noticed Fr Edward Mainwaring SJ who had served with Fr Wright as a camp missioner in Flanders. Disguised as a workman, Fr Mainwaring heard Fr Wright's confession, granted him absolution and then mingled back into the crowd. Fr Wright was executed before an estimated crowd of 20,000. To the onlookers he said: "As for you Catholics, fellow soldiers and comrades, as many of you as are here, I earnestly beseech you to join with me, and for me, in prayer till my last moment, and when I shall come to heaven I will do as much for you." Fr Wright was hanged, drawn and quartered. He was beatified by Pope Pius XI in 1929.

The Jesuits and the English Civil War

To religious dissenters during the English Civil War, Anglican chaplains to Royalist troops were little better regarded than the despised Catholic priests and King Charles was taunted that he led a "Popish Army". Chaplains with Parliamentary forces, although ranging in theology and religious conviction, were better organized and differed in function from Anglican and especially from Catholic chaplains. But as Margaret Griffin has pointed out, the presence of a Catholic priest with a British regiment or on the battlefields of the British Isles did not mean that he was an official army chaplain. The appointment of a Catholic chaplain would "have been political suicide". The presence of an Anglican chaplain was specified by *Military Orders and Articles* of 1643/44, whereas Catholic priests were unofficially attached to regiments at the personal behest, in the pay, and under the command of a Catholic colonel. They acted as chaplains, but their appointment was an *ad hoc* arrangement without reference to the Royalist Anglican Chaplain-General.

Jesuit pastoral administration was divided into geographical regions termed "Colleges" and the annual report of the College of St Francis Xavier (Wales and the West Country) for 1642–43 contained an account of Jesuits in the Royalist army:

> A fresh duty now devolved on the Fathers: that of exercising their sacred ministry in the Royal army. One of them ... was already expert in its particular duties, having lately come over from Belgium where he had been employed in the service of the soldiers and he resumed the work with great zeal and spirit ... To be nearer at hand to afford his services where they might be called for, when an engagement was expected he joined the ranks of the cavalry on horseback.

Following the example of their officers, Catholic soldiers "presented themselves to receive the Sacrament of Penance" so that they "might be better prepared for the dangers of the approaching conflict". The annual report continued that the chaplains were "engaged to remain" with the troops "and attend them in the dangers of their future warfare, as it was shown how much comfort was felt and courage shown in battle by those who had previously reconciled themselves to God in the Sacrament of Penance".

A Jesuit ministered at the siege of Gloucester in September 1643 when he went along the ranks to administer the Sacrament of Penance and continued to do this even though he was "thrice shot through his clothes". Before the Battle of Newbury, also in September 1643, "great numbers of all ranks, and among them some of the nobility, came to him to confession, beginning before daylight". The next day, "Catholic soldiers, having thus prepared themselves, fought with distinguished bravery, and many of them fell". Among those killed in the battle was Robert Dormer, Earl of Carnarvon who, it was recorded, "never marched without a priest".

Catholic chaplains in the English Civil War

Other Catholic priests, regular and secular, ministered alongside Jesuits in the Civil War. Fr Henry Turbeville served the Marquis of Worcester's troops, Fr Francis Blackiston OSB "devoted his services in assisting Catholic soldiers who had ventured their lives in the service of the King", while Fr Francis Pavier was killed while ministering at the Battle of Marston Moor in 1644. Fr John Huddleston, a missioner in Staffordshire, exchanged the duties of chaplain to the Earl of Derby's army for those of an armed gentleman volunteer. He helped to shelter Charles I when he was fleeing the Battle of Worcester; later, he became a Benedictine and received the dying King Charles II into the Catholic Church. The Irish Dominican Fr Vincent Dillon ministered to Irish troops at the Battle of Marston Moor in July 1644. He was captured and died in York in 1651. In Scotland, the Royalist Marquis of Montrose allowed Catholics from the Highlands to be accompanied by their Jesuit chaplains, Frs James Macbrek, William Grant, John Smith and Andrew Leslie.

Fr Philip Powell OSB was born in 1594 in Brecknockshire and studied law before joining the Benedictine community of St Gregory at Douai. He was ordained in 1618 and in 1622 left Douai for the English mission. In 1624, he became chaplain to a family in Somerset and, when the Civil War began, he moved to Devon. In 1645, he served for six months as chaplain to Catholic soldiers in General Goring's Royalist army in Cornwall, but after a heavy defeat at Taunton, Goring left his demoralized army for France, where he secured the command of English regiments in Spanish service.

On 22 February 1646, Fr Powell sailed for South Wales but was intercepted, recognized and denounced as a priest. He was sent to London and confined in St Catherine's Gaol, Southwark, before his trial on 9 June at Westminster Hall. He was found guilty of being a priest and was hanged, drawn and quartered at Tyburn. Fr Powell was beatified in 1929.

The Apostolate to the Military

The Jesuits established a coherent and identifiable system of military chaplaincy on the continent, but the *missio castrensis* could not be replicated in England. Jesuits and other chaplains ministered unhindered within the civil and military milieu of the Low Countries but lacked the same religious and legal freedom in England where there was no opportunity "to visit, console or encourage the faithful", be they civilians or soldiers. Military chaplaincy could not fully develop in England, but Jesuits and other priests brought the consolation of religion to people brutalized by military violence.

Figure 2: Fr Henry Morse SJ: Chaplain and martyr (Jesuits in Britain Archives)

2

From the Glorious Revolution to Culloden: Stuart and Jacobite chaplains

A Catholic king

The appointment of Catholic army chaplains during the reign of King James II (1685–88) was inextricably linked with parliamentary opposition to a standing army and public anti-Catholicism. For reasons of political expediency and religious sensitivity, Catholic army chaplains were not officially appointed or named on army lists and it is difficult to be certain of many aspects of Catholic chaplaincy in this period. However, Catholic officers in the army were named and James ignored the legal requirement for them to subscribe to the Test Act. Despite widespread fears to the contrary, he did not envisage the army imposing Catholicism on the state. To him it was a reserve force to be used in a crisis and protection against a political or dynastic coup.

The birth of James Edward, Prince of Wales, in 1688, and with it the prospect of a Stuart Catholic dynasty, was too much to stomach for the Protestant establishment. They had witnessed James reintroducing Catholicism into court, the universities, the army and the magistracy, and to prevent a further extension of this unwelcome development they called for Mary, James's Protestant daughter, and her husband, the Dutchman William of Orange, to assume the throne. William landed at Brixham in November 1688 by which time much of James's army had deserted and he had fled to France. In March 1689, James landed with an army in Ireland in an attempt to recover his kingdoms but was defeated at the Battle of the Boyne in July 1690. He returned to France, where he spent the rest of his life. One Catholic commentator wrote that "after a brief period of brightness, the Church in England was plunged into darkness with the flight of the King".

The army of James II

Under James II, the army grew from approximately 9,000 in 1685 to 35,000 in 1688, with separate establishments for Ireland (approximately 9,000 men in 1688) and for Scotland (a single regiment of foot). By 1688, the army was much more than a collection of regiments and had structures of command and control, logistics and training necessary for it to function as an effective army. As part of this increasing professionalism, duties were delineated and pay and conditions of service were stipulated, but a standing army with such features and officered by Catholics under the command of a Catholic king exacerbated the fear of Catholic influence.

Military Orders and Articles of 1643/4 laid down that all regiments, companies and troops should attend divine worship conducted by a chaplain. This was as much for military discipline as it was for religious motivation. Although the role of chaplain was not included in the list of General Staff Officers or in the Scots Establishment, "The Lord Primate of Ireland" was named as "Chaplain-General of the Army in Ireland". The Royal Regiment of Horse Guards, the Scots Troop of Horse Guards and the Irish Troop of Horse Guards each had a chaplain on the payroll. The 11 English Regiments of Horse, the Royal Scots Regiment of Horse and the three Irish Regiments of Horse similarly had chaplains. Dragoon Regiments had chaplains as did the Royal Regiments of Foot Guards, but the artillery was not supplied with chaplains. To the increasing number of soldiers who were religious dissenters, Anglican chaplains to James's army were little better than the despised Catholic priests.

Catholics in the army of James II

Although Catholics were excluded by penal laws from holding public, ecclesiastical and military office, Charles II had commissioned Catholic officers. James II saw the loyalty of the army as an essential prerequisite for the retention of his royal authority and, despite parliamentary opposition, "reliable" Catholics were freely granted commissions. In 1685, the king appointed George Douglas, the Catholic Earl of Dumbarton, as Lieutenant-General "over all Our Forces as well as Horse and Foot". The Catholic Lords Dover, Stafford, Bellasis, Carlingford, Hunsdon and Herbert became colonels of regiments, and the Catholic Irish Earl of Tyrconnel was appointed a general.

The number of Catholic officers in the army increased after 1685, but during James's reign the figure was never more than 11 per cent, while it has been estimated that 12 per cent of the rank and file were Catholics. There were Catholics in the regiments of Catholic colonels, such as the Earl of Dumbarton, the Duke of Berwick, Sir Edward Hales and Sir Henry Gage. There were also Catholics in Irish regiments. By 1686, 3,409 out of 8,629 officers and men in the Irish army were Catholics. In some cases, Protestant officers were replaced by Catholics but Catholic and Protestant officers were employed on equal pay.

Edward Cary: A Catholic "Chaplain-General"?

Edward Cary was born into a Catholic family in Long Melford, Suffolk. As a soldier, he fought on the Royalist side during the English Civil War but later studied for the priesthood at the Venerable English College, Rome, where he was ordained on 25 March 1651. He was sent to the English mission and ministered in the West Country. It was said that "he was in great esteem among his brethren" and in 1684 he was appointed Vicar-General of Cornwall. He would, therefore, have some experience of exercising authority over other missioners. Although there are references to the commissioning of Catholic officers, there is no mention of the appointment of Catholic chaplains and what is particularly special about Fr Cary are the references to him as "Chaplain-General".

Fr Anstruther refers to Fr Cary being "Chaplain-General for the benefit of Catholic soldiers", indicating that King James recognized the need for a priestly ministry among his Catholic troops and perhaps that he wanted Catholic chaplains to be organized and paid in the same way as Anglican chaplains. No Anglican chaplain was assigned the title of "Chaplain-General", although Anglican chaplains were in the majority, and studies of James II's army make no reference to Catholic army chaplains. That the king paraded his religion before his army, however, can be in no doubt. At the army's training grounds in York and Portsmouth and on Hounslow Heath, Catholic chapels were erected and priests were in attendance. To anti-Catholic elements in the army, this must have been particularly offensive and provocative.

More evidence of Fr Cary's military chaplaincy and rank is found in the annals of the Poor Clares at Rouen, where, it was recorded, from November 1695 until June 1696

> Mr Edward Cary, an ancient and able missioner, supplied our worthy confessor's place during his absence, excepting one month when he was obliged to go to Calais to receive King James' order, he being general chaplain of his army.

It would seem that Fr Cary left England on the flight of King James and served him in exile, but no other information is forthcoming. The English Catholic historian, Fr Hugh Tootell (alias Charles Dodd), assigned the title "Chaplain-General" to Fr Cary, and other Catholic historians have used the same evidence and nomenclature but provided no further details of Fr Cary's jurisdiction over chaplains either on the continent or in the British Isles.

Catholic chaplains in the army of James II

Although it is difficult to find firm evidence relating to the appointment of chaplains and their function among Catholic troops or be clear about their presence at engagements during James's reign (for example against the Earl of Argyll in Scotland in 1685 and against the Duke of Monmouth at Sedgemoor in 1685), it is possible to identify from a variety of sources some priests who ministered to Catholic soldiers in the army of James II.

At least five secular priests, other than Fr Cary, served as chaplains. Fr Thomas Churchill of the London District, for example, served with King James in France, Ireland and Scotland after William of Orange's invasion. He wrote:

> I followed his majesty at my own charge through France and Ireland, and to help the English that went to the assistance of (Lord) Dundee I went into Scotland. In going on this voyage, I was in two fights, the one by sea, the other by land; in both we had the better, but in the latter (the Battle of Killiecrankie, 27 July 1689) Dundee our general was slain. Then I endeavoured to get back to the King.

Fr Churchill was later captured and spent two years in prison.

Fr Peter Gooden of the Northern District, described as "naturally bold and intrepid", served on the mission in Lancashire, the county of his birth, after his ordination at Lisbon in 1670. In 1685, King James appointed him to be chaplain to the Duke of Berwick's Regiment of Horse at Chester, but after the flight of the king in 1688 he returned to the Lancashire mission. Fr Nicholas Trapps (alias Sebastian Giffard) of the London District was ordained at the English College, Rome, in 1675 and according to *State Papers* was commissioned as an army chaplain under James II on 17 December 1685. He then served "the considerable body of Catholic officers in Sir Edward Hales' Foot", which had been raised in Kent and commissioned in June 1685. Fr Trapps ministered to the regiment and also to garrisons at Chester, Bristol and Plymouth. In January 1687, Fr Christopher Turner was appointed by James II to say Mass for the Plymouth garrison. On 1 September 1688, Fr John Gildon (alias Worsley), who had studied in Lisbon, Douai and Paris, was commissioned chaplain to the Royal Regiment of Foot under the command of the Earl of Dumbarton.

Jesuits also served as army chaplains. Fr Andrew Poulton SJ served in "the capacity of army chaplain" to James II in Ireland, while Fr Louis de Sabran SJ, an army chaplain in Ghent from 1682 to 1683 and in Brussels in 1684, became Royal Chaplain to the Prince of Wales in 1688. Fr John Smith SJ of the Jesuit College of St Ignatius (London and neighbouring counties) is recorded as serving as an army chaplain in England in 1685, and Fr William Janion SJ, also of the College of St Ignatius, died in 1685 in England while serving the military under James II. Fr George Wise SJ served English and Scottish soldiers at Ghent during the period 1685–88 and Fr Joseph Plowden SJ served King James in Ireland from 1690 to 1691. Fr Plowden died in France in 1692 while ministering to sick and wounded troops. It is likely that Jesuits were engaged in attempts to convert Protestant troops in James II's army in England, Ireland and on the continent.

The last military attempt by King James to save his monarchy occurred at the Battle of the Boyne, Oldbridge, County Meath, on 1 July 1690. It was the decisive battle in the struggle in Ireland between James and William of Orange and the success of William's forces assured the Protestant Ascendancy in Ireland. Both armies were accompanied by chaplains. Catholic chaplains said Mass, heard confessions and administered the sacraments to the wounded and dying. On William's side, the Revd George Story accompanied Lord Drogheda's regiment, while the Revd Rowland Davis served as both a commissioned captain and a chaplain. His diary reads more like that of an army officer than a chaplain, but there are references to him leading prayers on horseback in a field, preaching sermons and burying the dead. Fellow chaplains, wrote Davis, worked in the hospitals among the wounded and the sick.

Jacobite chaplains

After the deposition of King James II, the Stuart cause remained strong in Scotland, northern England and Ireland and his son, King James III, who was in exile in France, attempted to regain the throne by means of a military coup originating in Scotland. The Act of Union of 1707 with England was bitterly resented in Scotland and the new Hanoverian regime was unwelcome. There was not only resistance to the Hanoverians among Catholics, Episcopalians and Presbyterians in Scotland but also among Catholics and some Protestants, including Anglican clergymen, in northern England. As one historian wrote, there was a "menacingly broad appeal of Jacobite ideology".

The first Jacobite Rising in Scotland was at the Battle of Killiecrankie in July 1689, when supporters of James II defeated a Scottish Convention force. A short-lived campaign was later led by the Earl of Mar who raised James's standard on 27 August 1715. His forces had initial success, but neither the Scottish nor the English Jacobites were a match for Hanoverian forces. James landed in Scotland on 22 December, but by this time his military campaign was effectively over and he left Scotland on 5 February 1716. Among Jacobite rebels captured at Preston were men from Lancashire, Northumberland and Ireland. It was recorded that the "Roman Catholicks . . . had the Sacrament administered by a priest".

Priestly involvement in politics was discouraged by the papacy, but this did not prevent clerical support for the Stuarts. Though sympathetic to Stuart claims, leading Scottish Catholic churchmen did not openly support Prince Charles Edward Stuart, the "Young Pretender", when he repeated his father's attempt to reclaim the crown, again via Scotland, 30 years later in 1745, but there were other Scottish priests who did and who served as chaplains to Jacobite forces.

The Jacobite incursion into England from Scotland in late 1745 provoked a firm English response. Conflict was inevitable and, having failed to persuade the "Young Pretender" to return to France, Bishop Hugh MacDonald, Vicar Apostolic of the Highland District, blessed Stuart colours and permitted his priests to serve as chaplains to Catholic Gaelic-speaking clans. Forty-two Catholic priests were known to have been serving in Scotland in 1745, some with very strong connections to Jacobitism through the clans.

One chaplain was Fr Allan MacDonald, born in the Western Isles in 1696, trained for the priesthood in Rome, Madrid and Douai, and ordained in Scotland at some date between 1736 and 1743. In 1745, Fr MacDonald accompanied the prince as his confessor and served as chaplain to the regiment of the powerful and Catholic Clanranalds. He wore an army uniform, bore arms and was styled "Captain". Fr MacDonald accompanied the prince's army at the Battle of Prestonpans on 21 September 1745. At the Battle of Falkirk on 17 January 1746, he rode along a line of kneeling soldiers and gave them a blessing before the battle. After the Battle of Culloden on 16 April 1746, he was with the prince until he reached Scalpa on 2 May. He was captured in South Uist and sent to London along with four other priests. He was imprisoned at Tilbury on a prison hulk before being sent to Southwark New Gaol. He was banished in 1747 and travelled to the Scots College in Paris via Holland.

Seventeen Catholic priests were listed as Jacobite clergymen in the 1745 Rebellion. Some were identified as chaplains, others as non-combatants, and a distinction seems to have been made between chaplains who wore military dress and bore arms and those who did not. Fr Aeneas McGillis, chaplain to the Glengarrys, ministered at the Battle of Prestonpans as did Fr James Leslie, who tended the wounded. Fr John Tyrie of Glenlivet joined the main Jacobite army at Edinburgh and marched with it to Carlisle before ministering to Gordon of Glenbucket's Regiment at the Battle of Culloden on 16 April 1746. He heard confessions before being injured and escaping. Fr Colin Campbell, a fervent Jacobite like Fr Tyrie, was killed in action at Culloden. Like Fr MacDonald they all wore highland dress, carried arms and were styled "captain".

Fr Alexander Cameron SJ of Strathglass served as chaplain to Cameron of Lochiel's Regiment. On the evening before the Battle of Culloden, wearing a tartan chasuble, he offered Mass on the battlefield for the regiment. He was taken prisoner at Morar in July 1746 and sent on HMS *Furnace* to London where he died on arrival. Fr George Duncan of Glenlivet was listed as a non-combatant. He was taken prisoner at Glenlivet in 1746 but released after a short imprisonment and went to Carlisle to look after Catholic prisoners. Fr Charles Farquharson SJ from Braemar, a non-combatant chaplain, was imprisoned at Inverness after Culloden, sent to Tilbury, incarcerated aboard one of the prison hulks, and banished in 1747. Another Jesuit and non-combatant chaplain, Fr John Ferguson SJ of Strathglass, was from Braemar. He was captured at Inverness, sent to Southwark and banished in May 1747. Fr Alexander Gordon from Aboyne served in the Prince's French Service. He was captured at Inverness on 17 April 1746 and died in captivity three weeks later. Fr John Farquharson of Strathglass surrendered after Culloden and was banished.

Some of those captured were released. Fr John Gordon of Aberdeen was captured and imprisoned at Carlisle on 30 December 1745. He was sent to Southwark but subsequently acquitted. Similarly, Fr Peter Gordon of Braemar was arrested at Aberdeen but discharged. Another non-combatant, Fr James Grant, was arrested at Barra and imprisoned at Inverness. He was sent to London but released in July 1747. Another chaplain, Fr John MacLauchlan of Kilchgoan, chaplain to MacLachlan's Regiment, escaped capture. Fr Alexander Forrester of the Uist mission was taken prisoner with Fr Allan MacDonald on the Isle of Skye in July 1746. He was sent to London and banished for life. However, he returned from France to Edinburgh in autumn 1748 before escaping to Ireland and re-entering Scotland in 1754. After Culloden, Fr William Reid of Mortlach was held in Edinburgh before being released in August 1746. From the Aberdeen district, Fr Patrick Leith joined the Jacobite army at some date before the Battle of Prestonpans where he tended the wounded. He then marched into England with the main Jacobite army and fled after the collapse of the rising.

The Jacobite force at Culloden, numbering between 12,000 and 14,000, was not completely Scottish, for there were many Irishmen in the army. Nor was it entirely Catholic, as Episcopalian clergymen also served as military chaplains in the Stuart cause. Two were executed for their part in the rebellion—the Revd Thomas Coppoch, chaplain with the Manchester Regiment, and the Revd Robert Lyon, chaplain with Lord Ogilvy's Regiment. English priests such as Fr John Sergeant of Lancashire ministered to Stuart forces as they marched south into England. Fr Sergeant was subsequently arrested and imprisoned at Lancaster Castle. As in the 1715 rising, northern Catholics rallied to the Stuart cause. The Manchester Regiment was raised in November 1745, but its existence was short-lived, and it was defeated at Carlisle in December. Twenty-seven officers and men were subsequently executed for their role in the rising.

Finally, Bishop Hugh MacDonald, who had blessed Stuart banners as the prince arrived in Scotland, served as chaplain to MacDonald of Clanranald's Regiment. After Culloden, he was with Lord Lovat in Morar, but whereas Lovat was captured and executed, Bishop MacDonald escaped and fled to France. He returned to Scotland in 1749. He was arrested in July 1755 and imprisoned in Edinburgh Castle but released on bail. In February 1756, he was sentenced by the High Court to perpetual banishment, but the sentence was not enforced and he remained in Scotland until his death in 1773. The number of priests at his disposal, however, was considerably reduced during the brutal aftermath of the '45, while penal restrictions on the Catholic community weakened the Church in Scotland even further.

Priests, politics and war

Priests who ministered to soldiers serving the Stuart cause in the seventeenth and eighteenth centuries identified themselves with a political ideology committed to the restoration of a Catholic monarchy and Catholic worshipping communities in the British Isles. Their ministry, supported by royal patronage during the reign of King James II, was regarded as treacherous by the state in the years following the Glorious Revolution.

It is possible to identify Catholic priests who served as army chaplains during the reign of James II and although the number of chaplains over which Fr Cary had nominal authority was small, the references to him as Chaplain-General appear to substantiate his position. However, there is no evidence of him ministering in a specific battle nor are his specific responsibilities defined.

That Catholic chaplains served the Jacobite cause in Scotland is well documented. In the early eighteenth century, the Stuart cause did not die and priests, particularly in Scotland, continued to recruit men for the cause and minister to Jacobite troops either as armed and uniformed chaplains or as non-combatant chaplains.

That a Catholic army chaplaincy was established, separate from a royal court chaplaincy and domestic chaplaincy, seems beyond doubt, but the advent of the Hanoverians and the enforcement of penal legislation ensured that Catholic army chaplains were superfluous.

Figure 3: Fr Alexander Cameron SJ before the Battle of Prestonpans

3

Patriot, military chaplain, educator and legislator: A chaplain with the Glengarry Fencibles

Catholics in the military in the late eighteenth century

Before and throughout the Napoleonic Wars (1793–1815), large numbers of Catholics served in the Royal Navy and the army. A Catholic Relief Act of 1778 had removed the worst excesses of anti-Catholicism, but Catholic priests were still forbidden to minister to sailors and marines on board ships and soldiers on the field of battle. The Vicars Apostolic of England and Wales and the Irish episcopacy agitated for an end to this injustice, arguing that as Catholics served and died for their country, they should be provided with the spiritual ministrations of their clergy. Their entreaties met with little success. However, at a local level and on land, volunteer priests served the needs of Catholic sailors, marines and soldiers. This ministry, occasionally undertaken with official permission, was mainly unpaid but increasingly remunerated.

"The Army", wrote an Irish bishop in 1813, "is not, in general, a school of virtue", yet their religion remained important to Catholic soldiers and sailors. Attempts to have an Act of Indemnity (which pardoned those not subscribing to the religious tenets of the Church of England) administered to Catholics on entering the army had failed and the Articles of War still applied in the case of religious practice. A refusal to comply with the Articles was a mutinous offence.

Bishop John Milner of the Midland District stated that the "morality and the practice of their religious duties will never be kept up while our youth mix with the Protestant officers and men as they have done in the regiments composed of all sorts of characters and sectaries". Catholic soldiers were compelled to attend Protestant services and, wrote Bishop Gregory Sharrock of the Western District, "were cruelly used if they frequent our chapels, even out of hours". It was, concluded Bishop Milner, "a tyranny exercised over our poor soldiers and sailors in the affair of their religion".

Local clergy ministered to troops stationed in nearby garrisons. In 1796, Fr James Worswick of the Northern District celebrated Mass for Irish soldiers at North Shields. At Portsea, Fr Joseph Knapp of the London District reported that on 2 May 1796 he had 200 Irish soldiers at prayers "with the officer at their head drawn up in order and returned publically". In June 1800, Bishop Milner informed Bishop William Gibson of the Northern District that his workload had increased due to the presence of 1,500 Irish soldiers. "I have hardly had time for anything else", he wrote. In 1815, Bishop William Poynter of the London District recorded that there were 700 Catholic soldiers at Newport on the Isle of Wight. The erection of military camps and incoming French Catholic émigrés led to an increase in the size of English Catholic missions and placed further demands on the local clergy. The military ministry of Fr Alexander MacDonell has to be considered in this context.

Fr Alexander MacDonell

Alexander MacDonell was born at Inchlaggan, Glengarry, on 17 July 1762 of a Scottish highland family with strong Jacobite affiliations. He was educated at the Scots Colleges in Paris and in Valladolid, where he was ordained in 1787. Returning to Scotland, Fr MacDonell served on the mission in Inverness and Perth and assisted many of his Gaelic-speaking co-religionists severely affected by the harsh economic conditions of the time. He managed to place some, suffering as a result of agricultural distress, in manufacturing opportunities in Glasgow and, contrary to laws of the time, opened a chapel for them. He also acted as their English interpreter. The French Revolutionary, or Napoleonic, Wars (1793–1815) adversely affected Scottish industry and exports and once again Fr MacDonell's highlanders found themselves without work. In such a situation, as many had done before, they joined the army.

"Big Sandy", as Fr MacDonell was affectionately called (he was six feet four inches tall with an "immense and herculean frame"), devoted much of his life to Scottish soldiers and their families, whether in Scotland, Guernsey, Ireland or Canada, at peace and in war. Undoubtedly, "Big Sandy" had charisma. As a priest and chaplain, he was conscientious, brave, politically astute and unafraid of adverse publicity, and he succeeded in advancing the interests of the Catholic soldier and the Church in an era when anti-Catholicism was still prevalent. Later, as Bishop of Ontario, he was committed to the development of the Catholic community of Upper Canada.

The Glengarry Fencibles and their chaplain

In spite of the legal difficulties and religious barriers confronting them, Catholics continued to join the armed services and corps were raised, especially in Scotland. In 1793, Fr MacDonell made contact with the young Protestant clan chieftain, Alexander Ranaldson MacDonell of Glengarry. Together they devised a scheme whereby unemployed highlanders would be offered to the British government as a Fencible, or light infantry, a regiment willing to serve outside England or Scotland, unlike other Fencibles, which were primarily home defence units. After a meeting at Fort Augustus in February 1794 that pledged Catholic loyalty to the crown, Fr MacDonell went to London to seek acceptance for the proposal. Successful, he returned to Glasgow and was greeted with displeasure by his bishop, who was distressed by the young priest's neglect of his primary mission. Fr MacDonell, however, was determined to follow the Glengarry chieftain, aspiring to bring him back to the Catholic fold and hoping to find employment for his flock.

In 1794, the chieftain and Fr MacDonell formed a Catholic military unit—the Regiment of the Fencibles of Glengarry—to give the chieftain a leadership role, and the highlanders work, an income, and a chance to fight in the war against France. The Glengarry Fencibles (as they are commonly known) were, like other Fencible regiments, formed to supplement the British army. It was the first Catholic regiment to be formed in Britain since the Reformation.

On 14 August 1794, Fr MacDonell became the first Catholic chaplain in the British army since the reign of King James II when, contrary to statute, King George III secretly commissioned and appointed him chaplain to the Glengarry Fencibles. This remains an unusual appointment in the annals of army chaplaincy and the circumstances surrounding this episode have never been adequately explained. Canadian Catholic historians maintain that this is a false claim resting "upon the insecure foundations of clan folklore and fiction" rather than upon "archival documentation and authentic history". They assert that Fr John McKenna was granted a salaried commission by Sir Guy Carleton in 1776 to be chaplain to the King's Royal Regiment of New York.

Fr MacDonell used whatever means at his disposal to recruit and equip the regiment. As it was not a regiment of the line, it was not equipped by the government (but it came under the auspices of the Secretary of State for War), nor could it be deployed by the government, but McDonell "offered to extend the service of the men under his influence to any part of His Majesty's Dominions where their service might be required". Such an offer proved acceptable to the British government.

At first, the regiment was not overwhelmed with Catholic recruits. Scottish Catholics had long been accustomed to joining non-Catholic regiments, but the Fencibles gradually filled up due to the efforts of Catholic clergy actively recruiting throughout the Highlands. It did not consist solely of Macdonell's or even Glengarry's tenants and men were recruited from all areas of the Highlands. Ultimately, the Fencibles recruited men from the Scottish Lowlands, Ireland, England and Italy.

In 1795, the embodied regiment was at last ready for service under its colonel and with Fr MacDonell as chaplain, it was sent to Guernsey as part of the plan to forestall a French invasion. There the chieftain and his officers quarrelled and the chaplain was drawn into an unseemly legal wrangle which led to his being briefly imprisoned before the dispute was resolved by court proceedings.

The Glengarry Fencibles in Ireland

With other Scottish and Welsh Fencible regiments, the Glengarry Fencibles were sent to Ireland in June 1798 at a time when over 10,000 Fencible infantry were involved in British attempts to quell the revolutionary disturbances which had been taking place in many counties but particularly in Wexford. The leaders of the rebellion, mainly members of the republican Society of United Irishmen, included Protestants, Dissenters and Catholics and their priests. Fifty thousand Irishmen took part in the rebellion and were supported by French troops, which added a new dimension to the conflict as France was already at war with Britain. Over 100,000 British regular army, Fencibles, militia, yeomanry and Hessians eventually put down the rebellion with great force and savagery. Wolfe Tone, the leader of the United Irishmen, took his own life in December 1798 after the rebellion had been ended.

The Glengarry Fencibles landed at Ballyhack, marched to Waterford and then to New Ross in County Wexford. Fr MacDonell accompanied his men on engagements into the bleak Wexford Mountains and did his utmost to offer spiritual and physical comfort to men of both sides. As the year wore on and many towns and villages were destroyed, the Fencibles were compelled to live under tents for the greater part of autumn and winter. Fr MacDonell considered it his duty to share the privations and sufferings of his men.

Under the influence of their chaplain, the Fencibles earned the respect of many Irish because of their good behaviour and their help in restoring Catholic churches ransacked by English troops and used as stables and barracks. *The Catholic Encyclopedia* recorded that Fr MacDonell's ministry had "an almost magical effect among the terror-stricken Catholic population". They witnessed a regiment of Catholics speaking Gaelic, and among them was a *soggarth*, or priest. An American bishop later wrote that "the memory of Father MacDonell is as green in those regions as the fields they cultivate. That holy, chivalrous priest saved the lives of many innocent Irishmen and restored their chapels to their original purpose."

However, the Glengarrys did not lose sight of their primary purpose and were dubbed "The Devil's Bloodhounds" by the rebels because

of their tenacity in searching out rebels in the Wicklow Mountains.
Following an episode at Derrynamuck, a rebel song was composed about
an encounter with the Fencibles and their clan:

> But the kilted foes around them set
> And fired the house of Connell,
> Those hungry Scots, the hounds of death,
> Ah, shame on you MacDonell!
> Spirits of the dead, the butchered of Glencoe,
> Look down with vengeful ire
> On you, degenerate sons, the murdering crew
> That sought the life of Dwyer,
> Of the freedom-loving Dwyer.

Michael Dwyer was a leading member of the United Irishmen and was
high on the list of those sought by the Fencibles.

The Catholics of Wexford in particular received some harsh treatment
from the British forces, which included Protestant Orangemen from the
north. Fr MacDonell wrote:

> The rebellion is now entirely at an end, but a set of bloody
> Orangemen still exercise their wanton cruelties upon the
> defenceless inhabitants if allowed and would force these
> unfortunate people to the mountains ... but for the protection
> of the British troops and for the earnest remonstrances of the
> Catholic clergy who have certainly contributed in a great measure
> to tranquilize the country, notwithstanding how much their
> conduct has been misrepresented by the Orange party.

Yet in a letter to his cousin, Fr MacDonell expressed his poor opinion of
some British soldiers who, like the Orangemen, also vented their fury
on the local inhabitants:

> The barbarous conduct of the soldiery in general ... exceeds
> belief. There is no species of cruelty, but they exercised on their
> unhappy victims of their fury, neither age nor sex was respected,

and there are instances of the heads of the husbands being cut off in defending the virtue of their wives and the arms of the mothers round the bodies of their daughters. I must, however, observe that the British troops in general behave extremely well, more especially the Scots Fencibles, some few individuals excepted.

But some Irish were unhappy that fellow Catholics were fighting for the British government and that their regimental chaplain was dressed in the Scottish plaid of a soldier (the Glengarry uniform had yellow facings) rather than the black suit of a clergyman. Irish priests, meanwhile, had taken a leading role in the Rebellion and therefore opposed Fr MacDonell's Fencibles and other British regiments. Some had been executed by the British authorities. To some Irish, the methods and behaviour of other Fencible regiments were less than exemplary.

In 1803, it was stated that Fr MacDonell's "zeal and attachment to government were strongly evinced while filling the office of chaplain … during the Rebellion in Ireland", and he had earned the respect and loyalty of the Glengarry Fencibles "by them having witnessed him bear arms and accompanying them during every duty during the late rebellion in Ireland". The Marquis Cornwallis, Lord Lieutenant of Ireland, was so impressed with the services of the Fencibles that he wished to have them enlarged and augmented as a regiment. Fr MacDonell's personal reputation, political usefulness and social standing meant that he became closely involved in the discussions over the proposal to enhance the regiment's status. He was also used as an emissary between leading Irish Catholics and the British government in the tortuous deliberations over the Act of Union which took effect in 1801 and created the United Kingdom of Great Britain and Ireland.

The Glengarry Fencibles in Canada

After the Treaty of Amiens in 1802, the Fencibles were disbanded. Two years later, Fr MacDonell accompanied some of them to Upper Canada, where there were already substantial settlements of Scottish Catholics.

Some Scots had fought on the Loyalist side in the American War of Independence, and the King's Royal Regiment of New York, for example, included many Catholics from the Highlands. Fr John McKenna, with strong links to Badenoch and Glengarry, and who had emigrated with many highlanders in 1773, served as their chaplain in a number of engagements.

Prime Minister Henry Addington had offered land in Trinidad to the Glengarry Fencibles in reward for good military service, but "no consideration on earth" would induce Fr MacDonell to persuade the highlanders to accept the offer. Instead, the Glengarrys who wished to eventually sailed for Canada and arrived at York (now Toronto) on 1 November 1804. Fr MacDonell continued to minister to his Gaelic-speaking compatriots and acted as both their priest and advocate.

Fr MacDonell immediately tried to convince the British government of the loyalty of the discharged Fencibles and also of the military necessity of using them to protect the colony against American attacks. He proposed a corps of Canadian Fencibles which would serve "the double purpose of forming an internal defence, and settling the country". He requested that "a portion of land should be granted to every man, after a service of five years, or on his furnishing a substitute, so that the same force might always be kept up, and the settlement of the country go on".

In 1807, Fr MacDonell urged that Glengarrys be enrolled in the local militia and Colonel Isaac Brock enthusiastically welcomed the suggestion. He was familiar with Fr MacDonell's military experience and the "naturally brave and loyal" highlanders so "firmly attached to the British constitution and government". Governor Sir James Henry Craig was less convinced. However, just before the outbreak of war between England and America in 1812, Brock had become administrator of Upper Canada and military commander, and he urged Fr MacDonell to visit York and seek approval for the raising of a Glengarry regiment. Governor Sir George Prevost, happy to have men of proven military skill and loyalty, did not wait for official approval and on 24 March 1812 ordered the formation of the Glengarry Light Infantry Fencibles. The regiment became part of the British army and, with Fr MacDonell as chaplain, soon recruited over 800 men and continued to recruit during the war. "The Chaplain", wrote Lieutenant John MacDonell of Glengarry, "having served in that capacity in the late Glengarry fencibles in Great Britain, Ireland and Guernsey, has a claim to the favour of Government".

Fr MacDonell was appointed chaplain on the understanding that he would not accompany the regiment in the field, but in fact he took part in several engagements against the Americans in the war that lasted from 1812 to 1814. At the Battle of Ogdensburg, in December 1812, it was reported that "the Reverend Alexander MacDonell was conspicuous by his efforts to encourage his clansmen in the field". As the Fencibles advanced across open ice towards the Americans, MacDonell held the cross aloft while on the other flank the Revd John Bethune, a Scottish Presbyterian minister and veteran army chaplain, held up the Bible.

Fr MacDonell was with the Fencibles in several other engagements— Fort Covington, Oswego, Sackett's Harbour and York. His ministry and his addresses inspired not only the Fencibles but also other regiments. It was said that he excommunicated a soldier who tried to run away, and another story relates that he carried a wounded Glengarry to the American border and demanded medical treatment for him. When not ministering in battle he was busy writing letters to military and political figures either on the nature and course of the conflict or on future developments in post-war Canada. His courage, determination and patriotism led one British official to assert that Fr MacDonell more than any other man had saved not only Upper Canada but had kept Canada in the British empire. For his efforts in the war, Fr MacDonell was granted an additional and substantial pension by the British government. "The good conduct of the Catholics of the County of Glengarry and other parts in Upper Canada during this war", wrote Fr MacDonell, "has procured them the approbation of the Government". The Glengarry Fencibles were disbanded in 1816 at Kingston, Ontario.

Bishop Alexander MacDonell—Vicar Apostolic of Upper Canada

After the war, in 1814, Fr MacDonell sailed to England to negotiate with Addington, now Lord Sidmouth and Home Secretary, for the formal recognition of the Catholic Hierarchy in Canada and the division of the huge diocese of Quebec. MacDonell had been appointed Vicar-General to the Bishop of Quebec, Mgr Joseph Plessis, in 1807, and in 1820 he was consecrated Auxiliary Bishop of Quebec and Vicar Apostolic of Upper Canada with the title of Bishop of Thabraca *in partibus infidelium*. Indicating the unique respect and favour which the former chaplain enjoyed, his episcopal ring was the gift of King George IV.

In 1826, the British government agreed to the division of the Diocese of Quebec and Bishop MacDonell became the first Bishop of Kingston, Ontario, with the title of Bishop of Regiopolis *in partibus infidelium*. He spent the rest of his episcopate establishing missions and building schools and churches across his vast diocese. His efforts on behalf of the Catholic community and the colony were recognized in 1831, when he was elected a member of the Legislative Council of Upper Canada.

Bishop MacDonell thought that one of the ways to pay for his projected diocesan seminary would be to encourage Scottish emigration to Canada and he returned to Scotland in 1839 in an attempt to make the necessary arrangements. He was not to return to Canada, however, for he died of pneumonia in Dumfries on 14 January 1840. The mortal remains of "Big Sandy" were transferred to Kingston in 1861. *The Catholic Encyclopedia* concludes its biography of Bishop MacDonell:

> His voluminous letters reveal the master mind of the organizer and ruler, and the singleness of purpose of the great churchman. His life was a striking example of the truth that in the Catholic Church piety and patriotism go hand in hand. In the year 1840, he died in his native Scotland, whither he had gone with the hope of interesting Irish and Scotch bishops in a scheme of emigration. In 1861, his remains were brought to Kingston by Bishop Horan and were interred beneath the cathedral. Bishop MacDonell in 1804 found three priests and three churches in Upper Canada.

By his energy and perseverance, he induced a considerable immigration to the province, and left at his death 48 churches attended by 30 priests. The memory that survives him is that of a great missionary, prelate and patriot—the Apostle of Ontario.

Many tributes were paid and memorials erected to Bishop MacDonell's life and ministry. In 1929, the Canadian government unveiled a plaque at St Raphael's Church, Glengarry County, Ontario. The inscription reads:

Historic Sites and Monuments Board of Canada.

BISHOP MACDONELL

In grateful remembrance of the eminent public services of the Honourable and Right Reverend Alexander MacDonell, 1760– 1840, as Patriot, Military Chaplain, Educator and Legislator. Here he lived and laboured with success for many years.

One of Bishop MacDonell's favourite sayings was that "every man of his name should either be a priest or a soldier".

Figure 4: Bishop Alexander McDonell: Fencible chaplain

4

"The devotion of this clergy
seems to be very great": Chaplains
in the Crimean War

The Crimean War

The Crimean War (1854–56) was fought by Britain, France, Turkey and Sardinia against Russia. The immediate cause of the war concerned the rights of Christian minorities to access Holy Places in the Turkish–Ottoman empire. The French promoted the rights of Roman Catholics while Russia promoted those of the Eastern Orthodox Church. The underlying cause was a bid to halt Russian expansion in the declining Turkish–Ottoman empire.

Spiritual provision for Catholic soldiers and sailors

A large proportion of the British army was Catholic but the Army Chaplains' Department, formed in 1796, was totally staffed by Anglican clergy. Presbyterian ministers and Catholic priests were granted "administrative parity" in 1835 and 1836 but were denied commissions. At the outbreak of the Crimean War, there were seven commissioned Anglican chaplains, but such a small number could hardly be expected to fulfil religious duties and instil patriotism, temperance and good conduct in an army at war.

In March 1854, Catholic MP Frederick Lucas argued that if Catholic soldiers were "hazarding their lives on behalf of their country", then "their reasonable interests should not be left uncared for". Anglicans received £14,436 to cater for the religious needs of their 74,335 soldiers, Catholics were allocated £2,702 for 41,000 soldiers, and Presbyterians £865 for 12,765 soldiers.

Only £2,000 was allocated for the religious needs of Catholics in the Royal Navy. There were 69 Anglican chaplains but no Catholic chaplains and Lucas opined that the Admiralty feared "the spread of Roman Catholicism more than any invasion". Sidney Herbert, Secretary of State for War, and James Graham, First Lord of the Admiralty, failed to offer a satisfactory response. Catholic priests were not allowed on Royal Navy vessels, but Graham agreed to discuss the provision of shore chaplains with the "Heads of the Roman Catholic Church". Bishop Thomas Grant of Southwark, the Hierarchy's intermediary with the government over the spiritual provision for Catholic servicemen, had been negotiating with the War Office and Admiralty since 1852 but had made limited progress. He moved cautiously, aware that strident claims could antagonize anti-Catholic public opinion and conscious of the fact that he and his brother bishops were struggling to find priests for their newly established and poor dioceses.

In April 1854, the Catholic bishops submitted a *Memorial* to Prime Minister Lord Aberdeen urging that "a greater number of Catholic chaplains be sent with our army to the eastern war and a sufficient number of the same with our navy". Aberdeen replied that "the arrangements which have been made for this service are based upon a due regard to the relative proportions of the several communions to which the men of that expedition belong". Sidney Herbert informed Grant that two Catholic chaplains would be allowed to accompany an estimated 10,000 Catholic soldiers out of 26,000 men bound for the Crimea. Their salaries were £150 per year plus a daily allowance of 3s 6d "to cover their own expenses in the field together with rations for a servant and forage for a horse and mule". In Herbert's opinion, Catholic chaplains were "in a good and proper position".

Catholic chaplains in the Crimean War

Born in 1824, John Wheble studied for the priesthood at St Mary's College, Oscott, and was ordained for the London District in 1847. He became a curate in Chelsea and moved in the highest circles of the English Catholic community, but the nature and context of his vocation changed when he went as chaplain to Catholic soldiers serving with the British army in the Crimea.

In March 1854, Fr Wheble now of the newly created Archdiocese of Westminster and Fr Denis Sheehan of the newly created Diocese of Southwark volunteered to go to the Crimea as chaplains and other priests had "declared their readiness to share in their dangers and their trials". Grant sought financial support for vestments for the priests and devotional books and other spiritual comforts for Catholic soldiers and sailors.

On 28 March 1854, Frs Wheble and Sheehan were welcomed to Malta by Catholic troops who were afraid "that they were destined to go to the East without any spiritual assistance". By April, Fr Sheehan was in Scutari "leading a soldier's life" and ministering to ten regiments of which "a very large portion" was Catholic. Fr Wheble was under canvas with the Gallipoli divisions until he sailed for Varna on 25 June. He served those able to take advantage of his ministry but troop movements compelled him to locate himself where he could be of most value. "By doing so", he wrote,

> I ... put myself in a very isolated spot, but still I had four camps in view, by which some advantage was gained, for my solitary encampment necessarily attracted the notice of the soldiers and enabled then to find me. There are many men who when free, are most anxious to attend daily Mass and obtain prayers.

He arrived at Varna on 27 June. Adversely affected by heat and poor rations, many troops succumbed to cholera and Fr Wheble was soon busy in the hospitals. "No Catholic has died in hospital without the priest seeing him", wrote a Protestant officer. "He is a constant visitor of the sick and he is always trying to find out where sickness is." Chaplains of all denominations were conducting burial services two or three times a day. The correspondent of the *Morning Post* wrote: "How these clergymen stand the work I cannot imagine." The paper reported that many Catholics "must fall sick, die and be buried without the solemnities of their own religion", and it continued, "If we accept the services of the Roman Catholic soldiers to fight our battles, we are bound in return to leave no reasonable necessity of theirs, either for flesh or spirit, uncared for." Amid sickness, hardships and preparations for war the chaplains performed their duties aware that when hostilities commenced, they would be seriously overstretched.

On 3 September, Fr Wheble boarded the *Tenambia* with the 55th Regiment, who treated him "with the greatest kindness and civility". He was given a berth but had to find his own bedclothes.

Bloody work is before us . . .

Fr Wheble now sailed for the Crimea, where he feared that "bloody work is before us and who will live to tell the tale God only knows". On 20 September, he and Fr Sheehan were involved in the Battle of the Alma. Fr Wheble wrote that "our brigade began the battle at the Alma, and suffered much. I had no idea we were so near the Russians when the bullets came whizzing and the round shot bowling along." A French chaplain informed him that they had sufficient chaplains to enable some to stay on the field of battle and give absolution to the wounded while others remained at reception points at the rear. Fr Wheble wrote: "Had our staff of clergy been sufficiently numerous, one of us ought to have followed the battle through for the sake of those who died on the field, and before they could be removed to the rear."

Chaplains were not allowed their own horses, and after undertaking exhausting marches they had to begin their clerical duties. *The Tablet* of 17 October 1854 contained a copy of one of Fr Wheble's letters:

> I simply marched at the head of the column and as soon as a
> poor fellow dropt I was ready to attend him; and before I had
> done all for him and the many others brought back, the army

had advanced far ahead. The battle was over, in fact, before either Sheehan or I had finished our work where the regimental surgeons were busy. We then both started to look for any on the field of battle, but all we came across before reaching the village were dead, and at the village were fresh batches of wounded, and the general hospitals were opened.

I did not cross the river till dark, when I had to find my way to camp. After a long search I found it, but little comfort awaited me there, for my servant had lost all my wraps, and I had not even a great coat to keep me warm during the night. I could not sleep, the cold gave one such cramps, and I gladly hailed the dawn of day. After attending some cholera cases, I went to the general hospital, and spent the day there with Rev. Mr Sheehan.

When night came on and it became impossible to distinguish any object, I returned to camp. The following day was passed again with Sheehan at the general hospital, and in addition to the wounded we had a terrible number of cholera cases to attend. Towards the night all the wounded English had been removed on board ship, and the wounded Russians were being brought in in crowds. I will not attempt to describe any of the horrors of war as witnessed by us among the wounded, dying and dead.

W. H. Russell, war correspondent of *The Times*, reported that

a Catholic priest was active among the dying and might be seen bending over the ghastly forms and whispering to the ears that were fast closing to earthly sounds . . . The wounded were laid out for amputation in a farmyard near the field of battle. Here they were supplied by a Catholic priest attached to one of the Irish regiments. The devotion of this clergy seems to be very great.

The Tablet included a soldier's letter on 28 October 1854:

Almighty God must have endowed Messrs Wheble and Sheehan with a supernatural strength to enable them to do the Herculean work they have. How I prayed to God to strengthen these

> two reverend gentlemen, when, the day after the battle I was
> employed in burying the dead. I saw these two under the hot
> sun, toiling with unceasing energy in their endeavours to assist
> and give consolation to the wounded and dying.

After his initiation into battle and observing its aftermath, Wheble was
feeling the strain. On 7 October, he wrote to Bishop Grant describing
the arduous conditions in which he was working:

> Former hardships were nothing compared with what we have
> had to undergo of late. No Mass for at least five weeks, and no
> chance at present. Had to sleep in the open air without tents,
> drenched with rain and heavy dews. No horse but had to march;
> besides, all hospital visiting before and after marching. Obliged
> to carry provisions and knapsack; but I was obliged to get the
> latter carried for me, or I must have left it on the road. No change
> of clothes for the last three weeks; almost in rags, and generally
> wet with perspiration, or rain, or dew. No extra provisions to be
> got to keep up one's strength. Cholera raging since the Battle of
> the Alma . . .

Fr Wheble visited regimental and general hospitals at Balaklava but could
not serve the artillery, engineers and cavalry hospitals. He made contact
with the 2nd and 4th Divisions, but most of the 3rd were in the trenches
and "no directions had been given for the remainder to assemble for
prayers". He had given up all hope of seeing "the long talked-of assistant
priests", even though Frs John Butt and John Bagshawe of the Diocese of
Southwark had recently arrived, and he was sad that he was "deprived
of the comfort of saying Mass . . . and unable to fortify the poor soldiers
by administering them Holy Communion".

    Aware that another battle was imminent, he administered general
absolution, "an unusual ceremony":

> After prayers, I addressed them upon the necessity of being
> prepared for the coming dangers by obtaining pardon of sin,
> and showed them how, though the integrity of the Sacrament

of Penance required contrition, confession, and satisfaction, yet there were many cases in which that integrity, as regarded the two latter portions, could not be complied with except in desire. I therefore demanded of them that desire, and the intention of, as speedily as possible, supplying the confession and satisfaction, and as proof of their intention I called upon them to renew their baptismal vows before I administered absolution to them. They did so with fervour; and when I then told all those who desired absolution to kneel down, all fell upon their knees ... even some who had not attended church parade or prayers ran forward in haste to participate in the blessings I then offered them in God's name. I fancy about 4,000 at least thus had a chance of preparing their souls for the scenes of strife which are again beginning, and I only regret that I was unable to do service at all the divisions ...

The death of Fr Wheble

The Battle of Balaklava began on 25 October 1854. There are no references to Fr Wheble's involvement in the battle, but it was to be his last engagement. On 3 November, on the hospital ship *Arabia*, he died of dysentery, "no doubt, induced by the labours and privations he had undergone in discharging the duties of his arduous and noble mission". In the cold and driving rain, Frs Sheehan and Bagshawe buried him in the hospital cemetery at Balaklava.

Catholic soldiers mourned his death. The *Freeman's Journal* wrote that the "gentle and unassuming" Fr Wheble was "exceedingly popular amongst all classes and sects in the British army" but especially among "the poor Catholic soldiers to whom he unceasingly ministered". *The Times* of 2 December 1854 reported that from general to drummer boy "everyman mourns him as a friend". The *Morning Chronicle* stated that "the loss of this exemplary Christian is a great one to the army. Nothing could exceed his amiable devotion to the suffering both in mind and body."

Fr Sheehan, himself suffering from dysentery and "in a general state of debility", wrote:

> Poor Wheble's death has made me very, very sad. If you knew how
> much everyone of his own loved him—how much, even every
> Protestant clergyman included of his own division respected him,
> and the good he accomplished, you would realize the loss religion
> has experienced . . .

The Tablet censured the government for not providing chaplains and
wrote that Fr Wheble's "grave will forever stand as a monument to the
niggardly and bigoted policy to which he has fallen sacrifice".

Other Catholic chaplains

By the end of 1854, Frs Sheehan, Bagshawe and Butt were joined by
Frs Michael Canty and James Doyle of the Archdiocese of Westminster,
Henry Clark of the Diocese of Southwark, John O'Dwyer from Ireland,
and Michael Cuffe and Thomas Moloney of the Archdiocese of Dublin.
In December 1854, Frs Doyle and Canty were attached to the 2nd and
3rd Divisions whilst Fr Clark remained at Scutari and Fr Butt was with
the Light Division. Throughout 1855 other chaplains arrived: Frs Joseph
McSweeney of the Archdiocese of Westminster, who had returned home
by August 1855; Michael Gleeson, an Irish Vincentian; John Vertue of
the Diocese of Southwark; Thomas Unsworth of the Diocese of Salford;
and Jesuits William Ronan, Jerrard Strickland, Patrick Duffy and Joseph
Sidney Woollett. The last contingent of chaplains landed on 3 November
1855. They were Frs Augustine Maguire of the Diocese of Cork, Joseph
Mahé and Patrick O'Callaghan of the Archdiocese of Westminster, John
Pauline of the Diocese of Nottingham and James Sheil of the English
College, Valladolid.

More chaplains led Fr Sheehan, as early as December 1854, to raise
the question of local clerical authority. He informed Grant that chaplains
were anxious to "have some sort of superior. The number of chaplains is
sufficiently large to make it difficult for us all to move together without
direction . . . claims to authority have been made . . . which have no
foundation." He urged the bishop to appoint someone who had some
standing with the government and "make the person chosen by your

Lordship the head also of our department". The appointment of a Senior Chaplain was an issue which remained unresolved at the cessation of hostilities, although 23 priests served as chaplains in the Crimea.

Casualties

Six chaplains died either in the Crimea or after their return to England. Fr Wheble's death was followed on 2 February 1855 by that of Fr Michael Canty and on 10 March 1855 by Fr Sheehan's. Henry Clifford, a Catholic officer, wrote:

> This is a sad day for me! I have lost my friend and good priest Fr Canty. Fr Butt gave him the last rights, but he died of the fever brought on by the hardships he has gone through visiting the sick.

Fr Butt, himself suffering from fever, was carried by a soldier to give Fr Sheehan the Last Rites. Henry Clifford had found Fr Sheehan's ministry "very comforting", especially before the battles of Alma and Sebastopol, when the chaplain gave absolution to men before they went into combat. Fr James Doyle died on his return to England in July 1855; Fr James Shiel died at Sebastopol on 15 August 1855; and Fr Jerrard Strickland SJ died in the Crimea on 26 April 1856.

The development of army chaplaincy

In a House of Commons debate on the war, Sir George de Lacy Evans urged the government to acknowledge the ministry of those chaplains "who had a more arduous duty to perform than the chaplains in any war of the same duration" and argued that they should be awarded decorations. Sidney Herbert felt that Anglican chaplains could be offered benefices or pensions but made no reference to other chaplains.

In April 1856, Prime Minister Palmerston stated that eleven commissioned Anglican chaplains were sufficient for 200,000 soldiers.

Within the year, however, the War Office announced an increase in the Army Chaplains' Department from 11 commissioned Anglican chaplains plus Officiating Presbyterian and Catholic chaplains to 20 commissioned Anglicans and 35 Presbyterian and Roman Catholic "Assistant Chaplains". In November 1858, the government made an even more significant concession when a Royal Warrant granted permanent commissions to Presbyterian and Catholic chaplains and introduced four classes of chaplains equating to the rank of colonel, lieutenant-colonel, major and captain. Pay and pensions were equal, and promotions were the responsibility of the Chaplain-General and Secretary of State.

Anglican, Presbyterian and Catholic chaplains eventually ministered in the Crimea to soldiers who appreciated their presence and acknowledged their courage. At a farewell dinner on 9 May 1856 for Sir Colin Campbell, commander of the Highland Division, three Presbyterian chaplains, one Anglican and one Catholic chaplain were present as a toast to "the chaplains" was proposed. The Anglican Principal Chaplain, the Revd Henry Press Wright, wrote that "the critics will find that the thermometer at 7 degrees below zero is an effectual cooler of all wretched theological disputes and a dripping bell tent peculiarly calculated to put a damper upon all unkind feeling". Chaplains had experienced "miseries so great" that they had "every incitement to unity but none to division". Fr Joseph Woollett SJ wrote that in the Crimea there had been no "religious controversies or discussions" among chaplains, that Catholic priests had been able to distribute tracts and other reading matter, and that "harmony was not to be disturbed by religious dissent". Chaplains of different Christian denominations laboured and died together in their wartime ministry.

In April 1859, the War Office informed Bishop Grant that priests he had nominated had been commissioned as Catholic chaplains in the British army. Six were Crimean veterans. In future, Grant wanted only "zealous and edifying men" worthy of the memory of those "who went to their reward in the last war". The ministry of Fr Wheble and other padres demonstrated Catholic patriotism and had drawn attention to the spiritual needs of the ordinary soldier, long regarded as a social outcast.

Commemoration

Six Anglican chaplains also died in the Crimea and their names, together with the six Catholic chaplains, are commemorated in the Royal Garrison Church, Portsmouth.

A memorial tablet to Fr Sheehan was erected in St George's Cathedral, Southwark. A memorial stone was also placed over his grave in the Light Division Cemetery, Crimea. It is testimony to the respect that the soldiers had for their priests.

THIS TOMB ENSHRINES IN ITS BOSOM
THE MORTAL REMAINS
+
IHS
of the
REVD DENIS SHEEHAN
Catholic Chaplain to the British Forces
The 88th Connaught Rangers have had the
honour of erecting to his Sacred Memory
this Monument, for with them he lived and
with them he died 10th March 1855
Aged 31 years
In the Battle Field he stood beside them
In their sickness and wounds he consoled them
Many a British soldier filled with hope
did pass to GOD and aided by the prayers and
fortified by the ministration of this
HOLY PRIEST
May he rest in peace
AMEN

At St Mary's College, Oscott, a chapel window is dedicated to the memory of Fr Wheble. It depicts him setting sail for the Crimea, giving absolution to soldiers, attending the wounded at the Alma, and his death on board the *Arabia*.

**Figure 5: Crimean War medals of Fr Joseph O'Dwyer
CF (Royal Army Chaplains' Museum)**

5

"A martyr to hardship and privations": Chaplains in the Indian Mutiny*

The East India Company, chaplains and missionaries

In 1857, British India was governed by the East India Company, whose army of Muslims, Hindus, Sikhs, Europeans and Anglo-Indians was British officered and operated alongside British army units. "By 1850", wrote Corelli Barnett, "India had become the greatest formative influence on the life, language and legend of the British army, for most British soldiers could expect to serve there, and for a long time. India, with its heat, stinks and noise, its enveloping dust, its glamour and poverty, became the British army's second home—perhaps its first."

The Company had provided Anglican army chaplains since the late seventeenth century and in the early-nineteenth century it renewed its efforts to spread Christianity and improve army chaplaincy. Chaplains were appointed to European and Eurasian Christians in the Company's army and in the British army, but the Company also paid for Presbyterian and Catholic army chaplains. However, only Anglican chaplains were on Company staff and they were in receipt of better pay and conditions of service than other chaplains. A large minority of the British army was Catholic, but their chaplains received lower salaries than both Anglican and Presbyterian chaplains. Catholic chaplains conducted their ministry under significant financial handicaps. For its part, the Company preferred even the Catholic Christian influence to that of indigenous religions.

---

*   The term "Indian Mutiny" is now contested. We have used it as it was used contemporaneously.

Catholic soldiers and their chaplains were at other disadvantages. They received nothing for the maintenance of their chapels, their children were denied Catholic schools, and on some stations Catholic troops were compelled to attend Anglican services. The *Bengal Catholic Herald* lamented that "nothing has been done for the Catholic soldier", and, in October 1857, *The Tablet* voiced a commonly held non-Catholic opinion about Irish soldiers and their chaplains. "The East India Company and the English government", it claimed, "don't care one farthing about . . . Catholic Chaplains, nor value their services in any manner whatever, except as a kind of useful spiritual policeman to keep the Catholic soldiers from getting drunk and breaking the peace."

The Indian Mutiny

The Mutiny began among some of the Company's Indian troops (sepoys) in April 1857 and lasted until July 1859. The pretext for the disturbances was the Company's introduction of the Enfield Rifle which sepoys had to use lubricated cartridges to load. A rumour spread that the lubrication included either pig or beef tallow. To have contact with either was an insult to Muslims and Hindus respectively and the rumour added to wider Indian concerns about the British dispossessing indigenous landowners, undermining traditional Indian society and spreading Christianity. The Mutiny was vicious and reports of atrocities and massacres, committed by both sides, shocked Victorian society. "The Mutiny came upon us without sign or warning", wrote a correspondent to *The Tablet* in 1884, but earlier and more perceptive observers could see many complicated reasons for the multi-faceted uprisings.

In April 1857, there were 47,000 British troops in India as opposed to 232,000 Indian troops in the Company's army and other Indian regiments. British reinforcements were sent but, wrote Sir John Smyth, "on the plains of India, a small British garrison . . . British civilians and . . . British families, sustained an ordeal of unparalleled drama, danger, anxiety, and hardship; and, for a time, the outcome was in considerable doubt".

Catholic agitation for army chaplains in India

Catholic agitation for army chaplains pre-dated the Indian Mutiny. It gained strength after the Restoration of the English and Welsh Hierarchy in 1850, but Catholic protests were weakened by differences between the Irish and English and Welsh Hierarchies over the nomination and deployment of chaplains to Ireland.

On the outbreak of the Mutiny, the Irish bishops reverted to a familiar ploy. They sent a memorial to Prime Minister Lord Palmerston stating that Catholic soldiers "now engaged in the bloody war in India, have not their spiritual wants supplied. Their numbers and their dangers call loudly for a considerable increase of priests to minister to these spiritual wants." Catholics were "shedding their blood for their country" and the bishops considered that they were entitled to parity of religious support. They would advise Irish Catholics not to enlist "unless they can get the consolation and support of their religion when they are on the field of battle or lying wounded and dying in a military hospital".

Yet, as Bishop Grant, the hierarchy's intermediary with the government, pointed out, Irish bishops were slow to provide chaplains. "It was intimated", he wrote, "that priests were wanted for India but the Irish bishops have offered neither priests nor collections towards sending them out." *The Tablet* asked if "there was any hope from Ireland" for chaplains for the thousands of Irish and Catholic soldiers sent to India. Bishop Grant concluded that the government would provide chaplains, but he could not find priests. Some English Jesuits were against sending "some of ours" to India "to be shot or carried off by cholera, fever, etc." and resisted moves to recruit chaplains from the Society. Some Irish priests in England publicly opposed the call for chaplains, thereby discouraging Irishmen from enlisting.

Episcopal criticism of government policy had been frequently voiced during the Crimean War, and in August 1857, *The Tablet* claimed it did not need to remind its readers "of the total apathy of the authorities with respect to all that concerns the spiritual consolations of the Catholic defenders of the state". In September 1857, it stated that "Catholic soldiers must go out, and Catholic souls must be periled" and it urged bishops to deprive home missions of priests "whom they can ill-spare".

Catholic chaplains in the Indian Mutiny

On 28 August 1857, Cardinal Wiseman was informed by the War Office that six priests would be sent as Officiating Chaplains to minister to Catholic troops in India, and he expressed the hope that bishops would provide "zealous priests", so that "Roman Catholic soldiers would not be left in want of spiritual aid". He also received authority from Rome to grant faculties to army chaplains.

The legislative process of introducing commissioned Catholic army chaplains was proceeding slowly and again Bishop Grant relied on volunteers. In September 1857, Frs Edward Lescher and John Kyne of the Archdiocese of Westminster and Fr William Stone of the Diocese of Southwark sailed from Southampton to Marseilles and then travelled to India "by the overland route", arriving in India in November. In October, Frs John Browne of the Diocese of Salford, Patrick Fairhurst of the Diocese of Liverpool, the Augustinian Timothy Crowther, and Charles Morgan, not attached to a diocese, set sail. In January 1859, they were joined by Crimean veterans Frs Michael Cuffe, Joseph O'Dwyer and Thomas Moloney. As *The Tablet* noted: "The poor soldiers will at length have the blessings of priests among them . . . clergymen of experience . . . worthy priests that served in the Crimea." Catholic soldiers, *The Tablet* continued, would welcome them in India with "the greatest kindness" and they would have "the deepest respect of the Protestant authorities".

On arriving in India, the chaplains found confusion about their role. Fr Lescher complained that their ministry was not properly recognized nor was there any military inclination to assist them. The army refuted this allegation: the spiritual worth of chaplains was recognized, they were mentioned in army orders, and every effort was made to assist them. It was "of profound regret" to the commander-in-chief that Fr Lescher failed to understand that the padres' duties were being conducted in the midst of a conflict and that spiritual assistance to troops and garrisons was subject "to the exigencies of war". Fr O'Dwyer wrote that both military and Company officials were unhelpful and a sense of muddling through was evident from the early correspondence of Fr Kyne. In a letter written from Calcutta to Cardinal Wiseman in November 1857, he remarked that he had nothing to model his work upon and that "each chaplain will have to use his own discretion in choosing where he is to work as well as in all other matters".

Chaplains were also unsure as to how Catholic troops would receive them, as attention to religious duties varied among the soldiers. Fr Kyne, who had served a poor mission in Clerkenwell before leaving for India, received a warm welcome from Catholic officers and men at Lucknow in January 1858, and he was presented with a horse by soldiers of the 88th Regiment (Connaught Rangers). He wrote to Cardinal Wiseman:

> The majority of the Catholics in the Camp are now on the right side and this is saying a great deal. They are exceedingly fervent ... the daily Mass is well attended. The Communicants are sometimes as many as 20 a day & upwards of 50 on Sundays. There is a crowd every evening at the Rosary and Sermon ...

The commanding officer ordered that a shelter be erected for services because the padre's tent was too small. The new "chapel" accommodated 300 and linen, furniture and ornaments had to be bought or borrowed. In February 1858, Fr Kyne wrote to Bishop Grant informing him that he had successfully ministered to new recruits arriving in India and was "convinced that his future work would be among soldiers, whose spiritual necessities are greater than that of any other class". He was "determined to continue even if it cost him his life". Fr Kyne was to witness "stirring events", but his "arduous labours" and "the effects of the climate" seriously impaired his health.

In June 1858, Fr Crowther wrote of the intense heat and discomfort he was experiencing. "Sickness and death are prevalent", he wrote, "and more fall by natural causes than by the edge of the sword." He was of the opinion that military operations were "more like a hunt of wild beasts", and, he concluded, "We are all weary of our life, and would fain return to the quiet usefulness of a home mission." Twelve months later, he wrote from Lucknow that the "raw youths that came out a year ago were now clergymen of experience", who received "the greatest kindness from the Catholic officers and men and the deep respect of the Protestant authorities". Such respect did not extend to pay and conditions, however, and he and other chaplains were weary of appealing and complaining about the discrepancies. Meanwhile, he wrote that Fr Lescher was with General Whitworth's column, Fr Browne was with Brigadier Horsford's force, Fr O'Dwyer was with Brigadier Eveleigh's Division, and Fr Daniel Brosnan of the Archdiocese of Southwark ministered at Allahabad.

In September 1858, Fr Stone wrote:

> I have everything quite opposite to the word comfort. Living under canvas during the wet season is very disagreeable, for the rain comes down in torrents, the ground all around is quite marshy and is one large graveyard, by the reason of the number killed and buried about it. Everything in my small tent is either wet or damp, my clothes in the morning when I put them on are quite wet from the heavy dew that falls at night.

He recounted that the "wind blows so strong" and that during a burial service a lightning strike had killed two soldiers at the graveside. Some chaplains failed to cope with conditions and climate and Bishop Grant was informed that some had taken to alcohol.

All chaplains were ill-prepared for the expense, living conditions, geography and climate of India. Fr O'Dwyer wrote:

> You can have no idea of what a miserable country this is. I mean the immense plain of Bengal. Here at Allahabad, everything but mutton is excessively dear . . . Fr Felix (an Italian Capuchin missionary) and I live in the verandah of the chapel . . . By means of mats and bamboo blinds we have contrived to form bedrooms.

The Company also employed European missionaries to act as army chaplains, and the term "padre" is taken from the British soldiers' reference to a Catholic missionary-chaplain. Fr O'Dwyer had stayed with Fr Felix, but he also mentioned Frs Zacaharias, Julius, Bernard and Androdatus. In January 1859, Bishop Grant was informed by the War Office that missionaries Frs John Knaresborough, Peter O'Rorke, Lewis Muscarello and Martin Van Der Ryt had been appointed chaplains in India, but he had received no further details. Since arriving from Ireland in 1848, Fr Nicholas Barry had ministered to the Company's Irish

Catholic soldiers and their families at Agra and his ministry continued through the Mutiny. Fr William Strickland SJ, dressed like a soldier and carrying a sword and pistol for personal protection, ministered to Sir Hugh Rose's Division and was the only chaplain with the Division. A soldier wrote: "I can assure you that he was a glad sight to some of our men, not only his own followers but others." Fr Cuffe, however, wrote that Fr Strickland "was more like an Aide-de-Camp than a missionary, always with the officers". Other missionary-chaplains were Fr L. H. Gard, Fr Bernard Paes, who ministered to the 56th Regiment, and the Capuchin Fr Josaphat who, "in danger from mutineers and wild beasts", struggled to attend to 500 troops. Fr William Gleeson, an Irish missionary at Agra, wrote that as he was tending a dying man, "shot by a cannon ball", his horse was stolen by the enemy. "I think I will go with the army to Delhi", he concluded.

All padres were overworked during the long sieges of the garrisons. Richard Holmes wrote of two Protestant army chaplains and an Italian Jesuit in a camp on Delhi ridge. Before an attack on 14 September 1857, one officer wrote that "there was not much sleep. Just after midnight we fell in as quickly as possible, and by the light of a lantern the orders for the assault were read to the men. Any man who might be wounded was to be left where he fell." Fr Bertrand, a Jesuit and "a fine looking man wearing a long beard and moustache", who "could hardly speak a word of English", blessed the Catholics in the 52nd Light Infantry and prayed for mercy "on the souls of those soon to die". He then went from regiment to regiment "giving quiet consolation". When he reached the 75th Highlanders, he asked the commanding officers for permission to bless the men saying: "We may differ, some of us in manners of religion, but the blessing of an old man and a clergyman can do nothing but good." There was widespread agreement and the padre continued his rounds. Like clergymen of other denominations, Fr Bertrand conducted himself bravely and his services were so highly esteemed that he was a guest of honour in the officers' mess. An Anglican padre called him "a pattern of a Roman Catholic priest whose services have been justly recognized". Catholic soldiers, however, welcomed English-speaking chaplains.

Casualties

Before the Mutiny, missionary-chaplains had already suffered. In 1845, the French Capuchin, Fr Francis, was killed by "friendly fire" whilst accompanying an infantry regiment into battle against Sikhs at Mudki:

> He was in the act of hearing the confession of an Irish soldier who had been mortally wounded when a body of English cavalry swept past, and one of the dragoons thinking the Rev. Father was a Sikh made a slashing cut at him with his sword and almost severed the head from the body.

The following day Fr Francis was buried "in the jungle".

In the Mutiny, the Revd Henry Polehampton, an Anglican padre, was shot and wounded during the siege of Lucknow. He later contracted cholera and died before the siege was lifted. The Italian Capuchin Fr Zacaharias, "the chaplain of Delhi", was an early victim of the Mutiny, shot by mutineers before the altar of his church. It was recorded that "no vestiges of his body nor any of the sacred vessels or vestments were ever recovered". The church was used as a stable until order was restored by British forces. It was cleaned up and reopened for divine services by Fr Bertrand.

The Italian Capuchins Frs Androdatus and Bernard were in the siege of Lucknow between May and November 1857. Fr Androdatus died in a military convoy between the garrisons of Lucknow and Cawnpore after the civilians had been evacuated. A survivor of the siege wrote: "I cannot describe the invaluable spiritual assistance and consolation the two Fathers afforded the besieged during their weary, anxious and painful captivity."

Fr Joseph Rooney left Ireland in 1847 with Fr Nicholas Barry to establish St Peter's College, Agra. Fr Rooney served at Kanpur, the site of a large garrison. In June 1857, Kanpur became the target of a rebellion culminating in the siege of Cawnpore, when hundreds of men, women and children in the encampment were massacred. Fr Rooney was hanged by mutineers after ministering to a wounded soldier.

Fr Patrick Fairhurst, one of the original padres to be sent to India by Bishop Grant, died at Lucknow on 16 June 1858. Born in Liverpool and educated at St Cuthbert's College, Ushaw, he was ordained on 23 September 1848 and was Rector of St Mary's, Birchley, before going to India. Fr Fairhurst was attached to the Indian Field Force and died of sunstroke during the siege of Lucknow. As Fr John Browne reported, Fr Fairhurst's life in India "had been one of constant hardship and discomfort" and his health deteriorated. He ignored medical advice and rode out to minister to men of the 90th Regiment. On his return he collapsed, and Fr Browne administered the Last Rites. On his death, Fr Fairhurst was buried in his priestly vestments "among the numerous graves of those gallant defenders" of the Residency. His funeral was attended by men and officers of the 23rd Regiment, but Frs Kyne and Morgan were too ill to attend. A monument to Fr Fairhurst was raised in the Residency grounds by Catholic soldiers. The inscription reads:

> Pray for the soul of the Rev Patrick Fairhurst who, to assist his Catholic brethren amid the perils of the great Indian Rebellion, left his home and fell a martyr to hardship and privations on the 16th June A. D. 1858. The Catholic soldiers of Her Majesty's 53rd Regiment here testify their admiration and gratitude.

Commissioned Catholic army chaplains

The chaplains' ministry in the Crimea and India influenced the promulgation of the Royal Warrant of November 1858, which allowed Catholic priests to become commissioned army chaplains. But the Warrant was also the outcome of persistent lobbying by Catholic MPs and the Catholic press.

Catholic chaplains were given the same rank, pay and conditions as Anglican and Presbyterian chaplains. *The Tablet* stated that "this then is equality, practical and theoretical". By April 1859, 19 Catholic army chaplains had received permanent commissions, some with seniority backdated. They were given the post-nominal "Chaplain to the Forces" abbreviated to "CF". Fifteen were paid by the government, but four serving in India were paid for by the Company. Only when they ceased to receive pay from the Company would they be paid by the government. Of those nominated for a commission by Bishop Grant, Frs Michael Cuffe, Thomas Moloney, Joseph O'Dwyer, Charles Morgan and John Browne were serving in India. (See Appendix I.)

The appointment of commissioned Catholic chaplains did not entirely satisfy Catholic demands, however. The provision of Catholic army schools and orphanages and widows' payments from Patriotic Funds were still causes of resentment.

In 1863, Cardinal Wiseman recalled that Catholic soldiers in the Crimea and India had been denied "the exercise of their religion" and the "benefit of Catholic chaplains", but an end had been "put to this vexatious inequality" in 1858. "It has come to be understood", he wrote, "that piety does not stand in the way of valour, and that soldiers who go to confession fight none the less bravely than those who do not." The Revd Henry Press Wright, Principal Chaplain, supported Wiseman's claim, writing that "when the fight becomes fierce and bloody, there is no cry 'Presbyterians and Roman Catholics to the rear' but the one universal shout is 'Forward, Forward!'".

Church and government reached agreement regarding the appointment, rank, deployment and conditions of service for army chaplains, but issues of ecclesiastical authority remained. Cardinal Wiseman could grant faculties—the licence to practise the ministry of a priest—to Catholic chaplains to the British army in Britain, but Bishop Grant remained responsible for nominating, with episcopal approval, and disciplining chaplains. In 1863, Rome gave Irish bishops ecclesiastical authority over British army chaplains serving in Irish dioceses, and Grant's correspondence with Archbishop Cullen of Dublin shows his sensitivity to this jurisdiction. Chaplains remained subject to the authority of their own bishop or religious superior but were required to obtain individual faculties from local bishops when serving in countries outside the British Isles.

In the army, Catholic chaplains were not subject to the authority of the Anglican Chaplain-General or any other chaplain of a non-Catholic denomination. Most importantly, from the army's point of view, Catholic chaplains were subject only to military discipline and ultimately answerable to the Adjutant-General.

6

Padres to prelates: Victorian chaplains who became bishops

Fr Robert Brindle

When he died on 27 June 1916, Robert Brindle, Bishop of Nottingham, was the most decorated Catholic chaplain to have served in the British army. Born in Liverpool on 4 November 1837, Brindle was ordained in 1862 and became a priest for the Diocese of Plymouth. On 12 January 1874 he was commissioned as Chaplain to the Forces and remained in the army until his retirement in 1899. In that year, he was appointed Auxiliary Bishop in the Archdiocese of Westminster and in 1901 he was translated to the See of Nottingham.

Chaplain with the Egyptian and Sudan expeditions, 1882–85

Fr Brindle served first at Woolwich and then Nova Scotia and, in August 1882, with Frs James Bellord, Reginald Collins, Joseph Corbett and W. C. Magill, was deployed with an expeditionary force sent to protect British interests in Egypt. *The Tablet* reported that four regiments—18th Royal Irish, 87th Fusiliers, and 104th and 74th Highlanders—were mainly Catholic, and Brindle was attached to the Royal Irish.

Fr Brindle was not at the British defeat of the Egyptian army at Tel-el-Kebir on 13 September 1882 as he was suffering from cholera. However, his ministry had a significant impact on other points of the expedition. The British used the River Nile to transport men and supplies, but when the water level was low and dangerous rocks were exposed, they experienced great difficulty in dragging boats upstream. Major-General Sir Garnet Wolseley offered a £10 prize to the unit which arrived first with its stores intact. Major-General Sir Evelyn Wood recalled, "I saw the little flotilla of boats flying the Irish flag toiling up the river. Fr Brindle got out when he pulled up to us, hot, tired, irritable, with his hands blistered and perspiration running down his face." Brindle had been pulling the stroke oar in order "to encourage them". The battalion made the best time over the 300-mile journey and won the prize.

In an attempt to reach Khartoum, Wolseley sent men by steamer up the Nile and despatched his Camel Corps across the desert. The Dervishes, as the Mahdi's troops were known, were repulsed near Metemmeh, but learning that Khartoum had fallen, Wolseley's column retired across the desert to Korti. The Royal Irish were sent to reinforce and protect the desert column and Fr Brindle, foregoing the use of a camel, marched with his men. When they arrived at the camp at Korti, Fr Brindle was seen "marching with the regiment, but the soles of his boots were gone, and rags rolled about his feet replaced them". Another Catholic army chaplain, Fr Charles Keatinge of the Diocese of Salford, wrote about the impression given by Brindle and the influence that he had upon the men.

One thing about which all agree is that Fr Brindle did his duty nobly; he was the only chaplain of any religion to cross the desert to Metemmeh and he marched the whole way "ever ready . . . to carry a man's rifle or give away a drink from his water bottle".

Throughout the months at their camp at Kurot, Fr Keatinge continued, Fr Brindle allowed no grumbling. Sir Evelyn Wood recalled that all ranks admired him and described him as "the most popular man in the Expedition".

Fr Brindle, now Senior Catholic Chaplain, had established a firm reputation. In the history of the Royal Irish Regiment, it was recorded that "his genial personality, his devotion to duty, his coolness in danger, his indifference to hardship, combined to give him a remarkable influence over the men, which he exerted invariably in the interest of the service". An observer recorded that "according to my experience, everyone that met him appreciated him. He was a wonderful man for making friends, and Lord Wolseley had a very high opinion of him." Brindle was awarded the British War Medal with four clasps for his service with the Nile Expedition. Other Catholic chaplains to receive campaign medals were Frs Keatinge, Emmanuel Morgan and James Bellord of the Diocese of Southwark, and Fr Frederick Gascoigne of the Diocese of Portsmouth. They, like Fr Brindle, ministered to men in battle, those wounded and those suffering from dysentery and enteric fever. They conducted many funerals which were "very simply carried out". Fr Bellord was wounded at the Battle of Tel-el-Kebir.

With Kitchener in Khartoum, 1896–98

Fr Brindle returned to England in 1886 and was stationed at Colchester and Aldershot for the next ten years, but in 1896 he was attached to Major-General Sir Herbert Kitchener's Anglo-Egyptian Expedition sent to conquer the Sudan and avenge the death of General Gordon at Khartoum in 1885. On his arrival in Egypt, the Revd Owen Watkins, Wesleyan Chaplain to the Forces and attached to the Royal Warwickshire Regiment, met up with Fr Brindle and other chaplains:

> I made acquaintance with my three brother chaplains . . . good men all, first and chief amongst them being that man beloved of all ranks, Fr Brindle of the Roman Catholic Church. No other man in the Chaplains' Department has seen so much service as he—no Nile campaign, it is said, is complete without Fr Brindle; and though over sixty years of age, he marches as gaily and carries himself as straight as any boy.

Watkins recorded that he became indebted to Fr Brindle "in many ways, for the old campaigner, if he has the will, can do much to help one who is inexperienced". This was a feature of the co-operation engendered during the campaign by Watkins and Brindle and also by the Revd John Simms, a Presbyterian chaplain, and the Revd A. W. Watson, an Anglican chaplain. All recognized their mutual dependence yet respected their denominational differences. As Watkins wrote, "Each in his own way spent his days for the good of the men and in the service of the God whose minister he was proud to be." Watkins wrote that on marches across the desert a chaplain's duties "were not pleasant, as men fell out of the ranks utterly exhausted and borne down with the heat of the sun". Medical officers and chaplains brought up the rear offering encouragement and providing assistance.

Once again Fr Brindle distinguished himself by his ministrations to the troops of all denominations and by his brave conduct. When cholera struck the camp at Sarras, Brindle worked tirelessly among the victims. The military artist Richard Caton Woodville recalled the "undaunted spirit" of Fr Brindle, his devotion to the troops and their response:

> All the Tommies loved him . . . It was he who carried the Tommies
> out of their quarters in his arms, placed them in the ambulance to
> convey them to the hospital when nobody else would come near
> them, as the cholera was raging and the men were dying like flies,
> and even many of the doctors themselves had died.

During the halt at Atbara, Brindle bravely crossed the desert to minister to a dying Catholic soldier in another camp about ten miles away. He walked at night, unarmed, across the perilous and enemy-infested desert of El Teb, administered the Last Rites to the dying soldier and stayed with him until the end. Then he tramped back across the desert to his own camp in time to say Mass next morning.

On Good Friday 8 April 1898, Brindle took part in the Battle of Atbara against the opposing Mahdist army and was subsequently involved in the successful Battle of Omdurman on 2 September. It was noted that in the three great attacks at Omdurman "the heroic priest was in the fighting line".

At the subsequent memorial service for General Gordon, Fr Brindle was one of the four officiating chaplains—Anglican, Catholic, Wesleyan and Presbyterian:

> After the British and Egyptian flags had been run up on the roof
> of the palace there followed a dead hush while the four military
> chaplains . . . came slowly forward and ranged themselves with
> their backs to the palace, just before Kitchener. The Presbyterian

read the fifteenth psalm, the Anglican led the rustling whisper
of the Lord's Prayer. Snow-haired Father Brindle, best beloved
of priests, laid his helmet at his feet and read a memorial prayer
bare headed in the sun.

The prayer was later officially printed and distributed among the troops.
In a letter to Lord Roberts on the effectiveness of chaplains during the
Second Anglo-Boer War, Winston Churchill recalled "the venerable
figure and noble character of Father Brindle in the River War".

The wounded were treated in field and camp hospitals, and the
chaplains passed day after day tending the wounded and burying the
dead. Services were conducted for the many soldiers who had died in the
battles at Atbara and Omdurman and in other locations from wounds,
heatstroke, exhaustion and disease. Burial mounds began to appear
"among the mimosa bushes, each with its wooden cross marking the
last resting place of another brave soldier". Desert cemeteries became a
feature of the campaign and marked the Lines of Communication.

For his service in the Khartoum Expedition of 1896–98, Brindle
received the campaign medal with three clasps. He was also awarded
the Turkish Orders of the Medjidie with three clasps, the Osmanieh with
four clasps, and the Khedive's Bronze Star. In November 1898, he was
gazetted as a Companion of the Distinguished Service Order (DSO). The
citation ran: "Rev. Robert Brindle, Chaplain to the Forces, 1st Class, in
recognition of his services in Egypt and the Sudan, including the Battles
of Atbara and Khartoum." The insignia were presented to Brindle by
the Officer Commanding in Egypt at a full-dress parade of the Cairo
Garrison on 20 December 1898.

In 1899, on his retirement from the army, Brindle was appointed an
Auxiliary Bishop of Westminster and travelled from Egypt to Rome in
March for his episcopal consecration as titular Bishop of Hermopolis
by Cardinal Satolli. While in Rome, his DSO was stolen and he had
to purchase another. The replacement was presented to him by Queen
Victoria on 11 May 1899.

Fr Brindle was Mentioned in Despatches three times, was much
decorated, received a Good Service Pension and had a fine reputation. It
has been suggested that he was nominated for a Commander of the Order

of the Bath, but it was not permitted to bestow this honour on a chaplain, especially a Catholic chaplain. Certainly, some of the troops he served were of the opinion that he should have been knighted. Kitchener, whose own reputation had been made in Egypt and the Sudan, maintained contact with Fr Brindle and wrote: "I often look back in memory to the old Soudan days when you used to lead the troops across the desert and wish those days back again . . . I was delighted to get your letter, and to feel that you still have a kindly remembrance of your old friend." Lord Wolseley kept a picture of Brindle on his mantelpiece and described him as "one of the finest soldiers in the British army".

At a dinner to mark his elevation to the episcopate, Fr William Alexander made the important distinction between Fr Brindle's priestly vocation and his army career:

> It is this happy blending of priest and officer—never permitting the latter to overshadow the former, but ever keeping your priesthood in the front rank which has gained for you the esteem and respect not only of your colleagues in the service, not only of those of your own faith, but of every officer and every man, no matter what might be his religious opinions, with whom you came in contact, so that it maybe said without exaggeration that the name of Father Brindle is to-day a household word throughout the British army.

Despite their fine records of service, bravery and pastoral commitment, no other chaplain-bishop matched Bishop Brindle's experience, decorations or public reputation. He was buried with full military honours in the crypt of St Barnabas Cathedral, Nottingham.

Other Victorian chaplain-prelates

The Catholic chaplains of the mid-to-late Victorian era laid the foundations for both the conduct of the priestly ministry to the Catholics in the army and the establishment of a Catholic presence within the Army Chaplains' Department across the British empire.

After the Crimean War, Catholic chaplains ministered in India, Burma, New Zealand, the West Indies, Egypt, the Sudan, Malta, South Africa, China, Hong Kong, Ireland and on home bases. They did much to enhance the status of Catholic army padres among senior officers, they converted many soldiers to Catholicism, and they provided a spiritual focus and welfare support for Catholic soldiers and their families. They earned a reputation for dedicated service and for bravery in battle and were part of Britain's imperial expansion. Fr Brindle was prominent in this development, but he was not the only Catholic chaplain whose outstanding service was recognized. Nor was he the only nineteenth-century Catholic army chaplain to be raised to the episcopate. As Michael Snape has commented, the Vatican recognized the practical value of choosing former army chaplains to be bishops in dioceses with a large military presence. Bishop Brindle and other former chaplains, however, were made bishops of existing sees—they had no jurisdiction over Catholics and chaplains in the military.

Fr John Butt, a veteran chaplain of the Crimean War, became Bishop of Southwark in 1885. He was born in 1826 at Richmond, Surrey, educated at St Edmund's, Ware, and ordained to the priesthood by Bishop Nicholas Wiseman, Vicar Apostolic of the London District on 15 July 1849. When the Crimean War broke out in 1854, Fr Butt was a priest of the Diocese of Southwark and answered the call of Bishop Thomas Grant for paid but non-commissioned chaplains to accompany Catholics in the Crimean Expeditionary Force. Like other chaplains—commissioned Anglican chaplains and Officiating Chaplains of other Christian denominations—Butt experienced the full horror associated with that particular war. He and other priests ministered at the Battles of the Alma, Sebastopol and Balaklava, and like the troops they were affected by a merciless combination of contagious disease, death, injury, privation and maladministration. During his Crimean ministry Fr Butt, stricken by cholera, was carried several miles to give the Last Rites to another chaplain. Fr Butt recovered and went on to become a Senior Chaplain to the Forces.

After the war, Fr Butt returned to his parish at St Leonard's in Sussex and then became chaplain to the Duke of Norfolk at Arundel. In 1885, he was consecrated as Auxiliary Bishop of Southwark and titular Bishop of

Melos. He succeeded Bishop Coffin as Bishop of Southwark later in the same year and assumed ecclesiastical control of army chaplains. On his retirement, Bishop Butt assumed the title of Bishop of Sebastopolis—an appropriate title for a Crimean chaplain.

Fr John Vertue, born in London on 28 April 1826, was one of the first Catholic priests to be commissioned into the Army Chaplains' Department after 1858. Ordained on 20 December 1851 for the Diocese of Southwark, he was commissioned as Chaplain to the Forces, 4th Class, with the rank of captain; his seniority was backdated to 24 June 1855, when he had been appointed Officiating Chaplain at Chatham. He was promoted Chaplain, 3rd Class on 18 May 1865 with the rank of major, promoted Chaplain, 2nd Class on 2 February 1870 with the rank of lieutenant-colonel, and finally promoted Chaplain, 1st Class with the rank of colonel on 2 February 1875.

On service in Bermuda, Fr Vertue worked tirelessly among soldiers and sailors stricken by yellow fever. He later received a special vote of thanks from the War Office and was promoted for "devotion to the welfare of the troops and conspicuous disregard of personal dangers". In 1865, he returned to England and was chaplain at Colchester until 1871. From there, he moved to Portsmouth, where he remained until 1876, when he was appointed to Malta. According to a contemporary observer, his tall and dignified appearance impressed those around him, and it was recorded that "Mgr Vertue's love of precision and correctness was carried into the matter of dress". Whereas Bishop Grant feared that chaplains would lose their priestly identity when a military uniform was introduced, Vertue had no such reservations.

> When engaged in the performance of his round of military visits, he wore a good suit of broadcloth, such as any priest would wear in the streets of an English town, and a chaplain's cap with flat peak and black braided band. When it was a full-dress military function, however, he wore a long frock coat with a colonel's crowns in gold braid on the collar, and a broad stripe of black braid on the trouser. Very often he was seen walking the streets in the full habit of an Italian priest, with buttoned cassock, flowing cloak, buckled shoes, and a wide beaver hat—a costume which

became him admirably. His garb always comprised, of course, the violet front of a Monsignore; and I think he also sometimes wore a violet cassock and skull cap—or zucchetto?

Not for nothing was Mgr Vertue called "John the Magnificent". Some regarded him as a "society priest", but he never neglected his duties and his visits to Catholic soldiers were "unremitting". He often "put out in his boat and scrambled up a steamer's side to give the consolations of religion" to a dying seaman. He also compiled a prayer book for the use of Catholic soldiers. In May 1882, Fr Vertue was appointed as first bishop of the newly created Diocese of Portsmouth and assumed responsibility for naval chaplains. He died in May 1900.

Fr James Bellord was born in London in 1846 and educated at St Edmund's College, Ware, and St Thomas's Seminary, Hammersmith. After ordination in 1870, Fr Bellord spent a short time on the mission at Deptford in the Archdiocese of Southwark before being commissioned as an army chaplain. He served in Bermuda from 1875 to 1877 and again from 1898 to 1892. In the Zulu War of 1879, he was present at the Battle of Ulundi and received the medal with clasp. In that campaign, he recovered the body of the Prince Imperial of France after an ambush. He subsequently presided, in full ecclesiastical dress, over the Prince's Catholic funeral and headed the cortege. Fr Bellord subsequently served in the First Anglo-Boer War of 1881 and also the Egyptian War in the following year. At the Battle of Tel-el-Kebir, he was severely wounded and was carried around in an ambulance so that he could minister to the wounded and dying. In consequence of his conduct, he was promoted Chaplain to the Forces, 3rd Class, and received the campaign medal and the Khedive's Star.

Fr Bellord later served at Aldershot where, in addition to ministering to the military garrisons in the district, he also began and financed the town mission of Fareham. While at Aldershot he was also in communication with Giovanni Bosco, founder of the Salesian Order. Fr Bellord had heard that the Falkland Islands was to lose its Catholic priest and urged Bosco to assume pastoral responsibility for the distant mission. "As for me", he wrote, "I am a military chaplain and do not enjoy freedom, but I would like very much to devote myself to the foreign missions."

After nearly 30 years' service, he retired from the army in 1899 as Chaplain to the Forces, 1st Class. In the same year, he was appointed Vicar Apostolic of Gibraltar with the title of Bishop of Milevum. One of his co-consecrators at the Dominican Church at Haverstock Hill was Bishop Brindle. At a reception to mark his appointment to Gibraltar, Fr Alexander said:

> We cannot but feel that in an English colony like Gibraltar, where the army is so fully represented, no better selection could have been made for its Bishop than that of an English priest and a chaplain in Her Majesty's army.

Bishop Bellord undertook his episcopate in Gibraltar amid troubles between the Junta of Elders and the Church authorities. Gibraltar became a Crown Colony in 1830, and the Elders assisted the Church in the development of its educational, social and charitable activities on the Rock. However, when they wished to exercise power beyond their authority they came into conflict with the Church. Bishop Bellord had an uncomfortable episcopate in the colony and resigned in 1901. At the time, he was involved in writing a new catechism but wrote to Fr Hudson at Notre Dame University in the United States that he "was unfit for anything". Nevertheless, in the following year the university published his *New Catechism of Christian Doctrine and Practice*. His *Meditations on Christian Dogma* had been published in 1898 and had established Bellord's reputation as an author on religious topics. Bishop Bellord died in 1905.

Figure 6: Bishop Robert Brindle: Padre to prelate

7

"No priest who made the sacrifice had cause to regret the hardships he endured": Boer War chaplains

The Boer War

The war between Great Britain and the South African Boer republics of Transvaal and Orange Free State broke out in October 1899. British garrisons at Kimberley, Ladysmith and Mafeking were besieged and the British suffered defeats at Stormberg, Magersfontein, Colenso and Spion Kop. But the British entered the Orange Free State capital of Bloemfontein in March 1900 and the Transvaal state capital of Pretoria in June 1900. Peace negotiations commenced, but they collapsed and guerrilla warfare continued. Boer assets were destroyed and Boer women and children were incarcerated in concentration camps. The Peace of Vereeniging was signed on 31 May 1902.

The British army was neither trained nor equipped for the war, whereas the Boers were tactically astute, mobile and skilled marksmen. The British sent 233,548 troops to South Africa from home and imperial garrisons, while volunteers from Britain, Ireland, South Africa, Australia, Canada, New Zealand, India and colonies supplemented regular army contingents.

By the end of hostilities, 448,435 men had served on the British side. A total of 7,582 imperial soldiers were killed or died of wounds, and 13,139 died of disease. The Boers suffered over 7,000 casualties while thousands of Boer civilians and Africans died in British concentration camps.

Catholics, the war and the army

Catholics generally supported the war. Cardinal Herbert Vaughan, Archbishop of Westminster, claimed that justice was on Britain's side: "The British empire was possessed of a great and sacred trust, not to be surrendered", and its Christian and civilizing influence had to be maintained by sacrifice if necessary. Bishop William Vaughan of Plymouth was off the mark, however, when he claimed, in December 1899, that the war had ceased and "our troops, to a certain extent, are no longer required". Irish bishops did not share such views: Irish nationalists tried to dissuade Irishmen from joining the British army, and some Irish clergy condemned "an unjust war made against the heroic Boers".

Financial inducements and the lowering of physical requirements resulted in steady recruiting for the army and militia and despite anti-imperial and pro-Boer sentiments, Irishmen throughout Britain and the empire volunteered. In 1901, there were 40,000 Catholics in the army. Many were in Irish infantry and cavalry regiments and in Irish militia battalions, and although it would be wrong to assume that all Irishmen in the army were Catholics, it is probably safe to say that most were. Large numbers of Catholics throughout the British Isles and empire also served. *The Tablet* reported that 6,000 Catholic soldiers were either killed or died of wounds and disease.

Bishops and chaplains

In July 1900, Bishop Cuthbert Hedley of Newport informed his clergy of the death of Fr John Moloney, a priest of his diocese and an Acting Chaplain in South Africa. Rather than encouraging his priests to volunteer, Hedley wrote that "all dioceses must do their share in providing chaplains". Bishop Francis Bourne of Southwark, responsible for recruiting and supervising chaplains, wrote to the bishops in February 1901 informing them that "eight to ten additional chaplains were needed for South Africa". Only two bishops released priests. In April 1902, the bishops decided that when a vacancy occurred among chaplains, "each diocese in turn should furnish a priest" and they asked Cardinal Vaughan to write to "Superiors of Regular Bodies, urging them to furnish priests if asked by the Bishop of Southwark".

Bishop Bourne liaised with the War Office over chaplains but had no control over numbers, conditions of service or deployment. Volunteers obtained permission from their bishop or superior and then applied to Bourne, who informed the War Office. Following nomination and acceptance, the War Office informed the chaplain of procedures, conditions of service, medical requirements, kit, remuneration, allowances and the reporting date and place. The priest was now in the army.

Catholic army chaplains in the Boer War

Chaplains were to oversee the spiritual and moral welfare of the men of their denomination. Methods varied according to circumstances and the personality of the chaplain, but he had always to conform to military requirements. Catholic chaplains considered their role as distinctive and were responsible only to the Senior Catholic Chaplain and their military superiors, not to a chaplain of any other denomination. Like commissioned chaplains, most Acting Chaplains in South Africa wore khaki uniform with Army Chaplains' Department markings on their collars, but others wore civilian dress with a Red Cross armband.

The Army Chaplains' Department had an establishment of 85, with the majority being Anglican. In 1899, there were 17 commissioned Catholic chaplains, but it was obvious that they could not maintain empire-wide commitments while ministering to the army in South Africa. Chaplains who could be spared from other duties were immediately sent to South Africa. They were Frs Reginald Collins (Archdiocese of Westminster), CF, 1st Class; Emmanuel Morgan (Diocese of Southwark), CF, 2nd Class; William Alexander and Edward Ryan (Diocese of Southwark) and Lewis Matthews (Archdiocese of Westminster), all CF, 3rd Class; and William Keatinge (Diocese of Southwark), CF, 4th Class. They were joined by Frs William Le Grave (Diocese of Portsmouth), CF, 1st Class; Robert Nash and Stephen Rogers (both Diocese of Southwark), CF, 4th Class; William Forrest (Diocese of Portsmouth), CF, 4th Class; and Daniel

Lane, CF, 4th Class and Albert Boddington, a probationary chaplain (both Archdiocese of Westminster). Thirty-six Acting Chaplains were appointed in England, 23 in South Africa, and some within the empire.

Commissioned chaplains in South Africa

Fr Matthews was padre to 1st Royal Irish Fusiliers. In October 1899, they were ambushed at Nicholson's Nek. In the mayhem, the chaplain was knocked over by stampeding mules and he recalled that the firing "was furious". A mistaken order to surrender, not given by the Royal Irish (the padre reported indignantly), was sounded and the Irish laid down their arms. Many were taken prisoner, including the padre, and the officers were separated from the men and taken by train to Pretoria. Over 500 officers and men of the battalion were freed by the British in August 1900 but Fr Matthews, as a non-combatant, was released earlier. He proceeded to minister to the Royal Dublin Fusiliers and was present at the Battle of Spion Kop where his comrade, the Revd Wainman, a Methodist chaplain, later recalled:

> With the other chaplains, I scaled the mountain, and a terrible sight it was. The dead were lying everywhere, and the enemy in numbers taking from them anything worth carrying away. To get graves dug on such rocky soil took more than one day, and it was a task I hope may never have to be repeated in the annals of this terrible war.

"My Soudan experiences were mere child's play in comparison", wrote Fr Matthews.

Fr Morgan ministered to Methuen's Division and described in detail the engagement at Modder River, where he buried many in shallow graves. Fr Collins, another veteran of the Sudan campaign, was Senior Catholic Chaplain with the 5th Division. He was Mentioned in Despatches and received medal clasps for Spion Kop, Pieter's Hill, the relief of Ladysmith, Tugela Heights, Laing's Nek and Belfast. He was also awarded the DSO in recognition of his services. After Spion Kop, he had a tetchy exchange

with Boer General Botha over the clearance of the British dead and
wounded from the battlefield.

Fr Le Grave became Senior Catholic Chaplain and saw action in
Natal, the Orange River Colony and the Transvaal. He too was awarded
the DSO and Mentioned in Despatches. Fr Keatinge accompanied
White's Irish Brigade at the Battles of Colenso and Spion Kop and the
Relief of Ladysmith. Fr William Alexander was with 2nd Royal Irish
Fusiliers before an advance on Pretoria when a Boer shell landed on his
tent—luckily, he was elsewhere.

General Sir George White mentioned as being "eminently deserving
of reward" chaplains who "showed the greatest zeal and self-sacrifice in
their attention to the sick and wounded as well as in their ministrations
to those in health". Lord Roberts acknowledged the "devotion to duty
of the several chaplains" and mentioned Frs Morgan, Ryan, Matthews,
Keatinge and Nash. Lord Kitchener mentioned the meritorious service
of Frs William Alexander and Stephen Rogers.

Acting chaplains in South Africa

Fr Simon Knapp's posting to 6th Inniskilling Dragoons caused
consternation as the battalion did not know what to make of a Carmelite
monk in their midst. His conduct and demeanour were such, however,
that he proved to be "not only quite the best specimen of Army Chaplain
... but also a charming companion". Fr Stephen Dawes OSB, one of eight
English Benedictine padres, made a similar impression and earned the
respect, admiration and lifelong friendship of officers and men of 1st
Connaught Rangers. One described him "as the best polo player in the
army, the best shot, and the best confessor when you are dying". Five
Jesuits of the English Province and one of the Irish Province served as
Acting Chaplains, as did missionary priests in South Africa such as the
Oblates of Mary Immaculate.

Bishop Thomas Whiteside of Liverpool did not invite priests to
volunteer but considered requests of those "disposed to apply". Frs
Charles Swarbreck, Austin Dobson, Henry Ainscough, Michael Melia,
William Rockcliffe and George Walmsley interpreted the bishop's call

as one for "volunteers to act as army chaplains and provide our gallant soldiers with the consolations of their religion". They volunteered and were accepted.

Fr Swarbreck's "Notes from an Army Chaplain's Diary", in *The Ushaw Magazine* of 1902, described his journey to South Africa and expeditions with 1st Royal Munster Fusiliers. They include "impressions formed at the time in the midst of new and exceptional circumstances".

Fr Swarbreck left Southampton on 11 March 1901. Even with five Catholic chaplains on the troopship, they could not do much amongst the many Irishmen on board and it was impossible to say Mass. On St Patrick's Day, "shamrock was prominent amongst the officers", and the "rev chaplains" attended the officers' dinner that night. Many officers were returning after leave and some were "loud in their praise of our chaplains and their work with the troops". On the second Sunday at sea, two Masses were said, a parade was held and the men were given scapulars. A passing ship, homeward bound, signalled "British colours completely victorious". Fr Swarbreck discovered that this was not entirely true and, as they approached Cape Town, he wrote: "I do not think that the chaplains were quite the calmest people on board; most knew, to some extent, what was before them, but our destinations were vague, and we began to realize what a very big place South Africa is."

They received orders from Fr O'Donnell OMI, the Acting Senior Catholic Chaplain. Fr Swarbreck and Fr Benedict Scannell were sent on the thousand-mile journey to Pretoria, passing encampments, convoys, and heavily guarded railway junctions, bridges and stations. On Holy Thursday, they reached Bloemfontein and, "dead tired and hungry", they visited the local church. "I shall never forget my feelings", wrote Fr Swarbreck, "as I knelt before the altar. Peace and quiet was there in the midst and bustle of war, and the people were kneeling round the Blessed Sacrament as I knew they were doing at home." On Good Friday, they "thoroughly observed the fast" and met up with the Cork Militia at Philjohn's Drift.

Fr Swarbreck's first encounter with Catholic troops was an impressive one. It was also a defining moment for him, as he began to minister as a chaplain, although not yet under fire. With Fr Scannell, he conducted a service from a railway carriage:

As many as could assembled round our carriage, and we said a few encouraging words and supplied them with medals, rosaries and such things as we had. Fr Scannell gave them a crucifix for the regiment and a delightful little episode followed. All the men knelt down and kissed the cross. You can picture it better than I can portray it—some thirty rough soldiers, bronzed with heat, and their khaki uniforms all stained and torn with long service, filled with faith, kneeling on the railway track late at night, and kissing the cross with intense devotion. It was a bright, moonlit night; and I hope I may never forget the rough faces of those grand Catholic soldiers. We concluded our little Good Friday ceremony with a public act of contrition, prayers to Our Lady, and, I suppose most unrubrically, a blessing. The men went back to their camp proud of their treasure, and glad to have seen the priest. It was also a consoling conclusion to a dreary day for the priests themselves.

They reached Pretoria and Fr Swarbreck felt "extremely proud" when he saw the British flag flying over the town. Fr Scannell was assigned to the General Hospital while Fr Swarbreck searched for the Royal Munster Fusiliers.

Fr Swarbreck and the Munsters left Bronkhorstspruit and embarked on the journey to Middelberg but were delayed as the railway line had been sabotaged. At Middelberg, the Munsters met up with Scottish and Australian contingents before setting off in a "magnificent convoy" across the veldt. The journey, slow but eventful, was Fr Swarbreck's initiation into warfare. Unable to get a horse, he rode on the general's cart while the Australian scouts "rode like wildfire". Amid skirmishes, they snatched sleep and food. At lunch one day, they were attacked by Boer snipers, but the Australians successfully overcame the threat. It was Fr Swarbreck's first close encounter with enemy fire, and he wrote: "Many may have heard the whiz of a bullet on its way to a target, but the hiss of a Mauser on its errand of death is quite another thing." Occasionally the convoy engaged in heavy fighting and at Oliphant River they suffered casualties. The padre attended the wounded and buried the dead.

Fr Swarbreck witnessed the effect of the war on civilians. "The women and children were a pitiable sight . . . they had been in the open a long time and their clothes were badly worn." Adding these to the convoy of men, guns, supplies and captured cattle slowed the journey and made them more vulnerable to Boer attacks. However, the mission was accomplished, Boer operations were disrupted, and they marched back into Bronckhorstspruit led by the drums of the Munsters.

The padre had few opportunities to say Mass. Once he said Mass in the open, with his portable altar resting on ammunition boxes and Tommies kneeling round him. "There was a high wind, almost a gale and it was bitterly cold . . . a number of them availed themselves of the opportunity of approaching the Sacraments." He heard an Australian's confession as they walked through the camp, but illness prevented him from burying a Catholic officer who had died of wounds.

Fr Swarbreck experienced more difficulties in celebrating Mass for the Munsters during May and June 1901, for no sooner had they stopped than they were on the move again. Long marches and intense cold took their toll on the men and spirits sank. Their main occupation seemed to be "devoted to clearing the district of all cattle" and as the number of beasts increased, the speed of the column decreased, making it a target for the Boers. Frequent engagements kept the convoy alert, but the presence of other British troops provided much-needed protection. Whit Sunday passed without Mass, as did Trinity Sunday. Through freezing winds and under the gaze of Boer scouts, the column, cold and unwashed, trudged wearily and miserably from "fontein to fontein". Washing was painful as "the grit was stinging and had bitten its way into the skin". At Vandyke Drift they halted, and Fr Swarbreck borrowed a hospital tent and said Mass for the first time in a month. They remained in their bivouac sheltering from the "awful storms of penetrating, gritty dirt". The Boers, meanwhile, tried to burn them out.

Two days later a unit of Australians was attacked as they slept. At the first volley, men leapt half-consciously to their feet, many of them only to sink back again as a second line of fire revealed the number and proximity of the enemy. Eighteen Australians were killed and 40 wounded. Mules and horses were shot as they rushed about wildly; others stampeded, taking ammunition and supplies with them. With depleted intelligence and few scouts, the dispirited convoy moved on under threat of another ambush. Their fighting capabilities were seriously impaired, and they were extremely vulnerable. They rested where they thought it was safe, but their "nerves were too highly strung for sleep". "The dread of night attack", wrote Fr Swarbreck, "had succeeded in getting to my nerves, and I lay tossing there fully dressed on the open veldt sixty miles from Middelberg. I really wished I was anywhere else in the world." Fortunately, subsequent Boer attacks were not particularly menacing. The convoy rendezvoused with General Blood's column and learned that they had successfully evaded traps set by Boer commandos. They continued to Middelberg, taking with them 300 Boer men, women and children.

From Middelberg, the Munsters accompanied a convoy carrying supplies across the veldt to Kitchener's force. They found 5,000 men in a huge camp and one night, as campfires burned, Fr Swarbreck heard a corporal going amongst the Munsters crying: "Turn out for the Rosary." "Out they came like a lot of delighted schoolboys", he wrote, "setting down a blanket for the chaplain" and kneeling round him. On their return to Middelberg and a well-earned rest, the drums of the Munsters and the pipes of the Seaforths played them into the town. Spirits rose, but Fr Swarbreck heard with dismay that they would be moving again the next day, so he arranged for Benediction in the local church. He wrote:

> I quite forgot our disappointment and the unhappiness of war, and it was not until afterwards that it struck me that the people present might have been a little scandalized at the unrestrainedness with which I sang at the *O Salutaris* and *Tantum Ergo*. It was delightful to minister in a church again.

They departed for Elands River Station on the Pretoria–Middelberg railway line, where they stayed guarding a section of the railway. "Possessed of fixed abode", Fr Swarbreck wrote, "I felt it incumbent on me to return to the ways of respectability, to wash daily, wear collars and say my office. Trekking had reduced one to the level of an all but perfect heathen." His acquaintance with the veldt was not renewed, and he remained in his "quaint parish by the line".

The cost

It was inevitable that chaplains, ministering in battle and among the sick would succumb. Fr John Moloney died early in the war. Fr William Rockliffe was wounded in a shell explosion whilst serving with Major-General Pole-Carew's division. Fr George Walmsley and Fr Henry Hepburne SJ contracted enteric and were invalided home. The Benedictines Frs Stephen Rawlinson and Bernard Sweetman of Downside Abbey also contracted enteric and were given sick leave in England, but they returned to the war. Commissioned chaplains Frs Morgan and Nash were hospitalized suffering from enteric and dysentery. Chaplains of other denominations also suffered, and three Anglican chaplains died during the campaign.

Post-war developments

The organization and management of the Army Chaplains' Department and the co-operation between Church and government received much criticism. A Catholic chaplain wrote: "Nothing could exceed the awful muddling in South Africa", while Catholic troops complained that they rarely saw a chaplain. Bishop Bourne set about tightening up the organization of Catholic chaplains and lobbied the Vatican to give him more control over them, as he felt they had overstepped their authority by ignoring local bishops in South Africa. On his translation to Westminster in 1903, he took with him responsibilities for Catholic military chaplains and in 1906 he was confirmed as Delegate of the Holy See for the British Army. Bourne felt that other bishops did not appreciate his task and their reluctance to provide army chaplains was an issue that was to resurface in future conflicts.

Acting chaplains returned to their missions, colleges and monasteries. They had ministered in extraordinary circumstances and most served with distinction. Their work did not pass unnoticed by the troops and by their ministry they confirmed the need for a distinctive Catholic military chaplaincy. They had assisted in integrating Catholic priests into the army, further refined the model of chaplaincy and enhanced the reputation of chaplains. Fr Swarbreck wrote:

> No priest who made the sacrifice had cause to regret the hardships endured, for each was amply repaid by the joy and consolation his presence afforded to the troops in the field, especially to the sick and wounded. I was particularly fortunate in being attached to an Irish regiment which was nearly all Catholic; at all events, my circumstances were such as to impress on me how much the troops appreciated the presence of the priest.

REV. CHARLES SWARBRECK.

**Figure 7: Fr Swarbreck, chaplain during the Boer War
(Courtesy of the Trustees of Ushaw College)**

8

"No one class of our people is perhaps so destitute of spiritual aid, none more in need of it": Chaplains to Catholic sailors and marines in the nineteenth and early twentieth centuries

Chaplains to the Royal Navy

In 1626, King Charles I ordered that Royal Navy ships should carry chaplains. In 1653, public worship became mandatory for all sailors and, in 1661, King Charles II further decreed

> that all Co[m]manders Captaines and other Officers att Sea shall cause the publique Worshipp of Almighty God according to the Liturgy of the Church of England established by Law to be solemnly orderly and reverently performed in theire respective Ships And that prayers and preachings by the respective Chaplaines in holy Orders of the respective Ships be performed diligently and that the Lords Day be observed according to Law.

Despite this instruction, sea-going chaplains were not always welcome, and religious observance was more a tenet of naval discipline than theological fervour. Chaplains conducted divine service, acted as schoolmasters and attempted to temper the sailors' worst habits, but little attention was given to the chaplain's role or his commitment to spiritual duties. Chaplains were clergymen of the Church of England, but not all were active in naval duties and absenteeism was rife.

In 1812, the Revd John Owen served as Chaplain-General of the Fleet and Chaplain-General of the Army, but the naval post was abolished in 1815. In 1859, the Admiralty decreed that "the Senior Chaplain of Greenwich Hospital will be recognized as the head of the Naval Chaplains, bear the title of 'Chaplain of the Fleet' and rank with a Rear-Admiral".

The struggle for Catholic naval chaplains

There is scant evidence relating to Catholic chaplains in the Royal Navy. In the late sixteenth century, English chaplains actually served the enemy. Fr Charles Tancard SJ served the Spanish Fleet "over a period of two or three years", and Fr John Smithson "accompanied the Spanish Fleet that sailed for England in November 1596 and died at sea". Fr Walter Rought, chaplain with the Royal Navy in the Second Anglo-Dutch War (1665–67), though on whose authority is unclear, continued his efforts to convert at sea: "From 1 apr 1665 . . . I went as chaplain on the St George against the dutch. I reconciled the duke of Buckingham and others on board." Fr Thomas Montfort SJ was chaplain to the Catholic Duke of York, commander of the Royal Navy, in a battle with the Dutch in May 1672, and it was recorded that "his brave conduct . . . won commendation for both himself and the Society".

Although Catholic army chaplains had been commissioned in 1858, the Admiralty opposed the employment of chaplains not of the Established Church. The Admiralty's policy was a constant grievance for Catholic bishops and politicians, who argued that if the Royal Navy needed Catholic manpower, then it should provide for their spiritual needs. For Catholics, it was a question of justice and common sense to employ Catholic chaplains and, as Archbishop Cullen of Dublin wrote to Bishop Grant of Southwark, "it would be easy to prevent Catholics from joining the Royal Navy".

Throughout the early-nineteenth century, appeals to the government to improve religious provision for Catholics in the Royal Navy proved pointless. That Catholic army chaplains served without causing discontent or inconvenience to military effectiveness and discipline had no effect on the Admiralty. That Catholic soldiers and seamen were voluntarily attending services conducted by Catholic army chaplains and civilian priests on shore bases throughout the empire left the Admiralty unconvinced that changes were overdue. Their Lordships remained convinced that non-Anglican chaplains would impair naval discipline and organization and would also cost money.

Yet the Admiralty slowly made improvements in providing for the spiritual needs of Catholic sailors and marines. Catholic priests had ministered to Catholic seamen at Havant and Gosport since the 1730s and, during the Napoleonic Wars, Portsmouth's Catholic community dwarfed that of the old centres of Hampshire Catholicism because of the presence of Irish sailors. In 1797, Fr James Graham "administered the rites of the Catholic religion for the seamen and marines of that persuasion at Chatham and elsewhere" and attended Catholic sailors to be executed for their involvement in the Mutiny at the Nore. The Admiralty paid him and other Catholic officiating clergy for their ministry but at a lower rate than Anglican ministers. In 1822, Fr J. O'Mealy received payment from the government for his ministrations to Catholic sailors and soldiers at St Patrick's Chapel, Sheerness. In 1846, a chapel was opened for Catholic pensioners at the Royal Naval Hospital, Greenwich, and in 1852 another concession was made when Catholic boys in the Royal Navy were no longer compelled "to receive Religious instruction in a creed at variance with their own".

In 1847, a hulk was provided in Bermuda where Catholic sailors and marines could attend Mass, and in December 1855 hulks moored in Portsmouth, Devonport and Sheerness were provided for Catholic worship with a chaplain "specially appointed to the spiritual care of the Catholic sailors". The Admiralty was "pleased to provide the means of attending Divine Worship" on board HMS *Thalia*, an old vessel moored in "a convenient position" in Portsmouth harbour "for the benefit of the Officers, Seamen and Marines professing the Roman Catholic faith". A pennant was to be flown on a Sunday indicating that a service "will be performed on board on that day" at 10.00, and a Catholic officer, selected by the Flag Officer, was to supervise the service and note the names of those attending. Seamen could row themselves to the hulk if a Catholic officer was unavailable. Catholic officers or seamen at Spithead not wishing to attend the Catholic service on *Thalia* would not be compelled to attend any other religious service on board ship, but it was not until 1859 that Catholic sailors were "dispensed from the hard necessity of attending the Protestant service".

It has been estimated that in 1851 the proportion of Irishmen in the Senior Service had risen to 20 per cent with many enlisting through the naval base at Queenstown (Cobh), County Cork. But for these men there was no religious provision while at sea, and their case was taken up by Irish MPs and bishops. In 1859, "a Memorial . . . respecting the treatment of Catholic Sailors in the Royal Navy" was presented to the government but met with no success other than confirmation that Catholic priests could minister to sailors at land bases but not at sea.

Missioners at home ports came under increasing pressures. In 1855, Frs William Woollett of the Diocese of Newport and Menevia, Henry Clark of the Archdiocese of Southwark and Joseph Stourton were appointed Officiating Chaplains at Portsmouth, Devonport and Chatham. At Devonport, the military Catholic population of 1,500 outnumbered the civilian Catholic population and imposed extra pressures on the clergy. At Chatham, in 1853, the chapel built for a congregation of 250 had to cater for over 2,000 sailors and soldiers. Missioners were faced with excessive workloads and problems relating to the size, cleanliness and hygiene of chapels, and fluctuating congregations. After 1858, the responsibilities for ministering to Catholic soldiers in Chatham, Gosport, Plymouth and Portsmouth were transferred to newly commissioned Catholic army chaplains on nearby garrisons. In 1866, Frs William Woollett and Foran started building a chapel for the military at Portsmouth.

In the early 1860s, 550 Catholic sailors of the Channel Fleet in Plymouth attended Mass at the floating chapel *Hutspur*. Fr Henry Lea of the Diocese of Southwark ministered on the hulk HMS *Clyde* at Sheerness, and sailors attended Mass at Plymouth Cathedral and St Michael and St Joseph Church, Devonport. However, when Catholics were attending to their religious duties, they remained subject to naval discipline and timetables. In some cases, an army chaplain, such as Fr Sydney Woollett at Kingston, Jamaica, heard confessions and said Mass for 200 Catholic sailors on board Royal Navy ships. He found the army and naval officers, some of whom were Catholic, most hospitable, and in exceptional cases they allowed religious observance to interfere with "Divisions" (a formal parade in a ship or on a shore base).

Other developments included the appointments, in 1867, of Fr Gauci Azzopardi and Fr Andrew Sceberras to be full-time Officiating Chaplains in Malta for Catholic seamen of the Mediterranean Fleet. In 1876, Frs Woollett and Joseph Stourton were appointed full-time Officiating Chaplains to Portsmouth and Devonport and their names appeared on *The Navy List* of 1870. According to the Admiralty, Portsmouth and Devonport were "exceptional", and the official listing of these chaplains was "not to be taken as a precedent". The *Navy List*, which included the names of many Catholic officers, stated that only Church of England clergymen could be full-time chaplains in the Royal Navy and Catholic priests were appointed to shore bases on a fixed allowance. In 1876, the bishops of England and Wales again made unsuccessful official representation to have Catholic priests put on the same footing as Anglican chaplains.

The agitation of Catholic Members of Parliament achieved some success in 1878, when an Admiralty Minute stated that whenever a large number of ships, or a squadron, was sent on service "for a considerable time", then a Catholic priest could, with the senior officer's approval, accompany the squadron. This did not mean that a priest would be allowed on board a fighting ship. The Catholic Union of Great Britain and the Hierarchies of Ireland and England and Wales petitioned Parliament for the Admiralty's implementation of the Minute, because it was frequently ignored. The cost of providing chaplains for the large number of Catholics in the Royal Navy, however, seems to have met more with Treasury opposition than Admiralty obstruction. In 1882, during the Anglo-Egyptian conflict, the Admiralty arranged that Fr T. O'Reilly, a Franciscan missionary, would minister to sailors and marines at Port Said, but it was not until 1887 that Fr Thomas Kent of the Diocese of Plymouth accompanied the Mediterranean Fleet as a full-time Officiating Catholic Chaplain, and from 1892 Fr Joseph Cassar ministered full time to sailors and marines on Malta.

In place of chaplains

In 1892, the Admiralty allowed the use of a Catholic prayer book, *The Guide to Heaven for Those at Sea*, but such concessions did not compensate for the withholding of authentic and consistent spiritual support by means of commissioned chaplains. The absence of chaplains in the Victorian navy placed added burdens on the shoulders of Catholic officers and surgeons, who arranged for sailors to attend Mass and receive the sacraments and occasionally acted as surrogate chaplains. Surgeon Richard McClement recorded that on Ascension Island in 1861 he conducted the burial of Dr McDonnell, one of his colleagues:

> The ordinary Catholic burial service was read by me, and responded to by Drs Roche and Farelly. Having finished the prayers and thrown the earth on the coffin, in the ordinary manner, the troops were ordered to fire three volleys, which being done, they formed into marching order and returned to the barracks, followed by the sailors, and, soon after, by the officers.

In 1894, Dr Daniel McNabb, a Catholic surgeon on board HMS *Undaunted*, performed the burial service for a Catholic seaman who had died on the passage from Aden to Colombo. It was, he reported, an impressive event, but there was no Catholic chaplain to administer the Last Rites or conduct the burial service.

Consequently, Catholic surgeons acquired a level of spiritual authority not shared by other surgeons and their experience of naval life was markedly different. Their value to the Admiralty and their influence on their fellow Catholics was substantial but unrewarded. Elsewhere, Captain Edward Charlton, a Catholic officer on HMS *Orlando* in the China seas from 1899 to 1902, reported that while at Wei-Hai-Wei the Catholics of the fleet would attend Sunday Mass at a shore chapel served by a French Marist Father.

Official co-operation was limited. Fr Bernard Carey, an Irish Holy Ghost missionary, who served as a shore-based chaplain from 1894 to 1898, was forbidden from boarding a Royal Navy ship on the Australia Station to tend to a dying Catholic sailor or to conduct any religious services. Two other Catholics had died on ships in Sydney Harbour, but Fr Carey was told his services were not required. His report noted that Catholic sailors had not been able to attend Mass and the sacraments for months. Again, where Catholics were allowed ashore to attend Mass, they remained subject to the primacy of naval law and commitments.

In 1890, official reluctance to appoint commissioned Catholic chaplains to the Royal Navy compelled Fr Francis Goldie SJ to write of Catholic sailors that "no one class of our people is perhaps so destitute of spiritual aid, none more in need of it". It was, he continued, difficult to get access to sailors and therefore difficult to estimate the number of Catholics among them, but he was convinced that there were many. He also claimed that though the spiritual wants of Catholic soldiers, paupers and prisoners were officially attended to, those of Catholic sailors and marines were not.

Voluntary organizations, meanwhile, provided facilities for worship and recreation ashore and religious reading matter for sailors and marines on ships. Well-funded and active Protestant lay missions were numerous in ports at home and overseas, but the Catholic community did little for bluejackets, marines and other seafarers. Into this vacuum of spiritual neglect, after 1891 and supported by Bishop Vertue, came the voluntary efforts of the Catholic Truth Society with pamphlets and Catholic literature for sailors and marines. Supplemented by increasing efforts of priests and laypeople living in and around naval bases, Apostleships of Prayer were established in ports and encouraged on board ships. Catholic bibles, prayer books and newspapers were distributed, and a Catholic naval club was established at Portsmouth. By 1890, a Royal Naval Catholic Association had been formed, and a renewed effort was undertaken to provide for the spiritual wants of all Catholic seafarers; in 1893 a Sailors' Club was opened in Tower Hill, London. Such voluntary efforts, however laudable, were not going to impact on Catholics in a huge fleet stationed all over the world. Institutional change was required.

Into the twentieth century

Initially, ecclesiastical responsibility for Catholic chaplains to the Royal Navy rested with the Bishop of Southwark, largely because the three great dockyards of Chatham, Portsmouth and Devonport lay within his diocese. With the creation of the Diocese of Portsmouth in 1882, responsibility for Catholic naval chaplains passed to its bishop, John Vertue, a former army chaplain, but in 1900 Cardinal Herbert Vaughan of Westminster, with Admiralty approval, assumed responsibility for Royal Navy Officiating Chaplains. In 1903, this passed to his successor, Archbishop Francis Bourne, and in 1906 the Vatican named Bourne as the Ecclesiastical Superior of Catholic chaplains to both the Royal Navy and the army.

The Admiralty insisted on defining Catholics as "dissenters", and despite the large number of Catholic officers and seamen, it continued to officially forbid Catholic services on Royal Navy vessels. In 1901, the Irish MP John O'Dowd claimed that it was necessary to persuade the House of Commons of the justice of the claim for Catholic chaplains in the Navy. This was not an unreasonable demand, he said, considering the number of Catholics in the Navy. It was "disgraceful for a great naval Power, such as England", to have such a large number of Catholics in the Navy "without making provision for having their spiritual wants administered to by the clergymen belonging to their own religion".

Some Catholic officers, meanwhile, had risen to senior rank. Lord Walter Talbot Kerr was appointed Rear Admiral in 1899 and First Sea Lord and Admiral of the Fleet in 1904. Andrew Kennedy Bickford was appointed Admiral in 1904, Sir Henry Coey Kane retired as Rear Admiral in 1899, and Edward Charlton was appointed Rear Admiral in 1913. Their religion and rank, however, had little impact on Admiralty policy regarding Catholic chaplains.

The number of Catholic naval chaplains remained very small, and in the decade before the Great War (1914–18) the spiritual needs of Catholic sailors remained neglected. Recent research, however, suggests that this was due to Treasury parsimony rather than to the Admiralty's theological opposition. The government preferred to pay Catholic priests capitation fees or fixed allowances for their ministry to seamen in port rather than as commissioned chaplains at sea but even this system was abused. In 1901, *The Tablet* reported that there were over 10,000 Catholics in the Royal Navy, yet there were only 21 Catholic chaplains working on 148 stations worldwide, with only two in England. There were also obvious disparities in the chaplains' pay and conditions. Anglican chaplains received £300 per annum, whilst Catholic chaplains received allowances ranging from £25 to £200.

Some concessions had been made to allow Catholic priests to sail with squadrons and on hospital ships but Catholic MPs, in a Commons debate on the supply of Catholic army chaplains during the Boer War, still felt it necessary to ask why there was no Catholic chaplain attached to the Channel Fleet, which had over 1,500 Catholic sailors. Three years later, the situation had not improved, and Cardinal Logue and the Irish Hierarchy felt compelled to state: "We now deem it our duty to advise Catholic parents not to allow their children to join His Majesty's ships until suitable arrangements shall be made to minister to the spiritual wants of Catholic seamen in the Fleet." Despite frequent Catholic complaints and threats about the recruitment of Irish sailors, the Admiralty saw little need to change its policy and practice, and the number of Catholic, Church of Scotland and Free Churches chaplains remained derisory.

The Admiralty's attitude towards Catholic chaplains was slowly changing, however. Catholic chaplains served the China and Mediterranean squadrons but not on fighting ships at sea, although senior officers could and did bend the rules and the Admiralty turned a blind eye. In 1901, Fr Frederick McClymont celebrated Mass on the battleship HMS *Goliath* on the China Station and was dubbed "the flying chaplain", as he went about his work rowing from ship to ship. *The Tablet* reported in 1901 that Vice-Admiral Sir Edward Seymour expressed concern that local clergy in Singapore and Hong Kong did not minister to his Catholic sailors. In 1903, Fr Hamilton MacDonald of the Archdiocese of Westminster celebrated Mass on HMS *Magnificent* and HMS *Sans Pareil* with the Home Fleet. Frs Edward Bray and Peter Grobel of the Diocese of Salford served with the Mediterranean Fleet and Fr Edward Mostyn of the Archdiocese of Southwark and the Dominican Fr Maurice Watson ministered at Hong Kong. Fr Watson, who spoke Cantonese, had been in China since 1904 and served in HMS *Tamar* and HMS *Bedford*. He transferred to HMS *Triumph* and remained with her until 1915, when the China Squadron ceased to exist. Another priest to minister in China was the Franciscan Fr Patrick Connaughton. Ordained in Hankow in 1913, he ministered to Royal Navy personnel on the Yangtse River. The *Catholic Directory* noted that Frs Watson and Bray were "chaplains for service with squadrons afloat"—presumably on stations where Catholic places of worship were rare. No mention was made of Fr Connaughton, or Fr Bernard O'Riley, who from 1912 was chaplain to the Simonstown Naval Base in South Africa. Wherever they served, naval chaplains received their priestly faculties from the Archbishop of Westminster and not, as senior officers were frequently reminded, from the Admiralty.

There were large naval bases and hospitals along the English south coast, in Ireland and in Scotland. Fr Thomas Kent served in Plymouth and Devonport, while Fr William Bolger of the Diocese of Southwark served at Chatham. Fr Hamilton MacDonald served on ships and at Portsmouth, until he became naval secretary to Archbishop Bourne. He had established the first Catholic Naval Cub in Portsmouth in 1910. One hundred and thirty priests received fixed allowances as Officiating Chaplains, and two were eligible for pensions from their naval service—Fr Kent, who had served since 1887, and Fr Joseph Cassar, who had served on a fixed allowance since 1892.

In Scotland, Benedictine monks of Fort Augustus Abbey ministered to Catholic sailors of the Royal Navy when the fleet visited the Western Isles and northern anchorages. In 1905, Archbishop Bourne and Bishop Chisholm of Aberdeen had arranged with the Admiralty that a priest from the abbey should act as an officiating shore chaplain to the fleet at Cromarty, Invergordon and Kirkwall. In 1908, at Lamlash on the Isle of Arran, Dom Odo Blundell OSB celebrated Mass on a Royal Navy ship. From 1910, Dom Odo and Dom Adrian Weld-Blundell OSB ministered as chaplains to sailors of battle squadrons at Cromarty Firth and also to sailors at Lamlash. Throughout 1913 and 1914, Dom Odo ministered at weekends at Lamlash and became an honorary member of the officers' mess. Such developments, though indicative of change within the service, had no immediate influence on the Admiralty's official stated position.

**Figure 8: Fr Peter Grobel: Naval chaplain
(Salford Diocesan Archives)**

9

"His life's work had been devoted to the Catholic soldier": The first Army Bishop

Catholic chaplains in the Victorian army

During the 40 years after the commissioning of Catholic army chaplains, 41 uniformed priests ministered to British forces in New Zealand, Canada, the West Indies, South and West Africa, Matabeleland, Cyprus, Malta, Gibraltar, Egypt, the Sudan, Burma and the North West Frontier of India. Fr Arthur Wallace, for example, had served in Canada and had quietly but bravely ministered to British troops in the Ashanti War of 1873–74. From 1883 to 1887, he was in Burma with the Royal Munster Fusiliers who, in addition to attacks from insurgents, lost over 100 men to another enemy—cholera—in a few days. Fr Wallace had slept in the hospital in case he was needed, and his devotion to duty was noted by those who appreciated such qualities. Individual Catholic chaplains consolidated the status and enhanced the reputation of all army padres through their active, courageous and often lonely ministry.

The effectiveness of that ministry was tested on the veldt of South Africa. The Boer War was the first conflict in which a large number of commissioned, acting and officiating Catholic chaplains ministered together. Their ecclesiastical superior in England was Bishop Francis Bourne of Southwark, whilst in South Africa they received faculties to conduct their ministry among the troops from the local bishops. In the field, they were responsible to the commanding officer. Padres were subject to a network of ecclesiastical and military jurisdictions.

Fr William Keatinge—army chaplain

William Keatinge was born in London on 1 August 1869. After studying at Downside and the Venerable English College, Rome, he was ordained for the Diocese of Southwark on 27 May 1893. Following a curacy in Wandsworth, Fr Keatinge was commissioned into the Army Chaplains' Department on 1 May 1897.

On the outbreak of the Boer War in October 1899, Fr Keatinge sailed from England to Durban with Buller's Natal Field Force. He accompanied the Field Force, which included 2nd Royal Dublin Fusiliers, 1st Inniskilling Fusiliers, 1st Connaught Rangers and the Border Regiment, at Colenso in December 1899 and Spion Kop in January 1900. In both battles, the brigade fought magnificently but suffered dreadful casualties, particularly 2nd Dublins. At the relief of Ladysmith, in early March 1900, the battalion was given the honour of marching into the town first, and Fr Keatinge was with them. General Redvers Buller rode in at the head of "his magnificent warriors, and leading, in the place of honour were the valorous Dublin Fusiliers, the poor but glorious remnant consisting now of 400 of the original battalion". Winston Churchill wrote: "What a sight. It made me weep and my heart throbbed wildly. The ragged, dirty, begrimed troops looked tanned and hard as steel." Lord Roberts, Commander-in-Chief, recorded in a despatch that "the devotion to duty of the several chaplains, civil as well as army, throughout the campaign, especially during the siege of Ladysmith and in the hospitals, has been frequently brought to my notice".

Other battles and long hazardous treks followed as Fr Keatinge and Fr Lewis Matthews, of the Archdiocese of Westminster, were deployed with the Dublins. Their duties, like those of all chaplains, continued when the army was at rest—in hospitals, tending the sick, administering the sacraments, burying the dead and visiting scattered outposts and garrisons. Their ministry was difficult and dangerous but was respected and appreciated by the men they served. At the end of the war, the Royal Dublin Fusiliers had suffered nearly 700 casualties. For his wartime ministry, Fr Keatinge was twice Mentioned in Despatches and received the Queen's South Africa Medal (QSAM) with five clasps. He was also promoted in the field to Chaplain, 3rd Class with the rank of major.

Ecclesiastical control and supervision of army chaplains

Throughout the Boer War, Bishop Bourne became increasingly frustrated at what he perceived to be the commissioned army chaplains' independence from his or any form of episcopal control. The nature of their ministry and the sheer distance from the British Isles removed chaplains in South Africa from Bourne's immediate supervision and the ecclesiastical arrangements in Southwark merely exacerbated the situation. South African bishops, in whose dioceses chaplains were serving, also considered the chaplains to be lax in their obligations to ecclesiastical authority.

In 1903, Bourne was appointed Archbishop of Westminster and subsequently arranged with the Holy See that episcopal supervision of army chaplains be transferred from the Bishop of Southwark to the Archbishop of Westminster, thus overturning nearly 50 years of control by Bishop Thomas Grant and his successors in Southwark. Ecclesiastical supervision of Catholic naval chaplains was already in the hands of the Archbishop of Westminster (transferred from the Bishop of Portsmouth in 1900), and in 1906 the Vatican formalized Westminster's control of both naval and army chaplains. Bourne took this role very seriously.

Commissioned army chaplains did not take kindly to Bourne's authoritarian views on their role. They were concerned that his attempts to prevent them from assuming military rank and wearing uniform would lessen their status in the army. The mutual antipathy between Bourne and commissioned army chaplains grew and continued into and during the Great War of 1914–18 and the outcome was to influence Catholic clerical and military relationships.

Catholic chaplains with the British Expeditionary Force, 1914

It is difficult to estimate how many Catholic soldiers were in the British Expeditionary Force (BEF) which sailed to France on the outbreak of war in 1914. Some scholars have calculated that there were approximately 33,000 Catholics in the British army of about 247,000 men and most were in the infantry which accounted for 57 per cent of the army. It has also been calculated that there were about 17,000 Catholics in the Army Reserve, mobilized at the declaration of war, while the Territorial Force would have also included Catholics. Irish sources calculate that 20,000 Irish Catholics were in the regular army.

The War Office assigned chaplains in proportion to the numbers of men in any given Christian denomination. In August 1914, there were 15 commissioned Catholic army chaplains, 88 commissioned Anglican and ten commissioned Presbyterian chaplains. The sudden and dramatic increase in the size of the British army, however, led to the commissioning of many more temporary chaplains who soon outnumbered clergymen holding permanent commissions. By the end of 1914, there were 70 commissioned and temporary commissioned Catholic chaplains in France.

Fifty-three chaplains immediately sailed to France with the BEF—30 Anglican, ten Catholic, nine Presbyterian and four Wesleyan. The Principal Chaplain was the Revd Dr John Simms, an Ulster Presbyterian minister, appointed by virtue of seniority. Simms was attached to 3rd Echelon General Headquarters, and arrangements had been made for an Anglican chaplain and a proportion of other denominational chaplains to be attached to each field ambulance and to each general, stationary and clearing hospital.

No consideration had been given to the chaplains' role; nor had arrangements been made for their accommodation, transport or rations. It was incumbent on each padre to do the best he could and rely upon the co-operation of military authorities. As Sir John Smyth wrote: "The Adjutant General's department was much too hard pressed to bother about chaplains. Indeed, as long as the wounded were looked after in hospital, the dead buried and occasional services held where possible, that was as much as could be expected of them." Catholic soldiers, however, expected more from their padres.

In the opening months of the war, the administration of the Army Chaplains' Department and the office of the Archbishop of Westminster struggled to cope with the increase in Catholic personnel and the rush of volunteer priests. Ministering to large numbers of men over huge distances, army chaplains were also subject to the impact of new strategy and tactics and the destructive power of new weaponry. Meanwhile, advances in war reporting and in newspaper coverage meant that the British public was regularly and quickly informed of the conflict and military developments. The Catholic population soon became aware of the exploits of Catholic soldiers and their chaplains, and Catholic opinion was to have a significant influence on the development of Catholic chaplaincy during the war.

Mgr William Keatinge—chaplain with the BEF

After the Boer War, Fr Keatinge served at Gosport, Portsmouth, Shorncliffe, Malta and Cairo. In 1907, he was created Privy Chamberlain (with the title of Monsignor) to His Holiness Pope Pius X and promoted Chaplain to the Forces, 1st Class, with the rank of colonel, in 1911. When war broke out in August 1914, Mgr Keatinge was Senior Catholic Chaplain in Cairo. He was recalled immediately and appointed Senior Catholic Chaplain to the ten Catholic chaplains accompanying the BEF of 80,000 men to France. He embarked with 7th Field Ambulance, 3rd Division.

Mgr Keatinge was with the BEF as it retreated from Mons in August–September 1914. "My chief work (when fighting is on)", he wrote, "is with the wounded and dying, and burying the dead. One can do very little for the healthy people. There are no parish services. Sunday is like any other day, marching or fighting. Occasionally we have Mass, and one hears confessions on every opportunity." In October 1914, a more detailed report of his experiences appeared in *The Tablet*:

> I have now been almost two months at the front. I left England on the 16th August and I came with my Field Ambulance? Unit?? at once and I have been at the front practically since the beginning of this show in Belgium and France. I was with the troops around Mons and Compiègne and all through the subsequent retirement ... During the retirement we were constantly on the march, but the marches were not long except once when we covered 43 miles in a day, the night and the next day ... my overcoat was left behind

in one retreat and is now doubtless adorning a worthy Prussian
... The worst thing is rain and during the retirement it seemed
to rain always—marching all day in pelting rain and no chance of
changing or drying at night ... We have been on the march now
again for five or six nights ... I don't dislike it. I am proud to find
that I am first rate on the march, better than most of them. They
are all surprised at the way I stick it out on these marches. Of
course, I have plenty of opportunities for talks with my men when
we are marching ... What I feel most in this campaign is that I
can do so little for my Catholic men. Occasionally I can get some
of them to Mass on a Sunday morning but there is no attempt at
a parade service and one never knows on Saturday night what
orders will come for Sunday morning ... Sunday morning no
Mass. Orders for an early start. My altar, of course, packed on a
wagon during the night and all were standing ready to march ...
As a rule one only has one's haversack with one: everything else is
in the valise which is generally on the wagon except at night, and
the haversack does not hold much ... In the retreat from Mons
practically the only wounded I saw were men slightly wounded,
men who could walk or even run! All the rest, dead and dying
together, were left on the field.

For his services under fire and during the retreat, Mgr Keatinge was
Mentioned in Despatches by Sir John French, the Commander-in-Chief.

Throughout late 1914 and early 1915, Mgr Keatinge worked with
Simms and advised the War Office on chaplaincy requirements on
the Western Front. Initially, Simms's command included chaplains of
all denominations, but in 1915 the Church of England was allowed to
form its own field establishment and Anglican chaplains were placed
under the field command of Bishop Llewellyn Gwynne. Thus, a dual
system of chaplaincy provision emerged on the Western Front. Other
denominations unsuccessfully demanded the same treatment. As Michael
Snape commented, "the fragile unity of the Chaplains' Department was
shattered".

Mgr Keatinge—Principal Chaplain in Salonika

Of all the British army's campaigns in the Great War, the Salonika Campaign is one of the least well known. Its origins lay in an attempt to enlist Greece to the Allied cause, aid Serbia's resistance to the forces of the Austro-Hungarian Empire and prevent Germany securing a land supply route to its Turkish ally.

In 1916, Mgr Keatinge was transferred from the Western Front to Salonika, where he became Principal Chaplain with the rank of Brigadier-General. It was the highest rank ever reached by a Catholic chaplain. He presided over a unified command system of chaplains, but his appointment was not entirely welcomed. He wrote to Fr Stephen Rawlinson OSB, a senior but Temporary Chaplain, on the Western Front: "As you may imagine, my position at the start was not an easy one, in view of the Church of England opposition to a Catholic Principal Chaplain."

Other Catholic chaplains were transferred from the Western Front, Egypt and Gallipoli, and at the Armistice in 1918, 45 chaplains were still serving in Salonika. Yet despite this apparently large number, the Catholics never filled their establishment. In July 1917, Keatinge wrote to Rawlinson, who had taken over Keatinge's role on the Western Front, informing him that he was 16 chaplains under establishment, but another ten chaplains were due to arrive. He was exasperated at the episcopal response to pleas for more chaplains: "How miserably our English (and Irish) bishops have failed in this war to rise to the occasion. They can't see beyond the petty wants of their own dioceses." Differences among the episcopate over military chaplaincy were to become acrimonious in their nature and significant in their consequences.

Episcopus Castrensis

The shortage of Catholic army chaplains was felt most acutely on the Western Front. Cardinal Bourne, Archbishop of Westminster and Ecclesiastical Superior of all Catholic military chaplains, failed to provide the necessary administrative framework to deal quickly with the numerous requests from priests for temporary commissions. To compound the problem, he was at the behest of the War Office for the recruitment and deployment of chaplains. Nevertheless, culpability for the shortage of Catholic chaplains was ascribed to the cardinal.

Bourne's authority over chaplains was disliked especially by the Irish bishops, who felt that they should be responsible for appointing Irish chaplains to predominantly Irish regiments. The fate of 2nd Royal Munster Fusiliers at the Battle of Étreux in 1914, where many British Catholic soldiers died without the ministry of a Catholic padre, served only as a sad precursor to what became an increasingly bitter dispute involving Bourne, the Irish Hierarchy, the British government and the Vatican over who should have control of Catholic chaplains in the British army. Opponents of Bourne, and also more objective voices, argued that a Catholic Chaplain-General or Bishop of the Army should be appointed.

The organization and deployment of Catholic chaplains on the Western Front exacerbated the shortage of chaplains. This could not be laid entirely at Bourne's door as he had no control over the deployment of Catholic chaplains but, as the war progressed, it became a greater source of dissatisfaction among chaplains at the front and also the wider Catholic community. Manpower shortages, a lack of organization and poor deployment were the distressing characteristics of Catholic army chaplaincy.

The result of this unseemly and protracted episcopal stand-off, accentuated by military and public Catholic unrest, was that on 30 October 1917 Mgr Keatinge was recalled from Salonika and appointed by the Vatican, with the agreement of the British government, as the first Catholic Bishop of the Army, or *Episcopus Castrensis*. On his appointment, he stated his priority: "In assuming this post of great responsibility my sole wish is to further and help the Catholic cause in our Armies, by every means in my power, and to help the chaplains in every possible way." He was consecrated titular Bishop of Metellopolis by Cardinal de Lai on 25 February 1918 in the chapel of the Venerable English College, Rome.

Bishop Keatinge's episcopal authority extended to chaplains to the Royal Flying Corps (later Royal Air Force) but not to the control and supervision of Catholic chaplains to the Royal Navy, which remained with the Archbishop of Westminster. Keatinge's episcopal appointment, however, came too late to materially affect the dire shortage of chaplains on the Western Front. By April 1918, Fr Rawlinson reported a shortage of 71 Catholic army chaplains on the Western Front. At the Armistice, over 5,000 ministers of all religious denominations had served as army chaplains. Of them, 819 were Catholic priests from dioceses throughout the British Isles and from male religious orders. Thirty-nine Catholic army padres had been killed or died during the war. Forty priests had served the Royal Navy; two had lost their lives.

The demobilization of army chaplains after the Armistice presented Keatinge with his first problem. In November 1918, 649 Catholic army chaplains were still in uniform. Bishops and religious superiors understandably wanted their priests returned quickly, but Keatinge was dependent on the military. The pace of demobilization was inevitably slow given the large number of priests and men involved.

Keatinge's appointment as Army Bishop may have been welcomed by army chaplains and some senior Catholic churchmen in England and in Ireland, but Bourne behaved with distinct coolness towards the new bishop. Meanwhile, other bishops with army camps, RAF stations and garrison towns in their dioceses questioned the nature and extent of Keatinge's episcopal jurisdiction and soon discovered that it was a canonical minefield. The decommissioning of hundreds of temporary chaplains and the disbandment of Irish regiments after the creation of the Irish Free State in 1922 left Keatinge with little to do except be responsible for the pre-war number of Catholic army chaplains and a few RAF chaplains. His army pension subsidised his episcopal income, but the War Office reduced his office accommodation and secretarial assistance. To add insult to injury, the English and Welsh, the Scottish and the Irish Hierarchies excluded him from their episcopal conferences except where military matters were to be discussed. Familiar with military precision, Keatinge wrote to Fr Stephen Rawlinson: "I have found out already that some bishops are not, to put it mildly, 'business-like.'" At one low point, he suggested that the Archbishop of Westminster should resume responsibility for army chaplains.

After retirement from the army in 1924, Keatinge remained, at the request of the War Office, as *Episcopus Castrensis* and, with the financial assistance of the War Office and Air Ministry, for the next decade he consolidated the position of Catholic army and RAF chaplains as they

80,000 weary troops were in the open and beginning to suffer from frostbite. The hospital ships "were overwhelmed", he recalled. Ships were crowded and medics and chaplains overworked as they sailed for Malta. Fr Aloysius Gribbin claimed that many Catholics died in the hospital ships without the ministration of a priest.

Catholic army chaplains

Army chaplains accompanied the Allied force from its amphibious landings in April 1915 to its withdrawal in January 1916. They ministered on narrow, murderous beaches and during unsuccessful attempts to penetrate into the Turkish hinterland.

Twenty-four Catholic army chaplains served in Gallipoli. The Senior Catholic Chaplain was Fr John Moth, Chaplain, 3rd Class of Portsmouth Diocese, who was commissioned in 1904. Another regular army chaplain was Fr William Murphy of Kildare and Leighlin Diocese, who had served as an Acting Army Chaplain at the Curragh Camp. He was given the temporary rank of Chaplain, 4th Class in August 1914. Mgr Peter Cavendish, a Maltese priest, had experience as an army chaplain in Malta and in Canada, while Fr Edward Mostyn of the Westminster Archdiocese had served as a naval chaplain on the China Station between 1903 and 1905. He was evacuated wounded soon after the Gallipoli landings began. These were the only priests with military experience. Others held temporary commissions as Chaplains to the Forces, 4th Class, and were attached to field ambulances, base hospitals, brigades and to Irish regiments. They were all in danger of death wherever they ministered. Among chaplains of all denominations there were exploits of bravery and examples of ecumenical co-operation. The Revd H. C. Foster, an Anglican chaplain attached to the Royal Naval Division, wrote later that all chaplains "lived together in godly union and concord".

The chaplains were under no illusions. One wrote that "to those of us privileged to attend the soldiers . . . this was a time of harvest before the storm of death". Another reported that over 1,000 Catholic soldiers received General Absolution before they embarked for their first assault.

Fr William Finn and 1st Dublins

Among the first fatalities at Gallipoli was Fr William Finn. His death presented Catholics with their first "martyr" of the war, firm evidence of their community's patriotism, and a propaganda coup. Conflicting eyewitness reports vitiated attempts to arrive at an accurate account of the padre's final hours, and accounts of his origins and death varied in accuracy and style.

William Finn was born near Hull in 1875, educated at Ushaw College, and ordained on 5 August 1900 for the Diocese of Middlesbrough. His first application to become an army chaplain was rejected by Bishop Lacey in October 1914, but in 1915 he was commissioned Temporary Chaplain to the Forces, 4th Class. Fr Finn became chaplain to 1st Royal Dublin Fusiliers.

The 1st Dublins were part of the 29th Division which was to land on five beaches (Y, X, W, V and S) at Cape Helles, while to the north ANZAC forces were to land at Gaba Tepe and at Anzac Cove, and French forces were engaged to the south. Central to the landing on V Beach was the *River Clyde*, a converted collier with machine guns on its decks, holes cut into its side to allow men to disembark, and towing barges full of heavily laden men. At 01.00, the *River Clyde* sailed to V Beach, which was 300 yards wide, crescent-shaped and with cliffs rising up behind it. Over 2,000 men from 1st Munsters, 1st Royal Dublin Fusiliers, 2nd Hampshire Regiment, the Anson Battalion of the Royal Naval Division, the West Riding Field Engineers, a Field Ambulance and a Signals Section were part of the amphibious landing. The *River Clyde* was to run ashore and allow its human cargo to disembark. At 5.00 a.m., as the naval barrage began, the *River Clyde* sailed into the sun towards V Beach. It was a Sunday morning. What followed was carnage and confusion. "Of all the landings", wrote Peter Liddle, "V Beach was to hold the strongest elements of tragedy, prolonged into a grimly sustained frustration of collective and individual heroism."

The death of Fr Finn

The Dublins landed in the first wave. Fr Thomas Harker of the Diocese of Hexham and Newcastle was on the *River Clyde* with 1st Royal Munster Fusiliers. He described the scene:

> The ... bay was alive with troops, snipers, and machine guns, while on both sides they had magnificent forts ... we began to land ... for three hours we had immediate sights of deeds of heroism and of such a shambles I hope never to see again. Men drowned, men dying without any hope of being assisted, and the only passage to shore was over the bodies of the living and the dead. The enemy's machine guns had naturally the easiest job in the world to range themselves upon the landing spots. Meanwhile the little boats were trying to land, but just as they reached the shore they were met with a fusillade of rifles and machine guns and the slaughter was appalling.

"Many anxious eyes were peering about over the protected bulwarks of the *River Clyde*", it was reported, and among them was Fr Finn:

> The sight of 500 of his brave boys lying dead or dying on that terrible strip of beach was too much for him, so heedless of the risk, he plunged down the gangway and made for the shore. On the way, his wrist was shattered by a bullet, but he went on and although lead was splattering around him like hailstones, he administered consolation to the wounded and dying, who, alas, were so thickly strewn around. For a time, he seemed to have some miraculous form of Divine Protection, for he went from one to another through shot and shell without receiving further injury. At last a bullet struck him near the hip, and on seeing this some of the Dublins rushed out to him from the protection of the sandbank and brought him into its shelter. When, however, he had somewhat recovered from his wound nothing would induce him to remain in safety while his poor boys were being done to death in the open. So, he crawled out again to administer comfort

to a poor fellow who was moaning piteously a little way off, and in the act of giving consolation to the stricken man, the heroic chaplain was struck dead by a merciless bullet.

Foster, who had befriended Fr Finn on the passage to the Dardanelles, wrote that Fr Finn did not expect to survive the landing at Helles: "'If you find my body,' he said one day, 'bury me simply, and say a prayer for my soul, old chap, and if you find any of my boys dying, get them to repeat a short act of contrition.'" Foster continued that Fr Finn's death was a great grief to him "and a great blow to the men who well-nigh worshipped him":

> When many of the Dublins fell wounded and bleeding into the water, Father Finn jumped in and tried his best to rescue them. Several bullets entered his own body. He fell just at the water's edge and, carried to cover, lived only a few minutes. ?? Seems two different accounts of Fr Finn's death—check with two papas above??

Fr Harker wrote that in Fr Finn's boat 40 out of 45 men never reached the shore. "He was hit in the boat and then four times more as he reached the shore and tried to crawl to shelter. He died after two hours' agony. I buried him myself." Fr Francis Devas SJ recalled that chaplains landed with their men under fire "and my friend, Fr. Finn was killed". "I heard his confession shortly before we went into action: he was a lovable little man and as good as gold."

On 12 June 1915, *The Tablet* gave a graphic account of the Fr Finn's final moments:

> Father Finn, the Catholic chaplain, who was so well liked in English circles, was one of the first to give his life in the landing at Sedd-el-Bahr. When appealed to not to leave the ship, he replied, "A priest's place is beside the dying soldier." He stepped on to the gangway, and immediately received a bullet through the chest. Undeterred, he made his way across the lighters, receiving another bullet in the thigh and still another in the leg. By the time

he reached the beach he was riddled with bullets, but in spite of the great pain he must have been suffering he heroically went about his duties, giving consolation to the dying troops. It was while he was in the act of attending to the spiritual requirements of one of his men that the priest's head was shattered by shrapnel.

Myles Dungan repeated this account and mistakenly claimed that Fr Finn was both Irish and the first padre to die in the war:

> Before the . . . landing, he had asked to be allowed to accompany the Dublins into what became an infamous massacre. He is reputed to have said, "The priest's place is beside the dying soldier; I must go." He certainly spent a considerable part of the day beside dying soldiers as there was an abundance of them at V Beach. He attempted to save a number of drowning and wounded men before being hit himself, in the right arm. He managed to get ashore and crawled around the beach offering help or consolation to the wounded and dying Dublins and Munsters. In order to give absolution, he had to hold up an injured right arm with his left. While he was blessing one of the men in this fashion, there was a shrapnel burst above him which blew part of his skull away.

Parnell Kerr claimed that through a night "of ceaseless imminent peril", "Fr Finn remained with his men, helping them and comforting them, giving those marked for death the consolations of religion, and the last services of a priest. Next morning, while still engaged in this work of mercy, he fell victim to a Turkish bullet."

A Catholic pamphlet stated that "there was not a newspaper that failed to chronicle the undaunted heroism of Father Finn", and, comparing the relative merits of Anglican and Catholic army chaplains, a correspondent to the *Manchester Guardian* wrote that Anglican chaplains "were too afraid of sacerdotalism" to be of any use. His description of Fr Finn's death was also more graphic than others:

> As usual, the Church of Rome reaps the fruit of her clear dogmatic teaching. Roman Catholics can understand and admire

their priest who . . . being wounded four times before ever he set
foot on land, continued ministering to the dying till his head
was blown off.

Whatever the contradictions in the accounts, the tragic circumstances of
Fr Finn's death had a strong impact on the Catholic community. To some,
his death was evidence of the Catholic commitment to the national cause,
while others sought to exploit his heroism and that of other Catholic
combatants.

In July 1915, Fr J. R. Meagher, of the Diocese of Hexham and Newcastle
and a contemporary of Fr Finn's at Ushaw, penned a poetic account of
the padre's death:

He did not turn his ears from that high call,
Nor parley with himself, nor hesitate.
Men would have held him; but he did not wait,
Albeit the air was thick with shell and ball.
He saw with tears his gallant Dublins fall;
His place was with them. Like a mountain spate,
His spirit o'erleaped its banks and laughed at Fate,
Knowing God's Providence that ruleth all.

Exaggerated, inaccurate reports and poetic verses did not appeal to Fr
Harker, who wrote to Cardinal Bourne's military secretary that "the
newspaper accounts and the stories told in a panegyric at Hull during
Finn's requiem are a fake. Good zealous priest that he was, he needs
no lies to endear his memory among the Dublins." Meanwhile, Foster
reported that a Presbyterian and a Catholic undertook to see that Fr
Finn's grave was properly tended. "He was buried close to the sea on V
beach, and a road had been made over the place. I think they managed
to get the grave marked off with a little fence."

As the Allies withdrew from the Dardanelles in late 1915, the *River
Clyde* was still anchored offshore. Thousands of Allied dead lay buried on
the beaches of the Gallipoli Peninsula. Peter Howson wrote that Fr Finn's
death, whatever the differences in accounts, illustrated to some the exact
nature of the padre's role in battle. The most important point for many

was that he "was with the men of the Dublin Fusiliers as they made their landing". Howson concluded: "If a single death raised questions about where their ministry should take them it must be seen in this context. It was during the course of an assault landing on a defended beach and thus something of a rarity in World War One."

Other Catholic chaplains at Gallipoli

Fr Thomas Harker was padre with 1st Royal Munster Fusiliers, 1st Lancashire Fusiliers and the Anson Battalion of the Royal Naval Division. He too was on the *River Clyde* and witnessed the mayhem and carnage of the landing. Men were shot scrambling ashore while others drowned under the weight of their equipment. The padre tended the wounded, gave absolution and assisted with "the disposal of the bodies of the officers and men".

Men dug in and stores were brought ashore. Mass was said by chaplains who survived the first landing and by those who arrived later. Altars were made out of ammunition boxes, trestle tables, packing cases or shelves cut into the wall of a cliff. The places may have been picturesque, but they were inconvenient and dangerous, as men huddled in a group were targets for snipers. Priests wore vestments or stoles and were easily seen.

Fr William Leighton of Diocese of Salford landed at Anzac Cove with 9th Royal Warwickshire Regiment. Fr Leighton "exposed himself freely in discharge of his duties . . . especially in the . . . attack on Hill 871" and for his courageous ministry, he was awarded the Military Cross. Fr John Linehan, also of the Diocese of Salford, was attached to 6th East Lancashire Regiment and moved along the beach carrying wounded men on his shoulders. He wrote that his experience and that of the men "is simply the limit of the most awful imaginings". Fr Henry Day SJ was attached to the Notts and Derby Yeomanry and recalled: "Ordinary risks and hair-breadth escapes are of daily occurrence, and unless materialized are thought nothing of. They are too numerous to recount . . . since for six weeks we have never been far from fire, either rifle or artillery." Fr Francis Devas SJ wrote: "I know what it is like to hear bullets whiz by you and see them spit in the earth at your feet."

Dom Bede Camm OSB, a Benedictine monk of Downside Abbey, and Fr Aloysius Gribbin of the Diocese of Salford, were army chaplains who spent some of their time working on troopships and hospital ships. When Fr Camm heard that men were embarking for Suvla Bay, he distributed "beads, medals, scapulars, etc, to the RCs in great number". Fr Gribbin was on the hospital ship *Dunluce Castle*.

Fr William Murphy and Fr John Mulderry of the Archdiocese of Dublin said Mass, buried the dead, tended the wounded, counselled the living, gave general absolution and throughout the campaign ministered in field ambulances. At Anzac Cove, the Rosminian Fr Frederick O'Connor was attached to 5th Connaught Rangers while Fr Peter O'Farrell of the Diocese of Ardagh was chaplain to Lord Granard's Irish Regiment. Fr Paul Hook, of the Diocese of Menevia and chaplain to 1/5th Royal Welsh Fusiliers, landed at Suvla Bay on 9 August and began work immediately at a Casualty Clearing Station. From his dugout, he looked over the beach to the sea "where some battle ships, destroyers & hospital ships are knocking about. To the right is a place where men & stores are landed. This place is shelled frequently." On 17 August, he wrote to his mother:

> On Sunday 8th we . . . came in for sterner things. When the lists are published in the papers you will find a number of people you know among killed and wounded, but I cannot give any names at present. We were not here many minutes before we had our baptism of fire. It is a weird sensation to hear the whine of shells over one's head.

The Allies decided to evacuate from the Dardanelles. One hundred and five thousand men withdrew from Suvla Bay in December 1915 and from Cape Helles in January 1916. It was a dangerous operation, but the evacuation was undertaken perfectly. Fr Gribbin wrote that "fortune favoured the exercise".

Fr Finn is buried in V Beach Cemetery, Gallipoli. The Sacred Heart Church, Hull, was built in his memory and paid for by his brother Councillor Frank Finn, former Lord Mayor of Hull. Fr Finn was one of 41 Catholic chaplains who died in the First World War; 39 were army chaplains, two were Royal Navy chaplains. The first chaplain to die was Fr Basil Gwydir, a naval chaplain and Benedictine monk of Douai Abbey, who drowned when the hospital ship *Rohilla* sank off the Yorkshire coast on 30 October 1914. Many deaths among army chaplains, including Fr Willie Doyle SJ, occurred on the Western Front.

**Figure 10: Fr William Finn CF: Gallipoli casualty
(Courtesy of the Trustees of Ushaw College)**

1 1

The Battle of Jutland:
Chaplains in ironclads

Catholic chaplains to the Royal Navy
before the First World War

As we saw in Chapter 8, the Admiralty was reluctant to commission Catholic chaplains in the Royal Navy and it maintained this stance well into the twentieth century. This was a source of discontent to Catholic prelates and politicians, who complained that the Royal Navy denied the spiritual rights of Catholic sailors and that the Royal Navy would be seriously understaffed but for the presence of Catholics, especially Irish Catholics, in its ranks. According to the Catholic argument, it was a both a question of justice and a matter of common sense for the Admiralty to address Catholic grievances.

During the First World War, Catholic prelates and politicians continued to demand that the Royal Navy appoint Catholic chaplains in the same numbers and on the same pay and conditions as those of the Church of England. As in the past, such entreaties met with little success. Notwithstanding these limitations, the Catholic chaplains who served the Royal Navy during the Great War did so with the same fortitude and bravery as their confrères in the army.

Royal Navy chaplains, 1914–18

In 1914, the Royal Navy had 648 warships of varying sizes, armament, functions and ages. Nearly 150,000 officers and ratings manned these ships, while there were over 46,000 in Naval Reserves. By the end of the war, the number of warships was 1,354; regular sailors had increased to approximately 186,000, while Naval Reserves had reached 110,000. Over 640,000 men served in the Royal Navy during the war, and many would have been Catholic.

As they had done for centuries, Anglican clergymen dominated Royal Navy chaplaincy. From the declaration of war until 1918, 174 Anglican Acting Chaplains were recruited for Temporary Service. The corresponding combined figure for Church of Scotland, Presbyterian and Wesleyan Officiating Chaplains was 13. The number of full-time Catholic Officiating Chaplains was 34.

The inadequate number of Catholic naval chaplains continued to cause dismay in Catholic circles. On the declaration of war, Catholics volunteered for naval service, but it was obvious that their spiritual needs were being overlooked. The *Catholic Times* lamented: "To questions asked as to whether measures will be taken by the Admiralty to meet the spiritual wants of Catholics in the navy the stereotyped reply that the question is under consideration continues to be given."

Chapels in ships

If assigned to a fleet, flotilla or ship, Catholic priests had to overcome the overt hostility of some officers and also the difficulty of ministering in large ships primed for war. But they were not the only ministers of religion who had difficulty in finding places in vessels in which to conduct services. Having a chapel or finding a space for worship in a crowded warship was a perennial difficulty for chaplains of all denominations. In *The Royal Navy Officer's Jutland Pocket Manual 1916*, it was stated that a chapel "was one of the best things that can be added to a man-of-war if space can be found". There were many places in a big ship but none appropriate for celebrating Mass or for special services. It was left to the chaplain to arrange with officers and men to identify a space and then "fit up all the essential parts". The chapel would inevitably be small and would only be suitable for services with small congregations or for individual counselling or confessions but to bring the religious community together in a corporate act of worship would require a bigger space and the permission of the commanding officer. Such permission was not always forthcoming.

The Battle of Jutland

For two years after the outbreak of war, the British Grand Fleet kept to the safety of Scapa Flow in the Orkney Islands while the German High Seas Fleet remained anchored in its own ports. In January 1916, Admiral Reinhard Scheer assumed command of the German fleet and planned to lure the British Fleet out of its anchorages into battle and destroy it. The British discovered the plan and prepared for a confrontation. That ensuing engagement was the Battle of Jutland, which took place in twelve hours, between 31 May and 1 June 1916, off the coast of Denmark. It was a sea battle of epic proportions which still interests the finest naval historians.

Just before 18.00 on 31 May, the fleets of Britain and Germany, totalling some 250 ships, engaged in combat. Fighting went on all evening with high explosive shells ripping into thick armour plating. Many ships were sunk; sailors burned to death or drowned in the icy sea. As darkness came, Scheer headed back to port and the British fleet, concerned about enemy submarines and minefields, refused to give chase. In the aftermath, the Germans claimed to have sunk more enemy ships, but the British maintained that Scheer had given up first and fled the scene of the battle. Britain had lost 14 battleships to Germany's 11. Germany lost 2,551 sailors, while Britain lost 6,077. The British public was astounded by the news. Huge sums had been invested in the High Seas Fleet, which was supposed to be the world's finest. Claims that Britain had been victorious at Jutland were greeted with scepticism.

Catholic chaplains at Jutland

Fifty-two naval chaplains were present at the Battle of Jutland. They served in battleships, battle cruisers, cruisers and five light cruisers from which they exercised spiritual responsibilities for squadrons. Catholic chaplains included the Redemptorist Fr Thomas Bradley in HMS *Tiger*; Fr William Meagher of St Cuthbert's, North Shields in HMS *Bellerophon*; Fr Stewart Phelan OMI of St Conleth's, Philipstown in HMS *Black Prince*; Fr Anthony Hungerford Pollen Cong. Orat. of the Birmingham Oratory in HMS *Warspite*; Fr Odo Blundell OSB in the Dreadnought HMS *Collingwood*; and Fr James O'Reilly of the Diocese of Gibraltar. Fr O'Reilly had served as an Acting Chaplain to the Royal Navy from 1905 to 1910 when he transferred to the Army Chaplains' Department. In August 1914, he transferred back to the Royal Navy and served with the Grand Fleet and battle cruiser squadrons. Given that the 151 combat ships making up the British naval strength would have included thousands of Catholic sailors, six was a ridiculously small number of chaplains and indicative of the Admiralty's continued opposition to the presence of Catholic priests in navy ships.

In December 1915, Fr Meagher had written to the President of Ushaw College telling him about the chaplain's duties in a Grand Fleet battleship and "other huge floating monsters".

He was lucky, he wrote, if he found a place to say Mass on any of the eight vessels that he had to visit, but he found that most of the Irish sailors were Catholic and "deeply religious men". Getting from ship to ship was "not the easiest part of a priest's life". When "seated in the stern sheets of the picket boat the danger is over. But to jump on and off it when the boat is bobbing up and down like a cork and at the same time trying to smash the gangway into matchwood, requires a certain amount of agility." The sailors, he wrote were given plenty to do and were generally contented, but they complained "that the Germans have not yet appeared". The time was fast approaching when they would have their wish granted. At Jutland, HMS *Bellerophon*, with Fr Meagher on board, took part in the battle as part of the 4th Battle Division but emerged undamaged.

Days before the battle, Fr Thomas Bradley had heard confessions and given Holy Communion to Catholics in HMS *Tiger*. He was to be busy throughout the battle and was slightly wounded. Like many others, he was experiencing his first action at sea and he recorded his immediate impressions: "The first two or three hours", he wrote, "were a very terrible experience. It was a 'bloody hell'. As this was the first time I had been under fire, the first few minutes made me feel full of a strange kind of funk—but after a time when we became very busy with the wounded one grew used to it." The ship was hit several times, and he heard the noise of shells tearing into metal and exploding. "The cries of the wounded and burnt men", he wrote, "were very terrible to listen to." Casualties were brought below to a Distributing Station where the padre helped others to tend the wounded, heard confessions and administered Extreme Unction. On other decks, he saw body parts and bodies with the clothes blown off. Where the dead were laid out, he wrote, "the sight was terrible". At the end of the battle, he returned "horribly tired" to what was left of his cabin. He found his mission crucifix still standing upright in its socket on the table. *Tiger*, badly damaged, returned to South Queensferry to be met by anxious relatives.

Fr Blundell was on board HMS *Collingwood*, a Dreadnought battleship which was in the middle of the battleline. At one point in the battle, *Collingwood* and the rest of the Grand Fleet disengaged and saw no further action in the battle. Prince Albert, the future King George VI, was a sub-lieutenant commanding a forward turret on *Collingwood* during the battle. Fr Blundell had already written to Cardinal Bourne telling him of the exhausting pressure he was under as he tried to minister to nearly 50 ships. Seeing how overworked the chaplain was, an officer had petitioned the cardinal to have an additional chaplain appointed.

The Australian naval chaplain Fr Patrick Gibbons, who was born in County Mayo, had been a chaplain since 1912 and was also at Jutland. However, he was not in a ship of the Australian navy. His ship, HMAS *Australia*, was in a dockyard for repairs and Fr Gibbons was assigned to HMS *Indomitable*, one of three Invincible-class battlecruisers which formed the Third Battlecruiser Squadron and had a wartime crew of nearly 1,000. In the battle, the ship was hit several times but not badly damaged and the chaplain heard confessions, in Maltese for the Maltese cooks, and later led the Rosary. He went about his duties in a casualty station and carried on hearing confessions long after the battle was over.

Fr Anthony Hungerford Pollen at Jutland

Fr Anthony Hungerford Pollen was born on 22 December 1860. His father had been an Anglican clergyman before he became a Catholic, and he was closely associated with Fr John Henry Newman when the latter was Rector of the Catholic University in Dublin. Anthony Hungerford Pollen was a pupil at the Oratory School, Birmingham, and after studies in Germany joined the Birmingham Oratory in 1883 at the age of 23. After his ordination in 1889, Fr Pollen taught at St Philip's Grammar School, Birmingham, and he became a naval chaplain in 1915.

At Jutland, Fr Pollen was attached to the recently commissioned battleship HMS *Warspite* in 5th Battle Squadron. At their first meeting, the captain of *Warspite* is reputed to have said to Fr Pollen: "I hope we shall get on, but I think it fair to tell you that I don't like Catholics", to which Fr Pollen replied, "I am sure, Sir, that we shall get on, as, to be candid, I detest Protestants." They did become friends and played golf together during the short intervals at Scapa when they could get ashore.

Warspite was heavily involved at Jutland. She was holed 150 times, and her steering and guns were damaged. As the fighting raged, some cordite charges caught fire in one of the six-inch casements on the main deck and several of the gun crew were injured and trapped. On hearing this, Fr Pollen immediately entered the casement and succeeded in bringing out two seamen but was badly burned himself on his face and hands. A Catholic priest later repeated an account he had heard from a seaman in *Warspite*:

> Yesterday a sailor whom the Navy dubs "ordinary" . . . fresh from the *Warspite*, came to see me and spun some fine yarns about the battle . . . One of them, if unknown to you as yet, cannot long escape publicity. It concerns the heroic deeds of the Catholic chaplain on that victorious ship. My sailor-boy, engaged about a turret and a 5-in. gun, did not see what had been done, but hearing of it afterwards proceeded to cross examine the doer himself and others too, till he elicited the following facts: Two boys who had to carry a shell to a gun-breech, removed the lid of its case too soon, with the consequence that the heat of the

battery, then very great, caused the shell, not to explode, which it does only in its proper time and place, but to catch fire and blaze up, and it seems when cordite does that it flares something like xylonite, celluloid, flannelette, &c., only I suppose with much greater intensity and wider extent, setting everything inflammable aflame. So the two boys were quickly blazing and would soon have perished like Nero's Christian victims wrapped in pitchy shirts. But Father Pollen was at hand, and embracing a boy in either arm he succeeded in pressing out the flames. That he saved the two lives was the verdict of all observers. That he suffered grievously himself was inevitable. It is said that he will recover notwithstanding his advanced years, and we may well rejoice at that, doubtful however whether he will care for health or strength or long life or the congratulations of all the world who has done so enviable a deed.

Surgeon Ellis of *Warspite* reported that "eleven cases, including Father Pollen, the Roman Catholic Chaplain, were brought down suffering from very severe and extensive burns of the face, body and limbs. They were so badly burnt that one could do very little to relieve them of their pain and shock." He continued: "Father Pollen stood the shock well and at no time whilst he remained a patient on board uttered any complaint that he was suffering." When the chaplain was stretchered off *Warspite* at Rosyth, his body was completely swathed in bandages with only holes for his mouth, nose and eyes. He was heard to whisper: "God bless *Warspite*." Despite the severity of the attack on *Warspite*, only four officers and 15 other ranks had been killed. It was said that the ship went into action with a statue of Our Lady of Lourdes installed in a place of honour on the lower deck and that the Catholic seamen attributed their escape to safety to Our Lady's intercession.

Fr Pollen was Mentioned in Despatches and awarded the Distinguished Service Cross for gallantry in action—the only chaplain to receive that decoration. *The London Gazette* recorded his action in the citation for the award:

Remarks of Rear-Admiral Evan-Thomas:

Rev. Anthony Pollen (Roman Catholic Chaplain).

The Reverend Anthony Pollen carried men injured by severe burns from the battery deck to the distributing station, he himself being severely burned at the time.

Aged 56.

Fr Pollen's bravery perhaps merited the highest award for valour, but his Commanding Officer recommended the Distinguished Service Cross, as he was not a commissioned officer. It prompted Fr Odo Blundell, who had conducted burial services on HMS *Collingwood*, to write to Mgr Bidwell, Cardinal Bourne's assistant in charge of chaplains: "I trust that you will allow me to express the hope that our Jutland and other war medals will be carefully watched."

Fr Stewart Phelan: A chaplain's death at Jutland

Fr Stewart Joseph Phelan was an Oblate of Mary Immaculate (OMI), who was born at Dingle, County Kerry, in 1879 and studied in England and Ireland before his ordination in 1903. For some time, he had been on the mission at Mount St Mary's at Richmond Hill, Leeds. In 1914, he volunteered as a chaplain in the Royal Navy and served initially in HMS *Collingwood*.

At Jutland, Fr Phelan was in HMS *Black Prince* with 1st Cruiser Squadron. At the first meeting of the two fleets, *Black Prince* had followed her flagship, HMS *Defence*, into action. *Black Prince* suffered damage as *Defence* was blown up and was left far astern after the Grand Fleet turned south. When a line of battleships was dimly seen ahead, it was thought that they were the British squadrons and *Black Prince* altered course to close them. At a half-mile range, however, the German recognition signal flashed out and the horrified Captain Bonham swung *Black Prince* away in a desperate effort to escape. It was too late. In the German battleship

Thüringen, the deadly efficient night action procedure that had been displayed at the head of the line went into play. Brilliantly lit by half-a-dozen searchlights, *Black Prince* was raked from stern to stem by a salvo of shells and lay a helpless wreck before she could even fire a shot in reply. As she drifted down the German line, ship after ship opened up on her, *Thüringen*, *Ostfriesland*, *Nassau* and finally the fleet flagship *Friedrich der Grosse* added her quota. *Black Prince* met the same end as *Defence*, blowing up with a tremendous explosion, vanishing with its crew of 37 officers and 825 men. *The Tablet* added Fr Phelan's name to the melancholy list of casualties:

> We add to the Roll of Honour of the great naval battle the name of Father Stewart Joseph Phelan, O.M.I., Naval Chaplain of the First Cruiser Squadron, who is known to have perished in H.M.S. *Black Prince*, on May 31, though his name did not appear in the first Admiralty list of officers of that ship. Father Phelan was thirty-seven years of age, and had been with the First Cruiser Squadron in the North Sea as Chaplain for over a year, first on the *Collingwood*, and later on the *Black Prince*. He was well known in Liverpool and Leeds, where he served the Oblate Missions. The last scene of his missionary labours was St. Conleth's, Philipstown, King's County, where there was a Requiem on Friday last week.

Fr Phelan was in *Black Prince* with the Revd William F. Webber, the Anglican chaplain, who was also killed in the battle. However, this fact is surprisingly not mentioned by Gordon Taylor, who recorded that the ship was sunk by superior German gunfire and that "her chaplain Webber, died with her". Fr Phelan is commemorated on the Portsmouth Naval Memorial. The Catholic dead of Jutland, whose bodies had been recovered, were buried at South Queensferry, and Admiral Beatty gave permission for a Requiem Mass to be celebrated by Fr Bradley in the dockyard.

On 5 August 1916, two months after the Battle of Jutland, Cardinal Bourne visited the Grand Fleet at Scapa Flow. The visit, organized by Fr James O'Reilly, Senior Chaplain at Scapa, was a unique occasion, for the cardinal became the first English prelate to board a Royal Navy ship since the Jacobite Duke of York, Cardinal Henry Stuart, had visited Captain Horatio Nelson's *Agamemnon* off Naples in 1798. Bourne was welcomed by Admiral Sir John Jellicoe and visited ships at anchor, but the realities of the chaplain's ministry cannot have escaped him, as his plans had to be altered due to sea conditions. He celebrated Mass in HMS *Venturesome*, paid calls to hospital ships, confirmed Catholic seamen and blessed the Catholic section of the naval cemetery. Later, the Cardinal addressed 1,000 Catholic seamen in a ship specially prepared for the occasion. There he exhorted the sailors to avail themselves of the sacraments and affirmed his belief in the righteousness of Britain's cause in the war: "As you look back hereafter upon these days spent in defence of King and Country and Empire, be able to say that you are better men in God's sight because you have been privileged to take part in so great a cause." In January 1917, the Cardinal visited British Catholic sailors with ships at Taranto off the Italian coast. Again, he urged them to "be true to their religion in thought, word and action" and begged them to frequent the sacraments. Irrespective of Bourne's visits and his patriotic words, the Admiralty felt no urge to increase the number of Catholic chaplains. This shortfall led to wide varieties in the frequency and quality of Catholic chaplaincy.

Fr Pollen's post-war ministry

After the war, Fr Pollen organized and conducted a naval pilgrimage to the Spanish shrine of St James the Apostle—Santiago de Compostela— when the British fleet, including HMS *Warspite*, visited Vigo. The Fleet also visited Palma, Majorca, then an island in the Mediterranean that few English people had heard of, and he invited the Palma Oratory Fathers to visit *Warspite*. After his service with the Royal Navy, Fr Pollen returned to the Birmingham Oratory. He died on 5 October 1940.

The Admiralty, meanwhile, maintained its opposition to the appointment of Catholic chaplains in Royal Navy ships. It was not until 1943 that Catholic priests were officially commissioned as Chaplains in the Royal Navy.

**Figure 11: Fr Stewart Phelan OMI: Naval casualty at
Jutland (OMI Archives Anglo-Irish Province)**

Military ministry and ecclesiastical diplomacy: Chaplains and missionaries in East Africa, 1914–19

Catholic interests and imperial interests

In the Great War, Britain and European nations continued to pursue their imperial interests in Africa. The Catholic Church was ever-watchful of these colonial ambitions, for through its European missionary institutes it wished to evangelize African peoples, establish religious and educational communities, facilitate the development of an indigenous priesthood and establish national ecclesiastical hierarchies.

European governments were content to allow missionaries to exercise social control through their spiritual and educational functions while missionaries accepted the protection of their governments. Missionary institutes also looked to the Vatican for approval and approbation and were as jealous of territorial boundaries as were their colonial masters.

In the Great War, senior Catholic military chaplains in Africa, like missionaries, found themselves serving temporal masters with a different world view from that of their spiritual authority.

The British East African Campaign

It was strategically important for the Allies to deny Germany access to her African naval bases and resources and, by mid-August 1914, expeditions had been mounted against German colonies in Togoland, Cameroon, South West Africa and East Africa. The major theatre of hostilities was

East Africa, where fighting began in August 1914 and ended 15 days after the Armistice had been signed on the Western Front in 1918. Over 126,000 men fought in the East African campaign: 3,443 were killed in action while 6,558 died from disease. It is estimated that deaths among indigenous porters and carriers numbered about 90,000.

The East African Expeditionary Force (EAEF) included regular army battalions and contingents from the West Indies, the Gold Coast, India and Mauritius. There were battalions of the King's African Rifles from Kenya, Uganda and Rhodesia, and in 1916 the Expeditionary Force was augmented by troops from South Africa.

Catholic army chaplains in East Africa

Eleven South African priests became either Officiating Chaplains or Acting Chaplains to South African forces. Some served in British East Africa; others served in South Africa and German East Africa and German South West Africa. Priests of British missionary institutes increased the number of commissioned army chaplains allotted to the EAEF.

The missionaries' knowledge of local languages, customs, cultures and geography was of great military value, but missionaries taken for army duties had to be replaced by others, a difficult task for missionary superiors, who saw their labours being destroyed by war. French and German missionary orders, especially, suffered more directly as some of their priests were obliged to leave Africa for conscripted military commitments in their home country. Missionary institutes were now seriously denuded of manpower at the behest of the imperial governments under whose protection they worked. German missionary effectiveness was further weakened by the internment and deportation of missionary priests and brothers. The deployment of British, French, Irish, Dutch and Italian priests outside their normal missionary territory also cut across ecclesiastical jurisdictions.

Fr James Dey—Senior Catholic Chaplain

Catholic chaplains ministered to men in the EAEF, but two of them assumed unexpected responsibilities. In 1916, in an attempt to bring order to Catholic army chaplaincy in the EAEF, the War Office appointed Fr James Dey as Senior Catholic Chaplain in East Africa. Fr Dey, a priest of the Archdiocese of Birmingham, was ordained in 1894 and commissioned into the Army Chaplains' Department in 1903. He had spent ten years in South Africa, and on the outbreak of war in August 1914 he was Chaplain to the Forces, 3rd Class. He accompanied the Connaught Rangers to France with the British Expeditionary Force, took part in the retreat from Mons and was subsequently stationed at a base hospital. His arrival in Africa caused confusion, as he was senior in rank to the Revd P. Guinness, an Anglican chaplain who had been acting as Principal Chaplain of the EAEF. The War Office decided that neither Dey nor Guinness could become Principal Chaplain but would work independently under War Office control.

Fr Dey arrived in East Africa on 14 March 1916 and after landing at Mombasa transferred to Nairobi. From his arrival to his departure in May 1917, he saw no military action. His work was entirely administrative, dominated and complicated by the shortage of chaplains, Catholic and ecumenical missionary politics, ecclesiastical jurisdictions, huge distances and the unique nature of warfare in East Africa. The range of his duties dictated an involvement in military, political and ecclesiastical affairs that far exceeded what might normally be expected of a chaplain of his rank. His presence, experience, administrative ability and awareness of missionary sensitivities were invaluable to his military masters. When he asked to be moved from Nairobi so he "could be better employed elsewhere", his request was refused.

Missionary chaplains

Fr Dey's first task was to ascertain the disposition of troops, discover how many chaplains were at his disposal and decide on their deployment. In the process, he learned of the missionaries' commitment to the military. Missionary chaplains were dispersed across vast tracts of country in their own missionary territories. Some had already experienced war. The British Mill Hill Fathers had missions in the Upper Nile Vicariate of Uganda and on the outbreak of war had assumed chaplaincy duties with indigenous police, soldiers and bearers. In September 1914, the Mill Hill Superior in London received news from Alwor that Frs Wall and Stam had been with the troops at Kisii Mission where a severe battle had taken place. The mission "was entirely and completely looted". Fr Philip Jackson ministered as Acting Chaplain in the Great Lakes Region while Fr Peter Rogan was Officiating Chaplain to hospitals and lines of communication in the Voi and Taveta districts. Fr Christopher Kirk, another Mill Hill Missionary, served on a supplies committee and acted as a recruiting agent among the African population for the Carrier Corps.

Other religious institutes provided chaplains. Fr David Brand SJ was chaplain to the EAEF in Southern Rhodesia and served from 4 August 1914 to 25 November 1918. Fr H. Demaison, a French priest, was serving 1st Division as an Acting Chaplain. The Irish Spiritan Fr Henry Gogarty was an Officiating Chaplain to military hospitals in Nairobi. The South African Fr Glynn was deployed with 7th South African Infantry in 2nd South African Brigade, while Fr Michael Costello was attached to 9th South African Infantry with 3rd South African Brigade. All had received War Office appointments.

In Uganda, the French White Fathers undertook chaplaincy duties without payment, and Dey learned that African porters at Entebbe would not join the Carrier Corps unless accompanied by a White Father. Facilitating such arrangements and negotiating rates of pay for Acting and Officiating Chaplains and other volunteers became part of Dey's duties. Italian missionary priests and nuns provided nursing and recreational facilities at military hospitals established in their mission grounds, and as Medical Officers praised their efforts Dey felt confident in requesting that they should be remunerated.

On completion of his survey, Fr Dey concluded that there was a shortage of chaplains. There were insufficient chaplains in the 2nd Division, which included the Loyal North Lancs Regiment (with an estimated 40 per cent Catholics), 2nd Rhodesian Regiment, East African Rifles and the South African Mounted Brigade, none of which had a Catholic chaplain. There were also, he noted, many Catholics in the Indian regiments. And since German missionaries in British territories had either returned to Germany or been deported to India (despite some having been declared neutral), Dey not only had to find priests for his own men; he also had to arrange for chaplains to German prisoners.

The military chaplain and missionary superiors

The shortage of manpower eased slightly in late March 1916, when Fr John Cosser, of the Diocese of Northampton and a commissioned chaplain, arrived from Egypt, but the delay in obtaining chaplains through War Office channels compelled Fr Dey to begin a series of visits to local Catholic bishops (normally missionary Superiors) to obtain more men. On 28 March, he visited Bishop Johannes Biermans, the Dutch Superior of the Mill Hill Fathers in Uganda, and was told that two British missionaries (Frs Jackson and Rogan) had already "been given" and were now serving. Many of Bierman's other missionaries, however, were Dutch and felt no obligation to serve the British military. In the absence of local success, Dey wired the War Office for three more commissioned chaplains, and on 21 April he was informed that Fr William Carroll of the Archdiocese of Liverpool and Fr Edward Collins of the Diocese of Cork and Ross would be deployed from Egypt to be "employed at your discretion", and that Fr William Flynn, of the Diocese of Portsmouth and a regular chaplain, would be transferred from France as soon as possible. If this was insufficient to meet his needs, then, Dey was told, he should "send further demands".

Dey's manpower problems eased considerably in May, when Frs Collins and Carroll and two other commissioned chaplains, Frs John Mulderry of the Archdiocese of Dublin and Richard Garrold SJ arrived at Kilindini. Fr Flynn arrived on 5 July but was immediately admitted to hospital suffering from sunstroke. The new chaplains were assigned to Divisional troops and Carrier Corps, at Casualty Clearing Stations, and in hospitals around Nairobi and beyond those ports and coastal areas where naval chaplains to hospital ships were available. Dey now had a cadre of chaplains on whom he could rely, and who were familiar with military routine.

Being from a variety of European nations and representing different religious institutes, local bishops, superiors and their agents were not always sympathetic to Dey's requests for priests. Many, however, were content to refer to him in times of difficulty or in dealings with the military. Superiors were reluctant to release men, and all were conscious of their ecclesiastical authority. Fr Dey had to exercise great diplomacy and always ensured that he obtained permission from superiors to deploy chaplains beyond their own missionary boundaries. Relations between European missionary institutes were also a problem, characterized as they were by national rivalry for missionary territory, a desire to demonstrate to the Vatican the success of their evangelizing labours, and attempts to gain the conversion and therefore the loyalty of the indigenous populations.

Dey's efforts to recruit bore fruit. In Uganda, Frs Fillion and Laplume, both French White Fathers, served as Acting Chaplains, while Frs Lafleur, Laberge and Michaud, also White Fathers, and Fr William Campling, a Mill Hill Father, were Officiating Chaplains. At Kampala, Dey received Bishop Biermans' permission to move Fr Rogan to Dar-es-Salaam. At Entebbe, in September 1916, he met with Fr Dirst, "the agent of the 5 White Fathers chaplains", with whom he discussed pay and promised to enquire about the release of Spanish and Alsatian White Fathers held in German East Africa. It was agreed that Fr Dirst would direct the chaplains in Uganda and inform Dey of their movements. Conscious of missionary sensitivities, Dey wired Dirst on 24 October 1916 to ask if Frs Fillion and Lafleur would serve in German East Africa. On another occasion, however, Dey found himself in a position of power when acting on behalf of military authorities. In January 1917, he visited Bishop Biermans again, but this time discussed the possibility of Mill Hill Fathers taking over missions vacated in German East Africa. Biermans was hesitant and wished for further details, to which Dey replied that the Assistant Adjutant-General had wired the Vatican and obtained approval.

Military and ecclesiastical authority

The early arrival from Egypt of the Irish Spiritan Fr Bernard Carey with the British West Indian Regiment on 19 August 1916 caught Dey unawares. Carey did not inform Dey of his arrival until 18 September when he promptly asked for leave. Dey refused his request. It was not the end of Dey's dealings with Fr Carey. In October, he received notice from GHQ at Morogoro about Carey's "insubordination". He may have been short of chaplains, but the Spiritan's ill-discipline caused Fr Dey serious problems. Fr Carey had differences of opinion with the military authorities, especially over the racial bigotry directed against West Indian soldiers and when he was rude to his commanding officer, he was dismissed. Fr Dey could not afford to alienate the military authorities and offered Carey no support but recommended that he be transferred to Europe. The War Office terminated Fr Carey's military career.

Other military–religious challenges confronted Fr Dey. In July 1916 Frs Michaud and Fillion informed him that their commanding officer would not allow them to accompany a column that included over 1,000 Catholics. A wire from Dey to the Assistant Adjutant-General solved the problem, but Fr Fillion complained that further obstacles were placed in his way by his commanding officer in the Great Lakes Region. Again, Dey successfully obtained redress. Fr Collins informed him that Catholics with the artillery at Mbuyuni had been compelled to attend Anglican Divine Service. On a different tack, Dey had to warn Frs Jackson and Rogan in November 1916 against interfering with relations between German missionaries and the Provost Marshal.

Dey discovered that missionary bishops were apt to conduct business through their own priests, as they had always done, rather than follow military procedures. In such cases, the British military command saw Dey as a useful conduit between their authority and his Church, and in January 1917 he was despatched to negotiate with a German bishop who had been asked to leave his mission. The bishop refused and would only yield to force in the presence of the local commander. Fr Dey took over the German church and asked the military authorities for priests to replace the expelled German missionaries. Political and military allegiance, it appeared, came before religious loyalty.

Yet on other occasions religious loyalty took precedence. As German missionaries left or were interned, their property and chapels were sometimes looted. It was distressing for Dey and other priests, and he complained vehemently to the military authorities to end this unwelcome practice. In December 1916, a missionary bishop informed him that an Anglican chaplain contemplated using a vacated Catholic missionary chapel for Anglican worship and, when the Senior Anglican Chaplain asked Dey if he could use an organ from a missionary chapel, Dey felt obliged to "warn him against requests of this kind".

Fr William Flynn—Senior Catholic Chaplain

In February 1917, Fr Dey was transferred to Salonika. His successor in East Africa, Fr William Flynn, wrote that "Major Dey received the DSO (Distinguished Service Order) before his departure in recognition of his excellent work with the E.A. Exped. Force". Fr Flynn was commissioned in January 1913 and had served on the Western Front. He was deployed with 15th Stationary Hospital at Morogoro, when he assumed Dey's responsibilities as Senior Chaplain. He was given the local rank of Chaplain, 3rd Class without extra pay.

During the next two years, Fr Flynn fulfilled a similar role to Fr Dey—liaising with military and missionary authorities, deploying and communicating with chaplains, negotiating pay and conditions for missionary chaplains, conducting funerals and organizing cemeteries, visiting hospitals, submitting monthly military returns, arranging for hosts and altar wine to be delivered to chaplains, and obtaining prayer books for soldiers, medical staff and porters. He also faced the same challenges as Dey—the dominance of military and colonial considerations, conflicting missionary loyalties, the shortage of priests, huge distances and a range of cultural and linguistic differences. Much of Fr Flynn's time was spent recruiting and deploying chaplains and it was, as Fr Dey had found out, a difficult task. He wrote many letters and paid frequent visits to missionary bishops to secure priests to serve European and indigenous troops and porters. In addition, the many military hospitals, which included separate ones for Europeans and for indigenous troops and porters, had to be served.

Enforced ecumenism

Ecumenical relations required attention when common grievances arose, where there was uncertainty, or when unwitting mistakes were made. As there was no Principal Chaplain, Senior Chaplains received incorrectly addressed mail. In May 1917, Fr Flynn advised Guinness to use the post-nominal "SCF (CofE)" to avoid confusion and, in June, Flynn, Guinness and Walker (Senior Presbyterian Chaplain) signed a common letter to the Adjutant-General requesting a Principal Chaplain for East Africa. The War Office took no action. Another issue, especially for chaplains, native soldiers and porters, was denominational identification. Guinness and Flynn agreed to issue identification discs to native soldiers and porters to ease the problem.

There were other occasions when ecumenical collaboration was helpful. One was establishing and caring for military cemeteries. In April 1917, Guinness approached Flynn to inform him that the cemetery at Morogoro was nearly full and that part of the nearby Muslim cemetery should be purchased. Wisely, it was not a suggestion that the military commander agreed to, but he did give permission for part of the German Christian cemetery to be taken over. Further discussions occurred over the use of denominational portions of cemeteries and the care of gravestones and crosses. In May 1918, along with other Senior Chaplains, Flynn was horrified to learn that the military were not preventing white troops from frequenting brothels. The Anglican chaplain wished to visit an area to ascertain the scale of the problem, but Fr Flynn thought that "the sight of a chaplain would do more harm than good" and, in any case, he considered it to be impossible to stop men visiting houses of ill repute. The chaplains persuaded the army to place guards on the brothels day and night to arrest all white troops going there.

English chaplains—German missionaries

Fr Flynn continued to liaise between military and ecclesiastical authorities. In March 1917, the British military requested that the Mill Hill Fathers assume responsibility for missions about to be vacated in German East Africa. This was a difficult and sensitive task for the Mill Hill Fathers, as they had always been on good terms with their German missionary counterparts. Although he could not staff the missions with his own priests, Bishop Biermans visited the German Benedictine Bishop Thomas Spreiter and begged him to cede his missions "with good grace", lest the British asked the Vatican to decide who had control. Bishop Spreiter agreed "for the good of the missions" and his Vicariate was handed over to a mixture of Mill Hill Fathers, Italian missionaries and army chaplains. Flynn saw both bishops on 31 March 1917 and arranged for the handover of chapels and property, while Bishop Spreiter remained under house arrest in Dar-es-Salaam. That was not the end of Flynn's involvement. When inspecting Dar-es-Salaam Cathedral, British officials noted that the German Imperial coat of arms was suspended above the main altar. Flynn was despatched to Bishop Spreiter who, fearing serious repercussions in Germany, asked for a written order for them to be covered and not removed. The British agreed.

Fr Flynn and other chaplains

Commissioned chaplains under Flynn's authority continued their priestly endeavours and accrued substantial military experience. Prior to their ministry in East Africa, Fr Richard Garrold SJ had served in France, Fr Arthur Allchin of the Archdiocese of Westminster had served in France and Egypt, Fr Louis Herlihy of the Diocese of Southwark and Fr John Mulderry had served in Gallipoli and Salonika, Fr John Cosser had served in Gallipoli and on hospital ships, Fr Collins had served in Salonika and Egypt, and Fr Anthony Barnett OSB of Ampleforth Abbey had served in Salonika. Fr Michael Galvin of the Archdiocese of Westminster was posted directly to East Africa following his commission in April 1916.

They and other chaplains ministered to the troops and porters in battle, and on wearying treks over vast distances and difficult terrain.

Although spared the trench warfare and slaughter of the Western Front, chaplains experienced sickness, hardship and deprivation, and they contracted a variety of debilitating illnesses which took them out of the line of duty for considerable lengths of time. When they returned, they continued their duties in the knowledge that the limits of their ministry were geographically extensive and often challenging, if not dangerous. For missionaries based in Africa this was a familiar situation but not for secular priests from the British Isles and not for most commissioned chaplains. The Benedictine Fr Barnett wrote: "I thought Salonika was remote, but East Africa is almost on the edge of the world."

Chaplains and missionaries

The provision of army chaplaincy to British and imperial forces in East Africa could not have been achieved without the aid of missionaries. *The Tablet* reported that missionaries working in East Africa assisted in caring for the spiritual needs of British and imperial Catholics and also of Africans who accompanied the British forces as soldiers, police or porters. The missionaries spoke native dialects and were aware of local customs. It was claimed that their ministrations "attended with very consoling results". Mobile and static military units, hospital clearing stations and general hospitals all had some form of chaplaincy. In reaching this position, the determined and devoted work of Frs Dey and Flynn was instrumental.

**Figure 12: Fr William Flynn CF: Chaplain
in Africa (Philip Murphy)**

"To serve, not to be served": RFC and RAF chaplains

The Royal Flying Corps

On 13 April 1912, a royal warrant established the Royal Flying Corps (RFC) consisting of a Military Wing, a Naval Wing, the Central Flying School and the Royal Aircraft Factory. The Air Battalion of the Royal Engineers became the Military Wing. The Naval Wing, with fewer pilots and aircraft than the Military Wing, was separated from the RFC in July 1914, when the Royal Naval Air Service (RNAS) was established under Admiralty control.

The ranks, organization and terminology introduced in the Military Wing reflected its army origins. Wings were commanded by lieutenant-colonels and squadrons were led by majors. On the outbreak of war on 4 August 1914 the RFC had 147 officers, 1,097 men and 179 aircraft. As the Military Wing developed and grew throughout the war, more army terms such as Brigadier-General, Divisions and Brigades were introduced. The RFC and the RNAS played significant roles in reconnaissance, bombardment and "dog-fights" in all theatres of war. "Barrage balloons", "aerodromes", "stations" and "seaplanes" became commonly used terms applied to this new and rapidly developing aspect of warfare.

In 1917, the War Council decided that a new independent air service—the Royal Air Force—be formed alongside the army and Royal Navy. This formation would make underused RNAS resources available for the Western Front and would end inter-service rivalry that affected aircraft procurement. The Admiralty urged that the RNAS should continue, be developed and be managed by naval officers and seamen.

The government, however, adhered to the principle of the independent status and identity of the Royal Air Force.

On 1 April 1918, the RFC and the RNAS were amalgamated to form the Royal Air Force (RAF) under the control of a new Air Ministry.

The post-war RAF

The demobilization of army and navy personnel after the Great War, together with the economic problems of the nation paying for the conflict and adjusting to a peacetime economy, made the nascent RAF a vulnerable target for successive governments wishing to reduce defence spending. The scaling down of the RAF was rapid. In 1919, the RAF had 4,000 combat aircraft and 114,000 personnel. By March 1920, only 3,280 officers and 25,000 other ranks remained. Huge quantities of equipment and land facilities were sold or returned to their original owners. The Women's Royal Air Force, which had also been created in April 1918, was disbanded, although the RAF Nursing Service, founded in June 1918, survived. It was established as a permanent branch of the RAF in January 1921 and became the Princess Mary's RAF Nursing Service in June 1923. The survival of a small, developing independent air force seemed highly unlikely in the face of naval and army attempts to reclaim their own air services and the urgent need for the reduction of government expenditure. Economic, political and military factors, therefore, became the weapons of those who sought to end the short-lived existence of the RAF as an independent service, but the need for a separate air arm that could profoundly alter future military strategy ultimately won through.

The formation of RAF chaplaincy

During the war, especially on the Western Front where formations were in close proximity, army and naval chaplains ministered to men of the Military Wing of the RFC and to squadrons of the RNAS. Fr Bernard McGarvey, for example, of the Diocese of Clogher, was commissioned in the AChD in March 1916 and served on the Western Front, where he won the Military Cross. *The Tablet* recorded that in June 1918 he was attached to five RAF squadrons in Italy. Fr John Rimmer SJ appears in Catholic military records as serving the RFC, but neither he nor Fr McGarvey appear in RFC or RAF records.

On 21 February 1918, the House of Commons agreed that the RAF should have its own publicly funded independent Chaplaincy Service, which was established in December 1918. The new Chaplaincy Service came under the direction and command of the Air Member for Personnel, and the Revd Henry Viener, an Anglican priest and RNAS chaplain since 1901, was appointed Chaplain in Chief. Reverend Viener was given the rank of Air Commodore while four Principal Chaplains or Staff Chaplains—Roman Catholic, Methodist, Baptist and Congregationalist—held the relative RAF rank of Group Captain. Subordinate chaplains, such Assistant Principal Chaplains or Station Chaplains, held the rank of Squadron Leader.

Fr James Dey and Royal Air Force Catholic chaplains, 1918–29

In August 1918, the War Office informed Fr Bernard Rawlinson OSB, Senior Catholic Army Chaplain on the Western Front, that the new Air Ministry was "in the process of organizing an independent chaplaincy service for the RAF" but that for the present, army chaplains would continue to serve RAF men attached to army formations. In future, RAF chaplains would serve stand-alone RAF units.

When the RAF was established, Bishop Keatinge, the *Episcopus Castrensis*, assigned the task of forming and supervising the Catholic branch of RAF chaplaincy to Fr James Dey, his Vicar-General. Fr Dey was a veteran of the Western Front, East Africa and Egypt, and when he left the army to join the RAF, he was Chaplain to the Forces, 2nd Class, with the rank of Lieutenant-Colonel. Fr Dey was commissioned in the RAF on 9 December 1918, after resigning from the army on 8 December, and was appointed Principal Roman Catholic Chaplain. As Principal Roman Catholic Chaplain, or Staff Chaplain, he was given the relative rank of Group Captain.

It was important to Bishop Keatinge, with his responsibility for the RAF, that Catholic interests were not overlooked in the new service, and Fr Dey's substantial experience of liaising with chaplains, religious orders, senior military officers and diplomats from his time in East Africa would be advantageous. Bishop Keatinge, meanwhile, attended meetings of the RAF Advisory Board on Chaplaincy Services, which provided a link between the denominations and the service, deliberated on matters concerning the Churches, helped to secure "the best kind of chaplain", and generally guided the RAF in the formation of its new Chaplains' Branch.

Compared with the large numbers of chaplains that Bishop Keatinge had been responsible for on the Western Front and in Salonika, the number of RAF chaplains was very small. They had all been commissioned as army chaplains and, as they ministered to the RFC, their names appear on RFC lists. The later publication of RAF lists, which included details of a chaplain's commissioning in the RAF, began after the formation of the RAF on 1 April 1918.

Including Fr Dey, six priests ultimately formed the nucleus of RAF Catholic chaplaincy. Fr Henry Beauchamp of the Diocese of Kildare and Leighlin was commissioned in the AChD in March 1916 and served on the Western Front as chaplain to the Argyll and Sutherland Highlanders. In 1917, he was awarded the Military Cross. Fr Beauchamp is on the RFC list and on the RAF list from 26 July 1919. Fr Denis Blackburn of the Diocese of Portsmouth was commissioned in the AChD in August 1914 and served on the Western Front. His name does not appear on the RFC lists, but he is on the RAF list dated 1 August 1919. Fr Matthew Dunne of the Diocese of Leeds was commissioned in the AChD in April 1918, and his name appears on the RFC list for 1919 and on the RAF list from 2 August 1919. Fr Robert Vincent O'Shaughnessy of the Diocese of Salford was commissioned in the AChD in July 1915, and served on the Western Front, where he was awarded the Military Cross. He was demobilized from the army in August 1919 when he transferred to the RAF. His name is on the RFC list and RAF lists. Fr Thomas Browne of the Diocese of Cloyne was commissioned in the AChD in 1916 and served with the 24th Division. He is on both the RFC list and on the RAF list from January 1922.

Fr Henry Beauchamp and the development
of RAF Catholic chaplaincy

In 1929, after ensuring the status of RAF Catholic chaplains, Mgr Dey (he was created a Domestic Prelate with the title "Monsignor" in 1928) retired and was succeeded as Staff Chaplain by Fr Beauchamp. The establishment of Catholic chaplains was four.

Henry Beauchamp was born in Rosenallis, County Laois, in 1884 and was educated at Carlow College and St Patrick's College, Maynooth. He was ordained for the Diocese of Kildare and Leighlin in 1908 and served as a curate at Portarlington until 1916, when he was commissioned in the AChD. He ministered at the Curragh, at Ripon and on the Western Front from 1916 until the Armistice, and he was the second Catholic chaplain to be commissioned in the RAF. In 1919, Fr Beauchamp was posted to RAF Halton, where his arrival was a source of great amusement. Having asked an airman to carry his luggage to his room, he gave him five shillings (25 pence) for his kind assistance. Later, in the Officers' Mess, he was formally introduced to the man who had carried his bags. It was the Commanding Officer! Other Catholic chaplains were posted to RAF Cranwell, which opened in 1918 with a flying training school, and to RAF Henlow, which also opened in 1918.

In 1935, Mgr Dey succeeded Bishop Keatinge as *Episcopus Castrensis* and found that his position vis-à-vis RAF authorities was unlike his status with the Admiralty. According to the Admiralty, Bishop Dey had "no official status but merely acts as a consultant and adviser to the Admiralty on behalf of the Archbishop of Westminster", who at the time was Archbishop Arthur Hinsley. However, the Archbishop of Westminster had no ecclesiastical authority over RAF chaplains, as this had been delegated by the Holy See to the *Episcopus Castrensis*. Any spiritual authority wielded by Dey over RAF chaplains related specifically to "the general supervision which the Holy See might wish to exercise" and bore no relation to the practical procedures that the RAF had in place for its Roman Catholic chaplains. These were the responsibility of the Roman Catholic Staff Chaplain. Bishop Dey's position was more spiritual while Fr Beauchamp's was administrative. Bishop Dey, however, had spiritual authority over Fr Beauchamp, and he attended the RAF

Advisory Board on Chaplaincy Services and spoke on issues affecting Catholic personnel. Relations between the two priests were always harmonious and respectful.

There was consistency and familiarity in the ranks of the chaplains. Fr Beauchamp provided continuity as Staff Chaplain and, for most of the inter-war period, he was assisted by two other Irish chaplains—Fr Denys Blackburn and Fr Thomas Browne. The ranks of the earliest chaplains were naturally thinned. Mgr Dey retired in 1929, Fr Browne also in 1929 and Fr Blackburn in 1938. Fr Dunne had left the service and his diocese and went to the USA in 1921. They were replaced with secular priests and priests from religious institutes. The Diocese of Salford was especially supportive, providing four chaplains, while the Pallotine Fathers also gave four and began the close relationship that Fr Beauchamp developed with religious orders and the RAF.

As part of the RAF's function was to provide reconnaissance, a policing function and air support for other services, Catholic chaplains ministered to RAF personnel both at home and overseas in the inter-war years. Fr Beauchamp served at the School of Technical Training at RAF Halton, Fr Graham Sutherland served at RAF Cranwell, Fr Cyril Smith served at RAF Upavon, Fr John Sherry SCA served at RAF Uxbridge, Fr James Done was attached to RAF Cosford and Fr Thomas Hourigan was based at RAF St Athan. Those who served abroad included Fr Dunne, who served in Egypt in 1920; Fr Thomas Browne, who was stationed in Egypt in 1925; Fr Blackburn, who served in Iraq and Egypt; Fr John Lavin (an officer with the Lancashire Fusiliers in the Great War), who served in Iraq; Fr Arthur O'Connor, who served at RAF Seletar, Singapore; Fr Patrick O'Connell, who served at RAF Iraq Command, Habbaniya; and Fr John Sherry, who ministered at RAF Abu Sueir with its Flying Training School near Port Said, Egypt. Numerically, Catholic chaplaincy to the RFC and subsequently the RAF remained small and relatively constant. From 1920 until 1938, the number of permanent Catholic RAF chaplains never exceeded five and never dropped below three.

In 1935, when rumours of war were in the air, papers were presented to the Staff Chaplains' Conference which detailed the development of the chaplaincy service by religious denomination. Negotiations on the respective numbers of chaplains had begun in June 1919 and ended in

January 1920. On the basis of what was agreed for army chaplains, the RAF establishment was fixed at 35 chaplains—Church of England 21 chaplains (14 home, seven overseas), Roman Catholic five chaplains (three home, two overseas), Presbyterians three chaplains (three home), Methodists four chaplains (two home, two overseas), and United Board two chaplains (one home, one overseas). Comparison with the army establishment was considered to be unhelpful because of the nature and growth of the RAF and the disposition of its personnel in smaller units.

Officiating Chaplains were employed to minister to isolated home stations and on stations abroad where Catholic facilities were rare. In 1923, Bishop Godric Kean, originally from the Diocese of Salford and an army chaplain in the Great War, was secretary to the Latin Patriarch of Jerusalem and also Officiating Chaplain for five years to the RAF in Palestine. Serving army chaplains were also called upon to minister to RAF units overseas. In 1931, Fr Peter Dorman of the Diocese of Southwark, based at Brigade Headquarters, Moascar, Ismailia, Egypt, informed Bishop Amigo: "I have a detachment of the Air Force 10 miles away in the desert. They come to Mass here on Sundays—and I go to see them when I can—and once a month I give them Mass. I go next Sunday at 8 o'clock." His visit to the RAF meant "a not too comfortable ride in a car across the desert", and he thought "flying would be easier!" Chaplains were also given permission to say more than one Mass per day. In 1938, Fr Patrick O'Connell was allowed to celebrate Masses for RAF personnel and Chaldean Catholics in the Middle East.

As the prospect of war increased in the 1930s, there was the likelihood that the RAF would grow and that more chaplains would be needed. In July 1935, the Staff Chaplains, "in view of the expansion of the Royal Air Force by the end of 1937", discussed the appointment of Auxiliary Air Force chaplains and submitted a scheme whereby an extra 22 chaplains would be commissioned on a phased basis from 1935 to 1937.

In 1936, the Staff Chaplains met to reply to an Air Ministry memorandum dealing with chaplaincy issues. They stated that the ratio of chaplains to men that had been set in the army in 1919 was 1:2,000, but was now 1:1,000; that "large concentrations" in the expanding RAF "only increases the real difficulty of our work"; that Officiating Chaplains have "too many other claims on their time"; and that Officiating Chaplains "lack a Service outlook and point of view with the result that their ministry is less acceptable and their influence for good is curtailed". Officiating Chaplains countered this view by saying that airmen were on military duties or were not available when the chaplain visited at the appointed time.

The Staff Chaplains were "strongly of the opinion" that "the only possible basis for the appointment of Service Chaplains is that of numerical strength", and the ratio of chaplains to men should be changed. They proposed that the Church of England ratio should be 1:1,200 men; that the Presbyterian, Methodist and United Board ratio should be 1:800 men; and the Roman Catholic ratio should be 1:500 men. Realizing that these agreed suggestions would influence RAF chaplaincy policy, the Staff Chaplains referred them to the Air Advisory Board.

From 1937 to 1939, Auxiliary Air Force chaplains were appointed, and by the outbreak of war they had been absorbed into the ranks of the permanent commissioned chaplains. The outbreak of war in 1939 led the government to further expand the RAF and also its chaplaincy service. In September 1939, the establishment of RAF chaplains was fixed at 100 with the number of Catholic chaplains being increased to 16.

Table 1: Appointments of Catholic Chaplains to the Royal Air Force, 1918–39

Year	Priest	Diocese/Order
1918	James Dey	Archdiocese of Birmingham
1919	Henry Beauchamp	Diocese of Kildare and Leighlin
	Denis Blackburn	Diocese of Cork
	Robert Vincent O'Shaughnessy	Diocese of Salford
	Matthew Dunne	Diocese of Leeds
1921	Thomas Browne	Diocese of Cloyne
1924	Francis Graham Sutherland	Diocese of Clifton
1929	Matthew O'Carroll	Diocese of Kilmore
1930	John Lavin	Archdiocese of Liverpool

Year	Priest	Diocese/Order
1931	Cyril Smith	Archdiocese of Liverpool
1934	Cyril Fay	Latin Patriarchate of Jerusalem
1935	Patrick O'Connell	Pallotine Fathers
1936	John Roche	Pallotine Fathers
1937	John Sherry	Pallotine Fathers
1938	Arthur O'Connor	Diocese of Salford
	James Done	Diocese of Salford
	Thomas Hourigan	Diocese of Salford
	John Thomas Pumphrey	Oblate of St Charles
1939 (Jan- Aug)	Michael G. Kelly	Pallotine Fathers
	Godfrey Richards	Diocese of Sioux Falls, USA
	Percy Bailey	Diocese of Shrewsbury

The Catholic community in the early RAF

RAF chaplaincy developed in a way which was quite different to that of the Royal Navy and army. Naval chaplains served ships or fleets frequently on the move and army chaplains were attached to regiments or divisions which could be moved relatively quickly. Naval and army chaplains were also deployed in combat situations. RAF chaplaincy developed around stations at home and overseas which housed semi-permanent facilities and where the support community were left behind when service personnel were deployed. RAF chaplains could not minister in air combat situations.

RAF stations were often located in isolated areas and lacked appropriate accommodation for religious purposes. In such circumstances, it was difficult to foster and develop a faith community. The large number and scattered locations of Church of England places of worship meant that Anglicans did not suffer quite as much other denominations, such as Roman Catholics, whose churches and places of worship were predominantly in urban areas. Nevertheless, Bishop Keatinge instituted a series of visits to all military bases. In June 1932, he informed Bishop Amigo that he had just completed a "visitation and Confirmation" at RAF Henlow.

Bishop Dey, Fr Beauchamp and other religious leaders in the RAF frequently discussed the issue of proper and adequate places for worship and, in 1936, a committee considered the provision of church buildings on RAF stations. "The need for church buildings had become so pressing" throughout the Royal Air Force that the committee called upon the Air Council to take action. The committee were, however, very practical and gave guidance to the Air Council as to how the problem could be addressed. For instance, the provision of one building used by all denominations or the multi-use of large spaces were suggestions. Whilst RAF authorities may have been sympathetic, government funding did not consider expense on religious facilities to be a high priority.

Fr Henry Beauchamp

After 1929, Fr Beauchamp oversaw the development of the RAF's chaplaincy service with tact and diplomacy. His friendly and outgoing character were to his advantage, and he collaborated and fostered ecumenical relations with chaplains of other denominations. In 1938, he was involved in the production of *Cross Beams*, a film about religion in the RAF.

Fr Beauchamp proved to be the ideal priest to establish RAF chaplaincy. At RAF Halton, his sense of humour and his personality were well known, and his wise counselling made him a "father figure". His sporting and hunting interests won him many admirers especially when, in 1924, he was admitted to hospital suffering from broken ribs after being thrown from his horse. He was, it was noted, "a born raconteur".

Having a small number of posts at his disposal, it was crucial that he chose the right priests to be chaplains, for they would be given command posts in war. To new chaplains he offered guidance and the following advice:

There is a service tradition that religion, politics and ladies' names must never be mentioned in an Officers' Mess and chaplains should take particular care to uphold this tradition. Sometimes religious questions are raised as a "leg pull". Chaplains must be careful not to discuss or argue on the matter. It is a grand thing to be able to talk about the right subject at the right time and in the right place.

These aspects of his personality and priesthood together with his organization, patriotism and great pride in the new RAF and its chaplains was to be to the service's advantage in the war that came in 1939.

When Fr Beauchamp reached the age of retirement in June 1938, the RAF asked him to extend his service until 1944.

Figure 13: Mgr Henry Beauchamp RAF: RAF pioneer

1 4

"Surprised at number of troops on beaches": Chaplains at Dunkirk

Blitzkrieg

Following Britain's declaration of war against Germany on 3 September 1939, a British Expeditionary Force (BEF) was despatched to France. At the end of September, 152,000 men had landed in France, and by April 1940 the BEF had grown to 380,000 men. Its war began in earnest when Germany invaded Holland, Belgium, Luxembourg and France in May 1940.

The pace and success of Germany's blitzkrieg forced the BEF to fall back from its defensive positions towards the port of Dunkirk. From there, between 27 May and 4 June 1940, approximately 338,000 Allied and French troops were evacuated in nearly 700 ships and smaller vessels from the beaches, breakwaters and makeshift harbours. However, 51st Highland Division, detached from the main body of the BEF, was pushed back at St Valery, where it was forced to surrender on 12 June.

A second BEF comprising British Armoured and Infantry Divisions and a Canadian Infantry Division had been despatched to France in May 1940, but all three were evacuated on 16–17 June. France capitulated on 22 June, and the first battle for France had ended. The BEF left behind thousands of guns, vehicles and motorcycles, and tons of ammunition and stores. Over 68,000 British troops were killed, wounded or taken prisoner during the retreat and evacuation. Winston Churchill remarked that "wars are not won by evacuation", while Sir John Smyth wrote that "the Allies had suffered a catastrophic defeat".

The organization of BEF chaplains

A unified chaplaincy command structure had been decided upon by the army in 1930 and Bishop James Dey, Bishop William Keatinge's successor as *Episcopus Castrensis*, agreed to this arrangement in 1938. He nominated the Senior Catholic Chaplain of the Aldershot Command to be "Assistant to the Deputy Chaplain-General in the Field", as he thought that this would make for "smooth working". The senior chaplains would be acquainted with each other and the appointment would not lead to the "jealousy and corresponding friction" that "would not make for efficiency".

The new command structure was implemented when the BEF sailed for France. The senior commanding chaplain was the Anglican Deputy Chaplain-General, the Revd A. T. A. Naylor, and the Assistant Deputy Chaplain-General was Fr John Coghlan, a priest of the Diocese of Meath and a veteran chaplain of the First World War. Fr Coghlan was the Senior Roman Catholic Army Chaplain. He had been promoted Chaplain, 1st Class with the rank of Colonel in 1938, and in March 1940 he was named as Bishop Dey's Vicar-General and raised to the ecclesiastical rank of Monsignor.

Fr Basil McCreton of Middlesbrough Diocese served as Catholic Staff Chaplain and Mgr Coghlan's assistant at General Headquarters (GHQ). Fr McCreton was commissioned on 1 March 1931. He served at Aldershot from 1931 to 1934, ministered to troops in Egypt, the Sudan and Palestine from 1934 to 1937 and was promoted Chaplain, 3rd Class in April 1939. He was described as "reliable in all circumstances, cool and able in emergencies, hard-working and enterprising".

Fr Joseph Stapleton, Chaplain, 2nd Class, became Deputy Assistant Chaplain-General of IV Corps, while Fr Peter Dorman, who had served in the ranks in the First World War, became Senior Catholic Chaplain with the 5th Division. Senior Catholic Chaplains had authority over chaplains of other denominations while Senior non-Catholic Chaplains exercised authority over Catholic chaplains. The scheme, however, was not to stand the test of war and it was discontinued after the BEF's withdrawal from France.

As in the First World War, temporary commissioned chaplains soon heavily outnumbered chaplains with permanent commissions. The campaign also resulted in the first casualties among the chaplains and the award of military decorations for their brave ministry.

The immediate shortage of Catholic army chaplains

In September 1939, there were 12 permanent and five temporary Catholic army chaplains. The War Office informed Bishop Dey that another 25 Catholic chaplains were required immediately to accompany the BEF, while another ten were needed to replace chaplains taken from home bases. The establishment of Catholic chaplains to the Territorial Army was fixed at 120, but only 50 were actually serving, and Fr Coghlan recalled that "at no time had we the number of chaplains allowed by the War Office". The primary consideration was to ensure that chaplains served the front-line troops, but this meant depriving Home Commands and Lines of Communication of chaplains. Shortages placed intolerable physical burdens and mental strain on individual chaplains, who had to do the work normally covered by two or three padres. "We were", wrote Coghlan, "always at least 60 below" establishment.

In October 1939, Fr Coghlan wrote to Bishop Dey to inform him that three Casualty Clearing Stations and ten hospitals were without Catholic chaplains. He compared this with the non-Catholic situation, where chaplains were present at all hospitals and Casualty Clearing Stations. He predicted that the war would be long and asked that chaplains appointed to troops in training should accompany them in action. He also requested that Dey obtain priests with parish or missionary experience; newly ordained men were enthusiastic, he wrote, but many lacked the organizational ability or experience required in the field. In March 1940, Mgr Coghlan reported that there were 83 priests with the BEF and suggested that arrangements be made for chaplains to minister to the likely prisoners of war. In April 1940, Dey informed the English and Welsh bishops that "160 secular priests and 130 regulars are now with our troops" at home and in France and were doing excellent work "in spite of the usual difficulties due to the fact that their 'flocks' are often scattered".

As Blitzkrieg intensified, the likelihood of casualties among the chaplains increased, and Dey felt compelled to ask the bishops for 50 more chaplains. On 7 May, he again wrote to the bishops to say that "many units are without spiritual assistance". He concluded: "The War Office is pressing me daily for priests and I cannot give them unless you provide them from your store." Dey wrote also to the superiors of religious orders asking "for contributions" and again the religious orders were generous. Forty-seven of 108 Catholic chaplains who served in France with the BEF were from religious orders.

Catholic chaplains at Dunkirk

Mgr Coghlan and Fr McCreton were with the administrative branch of the Army Chaplains' Department attached to the rear Headquarters Staff of the BEF at Arras. On 15 May, as the Germans closed in, orders were given to evacuate and the day was spent burning papers and destroying location lists. With difficulty, Headquarters Staff and padres tried to make their way from Arras to Bergues, a walled town six miles inland from Dunkirk. The roads were crammed with refugees and military vehicles. At Wimereux, they visited military hospitals, anointed soldiers and tried to get news of other chaplains. From Bergues, they could see Dunkirk in the distance, and clouds of black smoke could be seen rising from the port. Communications were increasingly difficult and it was hard to keep in touch with other chaplains. On 21 May, they slept in an evacuated house and managed to say Mass at dawn on the following day. On 22 May, they were ordered to leave for Dover.

With headquarters largely evacuated, Coghlan and McCreton discovered an Advanced Dressing Station but later attended British, French and German soldiers in a hospital in a cellar with about 20 beds. They were the only two chaplains with the force protecting Bergues. There were many civilian and military casualties as the Germans dive-bombed the town's wall defences. The padres tended the wounded, heard confessions, administered the Last Rites and buried men of all denominations in the Municipal Cemetery, Fr McCreton carefully noting the details and exact location of the burials. On 27 May, in the midst of withdrawal, confusion and destruction they met with Fr Gervase Hobson-Matthews, a Benedictine monk of Downside Abbey, who was arranging to evacuate some nursing nuns from his Casualty Clearing Station at Steenvorde near Cassel. Fr McCreton noted: "Hope he gets safely to Dunkirk; the road there is becoming very dangerous." On the same day, Mgr Coghlan arranged for his nursing nuns to be evacuated while Fr McCreton buried four men at the Croix Rouge British Military Cemetery.

On 29 May, Bergues came under heavy enemy shellfire and Coghlan and McCreton were ordered to leave. Fr McCreton recorded:

> Bergues beginning to look dilapidated. Although weather still fine, everywhere is covered with a pall of dust and smoke and streets are full of broken glass. Also, a queer fusty smell. Lots of military police and despatch riders rushing about.

They received orders to leave Bergues that night. Fr McCreton recalled:

> At Ypres Gate midnight. Giddins drove Mgr Coghlan and self in Humber. Main road to Dunkirk impassable, so convoy, including 500 men on foot, took devious track much pot-holed with half-broken bridges. Beautiful but dark night. No lights allowed or smoking. Heavy gunfire audible on both sides of gap, fields flooded by French. No incidents but repeated orders to switch off engines and wait. Expected planes to drop flares. Noticed a few A.A. guns in our convoy. Moved very slowly; everyone much keyed up.

At dawn on 30 May, they arrived at the beaches of Dunkirk. Fr McCreton recorded:

> Deserted car on dunes, as instructed, together with all our kit except a few files. Surprised at number of troops on beaches. Proceeded to jetty, but left it, and returned to St Malo beach

as jetty being shelled; 3 flights of Gerry bombers, 7 in each. Troops on beach not attacked, but planes kept 3 miles out over our destroyers; terrific A.A. fire and tracers from destroyers. Saw semi-submerged wrecks in harbour.

In the mayhem, they tried to get their car (its boot full of good quality cut-price wine) on to a ship but were refused. This caused Mgr Coghlan to vow that he would never speak to senior Royal Navy officers ever again. Back on the beach, they decided to try their luck in getting into a naval cutter to be taken to a destroyer. They agreed that the best way was to wade well out to sea and attract attention. They discarded all their kit, and Fr McCreton recalled that the sea was "tepid". At 07.30, they joined a group of about 30 men waiting to be taken to a cutter. They waited 30 minutes in the sea, but the cutter failed to return. As they waited, Fr McCreton noted that Mgr Coghlan had left his greatcoat on the beach.

Frantically waving, they attracted the notice of another cutter, and although it was overloaded, they were dragged on board. In the chaos, Fr McCreton noticed that there were badly wounded men trying swim to safety. The cutter, heavily overcrowded, ran aground but eventually it was freed and it sailed towards a tanker where its human cargo was unloaded. By 09.00, they were transferred to the destroyer HMS *Impulsive*. Fr McCreton was given brandy and tea and tried to dry his wet cigarettes. He also managed to retrieve Mgr Coghlan's greatcoat, which was being worn by "a villainous-looking Pioneer". He then fell asleep and slept heavily despite the loud noises round about him. *Impulsive* continued to pick up men until about 16.00, but on its way out of Dunkirk it struck a submerged ship. Badly damaged, *Impulsive* limped back across the Channel and reached Dover at 22.00. An hour later, Fr McCreton was on a troop train. He recalled that they were "fed and cheered on way, much to our surprise". He noted that his uniform was "dry but creased and fusty" with "trousers like wrinkled tubes". On 1 June, he arrived at Warminster, where he went to Hore-Belisha's Officers' Club.

Other chaplains at Dunkirk

Dom Gervase Hobson-Mathews OSB, of Downside Abbey, recorded
that Germans had machine-gunned the fleeing civilian population. "The
plight of the refugees is beyond description", he wrote. The Passionist Fr
Clem O'Shea was deployed to France with 118 Field Regiment, Royal
Artillery, and was attached to a Casualty Clearing Station (CCS) just
south of the Belgian border. As the Germans advanced, the CCS was
moved towards Dunkirk. It was slow going, with military and civilian
casualties, and they were strafed and shelled. On 26 May, the CCS was
instructed to fall back to Dunkirk and, in the midst of relentless bombing,
Fr O'Shea heard confessions, administered the Last Rites and helped
carry the wounded to the harbour's Mole, where they were loaded onto
ships and boats amid the chaos and confusion.

Fr John Roche was one of seven Redemptorists with the BEF. In
"heart-breaking hold-ups of traffic", he "directed a convoy personally",
escaping an ambush by enemy tanks. They endured days of "un-resisted
bombing" while waiting for embarkation.

Fr Gerard Lake SJ, originally deployed with 7th Battalion, Royal
Sussex Regiment, was slightly wounded when the train in which he was
travelling was bombed and machine gunned. Dunkirk had certainly
been a "tough spot", he wrote. Fr Maurice Roche of Brentwood Diocese,
commissioned on 9 October 1939, served with the BEF on the Maginot
Line and was reported missing in June 1940. He eventually returned to
London three weeks after the evacuation.

Catholic priests were not the only padres at Dunkirk. Bill Elmslie, on
board the minesweeper HMS *Dundalk*, recalled that on 1 June as they
pulled away from a makeshift jetty, he saw something that made a lasting
impression on him: "an Army padre, moving up and down the column
of patient men on the jetty, directing, helping, encouraging, selecting
soldiers for the boats, an inspiration to all by his utter calmness".

Decorations

Mgr Coghlan was created a Commander of the Order of the British Empire (the first Catholic chaplain to be so honoured in the Second World War—John Vertur was CBE) for his work in organizing Catholic chaplaincy services with the BEF, while Fr McCreton was awarded the Military Cross. The citation for Fr McCreton's award ran:

> He elected to remain although free to embark and eventually found himself at Bergues where he remained for eight days and until the place was evacuated. Under continuous enemy fire he encouraged all ranks, ministered to and consoled the wounded and buried the dead. He escaped from Dunkirk on the 31st of May.

Another Catholic padre was awarded the Military Cross. On 31 May, Fr Thomas Duggan of the Cork Diocese was attached to the 8th Durham Light Infantry (DLI), when his car became trapped between German positions and the DLI. The padre and his batman clambered out of the vehicle and made their way back to their own lines only for a French major to remonstrate with them for their foolhardiness. In his best French, and much to the amusement of the DLI, the padre lectured the Frenchman on the duties of a British officer and the use of army vehicles. The major stormed off. Fr Duggan set up a Regimental Aid Post (RAP), which he manned for the rest of the day in the midst of heavy enemy shelling. Fr Duggan was awarded the Military Cross and became the first padre to be decorated for bravery in the war. The citation ran: "His coolness, energy, courage and example were outstanding. He helped to maintain morale when the regiment aid post was heavily shelled and full of wounded."

For services in France and Belgium before and during the evacuation, some chaplains were Mentioned in Despatches. Two had been combat officers in the First World War. Fr Denham Fox of the Archdiocese of Liverpool had served in France and Russia while Fr Philip Adamson of the Shrewsbury Diocese had served on the Western Front. Two other padres to be mentioned were Fr John Clarke, a commissioned chaplain of the Archdiocese of Westminster, and Fr Henry Donnelly of Portsmouth Diocese.

Casualties and prisoners

Forty-two chaplains of all denominations were captured or reported missing at Dunkirk. Mgr Coghlan incorrectly informed the Jesuit Provincial that all the Jesuits had been evacuated safely, but Fr Vincent Gallagher SJ had been wounded when with elements of the BEF engaged in the defence of Calais. He was captured and spent the next four years in a prisoner of war camp.

Another chaplain to be taken prisoner was Fr Kenneth Grant, a priest of the Archdiocese of Glasgow, attached to the Cameron Highlanders. The 51st (Highland) Division was on its way back from training on the Maginot Line when the Germans invaded. The Division was cut off from the main BEF and was trapped at St Valery. Isolated and after strong resistance, the Scots were forced to surrender, and over 10,000 men were taken into captivity.

Over 400 chaplains were deployed with the BEF. Fifty-seven became casualties, seven were killed in action, one died of wounds, 34 were captured and eight were reported missing. In addition to Fr Gallagher and Fr Grant, Fr Michael Charlton CSsR was also taken prisoner. It was also reported that Frs Edward Hinsley of the Archdiocese of Westminster, Cyril Scarborough of Southwark Diocese, and Gervase Hobson-Matthews were missing. The War Office informed the Abbot of Downside that Fr Gervase had been missing since Dunkirk. His diary and stole were later recovered by the War Office but were subsequently "mislaid". Requiem Mass was offered at Downside on 31 March 1941 for Fr Gervase and four months later the War Office received information from the International Red Cross that his grave had been identified in Dunkirk Town Cemetery. Fr Gervase was the first Catholic military chaplain to be killed in the war. The *Catholic Herald* reported that he had been killed "in the fulfilment of his priestly duties among the wounded and the dying that lay exposed to unremitting enemy fire".

Fr John Hibbert of the Brentwood Diocese returned to England via Bordeaux. Dunkirk had seriously affected him, and he was declared medically unfit and released from military service on 24 July 1941. The Redemptorist Fr Augustine Teasdale also found the experience extremely unnerving and was in a state of almost nervous collapse when he was evacuated. The Salesian Fr David Hourigan, who was evacuated from Dunkirk with the Royal Ulster Rifles, was killed later, in 1943, while serving with 1st Airlanding Brigade in Sicily.

On 5 June, the War Office reported to Bishop Dey that 13 more Catholic chaplains had been evacuated. On 14 June, it informed him that there was no news of the Birmingham priests Frs Brian Withers, David Ford and Humphrey Bright, but the number of evacuees had reduced to a trickle and details of evacuated chaplains were still being received. By 16 June, 49 padres had returned. Such was the uncertainty and confusion that the War Office wrote to all priests waiting to be posted as chaplains "so that they will not be expecting to be taken forthwith". It continued: "The need for a considerable number of new R.C. nominations has been radically affected by the numbers returned from the B.E.F.", and these would have to be "absorbed".

After Dunkirk

Throughout the events leading up to and during the evacuation, Catholic padres, as well those of other denominations, displayed the courage that many came to expect of them. Catholic soldiers spoke highly of the calm demeanour of their priests in a highly charged and dangerous situation, for men were "on the very knife-edge of panic which is to be expected when an army has to retreat in face of the onslaughts of the enemy". Although many men were saved and lived to fight another day, the evacuation of Dunkirk was a humiliating setback for the British army. For the chaplains, the whole disastrous campaign had ended in death for one, injuries for some, and sheer exhaustion for those who returned.

Mgr Coghlan wrote to Archbishop Williams of Birmingham praising the Birmingham chaplains who had ministered at Dunkirk:

> Those who were with me in the B.E.F. (Bernard Navin, Humphrey Bright, Benjamin Cox, Michael Murphy, Brian Withers, Gerard Flint, and Joseph Griffin) were really outstanding examples of what priests should be. All of them are spoken of in the highest terms by the Formations to which they are attached, and the

respect and esteem in which they are held is due to their priestly zeal and hard work. I think it only right that Your Grace should know this because a Bishop should be proud to have such really Apostolic men.

Mgr Coghlan served as Principal Roman Catholic Chaplain and retired at the end of the war after 30 years of unbroken service to the British army. He saw no more active service after Dunkirk but dealt with the administration of the enlarged Catholic branch of the RAChD. In July 1940, Fr McCreton became Senior Catholic Chaplain, London Area, and was later posted to Headquarters, Eastern Command. He was appointed Senior Catholic Chaplain South Eastern Command in 1941 and promoted to Chaplain, 2nd Class in 1944. On 2 May 1944, he embarked for Palestine and became Senior Catholic Chaplain to the Mediterranean Expeditionary Force.

Figure 14: Mgr John Coghlan (front row, centre) with Senior Catholic Army Chaplains, 1940

1 5

From Scapa Flow to Hiroshima:
Naval chaplains at sea and on land

The Royal Navy at war

The Royal Navy in the Second World War was a formidable fighting force although much smaller than in the Great War. In 1939 it had 15 battleships and battle cruisers, 66 cruisers, 184 destroyers, 60 submarines and seven aircraft carriers. By 1945, it had 16 battleships, 52 aircraft carriers of varying sizes, 62 cruisers, 257 destroyers, 131 submarines and 9,000 other vessels. During the war, the Royal Navy lost 278 major warships and more than 1,000 smaller ships.

There was also an increase in naval personnel and many conscripts and volunteers were Catholics. In 1939, there were 200,000 men (including reserves and Royal Marines) and by 1945 there were 939,000. The Women's Royal Naval Service (WRNS) was revived in 1938, and there were 74,000 personnel in 1944. The Royal Marines reached a maximum of 78,000 in 1945.

The Royal Navy lost 50,758 men killed in action; 820 were reported missing in action while 14,663 were wounded. The WRNS lost 102 killed, with 22 wounded. Thirty thousand men of the Merchant Navy were killed.

Royal Navy chaplains

In September 1939, the Admiralty ceased to commission permanent chaplains to the Royal Navy and Royal Marines (Chaplains RN) and instead appointed temporary commissioned chaplains Royal Naval Volunteer Reserve (Chaplains RNVR) and non-commissioned Temporary Chaplains. Two Catholic priests were commissioned as Chaplains RNVR during the war; the remainder were appointed Temporary Roman Catholic Chaplains.

In 1939, there were 104 Chaplains RN, mainly Anglican. Twenty-three Church of Scotland ministers, 20 Methodists, 13 United Board (Baptist and Congregational) and six Presbyterians were given temporary commissions. In July 1945, there was a total of 416 Chaplains RN and Chaplains RNVR in addition to 118 non-Anglican clergymen who had been appointed as Temporary Chaplains for war service. At the end of hostilities, 534 chaplains were serving the Royal Navy and Royal Marines.

Naval chaplains wore no uniform, but in 1940 they were authorized, if they wished, to wear a special cap with a distinctive badge. This induced some chaplains, unmindful of naval tradition, to wear an officer's uniform with the chaplain's cap. Chaplains who considered themselves to be strictly non-combatant continued to wear clerical dress.

Catholic naval chaplains

The most significant wartime development for chaplains not of the Church of England was their change in status. In 1922, an Order in Council had decreed that from 1 September 1921 Acting Roman Catholic chaplains still in service or who entered service in October 1922 or after, were designated Temporary Roman Catholic Chaplains Royal Navy. In 1940, Cardinal Hinsley asked the Admiralty to appoint Catholic chaplains on a permanent basis and on the same terms and conditions as Anglican chaplains. In July 1943, the Admiralty announced that it would appoint chaplains who were not of the Church of England on the same conditions as their Anglican counterparts if in return the churches gave the Admiralty full control of their service.

In November 1943, an Order in Council decreed that Temporary Catholic Chaplains appointed before 3 September 1939 and still serving in November 1943 would be designated Roman Catholic Chaplains, Royal Navy. Catholic and other non-Anglican chaplains to the Royal Navy were therefore placed on an equal footing with Anglican chaplains, and the Admiralty's centuries of injustice and shabby treatment of Catholic sailors and their priests were brought to an end. Catholic chaplains who derived immediate benefit from the scheme were Frs Michael Egan, William Shepherd, Alfred Maxwell, Cyril Fay, Robert Catterall and John Dougherty. Frs William Purcell, Thomas Giles, Edward Dewey and William Driscoll were over 50 years of age, and the Admiralty would not include them in the new scheme but allowed them to serve until the age of 60 under existing rules.

As far as Catholic chaplains were concerned, the value of their ministry was now affirmed, and they received official recognition of their position within the Senior Service. However, there was still the distinction, applicable to all denominations, between Chaplains RN, Chaplains RNVR and Temporary Chaplains.

Catholic naval chaplains in wartime

During the war, 55 Catholic priests ministered alongside the ten Catholic chaplains serving full time with the Royal Navy and Royal Marines in 1939. Fr Patrick Scally, who had entered service in 1926, was mobilized as Chaplain RNVR on 27 August 1939. Six priests entered as Temporary Chaplains in 1939, seven in 1940, 12 in 1941, six in 1942, nine in 1943, 11 in 1944, and four in 1945. Only Fr Scally and Fr Walter Meyjes were appointed Chaplain RNVR. Three—Frs Leo Landreth, Valentine Elwes and James Bevan—had served as combatants in the Royal Navy during the First World War. Bishop Dey's Vicar-General for naval chaplains was Mgr Edward Dewey of the Diocese of Plymouth, who had entered service in 1921.

Despite their heroic efforts, the few Catholic chaplains could not possibly meet the religious and spiritual needs of the thousands of Catholic sailors and marines deployed at sea and on land. Fr George Pitt of Clifton

Diocese wrote that "there were so few of us, we were appointed to work for any ship that may need us". The Capuchin Fr Dunstan Dobbins was reported as doing "splendid work . . . unsparing himself" irrespective of a man's denomination. The personality, enthusiasm, piety and bravery of chaplains counted a great deal, but not all officers and men, Catholic or otherwise, admired or even respected them. The attention of senior officers and the responses of the men to a chaplain's needs, invitations and entreaties were not always positive.

During the war, chaplains ministered to the Home Fleet at Rosyth and Scapa Flow while others served on capital ships in the Battle of the Atlantic. There were chaplains in ships and also with Royal Marines in the Mediterranean, Malta, Crete, North Africa, Sicily and Italy. They served on the D-Day landings and the invasion of Europe and, as the war drew to a close, they sailed with the British Pacific Fleet. They also ministered in hospital ships and to sailors of the Merchant Marine.

On the hospital ship HMS *Oxfordshire*, Fr Pitt found that one way for sailors to have contact with personal prayer was the Rosary, recognized as a means of reconnecting men with their faith and reflecting, as individuals or in groups, on the life of Christ. Chaplains constantly appealed for rosaries for men who perhaps "had drifted away through little fault of their own". It was acknowledged that opportunities for Mass and Communion "are not so frequent as they would be had we double or treble the number of naval chaplains", but praying the Rosary and the wearing of Rosary beads around their necks was one way of sailors realizing "their companionship in the Church". Fr Pitt wrote that "wearing a rosary or a Cardinal's Cross around his neck does not make a man a saint . . . but they are great reminders of God's nearness to him". The Rosary was recited frequently in the most hazardous situations.

The Battle of the Atlantic

Ministering to the fleet at Scapa Flow was not for the faint-hearted. Fr Roderick O'Sullivan, who had already been torpedoed in 1940 on the *City of Benares*, served in HMS *Dunluce Castle*. He celebrated Mass in HMS *Iron Duke* and "to board it in foul weather", he wrote, "was a murderous trip". He also ministered to sailors and families ashore.

Fr Thomas Gilby OP entered service with the Royal Navy in 1939 and joined the battle cruiser HMS *Renown*. At Scapa Flow, he ministered to HMS *Renown*, *Hood* and *Repulse*, and other ships of the Home Fleet when at anchor, but rough weather often made visiting ships at anchor very difficult. *Renown*, which had its own chapel, sailed to the South Atlantic in December 1939 in pursuit of the German battleship *Graf Spee*, but, after its scuttling, the *Renown* returned to Plymouth. In April 1940, Fr Gilby's cabin was wrecked in an engagement in Norwegian waters with the enemy battleships *Scharnhorst* and *Hipper*. He had managed to put his "church gear away before the action", but his faculty papers had been destroyed. Searching the Atlantic for the German battleship *Bismarck* and for submarines which had caused so much destruction to Allied shipping, became a priority for the *Renown*.

Fr John Coughlan of the Archdiocese of Westminster sailed with convoys to Murmansk. He recalled that an essential part of his job was maintaining the morale of the ship's company when the battle was fierce, when men were killed, or when aircraft did not return. He was chaplain in a convoy that accompanied Winston Churchill to a meeting with US President Franklin Roosevelt.

Malta, North Africa and the Mediterranean

Surrounded by noise and activity aboard *Renown*, Fr Thomas Gilby reflected on the dangers experienced by those manning the convoys to Malta and the value of his ministry to them:

> Would praying for the safe passage of the convoy make any
> difference? How could we bend the wills of the higher powers

to consult our convenience and comfort . . . the comprehensive meaning of human life could not always be avoided, at least as a question.

Fr Walter Meyjes of the Archdiocese of Westminster sailed in HMS *Renown* from Scapa Flow to Malta in April 1942. He recalled his first operational experience when *Renown* "accompanied the American aircraft carrier *Wasp* through the Straits of Gibraltar in order to fly-off Spitfires to Malta". Fr William Devine of the Diocese of Derry had ministered at Loch Foyle and sailed with the Atlantic Fleet until 1943 before joining HMS *Hannibal* in the Mediterranean. Based at Algiers and then at Taranto, he regarded the whole Adriatic as his "parish". Fr Alban Brooks OSB in HMS *Rodney* and Fr Meyjes in *Renown* took part in the invasion of Sicily. Later, Fr Meyjes ministered to bases on the coasts of North Africa and western Italy and saw action at Anzio. Fr Patrick Dwyer of the Archdiocese of Liverpool and the Dominican Fr Peter Whitestone were deployed with the Royal Marines in North Africa.

Naval chaplains on D-Day

Royal Navy chaplains were heavily involved in OPERATION OVERLORD in June 1944. Men were prepared spiritually as well as militarily and chaplains were kept busy during the sea voyage, in the bombardment ships and in the major assault areas. The seaborne element of the invasion comprised 6,833 vessels, including 1,213 warships.

The Redemptorist Fr Gerard Costello, a naval chaplain since 1940, embarked with 48 Royal Marine Commando. They were to land on Juno Beach, and as they approached the shore there was a crescendo of gunfire and noise from the Allied naval bombardment and German defences. "One felt that one might be hit", recalled Fr Costello, but he jumped down the ramp, into the sea and onto the beach, where there was chaos. Men, self-propelled guns and tanks were met by enemy fire sweeping the narrow strip of sand. "Everywhere there were broken-down and blown-up tanks and people lying around; all sorts of indecent things", recalled the chaplain. He spent the day ministering to the wounded, including an officer he carried across a minefield to a medical post. By the end of the day, half of his unit had been wounded or killed. The chaplain buried the dead—British, French and German.

Fr Thomas Holland of the Archdiocese of Liverpool became a naval chaplain in 1943. He was sent to a Royal Marines Training Camp near Exeter, where he was introduced to the ways of the service and also inherited a "handsome chapel". Relations with other chaplains were cordial and everyone was aware that "the Big One"—D-Day—was imminent. Fr Holland's Liverpool confrère, army padre Fr Gerard Barry, who was deployed with Ack-Ack batteries, was certain he would die in the invasion. After a short retreat, Fr Holland visited Liverpool and wrote his will in St Mary's Church, Highfield Street.

He returned to his Royal Marines unit now on the accommodation ship *Ascanius*, moored in the Pool of London. It then headed with other vessels to Southend where they anchored. As they sailed towards France, the captain informed the ship's company that their destination was "J for Juno, the toughest of the beaches", adding, "God save the King!" With other chaplains, Fr Holland attended to men on accommodation ships and in Landing Craft Personnel Carriers. With fire-protection covering on his hands and face, the chaplain's action station was near the sick bay and his cabin was to be surrendered to the first casualty. As they reached Normandy, they dropped anchor opposite Juno, the middle beach of the British assault area, flanked by Gold and Sword Beaches.

The Royal Navy landed troops under the cover of a ship-to-shore bombardment. Fr Holland climbed down rope ladders over the side of a heaving ship onto a tossing landing craft while carrying his Mass kit and personal equipment. On Juno Beach, he occupied a tent next to a Beaufors gun emplacement and operated as the only Catholic chaplain in the area. He later said Mass for sailors and marines on a Mulberry harbour.

On British and Polish vessels, Fr Holland received assistance from senior officers while his fellow chaplains provided him with altar facilities. He also witnessed at first hand the effects of war. The Polish cruiser *Dragon* was severely damaged and was brought into a Mulberry harbour cradled between two destroyers. Fr Holland managed to get aboard *Dragon*, but there was little he or anyone else could do. "I saw

there sights that killed forever the 'glamour of war', if that ever existed",
he wrote. Elsewhere, he was informed that some of the Congolese crew
on *Thysville*, an accommodation ship, wished to be received into the
Church. This was a tricky problem for the chaplain, as he did not know
their state of mind or their sincerity. He lined them up and asked them (in
Pidgin French) about "their present desire" to be converted and told them
of their "future commitments". "A brief catechetical interlude" followed,
and the Congolese indicated their understanding of the Christian faith
by signs (one finger = one God; three fingers = The Trinity; both arms
extended = the Crucifixion). This accomplished, Fr Holland baptized
the men and gave them a certificate to carry with them.

Fr Holland's area of naval and marine chaplaincy responsibility
extended from Granville on the Cotentin Peninsula to Ouistreham on
the River Orne. While conducting his daily ministry of saying Mass,
censoring letters, tending the wounded and burying the dead, he saw
important personages arrive shortly after the landings—General de
Gaulle, General Le Clerc and Prime Minister Winston Churchill, who
made the famous "V" sign to all who could see him. A memorable
occasion for Fr Holland was when General Montgomery drove past in
his car, stood up and saluted him.

Despite near misses and accidents, Fr Holland survived D-Day and its
immediate aftermath. He was complimentary about those who planned
and executed the landing and invasion:

> I have never seen men work so hard, or so heroically against
> such odds, combining their relentless determination with
> supreme charity towards those who fell ... Each Service and
> regiment no doubt has recorded its Battle honours, its share in
> the achievement—except perhaps the Merchant Navy.

Fr Holland had words of praise and admiration for chaplains of all
denominations, but he particularly recalled the friendship of two army
chaplains—Fr Peter Firth and Fr Gerard Barry—who died in the landing
and in the breakout.

As naval units consolidated their positions along the coast, Fr Holland's
remit covered the enormous area from Ouistreham to Granville. As the

Allies moved inland, so too did Fr Holland and, near Bayeux, he again saw de Gaulle and Churchill. At a more personal level, he met Fr Rick Slevin of the Diocese of Salford; 22 years later he presided at Fr Slevin's Requiem Mass. By this time, Fr Holland was Bishop of Salford.

For ministering to the sailors and marines on assault vessels, as they landed and dug in under fire on Juno Beach, Fr Holland was awarded the Distinguished Service Cross for "his gallantry, skill, determination and undaunted devotion to duty to the Allied Forces on the coast of Normandy". He later became "RC Chaplain, Holland and Belgium" and "HQ Antwerp", and the whole Dutch coast was in his "parish". He encountered Dutch civilians who looked exhausted, pale and haggard. "Four years' occupation", he wrote, "had scarred both minds and bodies", whilst "moral standards had dipped below the horizon". The advance into Belgium and Holland he recalled as "the advance into agony". His naval confrère, the Oratorian Fr James Bevan, was with a unit that crossed the River Rhine into Germany for the final assault.

The Pacific Fleet

After Germany's defeat, the Royal Navy deployed the Pacific Fleet to Japan. A huge naval establishment was created in Australia from where, wrote Fr Pitt, "we ... confronted the Japanese navy ... they knew they were losing the war, but that made them all the more determined to fight to the death". Under Fr Thomas Moriarty OMI, Senior Chaplain at the shore depot HMS *Golden Hind*, were Mgr Val Elwes of the Archdiocese of Westminster, Fr Michael Barry of the Archdiocese of St Andrews and Edinburgh, and Fr Henry Leonard of the Archdiocese of Glasgow. Fr Matthias Bodkin SJ was on board HMS *Anson*, Fr Casimir Wilkins OSB was in HMS *Victorious*, and Fr Pitt was in HMS *Oxfordshire*. They knew, recalled Fr Pitt, that tremendous casualties were forecast if the Allies had to fight a sea battle and then invade Japan, but "the dropping of the atomic bomb came as a complete surprise to us all and seemed a great relief. So many thousand American and British lives would be saved by it."

After the dropping of the two atomic bombs and the Japanese surrender, Fr Matty Bodkin visited those cities which had suffered most from Allied attacks. "Hiroshima was totally destroyed with not one building standing. Nagasaki was different, it resembled many a European city destroyed by aerial bombing. The reason was the atomic bomb fell, not on Nagasaki itself, but on the great Mitsubishi armament factories 18 miles away." When he visited Tokyo, he was met "by the most dreadful sight I had ever seen". The station was gutted, the city was littered with tin huts and people gathered in thousands to barter for or exchange goods. Wooden houses had been obliterated . . . the general destruction of Japan was appalling . . . no devastation could be worse." However, Fr Bodkin found the priests at the Jesuit mission alive and well and the buildings almost intact.

The Royal Navy's hospital ships were soon involved in repatriating Allied prisoners of war who had suffered so much at the hands of their Japanese captors.

Casualties

Sixteen naval chaplains died as a result of enemy action during the Second World War—five were Catholic priests. Fr Thomas Bradley CSsR had served as an army and a navy chaplain in the Great War. In 1940, he rejoined the Royal Navy and was sent to East Africa, where he ministered on shore bases and on ships patrolling the Indian Ocean. Fr Bradley was granted leave to visit Catholic sailors based on Madagascar when his vessel, the SS *Hoihow*, was struck and sunk by a Japanese torpedo on 2 July 1943. Fr Thomas Brennan of the Diocese of Salford joined the Royal Navy in 1943. In 1944, his family were informed by the Admiralty that he was "missing presumed killed". Further information revealed that on 29 June 1944 Fr Brennan had been in the British steamship SS *Nellore* sailing from Bombay to Sydney, when it was sunk by a Japanese submarine.

Three other Catholic naval chaplains died in service. Fr Charles Lusby OMI died in the Royal Naval Hospital, Rainhill, Liverpool, on 23 May 1944. He entered the Royal Navy in 1942 and spent his ministry on shore-based establishments. He was buried in West Derby Catholic Cemetery, Liverpool.

Fr Michael Egan of Nottingham Diocese had served as a combatant in the First World War in both the army and the Royal Flying Corps. Ordained in 1925, he joined the Royal Navy as a chaplain in 1929 and served on Malta and in HMS *Rodney*, *Marlborough* and *Courageous*. During the Second World War, he was based at HMS *Pembroke* at Chatham, a shore establishment. He died on 25 September 1946 and was buried in Naval Reservation grave 133 RC, Woodlands Cemetery, Gillingham.

Fr Thomas Moriarty OMI died on 22 November 1946. Cork-born Fr Moriarty, who had served as an engineer in the Merchant Navy before ordination, entered the Royal Navy in December 1942 and was subsequently stationed at the Royal Marine Barracks, Ipswich. In 1945, he was transferred to HMS *Golden Hind*, a Royal Navy establishment in Sydney, Australia, where he became seriously ill. In 1946, he was taken to Malta and then to Chatham Naval Hospital, where he died after surgery. Fr Moriarty was buried in the Oblates' Cemetery at Inchicore, Dublin.

Figure 15: Fr Thomas Holland RN (right): Naval wartime chaplain (Salford Diocesan Archives)

1 6

"The Japanese went out of their way to obstruct chaplains in their work": Chaplains as Japanese prisoners of war

Twenty-seven Catholic army padres became prisoners of the enemy during the Second World War. Some were captured during the retreat from Dunkirk, some in the North Africa desert, while others were taken during the Arnhem raid. The Germans separated chaplain-officers from men and padres negotiated arrangements to minister to all ranks. The Italians seemed to offer more opportunities for chaplains to conduct their ministry to both officers and other ranks. Other padres, however, were captured by the Japanese. They suffered the same hardships, humiliation and brutality meted out to their fellow prisoners and were frequently prevented from practising their ministry.

Japanese prisoners of war

In 1939, the British Empire in India and the Far East included Malaya, Burma, Hong Kong, Ceylon, British North Borneo, Sarawak and Brunei, and the Pacific Islands of Samoa, Tonga and Fiji. Following defeats by the Japanese in Malaya, Singapore, Hong Kong and Burma during 1941–42, over 100,000 British, Indian, Canadian and Australian troops were taken into captivity. Many never returned. Japan had signed but not ratified the Geneva Convention of 1929 and failed to honour any obligations regarding the proper treatment of prisoners of war. Horrific scenes of Allied military and civilian prisoners suffering inhumane treatment at the hands of the Japanese emerged only after Japan had surrendered on 15 August 1945.

Religious life in the camps

Michael Snape has shown that somehow religious life survived and even flourished among prisoners in some Japanese camps and cites a number of factors that may have influenced this development. Varying tolerance of Japanese authorities between camps was an important factor. In Singapore, at Kuala Lumpur, and at Kanburi in the Thai jungle, churches and organized religious services were permitted. In this situation, it was possible to maintain the basic elements of Christian life and worship and eventually build temporary simple chapels and synagogues. A report on chaplaincy work in the Malayan camps revealed that in Changi Camp there had been 37,097 Anglican communicants by the end of October 1942, and Anglican chaplains had even established a theological faculty with classes in theology for potential ordinands drawn from all ranks. Eric Cordingley recalled that men had more time than usual for religious and spiritual matters, and padres had more opportunities to exploit such a situation. Fr Eric Green, a commissioned chaplain of the Diocese of Menevia, recorded that he said Mass daily, heard confessions, conducted confirmations and received many converts into the Church.

In some camps, the Japanese attitude to organized religion among prisoners was hostile. At Tanjong Priok on Java or in camps on the notorious Burma–Siam Railway, planned by the Japanese to carry supplies through jungle and mountainous terrain, services had to be held in secret and were attended by small numbers. Yet at Chungkai, a work camp north of Bangok, religious life was sustained. Once chaplains had arrived and a form of religious regimen introduced, a Catholic "church" was built and Christian life and organizations flourished. Another important factor influencing the development of religious life among the prisoners was their response to the brutal treatment they were subjected to and the high mortality rate, both of which compelled some men to look to religion for solace and consolation. Christian teaching and ethics also acquired a new meaning and significance in the midst of wanton brutality. And in the absence of recreational diversions, organized religious services provided alternative social gatherings. When religious services were forbidden, it was because the Japanese saw them as seditious and subversive, and they therefore became a focus of resistance and defiance. At the centre of these religious practices were padres.

In Hong Kong, 5,000 officers and men were incarcerated in the overcrowded and insanitary camp at Sham Shui Po. Prisoners died of overwork, under-nourishment, insanitary conditions, disease and torture, and some were murdered by Japanese guards. A large number of chaplains were also interned but, other than in Hong Kong and Changi, religious activities were severely limited. Suspicious of padres who tried to establish their ministries in the camps, the Japanese physically assaulted them, made them work as labourers, restricted religious services and confiscated all books.

Catholic army chaplains in Malaya, Singapore and Hong Kong

Before the arrival of army chaplain Fr Francis Carless of the Archdiocese of Birmingham in 1936, French missionaries ministered to Catholic troops in Malaya and in Singapore. In 1936, there was a proposal to build a Catholic church for the garrison at Changi in the northeast of Singapore, but this did not materialize. However, a Catholic church for the military community was opened at Tanglin in 1940, and the clerical establishment was increased substantially during the second half of 1941. By the time of the Japanese invasion, there were eight Catholic chaplains in Malaya and on Singapore: Frs Malcolm Cowin of the Diocese of Northampton, the Franciscan Aidan Jackson, Richard Kennedy SJ, John O'Mahoney of the Diocese of Middlesbrough, Edward Rowles of the Diocese of Nottingham, the Irish Spiritan Fr Kevin Whelan, James Ward of the Diocese of Clifton, and John Watson of the Diocese of Brentwood. This number was further augmented by the arrival of ten chaplains serving the Australian Division. Most of the chaplains would accompany thousands of British and Commonwealth troops into captivity.

In 1939, Fr Charles Winstanley of the Archdiocese of Liverpool was the only Catholic army chaplain deployed with British troops in Hong Kong. At time of the Japanese invasion, however, there were seven other commissioned chaplains serving in Hong Kong—three English and one

Canadian Anglican, one United Church of Canada, and two Catholic. Fr Eric Green replaced Fr Carless at Singapore in September 1938 before transferring to Hong Kong, and Fr F. L. Deloughery of the Archdiocese of Ottawa was deployed with the Canadian Brigade. From Garrison Headquarters, Frs Green and Deloughery ministered to Catholic troops scattered around Hong Kong, Kowloon and the islands.

The Irish Spiritan Fr Kevin Whelan had volunteered for chaplaincy duties while on leave in Ireland in the hope that he might serve a Nigerian regiment, but in early 1942 he was posted to Singapore. A week after his arrival, Singapore fell and Fr Whelan was interned with British and Australian troops. It was reported that his conduct was an encouragement and inspiration to all and for his service to others Fr Whelan was Mentioned in Despatches. Hugh Thwaites, a convert to Catholicism who later became a Jesuit priest, recalled that Fr Whelan was "indeed heroic", building a "church", visiting men in confinement, saying daily Mass, and soaking raisins in water in order to provide altar wine. But the strain took its toll. Spiritan records claim that Fr Whelan was released on the direct intervention of Admiral Mountbatten and that he emerged from the camp with his "health badly broken". It was recorded that he needed "much building up".

Fr John Watson had been a Territorial Army chaplain, and when war was declared, he was attached to 2nd General Hospital with 54th East Anglian Division. By September 1941, having arrived safely by means of heavily escorted troopship and without incident, he was in Malaya and was captured at the fall of Singapore. In 1942, along with Fr A. Jackson, five Australian Catholic army chaplains, one local volunteer Catholic chaplain and two Catholic chaplains from Dutch forces, Fr Watson was interned in Changi Camp. He later took part in the infamous "Death March" through Burma. In January 1945, his sister received news over a Japanese Overseas Service radio broadcast that Fr Watson had received her letters via the Red Cross in Tokyo. He was released from captivity in August 1945 but never spoke of his experiences at the hands of the Japanese.

Fr Eric Green

Fr Green was commissioned into the RAChD in 1938. He had served as an infantryman with the Rifle Brigade in the First World War and had won the Military Medal. When the Japanese invaded inadequately defended Hong Kong Island and the New Territories on 8 December 1941, Fr Green, stationed at Whitfield Barracks, visited forward companies of the Royal Scots. In the days that followed, he was evacuated to Hong Kong and from there took Holy Communion to the defensive positions held by 1st Middlesex Regiment. On 23 December 1941, he was captured by the Japanese and had his "hands up for two hours", but during the weeks after the Japanese takeover, on 25 December, Fr Green had a degree of freedom. He was able to minister at St Albert's Hospital, celebrate Mass in a Dominican chapel and say a Requiem for those killed, but on 25 February 1942 he was interned in Sham Shui Po Camp in Kowloon. There he was allowed his vestments and Mass kit and in the following months managed to say Mass, hear confessions and confirm prisoners. The influx of men wishing to convert to Catholicism was so great that the padre had to give general rather than personal instruction. At first, Mass was said in a small tent, but this was replaced by a bigger room to accommodate the 750 Catholics in the camp. Fr Green managed to decorate the church with Stations of the Cross and frequently held Benediction and the Rosary. He even managed to hold a Corpus Christi procession. The prisoners took full advantage of Fr Green's presence and the relatively tolerant approach of the Japanese. Fr Green celebrated Mass in the camp for the next three and a half years with altar breads and wine supplied by Italian priests in Kowloon.

Fr Green's limited freedom to practise his ministry in captivity, however, was not without incident or personal cost. Fr Deloughery later wrote up his experiences of his time in the camp with Fr Green. They shared their ministry and provided companionship for each other. In late 1942, Fr Green had the temerity to ask the Japanese commandant about the use of the money sent by the Vatican to ameliorate the prisoners' condition. Fr Deloughery recalled:

In November of this year Father E. J. Green, wrote to the Japanese and suggested that a portion of a sum of money donated by Pope Pius XII for the relief of allied prisoners in the Hong Kong Area be allocated to the Shamshuipo Camp for the alleviation of suffering and sickness in that camp. The Japanese contended that his letter insinuated that they were making improper use of this fund and Fr Green received a very severe beating at their hands. They clubbed him with sheathed swords till he was knocked out. As a result of this beating Father Green was confined to hospital for many weeks. It is of interest to note that the money donated by the Pope was subsequently used to purchase musical instruments and sports equipment for the various camps in Hong Kong Area.

Fr Green's diary contains no details of his personal injuries or the harsh treatment he received from his captors, but the Japanese threw him over the compound fence, breaking both his legs and severely damaging his back. He was confined to hospital on account of the maltreatment he received and by December 1942 all Catholic services for the thousands of British and Canadians became Fr Deloughery's sole responsibility. Daily visits to the sick continued and during Christmas week Holy Communion was taken to over 150 Catholics in the hospital. Additionally, Fr Deloughery was busy with preparations for Christmas and hearing confessions. Masses said, Holy Communions received, confessions heard and burials conducted bear some testimony to the relative tolerance of the Japanese in Hong Kong regarding the freedom of religious expression, but, as Fr Deloughery commented, the brutality of the camp authorities continued and attendances at services fluctuated depending on the demands for work parties, the presence of sickness in the camp, or the regular movement of prisoners to other camps.

In November 1942, Fr Green and Fr Deloughery had been allowed to visit Catholics in Bowen Road Military Hospital where Fr Deloughery was later a patient. Until he was sent back to Sham Shui Po Camp on 13 April 1943, he was able to say daily Mass and conduct services on Sundays for the Catholic staff and patients. This was the only time that Catholic services had been celebrated in the hospital for over a year. Later Fr Deloughery was transferred to the British Officers' Camp on Argyle

Street. The officers had been without chaplains for over a year, and it was in response to the repeated appeals for a chaplain that Fr Deloughery was transferred. He wrote:

> The officers had been told that Father Green was coming out, but the Japanese with their usual suspicious nature, thought they would cross them up, in case that Father Green might be carrying messages or bringing information to the Senior Officers of this camp, and so I was deposited in Argyle St. Camp, the only Canadian among some 500 British Officers.

Chaplains in the work camps

Prisoners and padres in the Japanese work camps were not treated in the same way as those in Hong Kong. The majority of commandants and guards in work camps were inhumane, sadistic and brutal in their treatment of all prisoners and were particularly hostile to the exercise of religion. Fr Malcolm Cowin, who had served with the 18th Division in Malaya, reported that "the Japanese policy regarding religion was much the same at Nong Pladuk as at other camps in which I have been stationed". There was no freedom of worship, the celebration of Mass was restricted for long periods, homilies were prohibited, and he was not allowed to visit camps where there was no Catholic padre. As a result, the chaplain was denied the opportunity to fulfil his sacerdotal role and "hundreds of Catholics died denied the Sacraments, the supreme consolation of their faith, and burial by the priest". What was particularly distressful and morale-sapping was that the Japanese forbade the priest to conduct the burials of the many prisoners who died:

> No transport was allowed for the bodies or burial parties, and the former, sewn up in sugar sacks, had to be carried to the cemetery on stretchers . . . a mile distant. At a time when morale was low and full freedom of worship would have been of incalculable value, the Japanese went out of their way to obstruct chaplains in their work.

The chaplain's exemplary behaviour, however, was inspirational. An officer of the Royal Artillery wrote that

> the man who inspired us all at the camps I was in was a Roman Catholic Jesuit priest called Father Cowin . . . He always wore his robes, he got badly beaten up, he wasn't in any way dogmatic, but he was there all the time, to help us when we were in distress. He was really quite wonderful.

In contrast, Eric Cordingley reported that at Changi "the funerals were always well carried out" at the military cemetery and were "military in character". Men were on parade, a wreath was made and a bugler on hand.

Prisoners and padres in work camps were starved of all material and spiritual necessities. Despite being subject to the same dreadful treatment as other prisoners, padres of all denominations tried as best they could to sustain morale and exercise their vocation. Their ministry and example did not go unnoticed. A report stated that Fr Cowin and the New Zealand Redemptorist Fr Burke

> carried out their work in spite of all the obstacles placed in their way by the Japanese. There can be no doubt in my mind (after three weeks continually hearing the testimony of so many people) that these Fathers have achieved something of which we may feel proud and grateful to God.

Like many others who suffered as a result of Japanese incarceration, Fr Richard Kennedy SJ was later reluctant to speak of his experiences. He had arrived in Singapore in 1941 and became a prisoner the day following capitulation to the Japanese. He was subsequently imprisoned in Malaya, Formosa and Fukuoka on the Japanese mainland before being transferred to Manchuria. In October 1943, he wrote that he was allowed "to function as a priest, to say Mass, administer the Sacraments, give lectures and instruction" and in late December 1943 wrote to his family that "Christmas in camp was quite enjoyable", as "we had better food, mock sports, and best of all I was able to say Mass". He had acted as a chaplain to a hospital, established a small library and worked on a farm. He described himself as "in the best of health", but when he was released on 19 August 1945, he weighed nine stone. An officer with whom he had shared a room considered converting to Catholicism because through Fr Kennedy he had come to admire the precision and certainty of the Catholic faith and worship. Fr Kennedy's visits to dying non-Catholics, however, did not endear him to non-Catholic padres, and the ecumenical distance between the denominations was maintained.

The Australian Marist Fr Lionel Marsden was a prisoner in a camp on the Burma–Siam railway, and Hugh Thwaites recalled aspects of his remarkable ministry. He was like "a living miracle", wrote Thwaites, and "we heard that he received many bashings from the Japanese". One evening, after the prisoners had returned from their work on the railway, they were told that Fr Marsden was about to offer Mass.

> He'd set up his little altar—two small crates covered with a white cloth with two candles burning. Around us were the tree trunks going up in the darkness, like the columns of a cathedral, and I remember thinking to myself, "St Peter's in Rome must be quite grand, but it's places like this that keep the Church going." There were, perhaps, a dozen of us at the Mass.

Fr Marsden told the congregation that "you're living through the most precious time of your lives". Thwaites concluded: "Now this was a time when we had cholera in the camp. Out of nearly 250 of us left, nearly 150 died. And yet he said that." In October 1943, Fr Marsden was returned to Sime Road Camp on Singapore. The camp commandant was relatively considerate, and he allowed the Catholics to build a chapel. The chapel was dedicated to Our Lady Help of Christians "and in memory of our deceased comrades in Malaya, the Netherland East Indies, Thailand and Burma, over whose remains there was no Christian symbol".

In Changi Camp, ecumenical disharmony sadly reared its head when Catholic padres were accused of undertaking "missionary work" by trying to convert men to the Catholic faith in contravention of army rules and regulations. In November 1942, the Revd J. N. Lewis Bryan, Acting Assistant Chaplain-General Far East and Senior Camp Chaplain in Changi, reported that 40 men had been "converted" and Anglican padres felt "very keenly about it". Padre Bryan was particularly concerned about the "missions" conducted in the barrack rooms and the hospital by Fr Bourke and complained to Fr John Watson, Senior Catholic Chaplain. Padre Bryan felt aggrieved that the "missions" mitigated the efforts he and other non-Catholic padres had made in "the spirit of co-operation" and cited the spiritual care they had exercised over Catholic prisoners when Fr Rowles "disappeared" and no Catholic chaplains were available. Fr Watson's reply was brusque: Fr Bourke was not an army chaplain but a missionary and therefore not under his command. Fr Bourke was subsequently moved from Changi, but the frosty relations between Bryan and Watson remained. Bryan wrote to the Assistant Chaplain-General that "Fr Watson is not the type of Chaplain the Dept. wants, or is accustomed to". However, padres generally eschewed ecumenical differences and ministered as they felt fit according to circumstances characterized by confinement, brutality, malnutrition, disease, exhaustion, overwork and despair. The role of the chaplain and the humanity of individual priests was defined and clearly visible.

When Changi Gaol was liberated, all denominations except Catholics, obeying the Church's directions, attended a General Service of Thanksgiving.

Little is known of Fr John O'Mahoney's incarceration except that he was held in camps in Malaya, Vietnam and Japan until his eventual release in August 1945. Fr James Ward was serving as a regular chaplain in Malaya when the Japanese invaded. He was wounded, taken prisoner and interned at Changi. As a result of his wound, his leg had to be amputated in May 1942.

Fr Eric Green was released from Sham Shui Po Camp on 17 August 1945. He resigned his commission on 20 February 1947 and returned to parish work in his Diocese of Menevia.

**Figure 16: Fr Kevin Whelan CSSp CF: Prisoner
of War (Spiritan Archives, Ireland)**

1 7

"If we are spared to return, we shall be all the better for the experience": D-Day chaplains

D-Day, 6 June 1944, and OPERATION OVERLORD

The Allied invasion of Europe began on 6 June 1944—D-Day. Planning was meticulous. Prior to embarkation, thousands of troops were confined in camps, military materiel was stockpiled in strategic locations, and rations and medical supplies were collected and prepared in readiness. At the close of 6 June, 83,000 British and Commonwealth and 73,000 American troops had landed in Normandy and the Allies were firmly ashore preparing to break out from the slender bridgehead. By the end of June, over 850,000 troops, 150,000 vehicles and 570,000 tons of supplies had been carried from England across the English Channel in an air and seaborne operation. By August 1944, over two million Allied troops had landed in Northern France.

Allied casualties were fewer than expected. At the end of D-Day, approximately 10,000 Allied troops had been killed, wounded or taken prisoner. By the end of OPERATION OVERLORD on 30 August 1944, the First Canadian and Second British Armies had suffered 83,045 casualties. 15,995 were killed, 57,996 were wounded and 9,054 were missing.

Army chaplains went through the same rigorous training procedures as the troops and wrote their wills before embarkation. Padres were given instructions ranging from loading to landing, from the contents of haversacks to the importance of transport, from battle to burials, and from necessary paperwork to the provision of "British churches" during the consolidation and reorganization period. Above all, the importance of the chaplains' role in the landings was emphasized. Chaplains were to inspire, encourage and sustain men during the landing phases; they were to serve those who required medical or spiritual assistance; they were to provide religious services as soon as practicable; and they were to carry and offer practical comforts. They were also to bury the dead and keep detailed records of burials.

So many chaplains were needed to accompany the huge military formations that they were organized into groups. D-Day was seen as the beginning of a much bigger military enterprise that would take the Allies across North West Europe and on to Berlin. Men and padres were in for the long haul. And just as there were many inexperienced soldiers at D-Day and in the ensuing campaign, so too there were many inexperienced chaplains who were to minister alongside veteran chaplains of Dunkirk, North Africa, Malta, Crete, Sicily and Italy.

Catholic chaplains on D-Day

Allied planning began in 1942 and 21st Army Group was formed in 1943 under the command of General Bernard Montgomery. Initially, Fr Basil McCreton was appointed as Senior Catholic Chaplain but was taken ill and replaced by Fr Richard Lester Guilly SJ. From October 1943 until February 1944, Fr Guilly acted as Senior Roman Catholic Chaplain until the arrival of Mgr Joseph Stapleton, recently deployed in the Middle East. Throughout the immediate planning for D-Day, Fr Guilly and subsequently Mgr Stapleton organized Catholic chaplains based on Forward and Rear Areas. Each Senior Chaplain (SCF) was responsible for sixteen chaplains in forward areas, Divisions and Brigades:

Forward Areas

HQ Second Army	Fr Richard Lester Guilly SJ	SCF (RC)
I Corps	Fr Cyril Patrick Crean	SCF (RC)
VIII Corps	Fr Herbert Henry Welchman	SCF (RC)
XII Corps	Fr Clifford Murphy	SCF (RC)
XXX Corps	Fr Charles Foley	SCF (RC)

Senior Chaplains in Rear Areas had responsibility for Lines of Communications, and for Catholic chaplains in hospitals, depots, workshops and support units. They were:

Rear Areas

	Fr Arthur Horner	SCF (RC)
11 L of C Area	Fr John Duggan	SCF (RC)
12 L of C Area	Fr Francis Coughlan	SCF (RC)

Such was to be the nature of the Normandy landings and the congested bridgehead it created that initially there were no rear areas.

Fr Cyril Patrick Crean

Cyril, or "Paddy", Crean was born in Dublin on 11 July 1908. His uncle, Major Thomas Crean, was an army surgeon who won the Victoria Cross in the Boer War and the DSO in the First World War. Paddy was ordained in June 1933 and worked at Our Lady of Lourdes Sanatorium, Dun Laoghaire, and as a curate in a Dublin parish before joining the British army as a Roman Catholic Chaplain on 10 March 1941.

One hundred and ninety-three Irish priests served as British army chaplains in the Second World War. Twenty-two were from Irish dioceses while the majority were from dioceses in England, Wales and Scotland. Others were from Irish religious and missionary institutes serving in Ireland, Great Britain and abroad (mainly in British African colonies). To get to England priests like Fr Crean, who resided in neutral Ireland, had to travel through Northern Ireland, as there were no direct sea routes from Irish ports.

Fr Crean's first posting in March 1941 was to Northern Command with 23rd Hussars of 29th Armoured Brigade, 11th Armoured Division. The Hussars were an armoured cavalry regiment raised in 1940. Fr Crean was with the Hussars from 1941 until 1943 as they moved from Northern Command to South Eastern Command and then back to Northern Command. In August 1943, he was sent to Scottish Command where he became Senior Catholic Chaplain to 1st Corps. He stayed with 1st Corps until they embarked for D-Day.

Fr Crean—D-Day Chaplain

Gordon Corrigan has described OVERLORD as "the most complex organization of war ever carried out, and the planning to get every man and every ship to the right place and at the right time and with the right kit was nothing short of extraordinary". D-Day was indeed a remarkable example of detailed military logistics and, like other men and chaplains, Fr Crean was astounded by the colossal size of the armada as it sailed across the English Channel to Normandy. "The trip over in that enormous convoy was a thrilling sight", he wrote.

Fr Crean landed on Juno Beach at Bernières-sur-Mer with the tank crews of 29th Armoured Brigade. Men and machines poured out of the landing crafts into organized chaos. The scene was one of tremendous noise and frantic movement. One man wrote that as they landed, "the air was alive with bullets and shrapnel". "All along the beach there were men lying dead and not just in the waves. Some of them still had their tin hats on. A lot of them had been overridden by their landing craft as they came off." Beachmasters attempted to move the men inland and clear the beaches for subsequent landings. On 22 June, Fr Crean recalled the landing and wrote to his father:

> I shall never forget my feelings when I stepped out of the landing craft to go ashore. I waded in with the rest with all my kit on my back from about knee depth. The beach was an extraordinary sight. You can't fully imagine it and I shall not try to describe it here.

To Fr Liam Breen, another Dublin priest, he wrote in August 1944:

> I landed on D-day in water waist deep and waded ashore into the midst of the most incredible sight in history. The fleet of ships was terrific and my first sight of France was of a Church steeple with

a hole clean through the side of it—a German plane appeared and as if by magic six of ours were on his tail and down he came.

On 22 June, he described his D-Day experiences to his father and emphasized the value of his ministry and that of other chaplains.

Dearest Dad,

Here I am sitting in my tent and it is still broad daylight. Overhead there is a plane droning—one of ours. Not far away our guns are firing and apart from that one might as well be in the Phoenix Park! After 16 days of this Second Front, thank God I am safe and well. We are in France as you know and everything is going well. I am overwhelmed with chaps all clamouring for the comforts of the Faith and I must say whatever dangers there may be and there are some of course, it is all well worth it. I have been up to the front quite a lot and been shelled once! However, God is good and though sometimes things get a bit hot at night I don't feel the least bit depressed or strained.

Our chaplains have been wonderful, and as must be expected I have had several casualties amongst them but only one fatal. I live in a tent and sleep in a slit trench! We have unwelcome visitors some nights and it is safer below ground. In a nearby town we have a gorgeous Church in which I say Mass for the lads at 6.30 every evening and they simply flock to it. The French priests are grand and I manage to carry on quite a brisk conversation with them. They are so delighted with the soldiers and the way they come to Mass . . .

I have had the most amazing experiences, some of them gruesome and sad; others frightening and some just exciting. Through them all thank God I have kept my old spirits and am enjoying it as much as anyone could enjoy such a grim business. I hope you and the family are very well and not forgetting me in your prayers. Of course, I did not expect to yet but I haven't heard from anybody since D-Day . . .

I had a great deal of travelling to do and tear along the French roads in my truck up to the front line often with relief chaplains, etc. Everywhere the boys are delighted to see the priest and always wave a welcome to you. I have a grand team of priests and all have been heroes and still are. The nights are a bit trying but thank God they don't get me down and I get quite a lot of sleep. My first real air raid was in France. What a noise. It was terrific. My Irish batman is a treasure as nothing frightens him and I can rely on him to drive through anything they can put over us . . .

. . . life is so full now that the only time I get for letters is at night and then I feel too tired to write. However, thank God so far I have managed to cope with everything including casualties amongst the chaplains and I honestly think the men in this show got every possible chance in the matter of their Sacraments . . .

. . . I am perfectly fit, never better. The food is absolutely grand and we get a daily slab of chocolate and sweets. Everything is grand and we are getting towards the end.

> your devoted son,
> Paddy.

Other Catholic padres on D-Day

Fr Maurice McGowan of the Archdiocese of Westminster was with Airlanding 195th Field Ambulance and many padres were with Casualty Clearing Stations (CCS), Casualty Collecting Posts and Advanced Dressing Stations. Fr Joseph Griffin of the Archdiocese of Birmingham landed on 6 June and immediately started tending the wounded and burying the dead. The Irish Jesuit Fr Alan Birmingham waded onto the beach and was directed to a CCS, where he was both padre and orderly. Over 700 wounded reached the CCS and the padre buried 250 dead. Fr Birmingham later described D-Day as "one of the best days of my life".

Fr Leo Donnelly, another Irish Jesuit, could see RAF planes "showering down the French shoreline" as his landing craft moved towards the beach in choppy seas. Many of the infantry were seasick. The naval bombardment began, and there was "an inferno of sound". They were late onto the beach, casualties were light, and "signs of destruction were concealed by the bustle of activity".

Fr James O'Sullivan of the Australian Diocese of Sandhurst was with 6th Duke of Wellington's Regiment. Their position was so open that the padre described them as "sitting ducks" and they suffered so many casualties they had to be withdrawn. Fr O'Sullivan administered the Last Rites to many of his men and covered the dead with their gas capes.

The Redemptorist Fr Dan Cummings was attached to 3rd Irish Guards. On landing, they dug trenches and were shelled by the enemy, the wounded received medical attention, and the padre administered sacramental and material comfort. Fr Cummings was called to minister to a Waffen SS man and, as he cut away the blood-stained tunic, he found a primed grenade in the soldier's pocket.

Fr Denys Rutledge OSB of Ampleforth Abbey, and veteran of Dunkirk, Malta and Sicily, wrote that following D-Day "the usual duties of a priest . . . are to be both enlivened and saddened by happenings peculiar to these unusual circumstances".

D-Day—the cost

Of all the casualties among Catholic chaplains from June 1944 to May 1945, more than 50 per cent were sustained on D-Day. Fr Peter Firth, of the Diocese of Lancaster and with 8th British Field Ambulance, died on D-Day. Fr Gerard Nesbitt of the Diocese of Hexham and Newcastle, attached to 8th Durham Light Infantry, was killed on 5 July. Fr Patrick McMahon, a Columban Father attached to 9th Battalion Royal Tank Regiment, died of wounds on 14 August. Fr Gerard Barry of the Archdiocese of Liverpool, attached to 8th Battalion, Scots Guards, was killed on 14 September.

Fr Philip Dayer of the Archdiocese of Westminster, who landed at Arromanches, was near Caen when the tank he was in was attacked and the driver killed. Fr Dayer was repatriated. Fr George Conlon of the Archdiocese of Glasgow, who landed with 51st Brigade, was wounded and repatriated in mid-June but was back in Normandy by 25 August. Fr James Graham, also a Glasgow priest, was wounded in the breakout. Fr Noel Stephenson SJ, Fr John Corbett of the Diocese of Salford, Fr Alphonso Coia of the Diocese of Lancaster, Fr Michael Murphy of the

Archdiocese of Birmingham, Fr John Meagher of the Diocese of Hexham and Newcastle, Fr Hugh Donaghey of the Diocese of Southwark and Fr Jack Devine of the Diocese of Elphin were all wounded.

Casualties among airborne chaplains of all denominations were particularly high. Of nine who dropped at D-Day, two were killed and two were wounded. Fr James McVeigh, of the Archdiocese of Westminster and with 6th Airborne Division, was taken prisoner when his glider crashed. Fr William Briscoe, of the Diocese of Shrewsbury and with 5th Parachute Brigade, suffered serious shrapnel wounds and his life was saved by naval surgeons aboard a warship which repatriated him to England.

Twenty-two army chaplains of all denominations were killed or died of wounds between D-Day and September 1944. As casualties occurred, padres covered additional units and became seriously overworked. Chaplains like Fr Crean, with forward units, were under great strain. As men of peace by inclination, profession and training, padres did not have the excitement of fighting in the battle to sustain them. But chaplains could never be seen to waver and had to be a constant source of encouragement and motivation. When others were at rest, the padre had to continue his ministry, as during this time he could be in touch with his men, dispense the Sacraments and celebrate Mass.

Retreats for the Rhine Army

Fr Crean wrote: "I have had the most amazing experiences, some of them gruesome and sad; others frightening and some just exciting." This sentence is repeated—see his letter to his father a few pages back. But 29th Armoured Brigade were to be involved in more heavy and costly fighting. Fr Crean was with them through offensives in Normandy, Northern France, Belgium and Holland and was in Germany at the collapse of Hitler's Third Reich. Germany was a broken and ruined country, and Catholic chaplains were warned about fraternization with Catholics among the former enemy. To the Church, rebuilding Catholic life and communities was a paramount objective.

Fr Crean had to arrange Mass centres for the many scattered units engaged in guarding vulnerable military points, clearing debris, rebuilding roads and bridges, and continually transporting supplies. Vital and urgent military tasks made attendance at Mass, and contacts with chaplains, very difficult for the troops. Fr Crean took every opportunity to celebrate Mass and hear confessions, usually in the evenings. He said Mass in ruined houses and partially destroyed churches. Often, he celebrated Mass "under the open sky which was visible through a gaping roof". Additionally, men wished to be received into the Church and some wished to reconcile themselves with God. Fr Crean and his confrères had to devise systems of tracking such men, as they were constantly being moved, with the result that their counselling and religious instructions were disrupted.

Chaplains were sensitive to the emotions of men, the majority conscripts, who were separated from family and friends and living among death and destruction. Army life gave little formal opportunity for personal thoughts. Fr Crean wrote: "It is difficult for those who have not experienced the atmosphere peculiar to army life to appreciate the anxiety which all soldiers experience for a little privacy." The soldier's life was "completely communal" and regulated by parades and rules.

A solution to the problem of finding privacy, spirituality and quietness was a Retreat House—something free, as far as possible, "from everything that suggested the army's everyday life". Fr Crean set about providing such a haven and with the help of the Archbishop of Paderborn, his brother chaplains and the army authorities, he succeeded. One half of the diocesan seminary in Bad Driburg was placed at his disposal, and beds and furniture were acquired. Soldiers willingly signed up for the three-day retreats, and between July and October 1945 over 450 men attended. There was daily Mass, prayer, lectures, reading and relaxation. Fr Crean and other padres were anxious to remind men who had so recently been fighting that it was their duty to return to a "virile" Catholic family life, "which the war has so seriously interrupted in the past six years". He concluded: "By these periods of prayer and instruction the hard work devoted by the chaplains in the field to the spiritual care of their troops, is to my mind, completed and rounded off."

Fr Crean MBE

Catholic padres were among the many chaplains who were decorated for their part in the D-Day landings and the campaign in North West Europe. Two Catholic padres were awarded the OBE, three were given the MBE and one was awarded the Military Cross. Twenty-seven were Mentioned in Despatches. Some also received French and Belgian decorations. For his services to the army in North West Europe, Fr Crean was awarded the MBE on 24 January 1946. The citation read as follows:

> Father Crean has been the Roman Catholic Senior Chaplain within I Corps throughout the campaign in North West Europe.
>
> Possessing a quiet, sincere and likeable character, he has always been on the best of terms with all ranks. He has never spared himself in his work and had afforded great assistance and comfort to many.
>
> He has made constant visits to the wounded, often in advanced medical posts and has throughout shown great keenness and organizing ability in arranging clubs and rest rooms, which have not been confined to those of his own creed. During the early days of the bridgehead he did invaluable work in locating the burial places and identifying the bodies of unknown airmen, who had crashed and had been reported missing. This work voluntarily undertaken by him must have been of inestimable comfort to the airmen's next of kin.
>
> He has been a strong rock to those of his own flock, and has throughout taken the greatest interest in all matters pertaining to the welfare of the troops. He has set a very fine example and has made a great contribution to the happiness and wellbeing of the men.

Chaplains of all denominations received the gratitude of their men and in some case the commendations of their commanding officers. Field Marshal Montgomery, quoting other military leaders, wrote: "I would sooner as go into battle without my artillery as without my chaplain."

Fr Crean—chaplain to the Irish Defence Forces

Fr Crean was demobilized on 10 May 1947 and became curate of the Parish of the Sacred Heart, Donnybrook, Dublin. He formally relinquished his commission in the British army on 16 March 1954 and was granted the honorary rank of Major (Chaplain, 3rd Class). His military exploits had not ended, however, for in 1955 he was appointed Head Chaplain of the Irish Defence Forces. In 1960, he accompanied the 32nd Battalion of the Irish army to the Congo, recently freed from Belgian control, as part of the United Nations Peace Keeping Force. He returned to the Congo with another Irish contingent in 1961 for a second tour of duty. The Irish were to find themselves not simply peacekeeping but also peace-enforcing, and they suffered casualties. With Fr Colm Matthews, Fr Crean was soon undertaking a ministry similar to that he had conducted in wartime Europe. In September 1962, Fr Crean retired from the Irish army. He died on 10 August 1973.

Figure 17: Fr Paddy Crean CF: D-Day chaplain (by kind permission of Dublin Archdiocesan Archives)

"Sky pilots": RAF chaplains in the Second World War

The Royal Air Force and its chaplains

In September 1939, the RAF had 175,692 personnel. By May 1945, there were 1,079,835 British, Commonwealth and Allied personnel in all branches of the RAF. In August 1939, the RAF had 1,911 front-line aircraft; by 1945 it had 9,200.

Bomber, Fighter and Coastal Commands operated independently and were generally located in rural areas on self-contained stations. Each station and squadron had its own *esprit de corps*. Pilots and aircrew had unique codes of comradeship and loyalty but relied on ground crew for the effectiveness of their aircraft. The character and morale of the station depended on the leadership of the station commander, the bravery and success of the aircrew, and the efficiency of the ground crew.

The RAF was a new breed of service personnel. Fighter pilots, flying and fighting as individuals, emerged as daring and confident while bomber crews, flying as a team, were dependent on each other and were regarded as more restrained. Ground crew—an indispensable factor in the equation—were skilled technicians and mechanics. These differences were manifest in the character of the station and in the nature of personal and group relationships.

The RAF had its own chaplains but, unlike Royal Navy and army chaplains, they did not accompany men in battle. Chaplains could not participate in fighter sorties or bombing raids and this restriction influenced the priest's relationship with service personnel. Like ground crew, chaplains endured tense and agonizing waits for the return of friends and comrades. News of missions altered mindsets and affected morale. Like those they served, chaplains were affected by battle experiences; some were taken prisoner and others died in service.

Catholic RAF chaplains

In September 1939, there were nine commissioned Catholic RAF chaplains, and the main objective of Fr Henry Beauchamp, Catholic Staff Chaplain, was to increase that number. Described as "a rich and picturesque figure", Fr Beauchamp had watched the new RAF develop as a service competing for its share of the defence budget in the inter-war years. Mgr Beauchamp, as he became in 1940, was very efficient and fiercely proud of the junior service; he became Bishop Dey's Vicar-General for the RAF.

Recruitment drives proved more successful among religious institutes than dioceses. Between 1939 and 1945, 72 per cent of the 204 temporary Catholic RAF chaplains were from religious institutes. New chaplains were instructed in their religious and military roles, and Mgr Beauchamp was anxious that the latter did not overwhelm the former. Mindful of the tasks they were asked to undertake, he warned that chaplains "should be careful not to take on so many duties that the religious welfare of their personnel suffers". They would be judged as priests, not as organizers of sports events, and they should seize every occasion that presented itself to show their bravery.

Initiation

The Irish Dominican Fr Hamilton Pollock, commissioned in 1941, was posted to RAF Uxbridge, where he learned RAF traditions, drilled, acquainted himself with *King's Regulations* and was taught how to behave like an RAF officer. He received a black bag containing a portable altar, vestments and Mass kit, and just as he determined never to lose his RAF identity card, he determined never to lose the black bag, for it was to be "the safeguard of his priestly vocation and the suit of armour that would protect him in this life of new-found freedom". The bag would allow him to "bring Calvary into aerodromes and airfields, on to landing beaches and into the enemy camp . . . he would open the miniature Cathedral to celebrate Mass and reveal the great Mystery of the Incarnation and the death of the Saviour of the World".

He examined his own "stock of courage and bravery", for his duties might result in his being in a "death zone". Yet "something worse than death" might happen, for military encounters could endanger his vocation. Death would not be in battle but in the loss of his priesthood. Military regulations and the company of airmen replaced Dominican rules and the company of his priestly brethren; the Roman collar was exchanged for "the collar and tie of the service". The freedom presented by the RAF would expose his vocation to many dangers, but thousands of young men had dedicated their lives to the service of their country, so he could do no less than offer his vocation to their service and that of the Church.

Religious provision was inadequate and chaplains used station buildings or relied on local priests for the use of ecclesiastical facilities. Fr Oliver Conroy CSsR, posted to the Shetland Islands, found it a culture shock after a London parish. Fr Oswald Earle SJ recalled that at RAF Pershore "we had no chapel". Fr John Burke of the Archdiocese of Dublin had to build a church, a club and priest's quarters at RAF Cosford. In 1939, Fr Peter Blake SJ found a "very lovely chapel" at RAF Cardington, but by December 1940 he was at RAF Halton, which had 15,000 men and eight chaplains of other denominations. There he began, with "great zest", "the task of coping with young Catholic men" and for the first time he encountered wounded aircrew "with appalling injuries and terrible burns".

RAF Catholic chaplains in Europe

In November 1939, Fr Thomas Hourigan was deployed to Nantes with British Air Forces in France Command. He ministered to scattered units but, as the Germans advanced in May 1940, he was evacuated from Dunkirk to Southampton. Army chaplains and others accused the RAF of being absent from the skies above Dunkirk.

In 1940, Fr Arthur Kavanagh SJ was in the south of England among "the Few"—Battle of Britain pilots who were "an exceptionally fine set of men". The pilot with whom he shared a room was killed in the battle. The arrival of Polish, Belgian and Czech pilots added to his work, but, as other chaplains discovered, it was difficult to develop a communal spirit given the brevity of relationships among men who "conversed daily with death". Fr Christopher Devlin SJ wrote that "the Few" personified the RAF "in its full and dazzling glory". Home stations were frequently targeted by the Luftwaffe and Fr Kavanagh tended casualties. Before and after bomber raids on Germany, he counselled aircrew and wrote to bereaved relatives.

Fr Pollock, posted to RAF Thornaby of Coastal Command, soon witnessed the dangers of flying. A Canadian aircraft dropped from the sky and exploded as it hit the ground. Two airmen were thrown from the wreckage. "They were lucky", wrote the chaplain, " . . . they were killed instantaneously". Others were trapped inside the plane, and the priest and doctor ran to give medical and spiritual help. They were too late, and three charred remains were dragged out. One had "RC" on his identity disc and Fr Pollock anointed his blackened skull. The following day, with the Union Flag draped over their coffins, the airmen were buried with chaplains of all denominations in attendance. On another occasion, a flag bearing the Swastika covered the coffins of German airmen shot down and brought to Thornaby for burial. The RAF were called "the Brylcreem Boys" and "the Glamour Boys", but on such occasions, the padre wrote, "there was little evidence of either Brylcreem or Glamour". A pilot who had befriended the chaplain was killed days before his wedding. Fr Pollock had to break the sad news to his friend's wife-to-be. He reflected: "Chaplains should be allowed to cry."

On D-Day, Fr Oliver Conroy CSsR landed on Juno Beach with elements of 2nd Tactical Air Force. Fr Peter Blake SJ, also with 2nd Tactical Air

Force, arrived at Amiens after D-Day and moved to Brussels, where he established retreat centres and visited stations in Belgium and northern France. Fr Frederick Hanson, a Columban Father, arrived in Normandy on D-Day+1. Fr John MacSeumais, an Irish Jesuit, commissioned in 1943, had experience of flying in gliders preparing for D-Day. Like Fr Leo Lennon OP, he was posted to Europe after D-Day to minister to the British Army of Liberation.

Chaplains were forbidden to fly on fighter sorties or bombing missions, though Fr Edmund D'Arcy SJ "wangled" an observation flight over the Battle of El Alamein. Fr Pollock proved another exception to the rule when, with Bomber Command at RAF Penrose, he encountered aircrew preparing to bomb Germany. He identified Catholics and provided spiritual facilities, developed friendships, encouraged them to attend the sacraments and blessed their military endeavours. After one mission, 58 men failed to return, and the chaplain wrote to the next-of-kin of Catholic airmen "to try to ease the blow". But "sorrow and mourning know no denomination" and Fr Pollock wrote to the families of all who did not return.

He was aware that he could not understand the nature of the aircrews' war if he had not experienced it, and so in response to jibes and encouragement, he decided to join a flight on a night raid over Essen. It was strictly forbidden, so before doing so, he made his confession to the local priest. A "sky pilot"—the colloquial term for an RAF chaplain— would be covered under Red Cross and Geneva Conventions, but as Fr Pollock removed his religious insignia before flying, he was now a combatant and, if captured, would be treated as such. He removed his dog collar and chaplain's insignia and, dressed as an observer, climbed into "the death trap".

In the air, the captain's carefree attitude, so evident on the station and in the mess, disappeared. Instead, he "was captain of the ship"—"C for Charlie"—and men were busy at their own jobs. There was almost complete silence "except for the deafening roar of the four engines outside". Over Germany, Fr Pollock recalled

> a bird's eye view of hell let loose. There were flares dropped by
> the path-finders, the flak that was coming up from down below,

and right in front hundreds of searchlights converging together like illuminated sticks on a witch's broom. "Those searchlights are trouble", said the pilot. "Father . . . if you are picked up in one of those you've had it." Scarcely had the words died on his Irish lips there was an explosion that . . . rocked C for Charlie. One of the other aircraft had been hit and exploded in mid-air.

"Someone swore a typical farewell", but there was no time for other thoughts except concentrating on the job in hand. The target came in sight, bombs were dropped, and they headed for home, dodging searchlight beams. When they landed, the chaplain was asked if he was "OK". He replied in the affirmative and headed straight for the chapel to give thanks for his "preservation". However, the Commanding Officer severely reprimanded pilot and priest. Five planes and their crews had not returned and the chaplain could easily have been killed. Yet now he could empathize with the aircrews and had nothing but admiration for the bravery of the men who risked their lives on their nightly missions. His admiration for Bomber Command "bordered on hero worship".

Crete, the Mediterranean, North Africa and Italy

In 1941, Fr Joseph Gill SJ was deployed to Crete and like others did not expect a German invasion, but by May the British were overrun. He received an hour-and-a-half's notice to quit "with orders to take no baggage but our greatcoat and equipment". "But", he wrote, "I counted my Mass set as the latter and so got it out." Separated from the commanding officer, Fr Gill took charge and led over 30 airmen down to the harbour. He was then evacuated to Alexandria.

Fr Thomas Hourigan SDB was based in the Middle East, and his "diocese" stretched from Cyprus to Kenya and, at certain times in the war, from Tunis to Tehran. As operations in the Middle East and North Africa increased, so too did the number of Catholic RAF chaplains. In August 1940, chaplains served at RAF Habbaniya (Iraq) and RAF Cairo, RAF Aboukir, RAF Ismailia, and RAF Abu-Seir (all Egypt). Among those who served in North Africa were Pallotine Fathers John Roche, Patrick

Sherry and Vincent O'Sullivan SCA, and they were joined by John Wright (Archdiocese of Westminster), Aelred Perring OSB of Ampleforth Abbey, Percy Bailey (Diocese of Shrewsbury), Gerard Horricks (Diocese of Southwark), Edmund D'Arcy SJ, Joseph Gill SJ, Hilary Carpenter OP and Lawrence Deegan (Diocese of Hexham and Newcastle).

In 1943, Fr David Lewis OP was in Sicily before crossing to Italy at Salerno. Five days later, he celebrated Mass in a church after months of saying Mass from his portable altar perched on petrol cans. The church, he wrote, "was surrounded by buildings pockmarked by shells", and as he said Mass, "guns bark outside and shells whine. There is the whoosh of bombs, the crackle of cannon and machine gun fire as Spitfires join combat with droning sneak raiders. Transport rumbling along the road outside blend into the symphony of war sounds." Inside, "in the dusk of the cool building, relieved only by a few candles on the altar", Fr Lewis and his congregation prayed undisturbed.

In 1943, Fr Pollock was posted to RAF Bizerta, Tunis, where he met a scene of devastation and military cemeteries—"the only places where order reigned". In the United Kingdom, the RAF Commands operated separately, defending the country and attacking German targets, but in North Africa the RAF flew in combined operations and the RAF station housed Bomber, Fighter and Coastal Commands. Fr Pollock was in contact with Allied forces and also with Italian and German prisoners of war. All were in a foreign land, and in such circumstances Allied and indigenous crime flourished. "Moral destruction", he wrote, "is the greatest evil wrought by war" and chaplains "not only had to plant the dead they had to replant the living". Not having a church did not worry him, for his chapel went with him on his motorcycle: "At times selected but in places not too dignified Mass was celebrated." Visiting hospitals "was a duty to be discharged and a most priestly one". As doctors and nurses carried out tender works of mercy inside, their fellow human beings did their utmost outside to inflict suffering and death.

In September 1943, Fr Pollock landed on Corsica. He recalled: "In all these operations it was the army who had to take the brunt. The navy landed them, the air force gave them umbrella cover, but the army had to stop the bullets." RAF men, wrote the padre, looked on with admiration as the soldiers embarked their landing craft. Fr Pollock was the only Catholic chaplain on the island.

He was then transferred to Sardinia and, as an Italian speaker, liaised with the locals and Italian prisoners of war. Although he had no respect for the Sardinian lifestyle, the occupiers, he wrote, behaved with no better moral code. He reminded airmen of the dangers of casual sexual relationships. Official attempts to prevent immoral liaisons and the spread of sexually transmitted diseases had little effect, and Fr Pollock's frequent remonstrations with commanding officers led to much unpleasantness. The Dominican protested against the setting up of a regulated brothel and forbade Catholic servicemen to frequent it or assist in its organization. He was reprimanded for voicing his disapproval.

Fr Pollock was posted to Italy for "the final bout". A tented station was soon in operation at Foggia, where a large hospital was erected. He was the only British chaplain alongside six American chaplains, and he discovered how their zeal positively influenced American service personnel. The padres organized a mission—"OPERATION SPIRITUAL"—which was attended by over 2,500 Allied troops.

The zeal of the American chaplains greatly improved the spirits of Fr Pollock, but their influence paled when, at San Giovanni, he encountered Padre Pio, the Franciscan who bore the marks of the Lord's stigmata. On one occasion, the chaplain encouraged Catholics to attend Padre Pio's Mass, and afterwards they all knelt to kiss the Franciscan's bleeding hands. Other Catholics and Protestants were later inspired to do the same.

In June 1944, the Americans entered Rome. It was a bittersweet moment for Fr Pollock as he had been a student in Rome before the war, and he was able to visit his Dominican confrères. A less joyful occasion was his visit to a site outside Rome where the mass graves of murdered Jews were discovered. The scene, he wrote, was "an example of the evil man can do when he allows himself to be guided by the savage hatred of his fellow man". He was convinced that the Germans were "capable of anything". Atrocities were committed "with deliberation and with full approval and authority".

Prisoner of war

Fr Patrick Rorke SJ was based at RAF Seletar, Singapore, when he was taken a prisoner of war by the Japanese and imprisoned in Sumatra. "When locked up", he wrote, "we had lost everything that makes up life at home. We existed in the direst and most sordid poverty, brought as low as any man can be brought." Fr Rorke had to forsake so much that "chained one to the world", but paradoxically he won the "freedom of soul". He was "emancipated from the quest for pleasures and comforts and discovered that such things are of no importance in a man's life".

Prisoners lived in the knowledge that they might be physically beaten and in fear that they might give in, lose their wits, or slide down "towards final sickness and hopelessness". Yet they combined for mutual assistance and comfort, pooled meagre resources, cared for each other and the sick, "and as for other things, they were of no account". Not all adopted this stoicism and there were those who stole and cheated and adopted a self-centred attitude.

In the last months of the war, according to Fr Rorke, men "began to lose the last treasure we had left to us: the likelihood of surviving at all". They feared that when the Allies invaded, they would be shot by the Japanese, who were then free to resist the invaders. But, as Fr Rorke wrote, "even this ceased to worry many men. We had waited so long and endured so much that we had learned not to fear death. And so, in a deeper way still, one found freedom of soul."

Fr Rorke sold or exchanged leaves from his breviary for cigarette paper and cloth from his vestments and altar linen for bandages. In return, he received eggs and other items of food. Despite Japanese reprisals, Fr Rorke took every opportunity to celebrate Mass and hold services in the camp.

Casualties

Five RAF chaplains died in the war. Fr Denis Ashill OP, attached to Bomber Command, died in Cambridge in December 1942 and is buried in Cambridge City Cemetery; Fr Michael Kelly, who had served on home bases, died in in August 1944 and is buried in Fordingbridge, Hampshire; Fr James Greany OMI died in February 1945 and is buried in Inchicore, Dublin; Fr Thomas Kenny of the Diocese of Perth, Australia died in September 1945 and is buried in Glasnevin Cemetery, Dublin; and Fr Bernard McCloskey of the Maynooth Mission died in the RAF Hospital Andover in December 1946 and is buried in Ballyshannon, County Donegal.

Reflections and appreciation

Fr Peter Blake SJ provided spiritual activities and "pushed" Catholic papers, books, debates and lectures. Fr Niall Corbett SJ was "regarded with admiration and affection", Fr Jerry O'Shea "brought interest and zest to his ministry", while Fr Geoffrey Sparrowe SJ "was a very popular chaplain" who did much "apostolic work". Fr Edmund D'Arcy SJ was known for "his approachability and getting things done". Fr Arthur Kavanagh SJ paid tribute to "a magnificent Service" and expressed "his gratitude to those who dared and suffered and died that we might live". Fr Oswald Earle SJ found his service in Palestine "a wonderful privilege", but for the men it had little significance. He was surprised, however, "to find the importance men attached to Confession".

Fr Pollock sought out an American chaplain for confession. He asked pardon if he had given any scandal as a priest and if he had preferred his own safety over the call of duty. If he had lacked courage, he asked for forgiveness on the score of human frailty, and his time as a chaplain he left to be judged by God. He reflected that he had "prepared hundreds of men to meet death" and perhaps "many of them were in Heaven through his priesthood". He prayed that he would be able to readjust "to the monotonous, humdrum life of a monastery after the excitement, glamour, freedom and devil-may-careness of Air Force life".

On Mgr Beauchamp's death in 1948, Air Marshal Sir Basil Embrey paid tribute to the Principal Chaplain's particular wartime contribution to the RAF. "His breadth of vision, priestly zeal and unflagging energy", he wrote, "devised and brought to fruition the scheme of the Moral Leadership Courses which time has proved to be of inestimable worth in the training and producing of leaders."

Figure 18: Fr Hamilton Pollock OP RAF: Sky Pilot

1 9

"The horrors which one reads about . . . are not exaggerated": Chaplains at Bergen-Belsen

The British Liberation Army

The Allies had advanced cautiously since the D-Day landings and as they moved into Germany and towards Berlin they met stern German resistance. On 7 May 1945, however, General Alfred Jodl, representing the German High Command, signed the document of unconditional surrender at Allied Headquarters, Reims. The Third Reich would fight no more. Hitler had committed suicide, the High Command had ceased to function, German forces lacked arms and supplies, and large numbers of German troops in Russia and in Eastern and Western Europe had been taken prisoner. Germany's industrial cities had been laid waste by incessant Allied bombing.

Whilst the Allies had expected strong German resistance, very few in the advancing British Liberation Army (BLA) and American army were prepared for what they encountered in the concentration and extermination camps of the Third Reich. Eventually they discovered the true horror that the Nazis had wrought, especially upon those of the Jewish faith, and also those they deemed to be racially inferior or who were considered to be a political and economic threat. Commanders, soldiers and chaplains came face-to-face with the Holocaust.

Catholic chaplains with the BLA

During March and April 1945 as British and American forces crossed the River Rhine and entered Germany, 164 Catholic army chaplains ministered to the Second Army and 21 Army Group. Senior Catholic Chaplains, Mgr Joseph Stapleton, Fr Matthew O'Carroll and Fr John W. Jones were attached to 21 Army Group HQ, while Fr Richard Guilly SJ, Fr Cyril Crean (I Corps), Fr Herbert Welchman (VIII Corps), Fr Clifford Murphy (XII Corps) and Fr Charles Foley (XXX Corps) were Senior Chaplains with Second Army. Fr Arthur Horner SJ was Senior Catholic Chaplain with Lines of Communication while Fr John Duggan was deployed with 11 Line of Communication Area and Fr Francis Coughlan with 12 Line of Communication Area.

During the preparations for D-Day and in the subsequent campaign, chaplains of all denominations were issued with strict instructions regarding fraternization with the Germans. The policy was that this must be avoided at all costs. For Catholic padres, the plight of the many Catholic Germans, their priests and their churches would present a particularly difficult dilemma, but they could show no favouritism towards their co-religionists in the defeated Reich.

The attitude and behaviour of German Catholics were not the only problems facing the chaplains. The Irish Jesuit Fr Laurence Kearns reported:

> The damage caused by R.A.F., artillery and tanks is immense. One can see whole towns wiped out. We have met many liberated prisoners and you can believe what you read of the concentration camps. Bestial cruelty was rife in them ... The majority of the people were ignorant of what went on behind the barbed wire ... The foreign workers were all delighted to be free at last.

Entering Belsen

By April 1945, many of the chaplains in northern Europe were veterans of Dunkirk, North Africa, Sicily, Italy and the D-Day landings; yet despite having witnessed death, injury and suffering on a large scale over a prolonged period, they were totally ill-prepared for what they encountered when they entered the concentration and extermination camps. Edward Hulmes has written that with

> the liberation of the camp at Bergen-Belsen by units of the British army, and the subsequent discovery of other extermination camps across Europe, a hitherto unsuspected level of human wickedness was revealed.

After his visit to Belsen camp, near the town of Bergen in Lower Saxony, Fr Charles Foley of Plymouth Diocese wrote to Mgr Coghlan: "There is no ability to describe it, nor do I wish to do so." He felt that German priests, ministers and people should be made to visit the camps, for what they witnessed would leave an "imprint forever on the German mind". Fr Laurence Kearns recalled that a general call had gone out for doctors, nurses and chaplains to report at once to Belsen. "That's how I saw hell on earth", he wrote.

Fr Michael Morrison SJ

Fr Michael Morrison was one of 18 English and Irish Jesuits deployed with the BLA, and in April 1945 he was attached to 32nd Casualty Clearing Station in northern Germany. Born on 5 October 1908 at Listowel, County Kerry, Fr Morrison was educated at Mungret College and entered the Jesuit Novitiate in 1925. He taught Maths and Religious Knowledge at Belvedere College, Dublin, and was ordained in 1939. He was commissioned into the RAChD on 19 May 1941 and was attached to 2/5th Battalion the Welsh Regiment before being deployed, in October 1942, to a General Hospital with the Eighth Army in North Africa. In the early days of the campaign to liberate Europe, he was deployed with 2/8th Lancashire Fusiliers.

Fr Morrison reported that on 12 April 1945, representatives of the Chief of Staff of the First German Parachute Army had approached the staff of the British VIII Corps to ask for a local armistice. Their objective was to discuss a truce during which the Germans would hand over to the British the concentration camps at Bergen-Belsen, near Hanover, holding 60,000 prisoners guarded by Wehrmacht, SS and Hungarian troops. There was typhus in the camps, and the German military wished the battle, now in full swing, to bypass Bergen-Belsen and declare it a neutral area. On 13 April, the German Chief of Staff again asked VIII Corps to take control of the camps with the assistance of the Wehrmacht guards, because the situation had deteriorated so badly that the German authorities were unable to manage it alone. The Wehrmacht, stated the German representatives, would assist the British army in the camps, but the British could do as they thought fit with the SS guards. Unlike Auschwitz, a camp liberated earlier by the Russians, Bergen-Belsen contained no gas chambers, but over 50,000 prisoners had died there between 1943 and 1945. As the war drew to a close, Josef Kramer, the camp commandant and former commandant of Auschwitz, was ordered by German authorities to kill all the remaining inmates.

On 17 April, senior British medical officers and chaplains inspected the Bergen-Belsen camps to ascertain the full medical, welfare and pastoral requirements of the internees. In the party were Fr Welchman, a priest of the Archdiocese of Westminster and Senior Catholic Chaplain, Fr Morrison and Orthodox Rabbi Leslie Hardman (who preferred to be called "Reverend" or "Padre") from Leeds, the Senior Jewish chaplain to Headquarters, VIII Corps. A couple of days later Fr Welchman reported to Mgr Coghlan:

> On entering the camp, a vast mass of pitiable humanity was seen sitting about or wandering in a dazed and lifeless condition, seemingly indifferent to the appalling stench and squalor of their surroundings.
>
> They appeared to be mentally degraded almost to a sub-human level. They watched their companions dying all around

them without a flicker of interest. Those who had scraps of food
ate it squatting unconcernedly beside naked corpses. All sense of
personal shame had been lost—men and women suffering from
dysentery, relieved themselves in the open. Seething crowds
fought for water from the Army water-carts, refusing to believe
the assurances of the troops that there was plenty for all and
more to come. The more active rummaged among the piles of
filthy rags stripped from the dead, jealously hoarding whatever
they could find. It was definitely established that cannibalism
had taken place.

A British officer reported that most of the inmates were little more
than skeletons with haggard, yellowish faces. Most of the men "wore a
striped pyjama-type of clothing, others wore rags, while women wore
striped flannel gowns or any other piece of clothing they had managed
to acquire". Many were without shoes, and most wore only socks and
stockings. "There were men and women lying in heaps on both sides
of the track. Others were walking slowly and aimlessly about—a vacant
expression on their starved faces."

For Rabbi Hardman, the experience of seeing his surviving
co-religionists was an incredibly powerful and sorrowful experience:

> Towards me came what seemed to be the remnants of a
> holocaust—a staggering mass of blackened skin and bones, held
> together somehow with filthy rags. "My God, the dead walk," I
> cried aloud, but I did not recognize my voice ... peering at the
> double star, the emblem of Jewry on my tunic—one poor creature
> touched and then stroked the badge of my faith, and finding that
> it was real, murmured, "Rabbiner, Rabbiner".

Fr Morrison arrived with 32 Casualty Clearing Station, 63rd Anti-Tank
Regiment, shortly after the initial inspection. When they entered the
camp, they found between "seven and ten thousand dead in the huts or
on the ground". On 18 April 1945, he wrote to the Jesuit authorities in
Ireland obviously overcome by the scale of horror he was witnessing:
"At the moment I am very busy. Our job is to look after a concentration

camp. The sights were indescribable. I saw between a thousand and fifteen hundred dead civilians lying about unburied." He added: "There are huge pits dug into which several hundred bodies are thrown and covered up." "Administering the Sacraments", he wrote, "is very difficult as none of the people speak English and no record of religion is kept." On 11 May he wrote:

> It is time I gave you some news from this place. It is Belsen Concentration Camp, which no doubt you have heard of. It got quite a bit of publicity on the radio, in the press and on the films I understand. But I think it is quite impossible to give an adequate idea of the frightfulness of the place when we first came. To begin with there are some sixty thousand people herded together in an area about half a square mile. Huts which could accommodate about 30–50 were made to hold over 500. Some of these huts had had three tier bunks with a narrow passage down the centre. In each bunk there were 2 and sometimes 3 people lying and it was not uncommon to find one or more of these dead. When we came in there were thousands of bodies lying unburied. Even walking down the centre passage one had to be careful where one walked so as to avoid stepping on the dead. More horrible still it was to see people crawling on their hands and knees because they had not strength enough to walk, or to see them totter along until they fell and remained there to die. My work for the first ten days was taken up solely with administering Extreme Unction from morning to night.

Fr Morrison reported that in February 1945 there had been 45 priests in Belsen. On 17 April, only ten were still alive, and four died within weeks of liberation. Of those who remained, few were able to walk. Fr Morrison managed to anoint 300 inmates a day, but then gave his stock of Holy Oils to the Polish priest and former internee Fr Stanislaus Kadjiolka. He and the other internee priests "eagerly welcomed the opportunity of exercising their sacred ministry again and were most anxious to assist the chaplain in his work in the camp". But the majority "were incapable of exerting themselves owing to their extremely feeble condition". Meanwhile, Fr

Morrison attended to burials. These, he wrote, did not take too much time as two graves held about 5,000 bodies each, and he was assisted by SS and Wehrmacht guards, some of whom made a point of throwing their military medals away. As Mass Grave number 2 was covered in, Fr Morrison and Rabbi Hardman said memorial prayers together over the dreadful scene with, where possible, the Christian victims being placed at one end of the grave and the Jewish victims at the other.

Only after he had administered Extreme Unction and buried the dead could Fr Morrison begin to give Holy Communion to inmates denied the Blessed Sacrament for four or five years. On Sunday 22 April, he was able to celebrate Mass in Belsen when those liberated, clad in rags, knelt in the pouring rain. Fr Guilly managed to acquire portable altars and Mass kit for several French priests. Fr Morrison wrote that the medical assistance that arrived was "totally inadequate".

By mid-May, Fr Morrison was able to report that there were seven British padres ministering in Belsen which was referred to as Camp 2. They were assisted by French, Hungarian, German and Polish priests, all striving to alleviate the plight of the internees. Four padres ministered at Bergen, three miles to the northeast of Belsen, and referred to as Camp 1. Their task was enormous.

At the end of May 1945, it was decided that Fr Morrison was in need of a rest from his harrowing ministry in Belsen. All the internees had been moved out of the camp and housed in military barracks. Fr Morrison wrote: "The work here has been physically the most revolting that I have ever been called upon to do, but it has also been the most consoling." Despite the coldblooded murder and distressing and dispiriting sights he had witnessed, he concluded:

> Belsen, despite its awful horror, will, I am sure, be a thought on which the minds of the priests who worked there will like to dwell. To have been "the ministers of Christ and the dispensers of the mysteries of God" to so many thousands in such dire need will be a consolation and a source of gratitude to God for their priestly vocation.

Fr Morrison was Mentioned in Despatches in the campaign awards.

Other chaplains at Bergen-Belsen

Two of the chaplains who were present at the liberation of Bergen-Belsen met up with another chaplain with the BLA, Fr Denys Rutledge OSB of Fort Augustus Abbey, on 7 May. They told him that during the first 14 days in the camp they had buried 12,000 dead, of whom 3,000 were dead when the British arrived. Internees were dying at a rate of 200–250 per day. Fr Rutledge wrote that those who were "first to visit Belsen . . . from this HQ are at a loss for words to describe what they found".

In *Indelible Memories of Belsen*, Fr Edmund Swift, a Jesuit of the English Province, recalled his entry to Belsen on 15 May 1945 and gave further gruesome details of the burials that took place. One grave, he recalled, contained up to 12,000 bodies, and on one day 2,300 bodies were laid to rest. "In total", he wrote, "at least 21,000 people lie buried in the Concentration Camp, their names unknown, all victims of the ravages of acute starvation, dysentery, typhus and T.B." He added that "regarding the total number of people held in captivity, no reliable check is ascertainable". The Vatican had attempted to compile information relating to the missing and prisoners in the camps, but the task was enormous and complex, as many Jewish prisoners had been compelled to use aliases. It was an important Vatican mission, wrote Fr Swift, and one that was "completely disregarded by certain critics of the reigning Pontiff".

Fr Swift and Fr Morrison met Fr Konopka SJ, formerly Provincial of the Polish Province. He was an internee and one of the "very few priests to survive the Horror Camp". He was looking for a cap to match "the very unclerical dress" that he was wearing, wrote Fr Swift. He "spoke rapidly and at great length in fluent Latin" presumably about "what he wanted us to remember about Belsen . . . I never saw him again".

Fr Vincent Fay of the Diocese of Salford corroborated the accounts of other chaplains and in May wrote to his family of the "indescribable horrors" he had encountered. "Believe me", he wrote, "the horrors which one reads about in Belsen camp are not exaggerated." He was attached to No. 9 British General Hospital and reported that there were 40,000 sick in Camp 1, and the padres ministered to 11,000 patients after he arrived on 3 May. "My work", he wrote, "does not consist of going into the huts;

Fr Morrison and some foreign priests do that." "Five minutes are enough for me", he continued, "but they are in there all day. I believe some are cracking up now." "Typhus is still very prevalent and almost all other diseases, especially TB and dysentery. The dead were thrown out into the road and afterwards thrown into a pit. People died as they walked or stumbled about." "Well, we tried to celebrate VE Day", he concluded, "but it was very hard to do much with 5,000 patients to look after."

Another Salford priest, Fr Herbert Rigby, arrived on 21 May. Fr Morrison wrote that by the time he left the camp on 27 May, "almost every Catholic had had an opportunity of receiving the Sacraments". Twenty-seven thousand people had been evacuated from Belsen, where they had been treated in the most inhumane fashion and deprived of all their basic needs. Requests for Holy Communion sadly had to be frequently refused because of the shortage of altar breads.

On 25 May, Fr Fay wrote that on the day before, Brigadier Hughes had "fired the first shot from a flame thrower which burned the last of the Belsen Horror Huts to the ground". At one end of a hut, there was a large German flag and a picture of Hitler. Shells were fired at both and destroyed them. "For the first time", wrote Fr Fay, "faces shone with joy at Belsen." The Baptisms of babies were also reasons for celebration, although the immediate prospects for the young and displaced were extremely challenging.

As soon as liberation came to Belsen, members of the Vatican Relief Commission in Europe were rushed from their headquarters in Paris to bring spiritual and medical aid to those who had suffered in the camp. Fr George Galbraith, of the Archdiocese of Glasgow and an army chaplain in the First World War, was a member of the Commission which confirmed the atrocities the Allies had discovered:

> In many of the huts there were three storied beds—two or three in each bed . . . doctors found it impossible to attend the patients as it was not possible to get near them. A chaplain, one of two French chaplains in the camp, said he had to climb up the beds and with difficulty administer the Last Sacraments. Dysentery was rampant and vermin increased. The camp was cosmopolitan—Poles in large numbers, Dutch, Belgians, Italians,

Czechs, Slovenes, Yugoslavs, Hungarians, Austrians, Greeks, German, French. The Jewish element predominated, 80 per cent Jews.

Fr Galbraith gave some statistics of the Nazi treatment of Catholic priests. Eighty priests, mostly Poles, died in Belsen, and in Dachau 1,200 priests died, 800 of whom were Polish.

The Catholic padres continued with their ministry to the BLA in and around Bergen; many were deeply traumatized by their experiences of the camps. Many German priests had been held prisoner and had been forced to work as orderlies. They wished to say Mass again, and the chaplains tried to make arrangements within the directives about fraternization.

Post-war ministry

Fr Morrison was one of 21 Irish Jesuits who volunteered as padres to the British Armed Forces in the Second World War. After demobilization, he was sent to minister in Australia but returned to his home parish of Holy Name, Manchester, and then finally to Belvedere College as a teacher of Mathematics. He was severely affected by his experience in Belsen but divulged little of what he had witnessed there. Fr Morrison's students had no idea of the dreadful sights he had witnessed as a padre. The British media released some images soon after the opening of the camp but, as Fr Morrison wrote to his sister in May 1945, "they do not reveal the real horror of the place". He added: "I expect the photos would not be published in the Irish papers." He told the Jesuit Provincial that the BBC reports "fall very short of giving a proper idea of the horror of this place". One newspaper reporter described Belsen as "the nearest thing I know to a spectacle of absolute evil". In the post-war years, the world began to fully realize the true extent of what had happened in the concentration and extermination camps of the Third Reich, but for Fr Morrison and many others such revelations failed to completely expunge memories of those barbaric times or ease minds and bodies of the horrors they had experienced.

Like many other priests who volunteered for ministry with the military, Fr Morrison had shown extraordinary courage and resilience in his chaplaincy duties. He went into the army, which he enjoyed tremendously, and into Belsen a fit and energetic priest, but after the war his health declined. Fr Morrison died in April 1973 and is buried in Glasnevin Cemetery, Dublin.

**Figure 19: Fr Michael Morrison SJ CF: Witness
to barbarism (Irish Jesuit Archives)**

The forgotten war: Chaplains in Korea

The Korean War

The Korean War began on 25 June 1950, when the Communist North Korean People's Army invaded the Free Republic of South Korea. Two days later, the United Nations (UN) called on its members to support South Korea by providing military assistance. By the end of August, the whole of South Korea, with the exception of an enclave round the southern port of Pusan, was in North Korean hands. An American landing at Inchon coincided with a UN offensive in the Pusan area and the North Koreans were driven back. By mid-October, Pyongyang, the North Korean capital, was in UN hands, but Communist China's entry into the war in support of North Korea changed the nature, intensity and length of the conflict. In November, Pyongyang was retaken by the Communists, and UN forces withdrew southwards towards the 38th Parallel, the border between the two Koreas. From late 1950 until May 1953, UN forces held back successive Communist offensives and eventually drove them back north of the 38th Parallel.

Truce talks between the UN and the Communists began at Kaesong in July 1951, but negotiations stalled, and in October 1951 the talks were relocated to Panmunjom and talks continued for another two years. An amnesty was declared in July 1953, and a demilitarized zone was established between the two warring sides. Over two million Koreans had died during the war. The Panmunjom peace talks continue to this day. Two nations live on one peninsula under two conflicting political, social and economic ideologies.

British forces in Korea

British forces involved in the Korean War included National Servicemen conscripted for two years' military service. Unlike their predecessors in the Second World War, they did not expect to be engaged in combat, but over 60,000 British troops served in Korea. Of them, 1,139 were killed in action, 2,674 were wounded and 1,060 were listed as missing or prisoners of war.

Five Royal Navy aircraft carriers were in action at different periods of the war with squadrons of the Fleet Air Arm engaged in aerial combat and ground attack sorties. Seventeen destroyers, six cruisers, five frigates and 17 support ships were also involved during hostilities. 27, 28 and 29 Brigades provided the British army's contingent supported by Commonwealth divisions. No RAF fighter squadrons were based in Korea, but the RAF flew transport planes and flying boats and its fighter pilots flew with the United States Air Force and the Royal Australian Air Force. The last British contingent left Korea in July 1957.

British veterans referred to Korea as "the forgotten war". The British public seemed preoccupied with austerity and domestic issues, while in 1950, the Catholic community was busying itself with celebrations commemorating the centenary of the Restoration of the English and Welsh Hierarchy. In Cold War Europe, Communist states threatened western democracies and behind the Iron Curtain the Catholic Church was persecuted mercilessly.

Catholic chaplains in the Korean War

After the Second World War, the number of British military chaplains was drastically reduced, yet in the immediate post-war period British troops were still deployed in India, the Middle East, Palestine, the Mediterranean, Malaya, Kenya, Hong Kong and occupied Germany. Chaplains of all denominations were still required.

At the outbreak of the Korean War, 94 Catholic chaplains were ministering to the British armed services. A Bishop of the Forces had not been appointed to succeed Bishop James Dey (who died in 1946), and Mgr John Clarke of the Archdiocese of Westminster, an experienced Principal Army Chaplain, continued as Apostolic Administrator of the Forces Bishopric. Fourteen of the 15 Royal Navy chaplains were long-serving with one, Mgr Edward Dewey, having entered service in 1921. Thirteen had served in the Second World War. Of the 41 army chaplains and 38 Royal Air Force chaplains, many had substantial wartime experience, whilst some new chaplains had entered on Short Service Commissions.

Among the Second World War chaplains who accompanied British forces to Korea was Fr Joseph Gardner of the Archdiocese of Westminster, who had been commissioned in the RAChD in October 1939. A senior officer wrote of Fr Gardner: "Although he was at all times a military figure, it is for his qualities as a priest that he was esteemed and respected by all." Fr Patrick Tobin of the Diocese of Clifton had served with the Guards Division in North Africa, Sicily, Italy, France and Germany. Fr William Briscoe of the Diocese of Shrewsbury, commissioned in the RAChD in 1942, had served at D-Day and Arnhem before joining the Royal Navy as a chaplain in 1946. Fr Harry Leonard of the Diocese of Paisley, who was commissioned in 1943, had served naval personnel and the Royal Marines. Fr John Ryan of the Diocese of Brentwood had joined the RAChD in 1942, and Fr Robert Woods of the Archdiocese of Glasgow was commissioned in August 1944 and attached to 28th Brigade in Korea.

Fr Louis Madden of the Diocese of Achonry and from Kiltimagh, County Mayo was commissioned in September 1944 and saw action in Italy and Austria. After completing parachute training in England, Fr Madden was posted to Kobe in Japan and then to Korea, attached to 28th Brigade. Korea, he recalled, "was a cold and bloody experience. We lived in holes in the ground. It was bitterly cold and wet, and the landscape was a sea of mud." Yet though the mud made life miserable it had a positive side—"It absorbed some of the impact from the mortar shells." He was wounded when a piece of shrapnel bounced off his chest, but the officer standing next to him was killed in the same explosion. Fr Madden recalled an act of great bravery performed by Sergeant Bill Speakman, attached to the King's Own Scottish Borderers, who was awarded the Victoria Cross for giving cover to his men. Fr Madden spent two years in Korea.

Fr Terence Quinlan of the Diocese of Southwark served as a navy chaplain after being commissioned in 1943 but served with the Territorial Army after the war. He obtained a Short Service Commission in the RAChD on 3 May 1950 and on 19 May was deployed with Far East Land Forces. He disembarked at Pusan on 29 August and remained in Korea until 29 April 1951. He was attached to 27 Brigade, which included 1st Battalion Middlesex Regiment and 1st Battalion Argyll and Sutherland Highlanders. Fr William P. Henry of the Archdiocese of Liverpool, commissioned in November 1942, was Senior Catholic Chaplain RAF in Korea. Fr Frederick Hanson, commissioned in the RAF in 1943, returned to Korea as a Columban missionary in 1950 and remained there throughout the war.

Fr Jim Petry of the Diocese of Southwark was another army padre. Ordained in 1948, Fr Petry subsequently joined the RAChD and served in Wales and Austria before ministering in Korea. From mid-1952, he was chaplain to 1st Battalion Durham Light Infantry and 1st Battalion Royal Fusiliers. After the Armistice had been signed, the Royal Fusiliers were able to relax and shortly afterwards entrained for Pusan. There, in the war cemetery, Regimental Chaplain Revd Freddy Preston and Fr Petry conducted memorial services for their fallen comrades. For gallantry and meritorious service in Korea, Fr Petry was awarded the MBE.

Other padres deployed to Korea were Frs Bernard McKenna of the Archdiocese of Westminster, George Smith and Bernard Boulton of the Archdiocese of Birmingham, Joseph Landregan of the Diocese of Salford, John Conway of the Diocese of Lancaster, and Donald MacMillan of the Diocese of Clifton. Fr Sidney Lescher of the Archdiocese of Liverpool, commissioned in 1939, became Senior Catholic Chaplain to British Forces Korea in July 1953.

Fr John Ryan—army chaplain in Korea

Fr John Ryan was one of many Irish padres in the British army. He trained for the priesthood at St John's Seminary, Wonersh, and was ordained for the Diocese of Brentwood on 11 June 1938. Fr Ryan served as a Territorial Army chaplain from 1938 to 1940, and in November

1942 he was released by Bishop Doubleday to serve as a full-time army chaplain. His first posting was to the 2/6 East Surrey Regiment (7 Infantry Brigade), and in December 1943 he was appointed Divisional Chaplain to HQ 9 Armoured Division. He was stationed at Colchester until June 1944, when he embarked for Normandy and thereafter the campaign in North West Europe. In the immediate post-war period, Fr Ryan took a short-service commission and served with the British Army of the Rhine (BAOR), where his duties included chaplaincy to the BAOR Training Centre and conducting retreats for troops who were now predominantly National Servicemen. He returned to Colchester in 1949. Mgr Clarke described his work as "splendid".

In June 1950, Fr Ryan took a regular commission and was appointed to HQ East Anglian District, Colchester, from where he was deployed to Korea. Bishop Beck, Co-Adjutor Bishop of Brentwood, wrote: "I expect you are delighted to have received your posting instructions for the force which is leaving for Korea." Fr Ryan was appointed chaplain to 29 Independent Brigade and arrived in Korea with Brigade HQ in late October 1950. The Brigade was very large, comprising six (as opposed to the usual three) major units, as well as many smaller support units. A great deal of Fr Ryan's time was spent with Royal Ulster Rifles, as well as the Royal Irish Hussars, Royal Northumberland Fusiliers, the Gloucestershire Regiment and 45 Field Regiment Royal Artillery.

On arrival in Korea Fr Ryan learned from Fr Robert Sherry, Senior United States Army Chaplain, that Pope Pius XII had given all Catholic chaplains in Korea the same faculties and had placed them under the canonical jurisdiction of an American Military Vicar, and so Fr Ryan, a British army chaplain, was now subject to American ecclesiastical supervision and control. United Nations armed forces had earlier been placed under the overall command of the American General Douglas MacArthur.

At first, Fr Ryan was based at Suwon, where he was able to use the damaged mission of the Columban Fathers, the largest Catholic missionary institute in Korea, as a Mass centre, and he positioned himself with 26th Field Ambulance. By November 1950, there had been many British casualties, and a brigade cemetery was established at Kaesong. Fr Ryan had the sad duty of burying many British dead brought in from widely scattered units. By late December 1951, as the UN forces were pushed back south of the 38th Parallel, Fr Ryan again found himself at Kaesong, but he found some comfort in that his units were not as dispersed as they had been. He celebrated Mass in the open, very often in bitterly cold weather but, he recalled, it had many benefits:

> In spite of all the difficulties, the lads are responding magnificently to their religious duties. As I am saying Mass so often in the open, the non-Catholic lads are getting their first sight of the Mass. At the same time the slack ones among the Catholics who are not attending have their consciences pricked.

Fr Ryan continued to give General Absolution and Holy Communion to the Catholics of 29th Brigade and to the Royal Ulster Rifles who had suffered heavy casualties during the fighting around Seoul in January 1951.

Padre Ryan visited the Gloucestershire Regiment on Hill 235 just before the Battle of the Imjin River began on 23 April 1951. The Chinese attacked a widely dispersed 29th Brigade and "the Glorious Glosters", surrounded, outnumbered and cut off, were hit very badly. They suffered many casualties and hundreds, including their Anglican padre, the Revd Samuel Davies, were taken prisoner. In the camp, Davies was harassed, bullied, beaten, brainwashed and humiliated. As an officer, he was prevented from mixing with other ranks and therefore unable to fully practise his ministry.

Another Chinese attack followed on 28 April, and a hole was punched in the central UN line. 28th Brigade was rushed to fill the gap and with them was Fr Louis Madden. 27th Brigade, including Fr Quinlan, was recalled from its planned move to Hong Kong and was also required to fill the gap. By mid-May, UN forces had begun to push the Chinese back north of the 38th Parallel.

On 1 May 1951, Fr Ryan was promoted to the rank of major (Chaplain, 3rd Class) and in July 1951 a Commonwealth Division of British, Australian, Canadian and New Zealand troops was formed and included 29th (British) Brigade. Assisted by Fr Woods, Fr Ryan stayed with the Division, and other Commonwealth Catholic chaplains, under a Canadian Senior Chaplain, ministered alongside them.

Kure

In October 1951, 29th Brigade left Korea and Fr Ryan left at first for the Commonwealth base at Hiro, Japan. In September 1952, he moved to nearby Kure where, as Senior Catholic Chaplain, he did much of his work in the military hospitals with occasional visits to bases in Korea. In March 1953, John Carmel Heenan, Bishop of Leeds, originally a priest of the Diocese of Brentwood and known to Fr Ryan, made a twelve-day visit to British and Commonwealth troops in Korea, Malaya, Hong Kong and Japan. At Kure and elsewhere, in addition to learning of the distressing rates of venereal disease among Commonwealth troops, speaking with men in detention centres, and observing troops in training for action in Korea, he learned that Fr Ryan and other Catholic chaplains were held in high regard for their ministry. The bishop made no observations on either the worth or effectiveness of the chaplains' work but did emphasize that he personally received "an especially enthusiastic reception" by men from Yorkshire regiments and that he addressed Catholic officers and men whenever he could. In speeches redolent of Heenan's mentor, Cardinal Hinsley, the bishop spoke of the Korean War as "a crusade" against Communism and a reaction to "influences that are determined to destroy the Christian way of life".

Bishop Heenan also visited British and Commonwealth chaplains other than those serving with the army. Serving with 41 Royal Marine Commando was Fr Harry Leonard. During the war he had served in HMS *Glory* and then in the Mandated Territory of Palestine after hostilities ended.

Other Catholic chaplains in Korea

In combat or in captivity, British Catholic troops in Korea were so desperately short of chaplains that they were frequently served by American and Commonwealth padres and by missionaries. There were 932 American Catholic priests who served as chaplains. Many Catholics of all nationalities in prisoner of war camps did not see a Catholic chaplain until they were released. In many cases, Catholic soldiers conducted religious services themselves.

Men of the Royal Navy fared little better. In February 1951, Fr Harold Shepherd, of the Diocese of Plymouth and Senior Roman Catholic Chaplain (Royal Navy), lamented to his predecessor Mgr Edward Dewey that there were no ship-based Catholic chaplains in Korea. Fr William Briscoe had earlier ministered to ships in Korean operational waters but had been recalled to Singapore. Catholics on HMS *Belfast* called upon Fr Francis Lyons, chaplain on the Australian aircraft-carrier HMAS *Melbourne*, to celebrate Mass for them. *Belfast*'s Anglican chaplain made all the arrangements. The Royal Marines were served by land-based naval chaplains like Fr Leonard.

Casualties among American Catholic chaplains and European missionaries were high. Six US military chaplains died, three in captivity. Among them was Fr Emil Kapaun with the US 1st Cavalry, who died in Camp 5. Fr Herman Felhoelter, a Franciscan, was the first US chaplain to die in the war, shot as he pleaded for the lives of wounded American servicemen. USAF chaplain Fr William Maher died in a plane crash on his return from service in Korea, while Fr Leo Craig OP was killed by a mine explosion in 1951.

The Irish Columban Fathers, veterans of the Korean mission, also ministered to Allied forces and suffered as a result. Six—Frs Peter Anthony Collier, James Maginn, Patrick Reilly, Patrick Brennan, Thomas Cusack and John O'Brien—were murdered by North Korean forces, while their confrère Fr Francis Canavan died in a Korean prison camp. Frs O'Brien and Brennan had served as British army chaplains in the Second World War. Fr O'Brien, from Claremorris, County Mayo, was a friend of Fr Louis Madden.

American and Canadian prelates visited the war zone. Cardinal Francis Spellman of New York, a former Military Vicar of United States Forces, visited American forces and their chaplains whilst Archbishop Maurice Roy, a former chaplain, Archbishop of Quebec and the Ordinary of Canadian Armed Forces, visited Canadian personnel. Other than Bishop Heenan, no British Catholic prelate visited Korea. When Mgr Clarke, Apostolic Administrator of the British Armed Forces, replied to public concerns about the spiritual welfare of Catholic national servicemen, he pointed out that religious facilities were in place wherever British forces were stationed, but he made no mention of Korea. He added that there was "no alarm", but subsequent comments from former and serving soldiers differed from those of Mgr Clarke, blaming the lack of religious fervour among the troops not on the influence and ministry of serving chaplains but on the absence of chaplains.

Only two British army chaplains, Fr John Conway of the Diocese of Lancaster, and Fr George Smith of the Archdiocese of Birmingham, were ministering to troops in Korea in the immediate post-war period. Their work on the Seoul and Pusan fronts was demanding but rewarding. They said Mass, conducted services, held "padre's hours" and ran catechism classes, but they could not reach all Catholic men. Bishops may have felt that National Service provided opportunities for the Church to contact young Catholic men, but the reality of army life and the lack of chaplains prevented padres and men from fulfilling these expectations, especially in Korea. Yet the two padres reported many conversions and men who for years had not been near a church at home but now regularly practised their faith. The percentage of those attending Mass, both padres reported, was higher than they would expect from an ordinary parish—and the number of communicants was also higher.

Released prisoners of war

At the cessation of hostilities, Allied prisoners of war were released. The war was particularly vicious, and UN prisoners of war suffered grievously at the hands of their North Korean and Chinese captors. The Americans described the Communist mistreatment of prisoners of war and wounded servicemen as constituting "one of the most heinous and barbaric epochs of recorded history". In the House of Commons on 7 April 1955, William Hamilton MP said that "it became apparent, when the main batch of prisoners of war was released from Korea in September 1953, that the men had been subjected to treatment which was unparalleled in our experience".

Freed British prisoners of war, still wearing camp uniforms, were taken to "Freedom Villages" and then to a British camp, where Fr Bernard

Boulton and Fr Jim Petry awaited them. Two altars were erected in a reception centre, and soon after their arrival Catholics were going to confession and receiving Holy Communion. Some of them had not been able to go to Mass or receive the sacraments for over two years. However, religious life had not been extinguished in the camps, despite enemy attempts at brainwashing and confiscation of rosaries and other personal objects of devotion. Catholics and non-Catholics had gathered in the camps for devotions on Sundays, Christmas, Easter and holy days, and religious study groups met frequently. An army psychiatrist said that religious activity was a major factor in preserving the prisoners' mental health.

Fr John Ryan

Fr John Ryan was Mentioned in Despatches for his ministry in Korea and the Far East. He had served longer than any other army chaplain in that theatre of operations. In June 1952, he addressed a memorial service in the Cathedral of the Immaculate Conception, Seoul, where a statue of St Teresa of the Child Jesus was dedicated to the memory of British Catholic servicemen killed in the war. The major cemetery for British war dead was the United Nations Memorial Cemetery in Busan, where more than 800 British servicemen were buried.

Padre Ryan arrived home aboard a troopship in September 1953 and went directly to Ireland for a holiday. On his return to duty, he was attached to Catterick Camp, Yorkshire, where from December 1953 he served as Senior Catholic Chaplain, Northern Command. He had oversight not only of chaplains but also garrison churches, service families and service schools. In October 1955, he became Senior Catholic Chaplain, Eastern Command, at Hounslow, Middlesex. Fr Ryan retired from the army in April 1956 and returned to the Diocese of Brentwood to resume parish work.

Figure 20: Fr William Briscoe RN: Naval chaplain in Korea

2 1

The Cold War: Chaplains with the British Army of the Rhine

British Forces Germany

British Forces Germany (BFG) was the term applied to the British military in Germany following the cessation of hostilities in Europe in 1945. BFG included the British Army of the Rhine (BAOR), British Air Forces of Occupation (BAFO) and units of Royal Navy and Royal Marines.

BAOR's function was to police and administer the British Zone of Occupied West Germany, but after the restoration of civilian government it became the command formation for the British army in Germany. With deteriorating Allied–Soviet relations, BAOR assumed a more defensive role and it became Britain's major contribution to the North Atlantic Treaty Organization. Snape referred to post-war Germany as "the European cockpit of the Cold War and the army's greatest overseas commitment".

In 1945, there were 80,000 soldiers in BAOR, in 1955, there were 77,000, and by 1965, there were 50,000. German reunification in 1990 and the withdrawal of Soviet forces from Eastern and Central Europe lessened the need for a British presence in Germany and in 1994 BAOR and RAF Germany (formed in 1959) reverted to British Forces Germany (BFG). BFG was phased out by 2010. By 2015, only 21,500 British troops remained and the last military base was handed to the Bundeswehr in February 2020.

For over 70 years, thousands of British military personnel and their dependants served and lived in Germany. As Dannatt commented, "a cocoon of Britishness was created".

Chaplains with the BAOR

In 1945, army chaplains remained in Germany to minister to British forces, liberated prisoners of war, inmates of concentration and death camps, and thousands of displaced persons. The Allies were faced with a devastated, dislocated and leaderless Germany and, in the USSR, a wartime partner determined to avenge years of suffering inflicted by the Nazis and intent on extending political control in post-war Europe. BAOR, formed in August 1945 out of 21st Army Group, addressed the restoration of political and social order and civilian life while simultaneously preparing for a further conflict with an erstwhile ally.

The Royal Army Chaplains' Department's (RAChD) participation in the moral reconstruction of Germany went alongside its role in moderating the excesses of war-weary troops ready for demobilization and home. The abolition of compulsory church parades in 1946 broke the traditional link between the army and religion, and the padre's work was further challenged by a post-war generation of National Servicemen with increasingly secular attitudes. However, as BAOR assumed a state of permanence with barracks, homes and hospitals, many service personnel and their families welcomed a support framework in which religion was a vital element. Military provision took precedence, but the material, medical and social requirements of service families were not overlooked. Chaplains of all denominations attended to the religious and educational needs of the British community.

The RAChD undertook the routine administration of army padres, and Catholic Senior Chaplains accepted this arrangement whilst remaining in control of denominational matters. Short Service Commissions alleviated the shortage of chaplains, but the RAChD in BAOR was always understaffed. Britain still had other overseas commitments and Principal Chaplains continually tried to increase the number of chaplains whilst balancing their deployment. Many clergymen took advantage of Short

Service Commissions to serve as chaplains as an alternative to or as deferred National Service. For chaplains who had served during the war or who accepted extended commissions, a posting to BAOR was normal. For chaplains commissioned after the war, a posting to BAOR was almost inevitable.

Post-war Catholic army chaplains with BAOR

Chaplains with the BLA which gave way to BAOR, were ordered to observe a policy of non-fraternization with the defeated Germans. Catholic chaplains in particular were warned about fraternizing with their co-religionists, especially Catholic priests, who were regarded by Allied leaders as Nazi sympathizers. Fr Clifford Howell SJ wrote to Cardinal Griffin to say that what he had heard and seen since the occupation aroused in him "a sense of impending disaster for the Catholic church in Germany".

Jesuit padres Richard Guilly and Maurice Dowling were deputed to liaise with the German Catholic Hierarchy, while Padre Joseph McVeigh and Fr Barnabas Sandeman OSB were appointed to the Religious Affairs Branch of the Control Commission for Germany established to supervise the restoration of normal life, including religious observance. Another Jesuit, Fr Richard Kennedy, wrote in March 1946 from Göttingen: "I am not quite clear what my job will be, but I expect it will be to try to organize Catholic life there."

As 21st Army Group entered Germany in April 1945, 164 Catholic chaplains were deployed with it, many of them experienced and battle-hardened veterans. Among them were Frs Herbert Welchman of the Archdiocese of Westminster, John Ryan of the Diocese of Brentwood, Gerry Malone of the Diocese of Salford, Clifford Howell SJ, Owen Evans of the Diocese of Leeds, Gerard Hiscoe of the Archdiocese of Cardiff, James O'Sullivan of the Australian Diocese of Sandhurst and Lionel Kearns SJ.

In 1946, the establishment for Catholic chaplains with BAOR was 24, but in 1947 this was reduced to 20, causing Senior Chaplain Fr J. O'Carroll "grave concern". Fr Patrick Taggart informed Archbishop

Amigo of Southwark in 1947 that even with an additional 35 chaplains on Short Service Commissions, one chaplain in BAOR was responsible for 1,200 Catholic men and a growing number of dependants, and the areas to be covered were extensive. In 1948, Fr Gordon Dick of the Congregation of the Sacred Heart of Jesus was chaplain during part of the ten-month Soviet Blockade of Berlin from June 1948 until May 1949. Padres of all denominations worked closely to provide continuous church services and pastoral support to service and civilian personnel. Fr Dick was succeeded during the Blockade by Fr Bernard Heseltine of the Diocese of Salford. Both were Second World War veterans.

Regular chaplains usually held positions of responsibility in BAOR. Fr Alfred Blount of the Archdiocese of Westminster joined the RAChD in 1936 and served throughout the war in the Middle East. He served in post-war India and with Middle East Land Forces before being posted to BAOR in 1950 where he was Senior Chaplain until 1953. Mgr Blount became Principal Roman Catholic Chaplain (Army). Fr Peter Brady of the Diocese of Kilmore joined the RAChD in 1942 and was posted as chaplain to BAOR in 1959, and again in 1968 as Senior Chaplain. Fr William Campling of the Archdiocese of Westminster joined the RAChD in 1941. He served with HQ 7th Armoured Division, BAOR from 1954, before deployment to Malaya in 1956.

One post-war padre was Fr Michael Dowling of the Diocese of Leeds. Attached to 33rd Armoured Brigade, he wrote to the Principal of All Hallows College, Dublin, in March 1955. His letter indicates the extent of his travels across West Germany and the nature of his work among conscript servicemen:

> Greetings . . . from the Fatherland.
>
> I am stationed at a spot outside . . . Paderborn. I cover four garrison towns, Paderborn, Detmold, Lippstadt, and Lemgo. With three Masses every Sunday: 9.30, 11.15 and 17.00 hours I do about 120 miles. With such a vast area I sometimes feel like wearing a mitre. As regards the work, it's exactly the same as a priest's work anywhere. Firstly, his Mass, then his visitation of the flock. There is a good opportunity in the Army to get men to

make a new act of the will, as it were, regarding the Sacraments and the Church.

Some of the lads give up when they leave school, but I find that those who give up never really got a chance to know God and particularly to know and love the Mass. Some bitterly complained to me about their being punished on Monday morning at school for missing Mass—that still goes on! Others are victims of the mixed marriage and so on, but all of them are good, really good at heart. I go from regiment to regiment during the week, say Mass in the morning for them, then interview them individually during the day, and hear confessions. The grace of God will do all the work for the priest. I find those lads who were educated in India have a great grasp of the Faith. As far as I can gather the Jesuit Colleges are very strong there.

Fr Dowling had joined the RAChD in 1954 and served with BAOR until his accidental death in October 1957 when he was Garrison Chaplain, Münster.

In the 1950s, the Catholic press in England aired concerns about the moral dangers facing conscript Catholic youth in BAOR. To many correspondents, the faith of Catholic soldiers suffered as church parades were abandoned and temptations were plentiful. Padres were well aware of the situation and a visit to the Communist and God-less East Berlin was evidence of an even worse moral climate. Chaplains worked hard through retreats and counselling sessions to counteract the effects of atheistic Communism. There were two Catholic army retreat houses, supported by the army, and chaplains conducted retreats and moral leadership courses. Between 1948 and 1950, there were 72 religious courses provided at the retreat centre at Bielefeld attended by 2,016 officers and men.

The number of Catholic military families increased considerably. In 1956, Fr Gerard Hiscoe reported that in the Osnabrück Garrison there were 100 Catholic families and 250 children. In addition to his work with Catholic soldiers through retreats, services and Padre's Hours, he was also responsible for the education and sacramental preparation of children, for instructing converts and for visiting families. Much pastoral work, he reported, was undertaken "outside recognized office hours".

Some BAOR padres had already completed National Service before their ordination. Fr Hugh Beattie of the Archdiocese of Glasgow was a National Serviceman from 1946 to 1948, trained for the priesthood, and joined the RAChD in 1961. He completed parachute and jungle warfare training before subsequently being deployed to Borneo, Cyprus, Aden and Bahrain. From 1968 to 1971, he was Senior Chaplain in Northern Ireland and in 1980 was appointed Senior Catholic Chaplain at BAOR Headquarters, Rheindahlen. Fr Bernard Funnell of the Diocese of Leeds had actually served as a National Serviceman in BAOR before training for the priesthood and joining the RAChD in 1975. Fr John Ward of the Archdiocese of Glasgow served as a medical orderly in Kenya during his National Service and, after being commissioned into the RAChD in 1976, he served almost continuously with armoured units in BAOR until 1984. He returned to BAOR in 1986 attached to HQ 11th Armoured Brigade.

The Cold War: Facing the Soviet threat

Major features of BAOR were its geographical size, the disposition of its units and the ever-present Russian military threat. BAOR had to be vigilant of an attack by Warsaw Pact forces from the east and, after the Blockade of 1948, watchful of the special status of a divided Berlin. Army chaplains carried out their ministry against this background.

In 1964, Fr Michael Holman of the Archdiocese of Westminster celebrated Mass at three centres in Germany 40 miles apart every Sunday in a "parish" of 16,000 square miles. He had joined the RAChD from a small parish in Islington and before studying for the priesthood had served two years in the Royal Navy.

Fr Larry Cosgrove of the Diocese of Lancaster had served as a chaplain with the Territorial Army before joining the RAChD in 1961. His tours of duty in Germany included attachments with the BAOR All Arms Training Centre from 1961 to 1963; with 16th Signals Regiment at Krefeld from 1965 to 1966; with Headquarters Infantry Brigade, Berlin, from 1967 to 1969; with HQ 20th Armoured Brigade and HQ 1st Division from

1971 to 1974; and finally in 1979 as Senior Chaplain at Headquarters, Rheindahlen. Interspersed with Fr Cosgrove's BAOR service were tours in the Persian Gulf, Borneo, Scotland, Singapore and Northern Ireland.

Fr Tom Bradley of the Archdiocese of Liverpool joined the RAChD in April 1966 and completed three tours of Germany. From 1966 to 1970, he was based with 12th Infantry Brigade in Osnabrück; from 1971 until 1973 he was based with 20th Armoured Brigade in Sennelager; and finally, he served at Minden as Senior Catholic Chaplain with 4th Armoured Division. In between these tours were postings to Singapore, the Royal Military Academy Sandhurst and Northern Ireland. For his exceptional qualities as a chaplain and his untiring service in Osnabrück, he was awarded the MBE in June 1970. In January 1980, Fr Bradley was killed near El Alamein in an accident unrelated to the military. He was buried next to Fr Gerry Weston, another army chaplain from the Archdiocese of Liverpool, who had been murdered eight years earlier by the IRA. Fr Weston had also served in BAOR.

Later BAOR padres

Fr Alf Hayes of the Diocese of Lancaster was commissioned into the RAChD on 5 September 1980. In addition to postings in Northern Ireland, Hong Kong, Home Commands and service in the Falklands War, Fr Hayes undertook six tours of duty in Germany. His first posting in 1980 was to Hohne with 1st Armoured Division, where he took over from Fr Gerry Cudmore, an Australian chaplain.

From Hohne, Fr Hayes covered Celle, Wolfenbüttel (in Lower Saxony near the East German border) and Hildesheim. Wolfenbüttel was a two-hour journey across country and Fr Hayes would leave Hohne at 14.00 on a Saturday, celebrate Mass in Wolfenbüttel for about eight people, then drive for another hour to Hildesheim for Mass at 18.00, again for about eight people, and arrive back in Hohne about 21.00. It was a long day and particularly hazardous in winter weather. Celle was approximately 20 miles away, and on Sundays Fr Hayes celebrated Mass there at 09.00 and at 11.00 in Hohne.

As always seemed to be the case, a major problem was the shortage of Catholic chaplains. There were only 14 Catholic chaplains for the whole of BAOR, which included four Armoured Divisions (125,000 personnel), wives and children, schools and other support services. Three Catholic padres were with 1st Armoured Division: Fr Adrian Poole of the Diocese of Middlesbrough was based at Divisional HQ, Verden, Fr Michael Jones of the Archdiocese of Liverpool was with 7th Armoured Brigade at Fallingbostel, and Fr Hayes with 22nd Armoured Brigade. They had care of twelve garrisons and stations, making it very difficult for them to provide adequate cover. Catholic chaplains with other Divisions had similar areas to cover. Fr Tony Paris, of the Archdiocese of Westminster and commissioned in 1988, was posted with HQ 22 Armoured Brigade in 1990, and the area he covered included Hohne, Celle, Hanover, Wolfenbüttel, Dannenberg and Helmstedt.

In 1980, there were 32 Catholic chaplains for the British army worldwide, while the non-Catholic Branch of the RAChD had approximately 180. Because of small Catholic numbers, Catholic padres were always attached to a Headquarters formation, be it Brigade, Division or District, unlike non-Catholic padres who always started their careers as Regimental padres. The nearest Fr Hayes got to being a Regimental chaplain was when he was with the Irish Guards in Münster. Although he was Brigade Chaplain, responsible for covering six major units and two logistics outposts, "the Micks" claimed Fr Hayes as their own.

A peculiarity of the Catholic chain of command within the RAChD was that in practice one did not exist. The Principal Roman Catholic Chaplain in London tended to fill gaps with whoever was available, and wherever the station, regardless of rank. Although posted to an HQ Formation, Catholic chaplains were sent to live in the garrison or station with the biggest population. On one occasion, a Catholic chaplain CF, 4th Class (Captain) acted as Senior Divisional Chaplain with a chaplain CF, 2nd Class (Lieutenant-Colonel) in one of his garrisons—a situation incomprehensible to non-Catholic chaplains.

Fr Hayes adapted to his ministry in an unfamiliar culture and in a military environment. Having worked in a parish for eight years and as a hospital chaplain for four years, Fr Hayes took that civilian-parish model with him when he joined the army. In the army, however, there were no parishes in the civilian sense and the provision of religious education was particularly difficult. All schools were secular, and Catholic children were taught religious education by padres, Officiating Chaplains, female religious and lay catechists. The population was essentially transient: the make-up of the congregation constantly changed and sometimes this could be quite dramatic. If a whole regiment was posted, a padre would lose most of his congregation, whom he had just got to know, and the following week a whole new set of faces from a new regiment would appear. Chaplains were also frequently posted with the result that "parish" programmes sometimes came to an abrupt end when the padre moved.

The prime function of the BAOR was to prevent an incursion by Soviet Bloc forces and British and Allied forces constantly trained for war. This demanded large-scale exercises, frequently involving a whole Division, with men and padres away from garrisons or stations for considerable periods. Exercises clearly illustrated the primacy of military considerations and padres experienced problems of transport, communications and support. They were not provided with cars, telephone and mail links were haphazard, and it was virtually impossible to contact other padres. Carrying only his basic kit, the padre prayed for and with soldiers and offered Mass when and where possible. When troops were on exercise, the church transport from the outlying quartering areas would not function properly, which meant that wives and families often could not attend Mass.

Initially, Fr Hayes, like many chaplains before him, found his ministry in Germany to be frustrating—hours of driving with very little to show for it. Eventually, it struck him that army chaplaincy was a ministry of sowing seeds. In 1998, as he was about to retire from the army, he wrote:

> Rarely would you expect to see the results of your own sowing, but you would often pick up the results of the work of fellow chaplains who had gone before you. In Münster, over two years, I received twelve soldiers into the Church, more than I'd ever received in civilian life in a similar period. Clearly those men's faith had been stimulated and nourished along the way, and I

happened to be the priest in the right place at the right time to
reap the harvest as it came to maturity.

Fr Hayes' first tour of duty in Germany was in a divided country
threatened by a hostile power. His last tour was conducted in a unified
Germany, a situation that had last occurred before the end of the war
in 1945.

BAOR: Final days and drawdown

Commissioned into the RAChD in 2002, Fr Alex Strachan of the
Archdiocese of Glasgow was one of the last Catholic chaplains posted to
BFG. He was with 4th Armoured Brigade in Osnabrück until 2004 and his
routine included celebrating Mass at St Edmund's Church within Brigade
Headquarters Camp; at St Barbara's, the parish church of Osnabrück;
in the small chapel at Oxford Barracks, Münster; and later at Detmold
Garrison and Sennelager. He recalled that there was no great hunger
for religion but no hard opposition either. While the military side of his
ministry included strenuous training exercises, there were times when
Catholic families required his presence and that of the female religious
attached to the schools and parishes.

Fr Ian Evans, of the Archdiocese of Dublin and commissioned into
the RAChD in 1993, was serving as Assistant Chaplain-General, Home
Command, with the rank of colonel (CF, 1st Class) when he retired from
the army in February 2017. In August of that year, while on the Reserve
List, he was recalled and posted to Germany as the last Senior Catholic
Chaplain with BFG and assumed responsibility for the dismantling of
the Catholic chaplaincy infrastructure.

At the height of BAOR's existence, there were Catholic garrison
churches and Mass centres in Hanover, Dortmund, Hohne, Detmold,
Münster, Osnabrück, Rheindahlen, Sennelager, Gütersloh and Bielefeld.
For decades, they were the centres of Catholic life for the military and
their families but the accelerated British drawdown from Germany in
the early years of the twenty-first century presented the Bishopric of the
Forces with the immediate problem of the future use of churches, their

furniture and fittings. Under Fr Evans' direction, Catholic churches in BFG were closed and vestments, plate and furniture were transferred to Catholic communities in Germany, Fiji and Ukraine.

In 2017, there were five churches, including two Mass centres, and a garrison church at Sennelager. In 2018, only two churches remained, St Peter's in Paderborn and Our Lady of Lourdes in Sennelager, providing accommodation for military worshippers of all Christian denominations. On 8 March 2019, Bishop Paul Mason, Bishop of the Forces, celebrated the final Mass at Our Lady of Lourdes.

Over 300 Catholic army padres served with BAOR. Some were with British forces entering defeated Germany in 1945, others ministered in an occupied and divided Germany, whilst a minority served within a reunified Germany.

Figure 21: BAOR chaplains 1996 (left to right: The Revds Fava, O'Keeffe, Rowland, Hernandez, Cummings, Vasey, Alker, Campbell, Barber, Kelly, Gosnell, Butler, Makings) (Mgr Phelim Rowland)

"We always have to carry arms when travelling": Chaplains in Malaya and Borneo

The Malayan Emergency

The Malayan Emergency was an anti-colonial, nationalist guerrilla war fought from 1948 to 1960 between British and Commonwealth forces and the Malayan Races Liberation Army (MRLA), the military wing of the Malayan Communist Party. The MRLA referred to the conflict as the "Anti-British National Liberation War".

The British declared a state of emergency in Malaya in June 1948. Internment, curfews and movement restrictions were imposed. From jungle bases, MRLA insurgents ("bandits" to the British) conducted campaigns of intimidation, raided police and military installations, and sabotaged tin mines and rubber plantations. Many MRLA fighters were former members of the Malayan People's Anti-Japanese Army, who had been trained and funded by the British to fight against the Japanese during the Second World War. Support for the Communists came mainly from the Malayan–Chinese population, most of whom lived in poverty, were subject to racial persecution and were barred from voting in elections. The MRLA failed to gain any substantial support from other sections of the Malaysian population.

In 1948, the 12,000-strong British garrison in Malaya and Singapore, part of Far East Land Forces Command (FARELF), consisted of British, Gurkha and Malay battalions. By 1956, there were 31,400 British and Commonwealth troops in Malaya, including British conscripted National Servicemen and volunteer servicewomen. The jungle campaign in which they fought involved being ambushed, avoiding land mines, wading through swamps, struggling through dense jungle, and fighting off insects and bloodsucking leeches. The Royal Air Force, operating out of RAF Tengah and RAF Butterworth, found that conventional bombing was largely ineffective against jungle-based insurgents and aerial support was largely limited to dropping supplies. Thirty-six thousand troops were carried by helicopters of the Royal Naval Air Squadron. Veterans of the Burma campaign described conditions in Malaya as worse than those they had experienced with Slim's "Forgotten" Fourteenth Army during the Second World War. The British raised local Malay auxiliary forces, developed rapid response units and supported civil attempts "to win hearts and minds" through a policy of detaching insurgents from their Chinese supporters by rehousing them in purpose-built "new villages". "Voice Aircraft" broadcast assurances to the Communist insurgents that they would not be ill-treated if they surrendered.

In August 1957, the Federation of Malaya was granted independence, but the Emergency continued until 1960. By 1959, it was possible to move around most of Malaya unarmed and unescorted, for while the word "Emergency" was still used, it no longer affected the lives of most Malays. Units were still operating in the jungle and chaplains were with them, but garrison life assumed greater importance with the cessation of active service conditions.

During the conflict, 519 British and Commonwealth soldiers and 1,300 police were killed, including RAF padre the Revd Alec Ross. Some were buried in Malaya; the ashes of others were repatriated. Communist losses were over 5,000 killed and 1,200 captured. As ever in war, acts of brutality, terror and wanton destruction were committed by both sides.

Army chaplains in Malaya

In the immediate post-war period, the British army was engaged in Germany, India, the Middle East, the Mediterranean, East and West Africa, and the Far East. In 1952, the greatest need for chaplains was in the Far East, where over 60,000 men were serving in the Korean War and the Malayan Emergency.

The Chaplain-General reported that conditions for troops in Malaya were harder than in Korea and complained that one chaplain attached to two infantry battalions could not conduct an adequate ministry to patrols deployed over hundreds of miles of hostile jungle. To get to know their men and minister to them, chaplains had to accompany patrols, visit isolated units and endure the stresses and strains of guerrilla tactics, the climate and jungle conditions. "Chaplains who are serving in the operational units", recorded the *Royal Army Chaplains' Department Journal* in 1955, "find that apart from the Communist Terrorists there are two other great enemies—the distance between Companies (the average battalion Chaplain travels 1,700 miles per month) and the tropical rain". D. W. Lewis recalled that a service on patrol was "a jungle rendezvous with God".

"The provision of more chaplains for Malaya", the Chaplain-General reported, "was a matter of the utmost urgency". The geographical extent of FARELF, over 1,500 miles from Hong Kong to Singapore, mitigated against the ease of supervision of chaplains whilst the army's other commitments made their replacement difficult.

Catholic army chaplains in Malaya

In 1948, there were 18 permanently commissioned Catholic army chaplains. Many were veterans of the Second World War. The Senior Roman Catholic Chaplain in FARELF in mid-1948 was Fr Eddie Stevens. Ordained for the Diocese of Portsmouth, Fr Stevens was commissioned into the RAChD on 4 September 1939 and served with the British Expeditionary Force (BEF) in France, the Tenth Army in the Middle East and the Eighth Army in North Africa. He landed in Normandy on D-Day and at the end of the war was stationed in Palestine. After the war, he returned to Southern Command, but in July 1948 he was posted to General Headquarters, FARELF, in Singapore. His subsequent deployments were to regions where geopolitical tensions had arisen out of the Second World War or where anti-colonial movements were gathering momentum. In 1960, Fr Stevens became Principal Roman Catholic Chaplain (Army).

Senior Roman Catholic Chaplains with FARELF were based in Hong Kong and Singapore. Fr Christopher McKenna of the Archdiocese of Westminster joined the Chaplains' Department in September 1939, served with the BEF in France, with Middle East Land Forces, with the British Army of the Rhine (BAOR) and was posted as Senior Roman Catholic Chaplain FARELF at Singapore from November 1953 until September 1956. Fr William Campling, also of the Archdiocese of Westminster, had been commissioned into the RAChD in 1941 and had served in the Middle East, Gibraltar and post-war Germany. He served in Malaya from 1950 until 1952 and then as Senior Roman Catholic Chaplain from 1956 to 1959. Fr Edward Ord of the Diocese of Hexham and Newcastle was commissioned into the RAChD in 1939 and had served in Italy and the Mediterranean before being deployed to Malaya from 1949 to 1952. He returned to Malaya as Senior Roman Catholic Chaplain in 1959 for a three-year posting. Fr Joseph Gardner of the Archdiocese of Westminster entered the RAChD in October 1939 and served in France, the Middle East and the Far East, after which he was appointed Senior Roman Catholic Chaplain in Hong Kong. Fr Patrick Tobin, of the Diocese of Clifton and a chaplain since 1940, had been with the British Liberation Army in Europe after D-Day. He was Senior Catholic Chaplain FARELF in 1958.

Catholic chaplains deployed to Malaya included Fr John Cairns of the Diocese of Leeds who was also a veteran of the Second World War. He arrived in Singapore with 2nd Battalion Coldstream Guards in October 1948 and served with the Guards Division in FARELF until September 1950. Fr Peter Brady of the Diocese of Kilmore was commissioned in 1942 and was twice Mentioned in Despatches in India and Burma during the Second World War. He arrived in Singapore in December 1948 attached to 48 Gurkha Infantry Brigade. Fr Brady stayed in Malaya until early 1952. In June 1952, Fr Anthony Antrobus of the Archdiocese of Liverpool, who had been commissioned in 1941, wrote from Malaya:

> The situation here is not good. There is no panic, but communism has blossomed overnight for everyone to see . . . there are plenty of murders in Perak and Johore but action is being taken.

He feared that strikes and attacks on the mines and plantations would cause economic and social chaos.

Fr Jimmy O'Sullivan, born in County Cork and ordained in 1941 for the Diocese of Sandhurst, Australia, joined the RAChD in 1942 and served in the Normandy landings and in post-war Germany. In 1952, he was posted to Malaya and served there until 1954 and was Mentioned in Despatches. Fr O'Sullivan was later appointed Principal Roman Catholic Chaplain (Army) in 1969. Fr Thomas Fehily of the Diocese of Motherwell was commissioned into the RAChD on 26 February 1953. After serving with BAOR, Fr Fehily served with FARELF from May 1956 until July 1959. He became Principal Roman Catholic Chaplain (Army) in 1973.

Fr Donald MacMillan of the Diocese of Clifton was commissioned into the RAChD in 1951. He was immediately posted to FARELF, served in Korea and completed his parachute training at Singapore in 1953. He served in the Emergency and became Principal Roman Catholic Chaplain (Army) in 1977. Fr Peter Flavin of the Diocese of Southwark served with BAOR before being posted to FARELF, where he served from June 1955 until November 1957. Fr Anthony Cluderay of the Diocese of Leeds had served with BAOR but was deployed to Malaya between November 1955 and October 1958. Fr George Smith of the Archdiocese of Birmingham and Fr Joseph Landregan of the Diocese of Salford also served in Malaya, while Fr Joseph Hughes, a Mill Hill Missionary, was deployed from the Suez Canal zone to the Engineer Training Centre, Kluang Garrison (north of Singapore in the state of Johore) where, from 1955 to 1958, he ministered to Rhodesian and East African troops.

Chaplains on operations

In January 1951, Fr Eddie Stevens wrote to the Principal of All Hallows College, Dublin, giving a detailed description of his extensive and frequently dangerous Malayan ministry. Like chaplains of other denominations, he made his way through jungle in oppressive heat and in range of a vicious enemy. His report encapsulates the chaplain's role and refers to the (unusual for chaplains) bearing of arms:

As no doubt you have seen in the papers, we have been having a lot of trouble out here. Our troops are now scattered all over Malaya, which (apart from the rubber estates and tin mines) is mostly very dense jungle. The communists have their camps in the jungle all over the country, and they have been doing a lot of damage. One is not permitted now to travel by road over most of Malaya. One goes by train and the train is preceded by a pilot train, which has an armoured carriage, and is always heavily guarded, because bridges have been blown up and lines tampered with. We have always to carry arms when travelling.

Malaya is about 900 miles long from one extremity to the other. I have only four chaplains to cover this huge area—with troops scattered everywhere. We still have Hong Kong and Ceylon, but, unfortunately, I no longer have chaplains to look after these places. The Irish Jesuits in Hong Kong are wonderful and most helpful.

In addition to all this "diocese", I run a considerable "parish" in Singapore and have many units to look after, hospital work, families, etc. In fact, I have rarely a spare moment. I am due home in July at the end of my three-year tour out here and I shall not be sorry to leave the tropics for a while.

His responsibilities included supervising chaplains in Malaya, Hong Kong and Ceylon, and this involved travelling either by air or by courtesy of the Royal Navy; when in navy ships he also acted as chaplain. Within the population of Malaya there were many Malay Catholics and also Catholics in the European and Eurasian communities. As in Hong Kong and Ceylon, there was a shortage of adequate church buildings, and much of the chaplain's time when not on operations with the troops was devoted to improving facilities for worship. Fr Stevens reported: "I rarely get a minute to myself."

Four Catholic chaplains were honoured for their ministry during the Emergency. Fr Peter Brady had served in Malaya since December 1948. His "parish" included a large part of the central Malay Peninsula, and his routine involved seeking out and bringing the sacraments to isolated units and detachments. He did this largely alone and with total disregard for his own personal safety. He was awarded the MBE, as his obituary stated, "for his exceptional ministry during the dangerous days of the Communist uprising".

Fr Thomas Berry of the Diocese of Paisley was ordained in 1945 and served in Malaya from September 1951 until 1953. Initially he ministered to Catholics of the Blues and Royals, the Cameronians, 13/18 Hussars and Royal Electrical and Mechanical Engineers (REME) at the Kluang garrison, where he organized the building of a Catholic church. His ministry consisted of base work with the Red Cross and soldiers and their families, and establishing places for worship and recreation. It also included a particularly active programme of visiting isolated units who were fighting bandits in the jungle. Later in the tour, he attended to the spiritual needs of men of the Royal Lancers, the Manchester Regiment and the West Yorkshire Regiment in the highlands of northern Malaya. The area he covered was very extensive and by bringing the sacraments to the troops, and by his presence, he sustained and raised the morale of all men and not only Catholics. For his endeavours, he "was universally respected", and the citation for his MBE read: "As a military chaplain in Malaya he travelled alone through bandit-infested territory, bringing to outlying camps the consolations of his religion to his own flock and his friendly charm and sympathy to solders of all denominations." He performed his duties, the citation continued, "with courage, zeal and enthusiasm".

The ministry of Fr Christopher McKenna, Senior Roman Catholic Chaplain FARELF from November 1953 until September 1956, was notable for a different but equally necessary dimension of the chaplain's ministry to soldiers and their dependants. In addition to undertaking chaplaincy duties with men on active operations in the jungle, Fr McKenna sought to improve facilities for worship and leisure in base areas. Above all, stated the citation for his OBE, he "was tireless in his devotion to the spiritual well-being of the Roman Catholics in his command". Mass attendance in the headquarters garrison increased, and Fr McKenna generated a spirit of devotion among men and their families. He initiated retreat programmes and developed links with local religious communities. His efforts included the building or refurbishing of garrison churches in Hong Kong, Singapore and Tanglin.

Fr William Campling, a Mill Hill Missionary who served two tours of duty in Malaya, the second as Senior Roman Catholic Chaplain, was described as "an officer of exceptional quality". He served when the Emergency was at its height and ministered to men on active service in the jungle. In his ministry to 17th Gurkha Division and other units, his devotion to meeting their spiritual needs, his outstanding zeal and overwhelming enthusiasm won the respect of many. His attention to the welfare of his men, it was noted, had a "marked effect on morale". His "parish" was widespread, and he frequently visited isolated detachments of troops in the jungle and also ministered to "the civilized centres" of large garrisons. His work involved travelling across difficult and dangerous terrain, but it was recorded that no matter what the circumstances or how difficult or arduous the conditions, Fr Campling displayed a cheerful spirit and an indomitable determination to serve all creeds and all races. The shortage of chaplains and the nature and extent of his work compelled him to agree with the complaint of the Chaplain-General, who wrote of the concerns felt by the RAChD with FARELF. Chaplains were understaffed, overworked, ministering in very difficult conditions, and morale was low. But they had to conceal these feelings in their attempts to fulfil their ministry. In September 1958, Fr Campling was honoured with the MBE for his service in Malaya between April 1956 and May 1958. The award was deserved, the citation stated, for an "outstanding contribution" that was "worthy of recognition". Another chaplain whose contribution was acknowledged was Fr Peter Flavin, who was Mentioned in Despatches in 1957.

Catholic Royal Navy and RAF chaplains

Although the brunt of the fighting in Malaya was borne by the army, the RAF, Royal Navy and Royal Marines played significant roles. The Royal Navy transported troops to the Far East and also supported land forces in Malaya. Catholic chaplains were not always available to sailors at sea, but Fr Harry Leonard of the Archdiocese of Glasgow, who had joined the Royal Navy in 1943, served in ships deployed to Malaya and Korea. Fr Leonard was awarded the OBE in January 1962. Fr Vaughan Morgan of the Archdiocese of St Andrews and Edinburgh was commissioned in 1962, served as chaplain in the aircraft carrier HMS *Ark Royal*, and was awarded the Malaysia Campaign medal. In 1956, Fr Frederick Hemus, of the Archdiocese of Westminster and commissioned in 1944, was chaplain to HMNB *Singapore*.

The RAF provided air support. Resupply increased the effectiveness of patrols; knowledge that casualties could be lifted out by a helicopter raised morale; and air strikes were extremely effective. RAF Catholic chaplains included Fr James McKeown of the Diocese of Ardagh who was commissioned in 1941. Fr Michael O'Brien of the Diocese of Clifton was also commissioned in 1941 and was Assistant Principal Chaplain on Singapore. Fr Gerry Monaghan, a Marist Father, commissioned in 1950, was based at RAF Changi, and Fr Kevin Mulhearn of the Archdiocese of Liverpool, commissioned in 1961, was awarded the Malaysia medal.

The Borneo Confrontation

In 1962, northern Borneo consisted of the British protectorate of Brunei and the colonies of Sarawak and North Borneo (Sabah). The rest of the island was made up of the Indonesian province of Kalimantan. Britain hoped to incorporate Brunei, Sarawak and North Borneo into the Federation of Malaysia, along with Singapore and the states of the Malayan Peninsula. President Sukarno of Indonesia, however, averse to British influence in the region, planned to extend Indonesian control on the island by adding Brunei, Sarawak and North Borneo to the rest of Kalimantan.

The "Confrontation" lasted from 1963 until 1966 while British and Commonwealth forces fought to secure the future of Brunei and North Borneo against a background of military incident and political uncertainty. It was the first time the army had deployed operationally since the end of National Service, but there were experienced commanders and soldiers from the Second World War, Korea, Burma and Malaya. Gurkhas were airlifted from Singapore and were joined by the Queen's Own Highlanders and 42 Royal Marine Commando. Eventually, 13 battalions of infantry, SAS units and support services served in Borneo. The conflict, consisting mainly of clashes in the jungle border areas, ended in victory for Britain and Commonwealth allies. The confrontation claimed the lives of 114 Commonwealth military personnel and 180 were wounded.

Catholic chaplains in Borneo

In 1964, Fr Lawrence Cosgrove of the Diocese of Lancaster was attached to 1st Battalion Royal Ulster Rifles in Sarawak. His "parish" extended 80,000 square miles and included leech-infested swamps, mosquito-ridden jungle and razor-backed mountains. He ministered to soldiers guarding a 1,000-mile-long jungle "border" to prevent incursions by terrorists in Brunei, Sarawak and Sabah.

Most of his time was spent travelling along earth roads or by RAF helicopters swooping low through jungle valleys near the border to avoid possible anti-aircraft fire from the Indonesian side. Occasionally, he travelled by boat on fast-flowing jungle rivers or slogged on foot through the steamy atmosphere of Borneo's rainforest. He said Mass in tents in jungle clearings or in the comparative safety of a wooden hut or a flimsy corrugated structure. In the jungle, Mass was said against a sandbagged defensive position, and he would talk with men in secluded corners and hear their confessions. As Fr Cosgrove said, "When a man spends weeks at a time on the border, he needs someone with whom he can discuss his personal problems."

Fr Hugh Beattie of the Diocese of Motherwell was padre to 3,000 men of 16th Parachute Brigade. Ordained in 1955 and commissioned in 1961, the diminutive Fr Beattie was regarded as a brave and resourceful padre. He had completed his National Service with the Royal Artillery and the Highland Light Infantry and was familiar with army ways. On many occasions, he would act as unofficial barber and thus engage with men back from jungle patrol. He would talk to the soldiers in front of him "about religion or anything else you cared to suggest", an Anglican chaplain recalled.

Other padres who served in Borneo were Fr John Kennedy of the Diocese of Hexham and Newcastle and Fr Desmond Swan of the Archdiocese of Westminster. Fr Swan entered the RAChD in 1961 and had served in Germany, Singapore and Hong Kong. From Kuching, Sarawak, "the Flying Padre" often covered a thousand miles a week in a helicopter to reach men on the border. Troops gathered round the padre for Mass, and the war, the jungle and insects were briefly forgotten. Services were held in huts, a table was an altar, and even in those primitive conditions, men would sit and think and pray.

Figure 22: Fr James O'Sullivan CF: Chaplain in Malaya

2 3

Colonial campaigns and strategic commitments: Chaplains in emergencies and counter-insurgencies

Palestine

The British Balfour Declaration of 1917 pledged that part of Palestine would become a "Jewish Homeland" and in 1922 a League of Nations mandate placed Palestine under British administration. As clandestine Jewish immigration into Palestine increased, friction between Arabs and Jews culminated in the Arab Revolt of 1936–39. During the Second World War, Britain restricted Jews entering Palestine and continued this policy until Britain's mandate ended in 1948. The Royal Navy's Palestine Patrol intercepted illegal Jewish immigrants, especially survivors of the Nazi Holocaust, entering by sea.

Britain's policy provoked armed Jewish resistance from Haganah, the main Zionist terrorist group, combined with Irgun Zvai Le'umi (National Military Organization) and Lohamey Heruth Israel (Fighters for the Freedom of Israel or Stern Gang). There followed bitter warfare between Jewish guerrillas, British security forces and the Arabs. In November 1947, the United Nations recommended the partition of Palestine into separate Arab and Jewish states.

From 1945 until 1948, 100,000 British troops were deployed to Palestine. Seven hundred and eighty-four British soldiers and civilians were killed in the conflict.

Catholic military chaplains in Palestine

Fr Michael Devlin OMI had served in the Middle East since 1944 and was Senior Catholic Army Chaplain in Palestine until 1947. Three chaplains were with 6th Airborne Division, six with 1st and 3rd Divisions, one was at Haifa and one at Sarafand. Fr Austin Treamer RAF, an Assumptionist, ministered in Jerusalem, while Fr John Burden SJ was at Jaffa. Fr Eddie Stevens and Fr Oswald Earle SJ RAF were deployed to Palestine at the end of the war. In 1946, Fr Joseph Murphy, an Irish Redemptorist with HQ 1st Guards Brigade, Nazareth, served dispersed detachments of the Coldstream Guards, Welsh Guards, King's Dragoon Guards and 4/7 Dragoon Guards.

According to Fr Earle, the religious significance that the country had for him and many Catholics aroused no interest in the majority of men, and their indifference was compounded by the political situation and by terrorist attacks. However, one commander cited visits to holy places organized by chaplains as "bright spots in the sombre life of the soldier", and these were "always most popular" with the troops. Whether the reasons for such popularity were religious or secular was not stated. Fr Earle was ambushed near Mount Carmel but escaped uninjured. It was difficult for him to establish any kind of routine and, with the exception of Acre, which had "an excellent Catholic congregation", it was virtually impossible for him to visit outlying installations.

Fr Devlin's *War Diary* recorded "nothing to report" between January and May 1946, but on 22 July a terrorist bomb exploded at the King David Hotel, Jerusalem, with horrific casualties. Fr Fergus Cronin SJ, in Haifa waiting for his release papers, wrote: "At present Palestine is like an armed camp, but with differences; for though all officers must go about in pairs, because of kidnapping, ordinary soldiers can go about unarmed." There was "an atmosphere of uneasiness everywhere", and he could not go to the top of Mount Carmel to say Mass but had to say it in his tent.

Fr Stanislaus Savage of the Archdiocese of Westminster had served in Italy and was with the post-war Central Mediterranean Force. On Sunday, 22 February 1948, he became a casualty in the Old City of Jerusalem. On his way to say Mass at the headquarters of 1st Highland Light Infantry, his jeep was stopped by Haganah terrorists, and a young

Jewish man opened fire on them. The driver was killed and the padre was wounded in the arm. Fr Savage lay as if dead and, after the attacker had fired more shots into the body of the driver, British troops were quickly on the scene. Fr Savage was treated in hospital and was soon back on duty. The HLI lost ten soldiers in the emergency and was the last unit to leave Jerusalem in July 1948.

Serving with the Royal Marines was Fr Harry Leonard of the Archdiocese of Glasgow. During the war he had served in HMS *Glory* and also in Palestine. He was the last chaplain to leave Palestine in 1948.

Catholic military chaplains in the Middle East

Between 1948 and 1956, over 70,000 British troops were stationed in the Middle East, Libya, Egypt and the Suez Canal Zone. Over 400 British service personnel died in the Middle East between 1950 and 1956, and 54 British troops were killed during operations in Egypt.

In 1947, there were six Catholic army chaplains in the Canal Zone, one in Tripolitania and one in Cyrenaica. Troops were scattered, communications were poor and there were no local churches or clergy. In 1954, when Principal Army Chaplain Mgr Alfred Blount toured the Middle East, he was met in Tripoli by Fr Patrick Thompson of the Archdiocese of Westminster, and at Benghazi by Senior Chaplain Fr Michael Murphy of the Archdiocese of Birmingham, both Second World War veterans. Fr Maurice McGowan of the Archdiocese of Westminster, commissioned in 1941, died in service on 18 June 1959 and was buried in the British Military Cemetery, Tripoli.

Army chaplains in the Canal Zone included Fr Daniel Kelleher MBE of the Archdiocese of Liverpool, chaplain with 1st Guards Brigade from 1950 to 1953. Fr Kelleher, noted his MBE citation, displayed a flair for "the spiritual leadership" of soldiers. In March 1954, Fr Michael Foley of Northampton Diocese wrote from the Holy Family Church, Moascar, to inform Mgr Blount that the security situation in the Canal Zone "has grown considerably worse" and "all the hard and fast regulations have come back in full strength". Recent arrivals Fr John Duggan of the Diocese of Hexham and Newcastle and Fr James Rattigan of the Diocese of Salford, however, were doing "excellent work". Fr Joseph Murphy CSsR was ministering to Mauritian troops serving with the British army, to German prisoners of war and to civilian contract labourers. Fr James O'Sullivan was with the Guards Brigade.

The Egyptian nationalization of the Suez Canal prompted the British and French governments to send forces to recover the strategic waterway and OPERATION MUSKETEER, a seaborne operation, was launched in October 1956. Over 100 Royal Navy and Royal Fleet Auxiliary ships were assembled including five aircraft carriers. Malta was used as a naval base, and the RAF operated out of Akrotiri and Nicosia on Cyprus, and Luqa and Hal Far on Malta. Royal Naval helicopters carried men and equipment while the Fleet Air Arm flew over 2,000 sorties. Reservists were recalled, and 16th Parachute Brigade and 3rd Commando Brigade made ready for a major operation.

Dom Nicholas Holman OSB of Downside Abbey, a Second World War chaplain, was recalled as an army chaplain and served in the Canal Zone and on Cyprus until 1957. Another Second World War veteran on MUSKETEER was Fr Louis Madden with 16th Parachute Brigade. Fr Madden met up with a local parish priest, Fr Eli Hash, with whom he had studied in Rome. As the British withdrew, Fr Madden arranged for the forces' rations to be left for Fr Hash's parish. Fr Michael Casey of the Archdiocese of Liverpool, veteran of BAOR and the Far East with the Irish Guards, was one of three padres with the Parachute Brigade in Cyprus. One battalion was dropped over the Canal Zone while another two went by sea. Fr Casey sailed with the Advanced Dressing Station (ADS) and worked with medics evacuating wounded by helicopters to waiting aircraft carriers lying offshore while other casualties were flown to Cyprus. As the invasion progressed, casualties lessened and, after the ceasefire, chaplains buried the dead and held services for their own denominations. After the ignominious withdrawal of British forces, Fr Casey returned to Cyprus.

Colonial campaigns

After 1945, British forces were involved in campaigns in colonies struggling to be free of British rule. In Snape's words, the army had the thankless task of "policing Britain's slow retreat from empire".

The campaigns, fought in differing climates and terrains, were characterized largely by guerrilla warfare. Termed "insurgencies", "risings", "crises", "confrontations" or "emergencies", they were dangerous, tedious and dispiriting for the British forces but, as ever, chaplains ministered to the military's religious, spiritual and pastoral needs. In all campaigns, there was a substantial number of National Servicemen within the British forces.

However, there were never enough chaplains. The army was involved in Germany, the Middle East, Cyprus, Borneo, Kenya, Nigeria, Aden, the Persian Gulf, Hong Kong, Singapore and Malaya. In October 1964, Mgr James O'Sullivan, Principal Roman Catholic Chaplain (Army), lamented that there were only 33 commissioned Catholic army chaplains.

Padres in Britain's African colonies

In both world wars, Catholic missionaries from British and Irish religious institutes served the British army in Africa. British authorities recognized that the missionaries' knowledge of the various colonies, languages and customs was useful, particularly in caring for and motivating African troops.

In West Africa, the Irish Holy Ghost Fathers (Spiritans) served as padres. Fr Cyril Donnelly, commissioned in 1942, served with African troops in Ghana, the Gambia, India and Burma until 1945. In 1956, he joined the Nigerian Army as a commissioned chaplain and served in Nigeria, the Cameroons and the Congo before his demobilization in 1964. Fr Michael Gilmore, commissioned in 1942, served with the Royal West African Frontier Force in Sierra Leone, Nigeria and the Middle East during the war, and ministered in the Gold Coast (Ghana) until 1952. He became Senior Chaplain in West Africa, and his work among Nigerian troops was described as "indispensable". In Kenya, Fr Thomas

Maher served with the King's African Rifles in the Second World War and continued until 1962. Fr Desmond Connaughton ministered to African troops in Egypt and Kenya during and after the war. Fr Francis Maher and Fr Joseph Hughes, Mill Hill Missionaries, and Fr Charles Mulholland, a Montfort Missionary, served East African troops, while Frs Daniel Spraggon, a Mill Hill Missionary, and Patrick Fitzsimons and Michael Convey of the Society of African Missions began service with West African troops in the 1950s. In 1954, the Principal Catholic Chaplain toured units of West Africa Command at Kanu, Kaduna, Lagos, Ibadan and Abeokuta.

Fr Bernard Navin, Senior Catholic Chaplain, East Africa Command, wrote from Nairobi in 1948 that he was responsible "for thousands of miles with four chaplains and 6–7,000 troops". Here members of the Kenyan Kikuyu, the Mau Mau, began a guerrilla campaign in 1952 against Europeans and Africans. Including elements of anti-colonialism, the rising was concerned with land ownership and the leadership of an independent Kenya. The 25,000 Mau Mau had few modern weapons, but two brigades of British infantry were deployed against them. Thirty-two European civilians and 1,800 Africans were killed by the Mau Mau, and 600 members of the security forces died in the conflict. Kenya was regarded as one of Britain's bloodiest wars of decolonization.

The emergency ended when Kenya was declared independent in December 1963. British troops remained, but the army's presence was drawn down. The British were called upon by the recently installed governments of independent Tanzania and Uganda to quell riots among their mutinous troops. British troops left Kenya in December 1964.

The Kenyan ministry was difficult for the chaplains, and climate, terrain, tribal animosity and the guerrilla campaign bore down as heavily upon the padres as it did upon the soldiers. British and African troops were deployed over wide areas and frequently in difficult forested areas. This made chaplaincy work exacting, but all padres attempted to provide opportunities for regular worship and the sacraments. In March 1955, a Motherwell priest wrote to a Senior Chaplain: "The work among the Mau Mau must have been very strenuous."

Fr Edward Gilligan of the Diocese of Southwark, commissioned in 1951, deployed with the Royal Irish Fusiliers from Korea to Kenya in

January 1955; Fr Peter Brady of the Diocese of Kilmore transferred to Kenya from Near East Land Forces in 1962; and Fr Joseph Daly of the Diocese of Portsmouth, commissioned in 1944, served in Hong Kong and Libya before being posted to Kenya in 1964. There he liaised with local clergy who were to assume post-independence responsibility for chaplaincy with the multinational King's African Rifles (later Kenya Rifles). Although peace had returned, the chaplain was still busy with British troops and their families, for the British presence included Brigade Headquarters, two infantry battalions and 3rd Regiment Royal Horse Artillery at Alanbrooke Barracks, Gilgil. For all denominations, there was the problem of disposing of church property and fittings. Other padres who served in Kenya were Frs John Mahony of the Archdiocese of Liverpool and Francis Robson of Hexham and Newcastle Diocese.

As Britain's African colonies moved towards independence and new countries assumed control of their own land forces, African priests began to take over from British padres as chaplains to African regiments. The pace of change, however, depended on the resources of missionary institutes and the development of the indigenous priesthood.

Cyprus

In the early 1950s, the Greek-Cypriot population of Cyprus demanded union (*Enosis*) with Greece. Britain, which had administered Cyprus since 1878 and had transferred its strategically important Middle East military headquarters to the island in 1953, rejected the Greek-Cypriot demand. In 1955, the National Organization of Cypriot Fighters (EOKA) began a guerrilla insurgency, organized anti-British riots, and launched a series of terrorist attacks. An emergency was declared by the British government, but the British response to events in Cyprus was hampered by the Suez Crisis. By 1956, there were over 17,000 British service personnel in Cyprus engaged in a continual round of cordon and search operations, roadblocks, curfews, law enforcement and riot control. Operations were directed against terrorist enclaves. EOKA extended their campaign to the towns, where they attacked British service personnel and their families.

In 1957, the *Royal Army Chaplains' Department Journal* reported that "at present conditions in Cyprus promise to be more settled and peaceful than they have been for a long time", but in 1958 it reported that

> Cyprus has been an uncomfortable place for many, but nevertheless a place where ministrations have been as needed as they have been appreciated. Movement restrictions ... have made the chaplain's work difficult to organize; armed escorts, two-vehicle roads, time restrictions—all these have not helped the chaplain to honour his programme, nor to seek out the lonely man or family.

As the situation deteriorated, it was reported that there was "inter-communal strife on a wider scale than any of us now here had ever seen before". Padres accompanied units on operations in places and in conditions to which some had become accustomed in post-war Palestine. Chaplains acted as wardens during curfews, "patrolling their areas and shepherding families in their homes". Eventually, after diplomatic negotiations, the Greek-Cypriots abandoned their demands for *Enosis*, and Cyprus became an independent republic in 1960. In the Emergency, 371 British service personnel lost their lives.

Catholic chaplains in Cyprus

Among the chaplains who served on Cyprus at the height of the emergency was Fr Donald MacMillan of the Diocese of Clifton, who was commissioned in 1951. He had served in Korea, Malaya and Bahrain and was with the Irish Guards in Cyprus during 1957–58. Fr Gordon Dick, a Josephite Father, was Mentioned in Despatches in January 1957 for distinguished services to troops on the island. Other chaplains included Frs James Fitzgerald and Robert Woods of the Archdiocese of Glasgow, Frs Christopher McKenna and Michael Holman of the Archdiocese of Westminster, Fr Michael Dowling of the Society of African Missions, Fr Michael Foley of the Diocese of Northampton, Fr Louis Madden of the Diocese of Achonry, Fr Joseph Daly of the Diocese of Portsmouth, Frs

Edward Gilligan and Peter Flavin of the Diocese of Southwark, and Fr Tom Bradley of the Archdiocese of Liverpool.

In 1959, Fr Edward Dempsey of the Diocese of Southwark was awarded an MBE for his ministry on Cyprus. Based at Dhekelia, he cared for the church, school and a Catholic community of about 300 including troops and their families. It was stated that during his two years on the island he had undertaken his ministry to the troops "consistently and deliberately" in the face of snipers, ambushes, booby traps and mined roads. His ministry in such "dangerous circumstances" earned him the respect of officers and men and did much to maintain their morale.

Aden

The Crown Colony of Aden, at the tip of the Arabian Peninsula, was an important element of British strategy in the Middle East. Royal Navy ships anchored at its deep port while RAF Khormaksar was one of the busiest RAF bases outside Britain.

An armed Arab insurgency against British rule began in October 1963. In response, Britain declared an Emergency in Aden and its hinterland, the Aden Protectorate. In 1964, Aden was home to 8,000 service personnel and their families, but the security situation deteriorated, and British service dependants were withdrawn by 1967.

Over 30,000 British servicemen were involved in the conflict in Aden. The army invested many resources into a situation dominated by vicious urban warfare, with troops engaged in cordon and search operations and manning observation posts and checkpoints. Elsewhere there was fierce fighting in the remote, mountainous and desolate Radfan region. The *Royal Army Chaplains' Department Journal* reported that "all chaplains in the Command have taken their turn 'up country'". One Anglican chaplain wrote: "The Radfan world is isolated by razor-sharp mountain tops, the roads and tracks are dangerous and each of the six main camps is a fortress. It is a world of sand-bagged tents, foxholes . . . ", and the Arabs "were hostile and ruthless". While the army conducted operations on the ground, the RAF operated nine squadrons including transports, helicopters, fighter bombers and the RAF Regiment. The Royal Navy provided Royal Marines and seaborne support.

The last 3,500 men of the British Garrison withdrew in November 1967, and the independent People's Republic of South Yemen was proclaimed. The emergency, which ended Britain's 130-year rule in Aden, was a gruelling experience for British forces. British casualties included 68 killed and 510 wounded. Seventeen British civilians also died.

Catholic padres in Aden and the Persian Gulf

Several of the chaplains who served in Aden were veterans of the Second World War. Fr Alfred Blount of the Archdiocese of Westminster was Senior Catholic Chaplain in Aden from 1947 to 1949; Fr Gerard Bankes of the Diocese of Middlesbrough was ministering to troops in the Radfan region in 1948; Fr Louis Madden spent three years in Aden; and Fr Peter Brady, veteran of Korea, Malaya and Kenya, was attached to Headquarters Middle East Command when he was posted to Aden in 1964. With other padres, he experienced bumpy flights to the dangerous isolation of the Radfan, patrols along mine-infested tracks, long hours of waiting and watching, the noise of battle echoing through the hills, and the silence of the desert. Newer chaplains included Fr Peter Flavin, who had entered the RAChD in 1953, and was deployed to Aden in September 1962 after service in Korea and Singapore. In 1966, Fr Hugh Beattie accompanied 3 Para to Aden after service in Borneo. His obituary stated that "the discomforts and hardship of desert and jungle never weakened his resolve to go wherever the soldiers went, holding Mass in the most unlikely places". In 1969, Fr Beattie was awarded the MBE. Fr J. P. Doherty, a veteran of the Italian campaign in the Second World War, was one of the earliest RAF chaplains to serve in Aden. Another RAF padre was Fr Aidan White-Spunner OSB. The RAF had churches for service personnel and families at Steamer Point and Khormaksar.

Fr Michael Holman of the Archdiocese of Westminster was commissioned in March 1964. After a posting to BAOR he was deployed to Middle East Command in October 1966. In Aden, he was attached to the Irish Guards and reported that the atmosphere was very tense and the British withdrawal likely to lead to a civil war. He tended to the needs of the 500 Catholic service personnel and realized that he might be the last Catholic padre to serve in Aden. By February 1968, he was at Sharjah in the Trucial States—an informal British protectorate—on the shores of the Persian Gulf and over 1,700 miles from Aden. There he embarked on the building of a garrison church but did not see its completion as he was posted to BAOR in June. In May 1968, Fr Thomas McAteer of the Archdiocese of Glasgow was Mentioned in Despatches for his ministry in Aden. Fr Joseph Bamber of the Diocese of Lancaster joined the RAChD in January 1966, and in June 1968 was posted to Land Forces Gulf at Sharjah. As the only Catholic padre, he served army and RAF units. As ever, the problem of transport loomed large, and Fr Bamber used a Land Rover to enable him to cover the extensive camp.

As the British withdrew from Aden, Fr Francis Walmsley was chaplain in HMS *Bulwark*, which had sailed from Singapore with Royal Marines, who were there to protect the army's withdrawal.

Figure 23: Fr Dan Kelleher CF: Chaplain in the post-war Middle East (image courtesy of The Royal Irish Fusiliers Collection, taken from *Faugh-a-Ballagh, The Regimental Gazette of The Royal Irish Fusiliers*)

OPERATION BANNER:
Chaplains in the Troubles

The Troubles

In 1955, the *Royal Army Chaplains' Department Journal* reported that Ulster "pursues the even tenor of its way, undismayed and undisturbed by the machinations of the IRA" (Irish Republican Army). By the late 1960s, however, Catholics in Northern Ireland were openly demanding civil rights and the IRA linked this movement with calls for a united Ireland and an armed struggle against the British presence in Ulster. In 1969, the *Journal* reported that tension was mounting and the army was trying to make sense "of a situation which the soldier who has not previously served here finds rather baffling". In 1971, the *Journal* noted, "the situation in that tragic Province is escalating very seriously". The Provisional IRA (Provos) had split from the Official IRA in 1969 and its guerrilla campaign met with an equally vicious and murderous response from Protestant paramilitaries. What began as street demonstrations became "The Troubles".

OPERATION BANNER

OPERATION BANNER was the British attempt to reassure Ulster's Catholics of their safety as communal violence worsened. It lasted from 1969 until 2007 and was the army's longest continuous deployment with its role evolving from peacekeeping to counter-insurgency. Initially, Catholics welcomed British troops, but this turned to hostility after incidents involving the army in Catholic deaths. In 1970, the B-Specials (Protestant police auxiliaries) were disbanded and the Ulster Defence Regiment (UDR)—consisting of Catholics and Protestants—was formed to support the Royal Ulster Constabulary (RUC), but the army was no longer seen as neutral by the Catholic community. The introduction of internment in 1971 further inflamed anti-British antagonism.

British forces engaged in guerrilla warfare on home soil. Seven hundred and twenty-two British service personnel were killed or died and 6,116 were wounded on deployment; 51 were murdered outside Ulster. The RUC lost 319 to terrorist violence. The Troubles claimed 3,466 military and civilian lives.

OPERATION BANNER was scaled down after the Good Friday Agreement of 10 April 1998, when the British and Irish politicians agreed on power-sharing governance within Northern Ireland.

Chaplains in Northern Ireland

In 1975, the chaplains' battle dress in Ulster was a clerical suit and they were warned to be vigilant and avoid routines. They were frequently in danger and however well-intentioned their actions or innocuous their reasons, chaplains had to be prudent not to inflame local sensitivities.

Church leaders condemned the violence and relations between padres and local clergy were generally harmonious. However, some senior Catholic priests expressed sentiments favouring the IRA, whilst some non-Catholic clergymen vocally supported the Unionist establishment.

The *Journal* recorded in January 1989 that

> the patterns of the past few months have caused us to look deeply at the relevance of a caring pastoral theology in the face of violence and violent death ... The task of ministry at this difficult time does not get any easier but the record shows that we remain at the frontiers of service.

Being at the "frontiers" meant that chaplains were caught in the middle—serving the military, exercising pastoral care in the community and encouraging reconciliation. Their actions aroused suspicion and hostility. Chaplains were part of the military which was seen by Republicans as serving an occupying force. Chaplains, some from Irish families, were also challenged by ethical issues surrounding the methods used by the army, paramilitaries and communities. The chaplains' role was difficult, but their clerical duties and pastoral responsibilities remained unchanged.

Catholic Royal Navy chaplains

Under the codename OPERATION GRENADA, the Royal Navy maintained a Northern Ireland Squadron to interdict the movement by sea of illegal arms. The Royal Marines conducted over forty tours of duty in Northern Ireland.

Fr Ian Hulse of the Diocese of Salford joined the Royal Navy in 1970, served in the Far East and completed the Royal Marine Commando Course before being deployed to Northern Ireland in 1974. He was struck by "the devastation of the inner-city areas and the utter waste and uselessness of it all". "The soldiers just never let up", he wrote. "When they're not on duty, they're asleep or having a meal . . . Sunday is whichever day of the week you can get to any given location—you just arrive and tell them that Mass is available." The chaplain celebrated Mass and attended to everyone's needs as he had done previously.

When questioned if he felt his position was anomalous—a Catholic priest serving troops seen by Irish Catholics as their enemies—Fr Hulse replied: "Sometimes one is able to do small things for the people—mainly in the areas of youth work, clubs, outings, and the like." But the chaplain recognized that Catholics were in a difficult position: "Many . . . would, I feel sure, like to receive what help we can offer, but there is always the danger of reprisals against them." Fr Hulse served two tours and in 1977 was awarded the MBE for his community work.

Fr Gerard Lavender of the Diocese of Hexham and Newcastle was commissioned in 1975 and completed the Commando Course. He served in Belfast and Bessbrook on tours between 1977 and 1979. Like other chaplains, he was involved with the community and once attended an ecumenical prayer meeting in a Belfast church. For Fr Lavender, it was a positive experience in the midst of desperate circumstances, and he subsequently kept contact with some of those who were present.

Fr Noel Mullin of the Diocese of Lancaster was commissioned in 1978 and also completed the Commando Course. In 1980, he was with 41 Commando in South Armagh, known as "Bandit Country". They were based in a converted, disused linen mill in Bessbrook, and troop movements were by Fleet Air Arm helicopter. Fr Mullin visited Marines in scattered locations and shopped for them. He also called on community leaders, and early in the tour he was asked by the local parish priest if he had brought his golf clubs!

In 1981, with 45 Commando, Fr Mullin was based near the military wing of Musgrave Park Hospital, Belfast. He was a regular visitor there and also to the Royal Victoria Hospital. The former was for pastoral reasons, the latter for relaxation as this was at the invitation of a consultant to enjoy time in the "consultants' mess". During this tour, the Commandant-General of the Royal Marines, Lieutenant-General Sir Steuart Pringle, was seriously injured when a car bomb exploded near his home in London. This heightened tension as Pringle had some years earlier been the Commanding Officer of 45 Commando.

Fr Jim Allen, also of the Diocese of Lancaster, was commissioned in 1978 and had served in Hong Kong and Cyprus before being deployed to Northern Ireland in 1979. From Shackleton Barracks, Ballykelly, he had the use of a Mini, enabling him to visit Marines in different locations. He met up with the local clergy, but this was usually a tense affair as they did not want to be associated with a British chaplain, especially a Royal Marines chaplain.

During Fr Allen's second tour, he was based at Bessbrook in "Bandit Country". He moved about by helicopter and visited Marines posted along the border. On one occasion, poor weather compelled him to drive through Newry in a back of a "pig" (armoured vehicle) wearing clerical dress and surrounded by Marines carrying their SLRs (Self-Loading Rifles).

Catholic army chaplains

In 1967, Fr Peter Flavin of the Archdiocese of Southwark was based at Army Headquarters, Lisburn. He noted that the proximity to England added a surreal dimension to the deployment, for it was active service within the United Kingdom. Fr Hugh Beattie of the Diocese of Motherwell served in Ulster from 1968 until 1971. In May 1969, he wrote that he celebrated Mass in several locations as troops were scattered and intimated that the Protestant Orange Order marching season in July could literally be "explosive". He wrote, "The Catholic chaplain can be either everything or nothing here depending on the point of view; there is no in-between." Another chaplain wrote: "One has to be a bit of an acrobat and very dispassionate."

In 1969, Fr David Gibson of the Diocese of Plymouth was with 24th Infantry Brigade at Ballykelly. Some Protestant officers questioned his loyalties and his ministry was conducted in a hostile environment. "This is a weird job", he wrote. "Much of the time is spent wandering around the troops on street corners, dossing in odd corners of queer buildings and the school . . . in the Bogside where the Military Police and Grenadiers hang out." He was always on the move and his car overflowed with documents, letters, maps and, of course, his Mass kit.

In the 1970s, the Senior Army Chaplain was based at Army HQ, Lisburn, with brigade chaplains at Derry and Armagh, and a chaplain at the Royal Victoria Hospital, Belfast. In 1973, the Senior Chaplain Fr Donald McMillan of the Diocese of Clifton noted that morale was "very high" among padres and troops. There were no "disturbing signs of decline", he wrote, but an indication of the pressure on padres occurred in 1973 when a Belfast Catholic priest claimed in a Dublin newspaper that a Catholic army chaplain was an "informer for the Crown". The continuous strain on soldiers and chaplains meant that the army introduced short, rolling tours of duty—an arrangement that placed a strain on logistics and on padres. Fr Tom Bradley of the Archdiocese of Liverpool served three tours, whilst Fr Timothy Kelly OSB of Douai Abbey served in Derry in 1973 and at HQ Lisburn in 1978, with chaplaincy responsibilities for the whole Province and local medical facilities. It was said that "he trod the sectarian tightrope with humour and compassion in the most difficult of times".

Fr Bernard Funnell of the Diocese of Leeds, who was commissioned in 1975, had served in Germany and Cyprus before being deployed to Ulster. There, he drove over 23,000 miles visiting soldiers, families and schools in 27 different locations. My "Sunday journey", he wrote,

> began after Saturday lunch, heading east for an evening Mass at Downpatrick. After a night on an RAF bed, Masses followed at Ballykinler, Portadown, Armagh and finally Omagh. A total of 150 miles. Every mile was one of tourist beauty. Fermanagh was like I imagined Finland to be, beautiful lakes and few people. In County Armagh, whilst the milk churns at a farm gate were a worry, boxes of apples were for sale with a trusting plate to receive money.

Picturesque scenery, however, concealed an undercurrent of violence, and Fr Funnell continued: "Nationalism is not a love of one's country, but exists only when there is another group to hate."

The padres' contribution was recognized. In 1979, Fr Austin Griffin of the Archdiocese of Liverpool received a Commendation for Gallantry for his outstanding ministry. Fr Kevin Vasey of the Diocese of Hexham and Newcastle, a padre since 1979, went to Lisburn in 1988 as Senior Catholic Chaplain. He was awarded an OBE for his work in establishing links in the nationalist community which, with the later work of others, paid future dividends as the peace process developed.

For a few weeks in 1982, Fr Alf Hayes of the Diocese of Lancaster was with 1st Light Infantry in Belfast, and in 1984–85 he was chaplain to 8 Infantry Brigade and responsible for South Armagh and Fermanagh. From 1995 to 1997, he was Senior Catholic Chaplain at Headquarters Northern Ireland and experienced violence soon after his arrival in Lisburn. In a ceasefire, called during peace negotiations, the IRA entered Thiepval Barracks disguised as workers (or workmen?) and planted two bombs. One soldier died as a result of the first bomb and, later, a second bomb exploded at the medical centre next to the chaplaincy. Fr Hayes had been in the chaplaincy centre but was out walking with another padre as the second bomb exploded. When they returned, the office was wrecked and littered with glass from broken windows.

Fr Hayes had another lucky escape. Driving through the Glenshane Pass, his car broke down, and he was helped by six men. His car was taken away, and as he waited for it to be repaired, he was sheltered from the rain by a family whose daughter was leading an anti-British protest in Armagh Prison. The padre was careful not to reveal his identity, but he recalled: "I'm sure they knew I was an army chaplain."

Fr Stephen Alker of the Archdiocese of Liverpool served in Northern Ireland in 1984 and 1985. Initially based with 8th Armoured Brigade, he visited an infantry battalion and UDR Mass centres across four counties. He visited men in isolated areas, at Vehicle Check Points and at border crossings, and he ministered to the Royal Highland Fusiliers on duty at the Maze Prison. He usually travelled alone, and visiting urban street patrols was particularly stressful. Troops were in cramped and heavily protected military facilities, and it was a morale boost for the men to see a padre. For days, Fr Alker was unable to celebrate Mass and obtained consecrated hosts from Armagh Cathedral so he could bring the Blessed Sacrament to the troops. A papal indult allowed military chaplains to recite five decades of the Rosary instead of reading the Divine Office. Mass and Padre's Hours were often replaced with informal contact with troops. One aspect of his ministry was the support that chaplains of all denominations gave to each other, showing their closeness and solidarity as brothers in Christ.

In March 1988, shortly after two soldiers had been murdered in West Belfast, Fr Christopher Keen of the Archdiocese of Southwark reported on the chaplains' work in Ulster. He wrote that there was tension, anger and sadness among the security forces that violence continued while political and religious leaders failed to influence the situation. Fr Timothy Forbes-Turner, also of the Archdiocese of Southwark, covered an area from Derry to Enniskillen and Omagh, and pressure on him was increased by the fact that his vehicle was recognized by both sides, and whilst superficially the situation appeared normal, "a little spark and events can change drastically". He reported that "while one may drive through beautiful countryside and the beautiful setting of the various colours or shades of green . . . the heavy military presence was a stark reminder of the unsettled situation". He concluded by saying that there was a willingness among ordinary people to try to lead a normal life and a strong sense on the part of those in the military that they remained professional in a very difficult situation.

Fr Phelim Rowland of the Archdiocese of Westminster and a Falklands veteran completed three tours of Northern Ireland. In 1989, he was posted to HQ 8 Infantry Brigade based on the Waterside of Derry City. "The very lovely vista betrayed a very sad history of a divided city and a litany of violence", he wrote. "It was a place of high intensity terrorist activity." His responsibilities were the barracks and army locations in Fermanagh, Derry and Tyrone. He lived in Ebrington Barracks, home to the Royal Hampshire Regiment.

With his Irish background, Fr Rowland understood the religious and political nature of Ulster. The army saw the border as a restriction; the locals saw it as an irrelevant nuisance. Many local associations and institutions were pan-border, not least the Church of Ireland and the Catholic Church. Many local priests were citizens of both Ireland and Northern Ireland, having studied at Maynooth in Ireland but working in the north. It was not unreasonable to have a nationalist outlook without being a terrorist—a subtlety some army units failed to understand.

Fr Rowland criss-crossed the two cultures and was usually welcomed by the locals, but no amount of goodwill could conceal the fact that the army was an unwelcome presence, albeit necessary to give stability. The price was vehicle checkpoints, armour-plated Land Rovers and armed police. Catholics saw the RUC and UDR as unsympathetic and bigoted. The padre was told that Catholics were not to be trusted. Catholics told him that "nothing good ever came from England". These extreme generalizations, he felt, had some truth. Above all, Ulster was in a time-warp where one's surname and school really mattered.

Fr Leonard Purcell of the Archdiocese of Glasgow was commissioned in 1990. He served with 3rd Light Infantry in West Belfast, 1st Irish Guards in Fermanagh and 3rd Infantry Brigade in Portadown. Northern Ireland was still an operational theatre, and chaplains were still subject to the same dangers and security constraints that had affected troops and padres since the 1970s. Ulster did not appear like a war zone, but danger was never far away, and the Roman collar did not guarantee safety. It was best to admit that you were an army chaplain, for pretending otherwise would arouse suspicion. Like the troops, he was always in danger. On 2 December 1993, with Anglican padre the Revd Mike Halshall, Fr Purcell attended an Artilleryman shot by a sniper at Keady. On 30 December 1993, with Anglican padre Kingsley Joyce, he attended a Guardsman shot by a sniper in Crossmaglen. On 14 May 1994, he attended a soldier killed in a bomb explosion in the base at Keady.

Fr Francis Barber of the Diocese of Salford, commissioned in 1993, was deployed with 8th Infantry Brigade when the Real IRA (another splinter group) detonated a bomb at Omagh on 15 August 1998, the Feast of the Assumption and a children's carnival day. Twenty-nine people were killed and 220 injured. The bomb caused the largest loss of life of any terrorist incident in the Troubles. Military, medical and emergency personnel at the scene were deeply traumatized by the scale and nature of the casualties.

One week later, a day of reflection was held, and vigils were kept all over Ireland. In Omagh, 40,000 people took part in an emotional service. Welcomes were spoken in English by Fr Kevin Mullan, in Irish by the Presbyterian the Revd Robert Herrin, and in Spanish by Fr Barber, specifically for the Spanish community living in and around Omagh. For his ministry after the bombing, Fr Barber was awarded the Queen's Commendation for Valuable Service.

Fr Gerry Weston—a victim of the Troubles

Gerard Weston was born in Liverpool in 1933, trained for the priesthood at St Joseph's College, Upholland, and was ordained for the Archdiocese of Liverpool in 1960. He was commissioned into the RAChD in 1967 and served in Germany, the Persian Gulf, Kenya and Northern Ireland.

Fr Weston was Regimental Chaplain for 16th Parachute Brigade and frequently went into the dangerous areas of Ballymurphy and Turf Lodge, Belfast. The Revd Anthony Appleby, an Anglican padre, worked with Fr Weston to try to reconcile opposing communities, and they were regularly seen together as they went about their task. A paratrooper wrote later: "To us mere soldiers, we were all impressed at their courage." He added: "The IRA didn't like it and put it about that they weren't really priests but Special Branch spies." Fr Weston's commanding officer said:

> Padre Weston was an absolutely tremendous Roman Catholic priest; he did a tremendous amount to try and bridge the gap between the Catholic community and the Catholic Church and our soldiers. He was continually going around into Catholic estates to try and achieve this, very often by himself and obviously unarmed.

The padre was in great danger and, for his own safety, he was ordered from Northern Ireland.

On 17 February 1972, Fr Weston was awarded the MBE for his community work in Northern Ireland. Seven days later, he drove to the Officers' Mess of 16th Parachute Brigade, Aldershot. As he got out of his car, a 200 lb bomb exploded, killing him instantly. Six civilians were also killed. The Official IRA claimed responsibility for the bombing, stating that the attack was in retaliation for the actions of 1st Battalion Parachute Regiment during the afternoon of Sunday, 30 January 1972, during which troops opened fire on civil rights protestors in the Catholic Bogside area of Derry. Fourteen civilians were killed, and the incident became known as Bloody Sunday. The IRA anticipated the deaths of officers at Aldershot and declared that civilian casualties were regretted as the target was the officers responsible for the Derry outrages.

Fr Weston became the second Catholic chaplain to be killed on British soil. The first was the Irish Vincentian Fr William Gilgunn, killed in 1942, when his vehicle was strafed by a Nazi plane flying over Rye in Sussex.

Padres were not the only ones in danger. Bishop Gerard Tickle, Bishop of the Forces, received a letter bomb at his London home. The bomb, which failed to explode, was sent in retaliation for Bishop Tickle's complimentary remarks about British troops when he visited Northern Ireland in 1973. The IRA regarded his comments as an endorsement of the army's actions on Bloody Sunday.

On 26 November 1997, Bishop Francis Walmsley, Bishop of the Forces, and a former naval chaplain, blessed a commemorative window at St Patrick's Church, Tidworth, to the memory of all military chaplains, and to mark the twenty-fifth anniversary of Fr Weston's death.

Figure 24: Fr Gerry Weston CF: Victim of the Troubles

2 5

"Nothing prepares you for the reality of military violence": Chaplains in the Falklands War

The Falklands War

The Falklands War began on 2 April 1982, when Argentina invaded and occupied the British Overseas Territories of the Falkland Islands and South Georgia. The United Kingdom sent a naval task force— OPERATION CORPORATE—to restore its sovereignty.

To fight a war 8,000 miles away appeared an impossible logistical challenge for British forces. It was assumed that the affair would be resolved peacefully, but Britain was as adamant to recover the Falklands as Argentina was to keep them.

OPERATION CORPORATE: Catholic chaplains

Four Catholic chaplains in the Royal Navy and Royal Marines sailed with the Task Force: Fr John Ryan MBE RN of the Archdiocese of Southwark (commissioned 1972), Fr Chris Bester RN of the Archdiocese of Birmingham (commissioned 1976), Fr Noel Mullin RN of the Diocese of Lancaster (commissioned 1978) in 3 Commando Brigade Royal Marines, and Fr Phelim Rowland RN of the Archdiocese of Westminster (commissioned 1979). Army chaplain Fr Alf Hayes of the Diocese of Lancaster (commissioned 1980) accompanied 5th Infantry Brigade.

Towards the Falklands

In Holy Week 1982, Fr Phelim Rowland was chaplain to HMS *Yarmouth* when it was ordered to resupply and collect ammunition at Gibraltar. At the Chrism Mass of Maundy Thursday, Fr Rowland and his congregation prayed for peace. On Good Friday, they set sail for the Falklands. The padre recalled: "It was all so unreal, watching a vast armada of ships storing and reorganizing in balmy heat and turquoise seas."

Fr Chris Bester was in SS *Uganda*, a P&O educational cruise ship converted into a hospital ship. She sailed from Gibraltar "to the warm zephyrs off the Moroccan coast", refuelled in Freetown and, with "numberless grey funnelled ships", anchored off Ascension Island. With the Revd David Barlow, the Anglican chaplain, Fr Bester established a daily routine of Eucharistic services, Compline, Bible study, and fellowship and meditation.

The Task Force reached the Falklands and action started on 1 May when British warships went searching for Argentine submarines. Fr Rowland visited ships by helicopter. On 5 May, he wrote: "The weather is awful with either fog or high winds and rain. The fog tends to keep the air raids away, so it has some blessing." As they entered the "total exclusion zone", he circulated among the flotilla celebrating Mass, giving absolution and visiting men.

General Belgrano and HMS *Sheffield*

"And so it was that I found myself at war", wrote Fr Rowland, but "nothing prepares you for the reality of military violence." That violence was wrought on the Argentine cruiser, *General Belgrano*, and the destroyer, HMS *Sheffield*. Fr Rowland wrote:

> 2nd May was quiet until the evening when we heard on the World Service of the sinking of the Argentine cruiser, the *General Belgrano*. It came as a great shock—especially with the news of the great loss of life. We still hoped that it would bring the Argentines to their senses and end hostilities. We awaited some

reaction. It came at 1430 on Tuesday, 4th May. The action stations buzzer sounded and we were warned of an air raid closing. Then we were told that HMS *Sheffield* had been hit. HMS *Yarmouth* was ordered to close, and again launched off our "chaff" rockets. The Officer of the Watch saw an Exocet missile pass us on the starboard quarter at about 600 yards. We very quickly found out it was such a missile which hit *Sheffield*.

Yarmouth's crew saw smoke rising from *Sheffield* and flames escaping from a hole in her side. As she closed in, *Yarmouth's* torpedo alarms sounded and she was forced to take action against possible submarine attack. *Yarmouth* then returned to the *Sheffield* whose captain gave orders to abandon ship. *Yarmouth* collected survivors and headed back to the Battle Group. Fr Rowland wrote that "it was a shell-shocked group of officers that ate their 'pot mess' that evening, sad beyond words—and angry. I remember saying a prayer over the ship's main broadcast system for the twenty men killed—and those injured."

Next day, he accompanied *Sheffield's* survivors to Fleet Auxiliaries and in the evening conducted an impromptu service for the dead. It was a sorrowful occasion and *Yarmouth's* entire company was present. *Sheffield's* survivors " . . . were still stunned and deeply saddened at the loss of life—and the loss of their ship", wrote Fr Rowland. On 9 May, *Yarmouth* towed *Sheffield* towards the Carrier Group, but on 10 May, severely damaged, she sank in bad weather and in range of the Argentinian air force. Fr Bester wrote that "*Sheffield* was the most unhappy sight I have ever seen. I went . . . to be with the survivors. They were shocked, but happy to be alive."

Fr Rowland's duty was to all belligerents, and he was transferred to HMS *Invincible* to minister to Argentinian prisoners. He recalled that some believed they would be shot as spies. "We celebrated Mass together and I gave them General Absolution. The prisoners were well looked after, well supplied with cigarettes and chocolate from the ship's company, and kept—ironically—in the ship's chapel."

Fr Rowland remained in *Invincible* for a week before transferring to the flagship, HMS *Hermes*. The ship was a hive of activity as the amphibious group had arrived and the invasion to retake the islands was imminent. The Task Force Commander, Rear Admiral John "Sandy" Woodward, wrote Fr Rowland, "looked tired and drawn but nevertheless confident that success would be achieved".

Falkland Sound, San Carlos Water and naval losses

Early on 21 May, British forces achieved tactical surprise and troops landed mostly unopposed on four beaches around San Carlos Water. At 08.45, the first air raid warning was heard. The bridgehead had been secured, but there followed waves of Argentine air attacks. HMS *Ardent* was sunk, HMS *Argonaut* and *Antrim* were badly damaged, and HMS *Brilliant* and *Broadsword* were slightly damaged. Two Marine helicopters were lost to ground fire and one RAF Harrier was shot down. On 23 May, in the continuing Battle of San Carlos Water, HMS *Antelope* was hit and sank the following day. Three Royal Fleet Auxiliary (RFA) landing craft received direct hits, but the bombs failed to explode. As the build-up ashore continued, there were more losses, and on 25 May HMS *Coventry* was sunk.

On 4 June, Fr Ryan wrote from San Carlos Water: "It is all so sad and horrible... We have a little cemetery here for the British and Argentinians, but hopefully it is only temporary. I bury the dead every day at 16.00." He arranged for an Argentinian chaplain, who was a prisoner of war, to tend to his own wounded and anoint them. They concelebrated Mass every evening for British and Argentinians. "The sign of peace is very meaningful", wrote Fr Ryan.

Fr Rowland returned to *Yarmouth* which, with *Glamorgan*, was tasked with inshore bombardment. The bombardment group sailed in at dusk and pounded Argentine positions through the night in support of British troops advancing on Mount Kent and Tumbledown. Later, on the night of 11–12 June, *Glamorgan* was hit by an Exocet missile, and 14 sailors were killed. *Yarmouth* provided firefighting and medical support to *Glamorgan*'s crew.

Yarmouth underwent repair and maintenance before rejoining the Task Force. She then bombarded enemy positions west of Port Stanley, sailing 200 miles each way to carry out bombardments by night and arriving back at the Battle Group by day to be replenished with fuel and ammunition.

Royal Marines chaplain

Fr Noel Mullin completed the All Arms Commando Course in 1979 at the Commando Training Centre Royal Marines and was awarded the coveted Commando Green Beret. In January 1980, he successfully completed the Arctic Warfare Training Course with 45 Commando inside the Arctic Circle. On Good Friday 1982, he sailed in the requisitioned and modified liner SS *Canberra*, as chaplain to 2,500 men of the augmented 3 Commando Brigade RM and 400 of the ship's merchant seafarers, together with the embarked RN Naval Party. Two RN Surgical Support Teams, the musicians of a Royal Marines band (stretcher bearers) and various small detachments were on board.

There followed training, briefings, planning and preparations for all service contingents and crew. Fr Mullin celebrated daily Mass and with his three Anglican colleagues also conducted ecumenical services. Each Sunday, there was a joint Liturgy of the Word followed by separate Eucharistic celebrations.

Service personnel and crew sought individual meetings with Fr Mullin or requested the Sacrament of Reconciliation. One Royal Marine NCO sought counsel regarding his response if one of his men was injured and dying in combat and the chaplain was unavailable. "When we are advancing in the field, what can I do to assist and comfort a dying marine?", he asked. "Do I cradle him and hold him, do I remind him of his mother's love, do I say an *Our Father*?" The NCO was subsequently decorated for his courageous leadership and making an outstanding contribution to operations in combat. He led reconnaissance patrols through unmarked minefields prior to 42 Commando's successful assault on Mount Harriet.

Meetings on the outward journey facilitated co-operation and understanding between chaplains and medics. The result was sensitive and constructive working relationships, both at sea and subsequently in the field hospital. Fr Mullin accompanied the senior RN Medical Officer and inspected the large and, by now, empty freezer spaces in the ship to ascertain their suitability as storage for bodies if the dead were to be repatriated. It was, however, decided to follow the tradition of burial where the men had fallen.

Canberra had carried over 2,000 troops and their equipment 8,000 miles, and on 21 May she entered San Carlos Water to disembark units in the amphibious landings. To Fr Mullin, this was one of the most notable days of the campaign, with numerous warships and auxiliaries in Falkland Sound and San Carlos Water. Such was the frequency and intensity of Argentine air attacks that San Carlos Water earned the nickname "Bomb Alley".

The landing was successful but was accompanied by deaths, casualties and the loss of aircraft and ships, including HMS *Ardent*. *Ardent* survivors were transferred to *Canberra*; 22 of her company had been killed. Casualties from other locations were received into *Canberra*'s converted hospital ward, and Fr Mullin offered counselling and the sacraments. Shock and pain were widely visible. In the evening of 22 May, Fr Mullin conducted the burials at sea of four Royal Marine aviators who had been killed. On 23 May, he conducted a Service of Remembrance and Thanksgiving for the men of *Ardent*, and all who approached in good faith were admitted to the Eucharist.

Casualties were brought to *Canberra* until the field hospital could be established and Fr Mullin remained onboard. Three days later *Canberra* rendezvoused with the liner *Queen Elizabeth 2* off South Georgia in order to embark 5th Infantry Brigade. The chaplain took the opportunity to go ashore at King Edward Point to visit M Company 42 Commando. They had taken part in the action to liberate South Georgia and were now securing the location against possible further incursion. M Company were thirsty for information regarding the earlier amphibious action and, as a witness to the events of 21 May, Fr Mullin briefed them. He also celebrated Mass and held a general service before setting out the next day with the Company Commander to visit Marines in distant observation posts. Having taken the opportunity to visit Shackleton's grave in Grytviken, Fr Mullin took a boat out and rejoined *Canberra* at anchor to become acquainted with 5th Brigade during the passage back to the Falklands. He was also able to welcome his friend and diocesan colleague, army chaplain Fr Alf Hayes.

Back in San Carlos Water and participating in a brigade amphibious landing for the second time, Fr Mullin experienced the frisson of going ashore via HMS *Fearless* in a small, fast Rigid Raider craft onto "Red Beach". There he joined up with the Commando Logistic Regiment in Ajax Bay. The regiment had just suffered casualties and fatalities in Argentine air attacks. Fr Mullin tended to British and Argentine wounded in the hospital, cared for Argentine prisoners, celebrated Mass, dispensed the sacraments to men from the opposing forces, and buried the dead. During Masses, celebrated in the prisoner of war compound next to the field hospital, he witnessed genuine exchanges of signs of peace between British personnel and their Argentine prisoners. He conducted burials for British and Argentine dead, borne to their graves by their comrades and afforded equal dignity. While observing the requirements of the Geneva Conventions, the conduct of leaders and men in relation to both prisoners and the hospitalized was, he wrote, "unimpeachable".

Following injuries inflicted on units of 3 Commando Brigade as they advanced east towards Port Stanley, the decision was taken to insert a small surgical team, including Fr Mullin, into a forward position and he took an overnight passage in a Landing Ship Logistics Boat from San Carlos round to Teal Inlet. Even after enduring bombing raids while in *Canberra* in San Carlos Water and ashore, the slow journey from the ship to the settlement was for the chaplain "the most vulnerable experience to date". The lengthy passage from ship to shore was by mexeflote, a slow moving, unprotected flat landing craft which could be clearly seen from the air by attacking aircraft. The team, however, was spared. At Teal, Fr Mullin's accommodation was a shepherd's hut shared with Special Forces. The body of one of their fallen colleagues was retrieved from an exposed forward position and he was afforded the rites of Christian burial conducted by the priest.

A few days later, Fr Mullin (call sign "Brimstone") was ordered to return to Ajax Bay. "If the insertion to Teal Inlet was the most scary", he wrote, "the extraction was probably the most exhilarating." The helicopter flight back "was fast and low, contouring every mound and dip, keeping just above ground in order to avoid detection by hostile forces". The aircraft door was open and, together with the rush of cool air, the chaplain felt that he could have reached out and trailed his fingers along the ground!

Shortly after his return to Ajax Bay the field hospital became extremely busy. On 8 June two Fleet Auxiliaries, *Sir Galahad* and *Sir Tristram*, carrying troops, ammunition and fuel, were attacked by Argentine aircraft off Fitzroy, causing the most fatalities and injuries suffered by British forces in the campaign. Forty-eight men were killed in *Sir Galahad*; five crew members and 43 soldiers, 32 of whom were Welsh Guards. Two merchant crew were also killed in *Sir Tristram*. In total, over 100 were injured, traumatized and burned. Many were helicoptered to the Red and Green Life Machine—the field hospital in Ajax Bay. The pain and shock were extensive and horrific. The time Fr Mullin had spent with medics in *Canberra* sailing south now yielded fruit. Large numbers of men suffering life-changing injuries were cared for with remarkable success in a disused meat-processing refrigeration plant with undetonated 1,000 lb bombs in its roofing.

Following the successful British assault on peaks surrounding Stanley and the recapture of the capital, General Menendez, the Argentine Governor, signed the surrender. Fr Mullin and the Commandos embarked for passage from Ajax Bay to Stanley with hundreds of men lying on crowded decks. The senior RN officer invited as many as possible in the constrained facilities to take a shower. For Fr Mullin, it was bliss to enjoy the first shower in weeks and put on clean clothes, which had remained wrapped throughout the campaign in his bergen rucksack.

After disembarking in Stanley, Fr Mullin, Marines and other liberators were beneficiaries of the hospitality of Mgr Dan Spraggon, a Mill Hill Missionary, former army chaplain and parish priest of Stanley, who gave an account of recent events which had befallen his parish. He showed the chaplain a book, still on his bookshelf, with an Argentine bullet lodged in the spine. Mgr Spraggon prepared large, slow roasts of lamb which he gave to the Marines—very popular with men who had lived off meagre rations in battle conditions fighting against defensive positions in hostile terrain and inhospitable weather.

Catholic army chaplains

In 1982, Fr Alf Hayes was one of 30 Catholic commissioned army chaplains. On 12 May 1982, he was one of three infantry brigade chaplains who sailed from Southampton on the liner *Queen Elizabeth 2*. The Revd Peter Brookes, an Anglican chaplain, was attached to the Welsh Guards; the Revd Angus Smith, a Church of Scotland padre, was with the Scots Guards; and Fr Hayes was attached to the Headquarters and Signal Squadron. They prepared the men spiritually for the conflict ahead. Amid intense military preparations, Fr Hayes celebrated Mass and with the other padres managed to transmit a "Thought for the Day" over the ship's radio, produce the Brigade's daily newspaper and organize leisure activities. As they got nearer to battle and tension grew, more men attended church services.

Three weeks after leaving Southampton, 3,000 men, including Fr Hayes, executed an unopposed landing at San Carlos Water from *Canberra*, which they had boarded at South Georgia. Fr Hayes dug in and based himself with a Field Ambulance before accompanying Brigade Headquarters as it advanced to Darwin and Goose Green. One thousand four hundred Argentines had surrendered and the padre was tasked with locating and burying enemy dead, some of whom were unidentified, in a mass grave at Darwin. With an Argentine padre, Spanish-speaking Fr Hayes later concelebrated a Requiem Mass on 5 June at Goose Green for Argentine prisoners. He then flew by helicopter to say Mass for 2 Para. His altar was an upturned oil drum. About 30 soldiers, all bearing the marks of combat, gathered around in the freezing cold.

The chaplain then walked with 2 Para to Fitzroy and to the battle for Stanley. His workload increased with the devastating air attacks on the Fleet Auxiliaries *Sir Tristram* and *Sir Galahad* at Bluff Cove. The Welsh Guards had suffered many casualties and Fr Hayes was occupied for many hours tending the wounded and dying at the Field Ambulance Dressing Station.

At the battles for Stanley on 12 June and Tumbledown on 14 June, Fr Hayes and Fr Ryan tended both British and Argentine casualties, Catholic and non-Catholic. The Scots Guards had suffered heavily and the chaplains tended the wounded. Fr Hayes recalled that he saw doctors perform miracles of surgery. He then transferred to the assault ship HMS *Fearless*, where he spoke with senior Argentine officers and witnessed Argentine soldiers suffering from both battle and self-inflicted wounds. The following day he flew to Ajax Bay where he and Fr Mullin tended to Argentine prisoners. Eventually he reached *Uganda*, where, with Fr Chris Bester, he cared for over 750 British and Argentinian casualties. Wounded Argentine prisoners were thankful for the treatment they had received from the British and desperate to go home.

The cost of victory—reflections

Argentine forces surrendered on 14 June. In the campaign, 255 British personnel and three islanders had been killed; 775 were wounded and 115 were captured. The British loss of life was the greatest since the Second World War. Argentina lost 650 men and 11,000 were taken prisoner.

Chaplains had accompanied service personnel through weeks of intense fighting. They witnessed fear, courage, fortitude, resilience and humour, ministering to the injured in field hospitals and in ships and burying the dead at sea and on cold, wet, windswept hillsides. They had experienced the horror of war and exercised their ministry in extraordinary circumstances and conditions.

Yarmouth, *Exeter* and *Cardiff* sailed ahead of *Invincible* as the Task Force headed home. Fr Rowland reflected on his ministry: "I was needed and used as a priest. I saw professional men doing what they consider a professional job. I discovered few who enjoyed the realities of war. We all know war is futile and negative."

Chaplains of all denominations, British and Argentinian, bravely carried out their ministry. Some were broken by the Falklands experience. Some could not carry other men's burdens and their own. For others it was the making of them. "The mental scars of such events", wrote Fr Rowland, "live long and for some never leave. Locked away in the person's mind, those sometimes terrible events cannot be put into words or divulged even to those you love most in the world."

Reconciliation

When Argentine troops invaded the Falklands, they carried a statue of Our Lady of Lujan with them and placed it in St Mary's Church, Port Stanley. At the end of the war, the statue was taken to the Catholic Forces Cathedral of St Michael and St George in Aldershot and installed as a memorial to all those who died in the Falklands War.

In October 2019, in the presence of Pope Francis, the statue was handed back to Bishop Olivera, the Argentine Military Bishop, by Bishop Paul Mason, the Military Ordinary of Great Britain. A replica statue was presented to Bishop Mason by Bishop Olivera to be kept in the Cathedral in Aldershot.

Figure 25: Fr Noel Mullin RM (left) and Fr Alf Hayes CF (right): Falklands chaplains (Mgr Noel Mullin)

2 6

"The prospect of war does not bear thinking about": Army chaplains in the Gulf Wars

The First Gulf War

The First Gulf War (August 1990—February 1991) was the result of an international response to Iraq's invasion of Kuwait and its threat to invade Saudi Arabia. A United States-led operation to free Kuwait was named OPERATION DESERT STORM and the prevention of the invasion of Saudi Arabia was named DESERT SHIELD. The United Kingdom's contribution, OPERATION GRANBY, was the largest deployment of British troops since the Second World War. Over 53,000 British servicemen and servicewomen served, and 47 British service personnel were killed in the conflict.

Army chaplains in the First Gulf War

By January 1991, 29 British army chaplains were serving in the Gulf conducting their ministry in intense heat, amid endless swathes of sand and in sight of burning oil wells. The immediacy of battle concentrated minds, and a unity of spirit and purpose soon developed. Maintaining cohesion and morale was essential for the chaplains as was the readiness to fulfil their sacramental role, attend casualties and receive the dead. Sought out by individuals for personal advice, padres counselled soldiers of all ranks and responsibilities.

British commanders, anxious to ensure that the chaplains' work was not restricted and Christian religious services were allowed in Muslim countries, issued instructions that chaplains should cover the crosses on their uniforms and be styled "Morale and Welfare Officers". Such instructions, designed to offset possible Muslim sensitivities, were regarded as unnecessary and misguided by those padres who experienced no limitations on their work during the conflict. Helpful arrangements were made by Muslim authorities for a Christmas service to be broadcast to troops in the Gulf and for this to be shared with Fallingbostel in BAOR and Aldershot in the United Kingdom.

Catholic army chaplains in the First Gulf War

In 1990, there were 29 Catholic army chaplains. Six served on OPERATION GRANBY and the Senior Chaplain was Fr David Mead of the Archdiocese of Birmingham, who was commissioned in 1975. Other chaplains were Frs Alan Finley of the Diocese of Clifton (commissioned 1986), Sean Scanlan of the Archdiocese of Southwark (commissioned 1986), David Kelly of the Archdiocese of Westminster (commissioned 1987), Michael Weymes of the Diocese of Hexham and Newcastle (commissioned 1988) and James Duddy of the Diocese of Motherwell (commissioned 1990). Fr Phelim Rowland of the Archdiocese of Westminster (commissioned in the RAChD after service in the Royal Navy) was based on Cyprus and was told to prepare for casualties.

The time before battle is a period of acute stress and chaplains reported a steady increase in troops attending religious services. According to one padre, "Nothing concentrates the mind as firmly . . . as the threat of a bloody war around the corner", and chaplains were sought out for confession and counselling. The confidential dimension of a priest's vocation allowed individuals to admit to him that they were scared. Fr Mead recalled: "None of us knew how things would turn out. And it must be said that they were not really scared for themselves—they were soldiers, after all—but for their families back home."

Fr Mead was billeted with 22 Field Ambulance. The unit totalled only 650 personnel at maximum, and so padre and soldiers were able to develop a close bond. He travelled on a regular basis with another padre to outlying units, and there developed an ecumenical dimension to their ministry. There were occasions when Catholics and Anglicans held joint liturgies, and such collaboration became a feature of the padres' work. Some soldiers, unsure of committing themselves, hovered around the tent-chapel during services, but "in their own way", wrote Fr Mead, "they were there". The padres had earlier approached the Commanding Officer (CO) to ask for a "Quiet Tent/Chapel", where, if the situation deteriorated, soldiers might have somewhere to pray, think and grieve. The CO was not in favour, but a number of senior ranks supported the padres and a tent was obtained. One night, as Fr Mead went into the tent, a young soldier was sitting there on his own. He looked at the padre and said: "Just my contribution to peace, sir."

Alongside Fr Mead's location in Saudi Arabia was a prisoner of war holding area. One Iraqi prisoner told him that when their position was overrun, they had nothing with which to defend themselves, because the day before they had been told they were quitting Kuwait and they had fired everything into the air in jubilation!

In September 1990, Fr Alan Finley deployed with 33 Field Hospital, Al Jubayl, Saudi Arabia. Before battle commenced, there was a sense of optimism that Iraq might withdraw from Kuwait but hopes for a settlement were to be dashed and prayers for peace continued alongside preparations for war. "The prospect of war", wrote Fr Finley, "does not bear thinking about."

There were concerns that padres celebrating Christian liturgies in Muslim countries might offend the very people they were fighting to liberate, but Fr Finley encountered no such problems. He celebrated daily Mass for the medical staff, those in the surrounding camp and troops in transit. His work involved visiting and saying Mass for troops in the wider vicinity and isolated positions, and he struck up a friendship and a working partnership with the Revd Christopher Walker, an Anglican padre. Their co-operation was noticed and respected by troops and commanders. Combatants in forward positions welcomed Fr Finley's attempts to maintain their morale. "Even the most hardened soldier is grateful for prayers at a time like this", wrote the padre.

Fr Michael Weymes deployed with 14th/20th Hussars Battlegroup in August 1990. At the end of the 100-day war, he entered Kuwait City to contact the local bishop and collect the Holy Oils for the coming Easter season. Noticing the plight of many civilians, the padre and commander arranged for food and aid to be taken into the city, and on 12 March 1991, they accompanied a truck filled with food and other supplies into the cathedral compound. The bishop introduced the padre to his multinational curates and to members of his non-Kuwaiti flock. The bishop then entertained the padre and the British troops to tea and told them of the harsh treatment the Iraqi invaders had meted out to Kuwaitis and the devastation they had wrought on Christian places of worship. On Easter Sunday, Fr Weymes returned to Kuwait City to celebrate Mass for the local ex-pat community.

Fr David Kelly, like other padres, was there for Catholics, those of other faiths and those of none. He made himself available as a listener at a time and in circumstances that were challenging for young people at war. Fr James Duddy, who had served as a Territorial Army padre, was chaplain at the British army hospital in Riyadh.

The Second Gulf War: the invasion of Iraq

OPERATION TELIC, the United Kingdom's military operation in Iraq between March 2003 and April 2009, is also referred to as the Second Gulf War. The intention of the American-led Allied campaign was the removal of Saddam Hussein, dictator of Iraq, who, it was alleged, was using chemical weapons against minority groups.

A total of 46,000 British military personnel took part in the invasion. 8,400 army and Royal Air Force Reservists were called up for service. In the campaign, 179 servicemen and servicewomen died and over 3,500 were wounded.

The British invasion and subsequent operations were confined to Southern Iraq and the city of Basra, where 5,000 military personnel were accommodated. The security situation was tense, dangerous and deadly, with civil unrest exacerbated by religious differences and the influx of foreign fighters. The Allied intention to hand over a peaceful and organized Iraq never materialized. In 2007, British bases were transferred to Iraqi forces, and by 2008 the number of British personnel in Iraq had fallen to 4,100. The majority of British forces were withdrawn from Basra on 30 April 2009. Remaining British military advisers were withdrawn in 2011. OPERATION TELIC lasted 2,232 days.

Army chaplains on OPERATION TELIC

In January 2003, the Chaplain-General told chaplains preparing to deploy to Iraq that soldiers would look to them for moral and spiritual guidance "in this as in previous conflicts". The calling of padres was to be with people "in the messy, grey areas of life", and such places could be dangerous, difficult and compromising. Chaplains, he warned, could feel very vulnerable. Yet it was important for chaplains to be there, wrote Bishop Tom Burns, Bishop of the Forces, for "a chaplain's presence makes itself felt amid a dangerous and unstable environment, where often values could so easily be set aside in the fog of war".

Thirty-seven army chaplains deployed to Iraq. For some, it was the first experience of war; for all, it tested the workings and robustness of the newly introduced Convergence model of chaplaincy (see Chapter 32). Chaplains conducted services, counselled, supported surgical teams, prepared for the dignified repatriation of the dead, communicated with isolated troops and made contact with other padres. In all of this, the friendships and acquaintanceships they developed with other padres and service personnel bore fruit. An important development was the carrying of Muslim prayer cards.

Catholic army chaplains on OPERATION TELIC

Catholic chaplains from all three services were initially deployed on OPERATION TELIC. Army chaplains included Frs Anthony Paris and Nicholas Gosnell of the Archdiocese of Westminster, Michael Brown of the Diocese of Motherwell, Nicholas Farrell of the Diocese of Leeds, Mark O'Keefe of the Diocese of Plymouth, David Smith of the Diocese of East Anglia, Ian Stevenson of the Diocese of Paisley, Alex Strachan of the Archdiocese of Glasgow, Andrew Lloyd of the Diocese of Shrewsbury, Daniel Hernandez of the Diocese of Gibraltar, Paschal Hanrahan of the Diocese of Killaloe, Peter Madden of the Archdiocese of Birmingham, John Nelson of the Diocese of Portsmouth, Daren Brown of the Diocese of Nottingham and Steven Forster of the Diocese of Hexham and Newcastle.

Wartime ministry

Fr Tony Paris, commissioned in 1988, was Senior Chaplain with responsibility for Divisional and Catholic padres. A difficulty he soon encountered was convening padres serving dispersed units, and changes of location aggravated the problem. The situation reports he received from other chaplains enabled him to piece together a composite picture of their experiences and effectiveness. In his own unit, he was called upon to deal with casualties "and a great deal of fear and sadness".

On the Sunday before hostilities commenced, Fr Nick Gosnell, commissioned in 1998, spoke to 120 soldiers of 3rd Battalion Parachute Regiment. In a tent, with a table with a single candle as an altar, they sang "The Lord's My Shepherd", and although they prayed for peace, all thoughts were on war. "Our time to shine, to be glorified, is now", Padre Gosnell said, and asked the troops to trust in the Lord, whatever the next few days might bring. "We cannot know the future or what God has in store for us. All we can do is be faithful." Speaking for himself and his two fellow padres attached to 16th Air Assault Brigade, Fr Gosnell said: "If we are not here next Sunday, it's been a privilege for us to worship with you."

The build-up to the invasion was tense as the thought of conflict and its potential consequences cut across group and personal preparations. In northern Kuwait before the invasion, Fr Alex Strachan, commissioned in 2001, was with a medical squadron and recalled that "sharing basic facilities, in common with all ranks, helped unite the squadron. Living in the same space without partitions, accelerated the mutual familiarization process." Participation in briefings, clinical training, "digging and hammering", recreational sport and even disposal of rubbish generated an acceptance and integration of the chaplain. Fr Strachan added that "during this time many people were glad to share their deepest thoughts and feelings with me, at both the purely humanistic and the religious and theological level". Collective cohesion and individual isolation went hand in hand.

Fr Michael Brown, commissioned in 2001, adapted to the desert environment. Morale was high, and there was confidence that the outcome of the conflict would be successful. The troops welcomed him and to his surprise accepted sacramentals, pocket-sized New Testaments and prayer cards. Others came to him for counselling and assistance with all kinds of problems. Most, he recalled, left him "with their spirits raised".

Wearing body armour and helmets, padres frequently accompanied patrols. They came into contact with Iraqi opposition, unexploded roadside bombs, improvised devices and, inevitably, fatalities on both sides. They encountered frightened Iraqi adults and children; they were badgered for water and supplies.

Padres were placed with Dressing Stations and field and base hospitals and casualties increased as the war progressed. Fr Strachan summed up the effects on him and others:

> The flow of admissions, whilst demanding... never overwhelmed us... I saw a sample of the many phenomena war produces; the horrific, the frightening and worrying, the sad, the comical, the awesome, the banal and the disgusting; not too much of any single category, but enough to teach a sobering lesson, enough to hasten the emotional development of many including myself.

For padres in the field and medical units, the sights were disturbing and the experiences dangerous. They adjusted to grief and enabled grieving soldiers to carry on with their duties. Padres arranged field burials of British and Iraqi soldiers, attended the exhumation of missing soldiers from shallow graves, helped identify the dead, and offered prayers for the deceased in Dressing Stations. Fr Andrew Lloyd, Force Senior Chaplain in Basra, conducted 19 repatriation ceremonies. All this was carried on in a situation where there were problems relating to kit, transport and mobility, communications with other padres, and personal and ecclesiastical accommodation. But, as one chaplain remarked, "Readiness to accept the imposed privations sustained active ministry."

Padres were deployed on OPERATION TELIC after the introduction of the converged model of army chaplaincy—the All Souls Ministry (see Chapter 32). Sensitivity was necessary as Catholic padres did not wish to alienate chaplains and troops of other denominations. Padres celebrated daily Mass, explaining that it was open to all, but that Holy Communion would be distributed according to the norms of the Catholic Church. Sizes of congregations varied, and troops of various denominations attended Mass and Non-Eucharistic Services. Preprinted Mass sheets were used, and reusable copies of Field Services were available. In some cases, a Lectionary and Missal contained within one volume and covering the liturgical year was distributed, while white and purple stoles were used as vestments. The All Souls Ministry raised complex issues. Non-Catholic personnel complained that a Catholic service did not meet their spiritual needs, while Catholic personnel complained that they could not always access a Catholic padre and their denominational identity was weakened.

Fr Tony Paris and Fr Danny Hernandez were awarded the Queen's Commendation for Valuable Service, which recognized their meritorious service during OPERATION TELIC.

Reflections

In July 2004, Fr John Nelson was at Shaibah Base with a Field Hospital. One afternoon he led a service for a soldier who had died from wounds. The service was for the medics who had worked hard to save the soldier's life. After a Gospel passage, prayers and a brief address, a sergeant approached Fr Nelson and asked: "Padre, do you believe all that stuff you were saying?" The padre replied that he did. The soldier's response was not what Fr Nelson expected: "Well I don't, but it makes a difference to me that you do."

Fr Strachan's ministry transcended medical and welfare work and "even the nominally religious seemed to welcome sincere and sensitive Christian intervention". Some troops took a greater interest in religion through more frequent contact with padres. Others "preferred to live at a distance from their chaplain".

Fr Danny Hernandez, commissioned in 2000, completed two tours of Iraq. In October 2004, he was attached to the Royal Regiment of Artillery at Shabah Logistics Base and with fourteen other chaplains had care of 8,000 personnel. Padre Hernandez recalled that troops appreciated his presence, especially on patrol, regarding him as a sign of good luck. For the chaplain, it was an opportunity to share the work, fears and anxieties of the soldiers. On a mission, they became aware of religion and often accepted the Rosaries he had made out of parachute cord. In combat, he suggested, soldiers were living out the gospel by caring for each other and often laying down their lives for their comrades.

In 2006, Fr Steven Forster was attached to 1st Battalion, The Princess of Wales's Royal Regiment, on OPERATION TELIC 6. On completion of his tour, he wrote that the biggest challenge was the need to be adaptable. Common ground between priest and soldier is that they are both called and pledged to a life of service. For the priest, that is of service to God and his people, for the soldier it is in service to monarch and country, and that is never more evident than on operations. "What is obvious", reflected Fr Forster, "is that self-obsessed or self-centred personalities do not make good soldiers as equally it is true that such people fail to make good Christians."

The previous August, during the intense heat of an Iraqi summer, Fr Forster was in Camp Abu Naji with C Company of 1 Prince of Wales Royal Regiment, where they held a memorial service for a soldier who had been killed earlier. Leading prayers and conducting a memorial service was what a padre's role was about, but that particular day illustrated, for Fr Forster, the diversity of military life. The Company decided to pull a Challenger II Tank over 400 metres to raise money for a charity nominated by the dead soldier's family. The padre joined in. "It was hard, it was fun, it was bizarre", he recalled.

Fr Nick Farrell, commissioned in 1999, deployed to Iraq with the King's Royal Hussars in 2005. His entry in the *Regimental Journal* summarized the reality of the war for those involved and their families, friends and colleagues at home. The deaths of five soldiers "sent shock waves through the Regiment" wherever it was:

The Compassionate and Medical chain worked extremely well and the Regiment was soon able to focus back on operational work. The incident will go down in the Regiment's history and those involved will not be forgotten. The hard and sustained work of those who remained in Tidworth to form the Rear Party must not be forgotten. Without them the work out in Iraq would not have been nearly so successful, and the families would not have been as well cared for as they were. One of the marvels that I really came to understand on tour was the way that all of the parts, sub units and attached arms of the Regiment work so well together to complete the jig-saw which makes the Regiment run so smoothly and effectively.

It was with a sigh of relief that the Regiment returned to homes, families and loved ones in the UK. The Operation drew to a close with a Service of Thanksgiving and Remembrance, where once again the Regiment gave of their best in every way. I must say without reservation that they are a fine Regiment and a wonderful group of people who I am very proud and honoured to have ministered to on this tour of operations.

Although OPERATION TELIC raised moral and ethical questions among people and politicians in the United Kingdom, padres expressed no doubts about accompanying British forces. Like the personnel they served, they experienced a range of emotions and suffered from the symptoms of stress, fatigue and fear. In all of this, they had patiently, faithfully and genuinely conducted their ministry. That ministry was appreciated in many ways. As Fr Strachan recalled:

Some individuals were strengthened and comforted by a minister of religion being attached to their unit. Others found support on receipt of pastoral care. Or, again, the "humanistic" relations a chaplain can foster in the military environment seemed apt to those simply facing the ordinary matters of adult life. Signs of gratitude, respect and affection for the padre . . . resulted from this.

British withdrawal from Iraq

Fr Paschal Hanrahan of the Diocese of Killaloe, commissioned in 2005 and deployed to Iraq in 2006 and 2008, was the last chaplain in Iraq. On 30 April 2009, he conducted a memorial service at Basra Air Base to mark the end of the British deployment. It was a service charged with pride and emotion during which the names of Britain's 179 war dead were read out. To the assembled troops Padre Hanrahan said:

> Each name is unique and each name tells a story, the story of a son or a daughter; a husband or a wife, a father or a mother. Each will invoke powerful memories, not least for the family and loved ones back home, who are very much in our thoughts and prayers today.

Figure 26: Fr Richard Madders RN: First Gulf War chaplain meets Pope St John Paul II (Mgr Richard Madders)

2 7

"Body armour and extreme vigilance were always at a premium": UNPROFOR and SFOR chaplains in the Balkans

UNPROFOR and SFOR: The Balkans

In February 1992, the United Nations sent a multinational protection force (UNPROFOR) into the Yugoslavian constituent republics of Croatia, Serbia, Kosovo and Bosnia-Herzegovina. UNPROFOR's objectives were to protect civilians, provide humanitarian assistance, reduce internecine tensions and stem the fighting inside and between republics striving for independence. The major protagonists, ranged along ethnic and religious lines, were Bosnian Muslims, Orthodox Bosnian Serbs and Catholic Croats.

UNPROFOR was restructured in March 1995 when separate protection and prevention forces were established in Bosnia-Herzegovina and Croatia. UNPROFOR remained in Bosnia-Herzegovina until December 1995 when it was replaced by NATO's Stabilization Force (SFOR) and EU military missions. A total of 39,000 UN troops had served in UNPROFOR.

OPERATION GRAPPLE was the codeword used for the British commitment to UNPROFOR. In total, 2,400 British personnel were deployed essentially to provide protection for aid convoys and elements of all three armed services were eventually involved. The 1st Battalion Cheshire Regiment, with detachments of the Royal Irish Regiment, Royal Lancers and the Royal Engineers, deployed with armoured vehicles in October 1992 through the Croatian port of Split.

NATO air forces were also deployed to protect the civil populations and enforce United Nations resolutions and international peace agreements. Flying on night missions from stations in the United Kingdom, the RAF contributed to the longest airlift in history in order to relieve the siege of Sarajevo and provide intelligence, ground attack and airlift support to NATO forces. The Royal Navy provided fire power and support from the Adriatic.

UNPROFOR troops, there as peacekeepers with strict Rules of Engagement, soon found themselves in a situation where the Geneva Convention was not recognized and peacekeepers were viewed with suspicion by all opposing factions. British forces, like those of other nations, witnessed widespread racketeering of UN aid, war crimes and the very worst atrocities committed in a war that was a manifestation of deep-rooted ethnic and religious hatred. Concentration camps and mass graves became features of the conflict. From 1992 to 1995, an estimated 100,000 people were killed, the majority of whom were Bosniaks (Bosnian Muslims). In July 1995, Bosnian Serb forces killed an estimated 8,000 Bosniak men and boys in and around the town of Srebrenica, a UN "safe area". It was the largest massacre in Europe since the Holocaust. Fifty-nine British soldiers and one Royal Marine died in the Balkans.

Five British army chaplains were involved at any one time with UNPROFOR—two Anglican, two Church of Scotland and one Catholic. Their tour of duty lasted six months. The geographical extent of peacekeeping operations meant that it was impossible for one chaplain to minister to all soldiers of his denomination and so there was a good degree of ecumenical and international co-operation.

Catholic chaplains

Catholic army chaplains on operational tours with UNPROFOR and SFOR included Fr Tony Paris, Fr David Campbell and Fr David Kelly of the Archdiocese of Westminster, Fr Stephen Alker and Fr Martin Caddell of the Archdiocese of Liverpool, Fr Bernard Massey of the Diocese of Clifton, Fr Ian Evans of the Archdiocese of Dublin, Fr Frank Rowe of the

Archdiocese of Birmingham, Fr Francis Barber and Fr Anthony Barry of the Diocese of Salford, Fr Matthew Despard of the Diocese of Motherwell, Fr Mark O'Keefe of the Diocese of Plymouth, Fr Andrew Lloyd of the Diocese of Shrewsbury, Fr Tom Butler of the Diocese of Lancaster, Fr Leonard Purcell and Fr Donald Cumming of the Archdiocese of Glasgow, Fr Richard White of the Diocese of East Anglia and Fr Michael Fava, Fr John Humphreys and Fr John Nelson of the Diocese of Portsmouth. Fr Richard Madders RN of the Diocese of Arundel and Brighton served in Royal Navy and Royal Fleet Auxiliary ships engaged in related operations in the Adriatic.

Catholic chaplains with UNPROFOR

The first Catholic chaplain to the British forces with UNPROFOR was Fr Stephen Alker. Ordained in 1978, he became a Territorial Army chaplain in 1981 with the Royal Army Medical Corps (Volunteers), before being commissioned as a permanent chaplain in the Royal Army Chaplains' Department on 26 July 1983. Fr Alker had served with the army in Germany, Cyprus, Australia and in Northern Ireland before being deployed to Bosnia in October 1992.

In late September 1992, Fr Alker was given two weeks' notice to leave 11th Armoured Brigade at Minden in Germany and prepare for deployment to Croatia. With others, he arrived at Split Airport in the dead of night and drove to Divulje Barracks and their planned accommodation. The barracks had been trashed by outgoing Serbs and for the next few weeks living and sanitary conditions were extremely primitive. As Brigade RC Chaplain, Fr Alker was attached to the headquarters of the British force and alongside the Revd Tyrone Hilary, the Anglican padre, and the Revd Neil Cameron of the Church of Scotland, he began his Balkans ministry. The British force comprised 1st Battalion Cheshire Regiment, a Squadron of 9/12th Lancers and elements of the Royal Irish Regiment, the Royal Corps of Transport, the Royal Army Medical Corps and the Royal Air Force; in all, some 2,400 personnel. They were equipped with Warrior armoured personnel carriers and Scimitar armoured reconnaissance vehicles. Their task was to escort UN convoys delivering aid to Muslim and Croat villages and refugee centres. In their work, they frequently drove through villages destroyed by shellfire.

As the mission developed, the struggle for space and facilities eased. The padre received the services of an interpreter, but despite protests he was not provided with transport. Assistance came through the Archbishop of Split who provided Fr Alker with a car from the local seminary. Transport was essential as the extent of the theatre meant that padres found it difficult to maintain regular contact with outlying and isolated units. Such was the infrequency of his visits, once in every four to six weeks to some units, that Fr Alker encouraged Catholic soldiers to attend non-Catholic services. Some Royal Engineer and Royal Signals units were so isolated that the only means of getting to them was by helicopter. Visiting isolated units or checkpoints involved all padres and their drivers travelling huge distances on poor and very dangerous roads. Body armour and extreme vigilance were always at a premium. Fr Alker experienced live fire on a couple of occasions during his travels through the mountains in convoy.

Fr Alker recalled that he was welcomed by the troops but attendance at Mass and the Sacrament of Reconciliation was fitful. The results of his visits could be either dispiriting or warming for the padre. Despite his having travelled 50 miles for 17 hours in blizzard conditions, wearing Arctic gear, and having given advance notice of his arrival, no one turned up for Fr Alker's Mass at Tuzla. Yet on another occasion, having previously met men and shared leisure time with them in the same location, Fr Alker had over 40 at his Mass.

The effects of the war on the indigenous populations were cruel, severe and bitter. At Jajce, fleeing Bosnians were fired on by Serbs. Army patrols and medics had to attend to dead, wounded and dying civilians. In such instances, Fr Alker had to counsel traumatized officers and men. As houses were destroyed, families were forced to live in cramped and insanitary conditions in gymnasia and public buildings. Places of worship were common targets for the extremists, and mosques and churches (both Catholic and Orthodox) were desecrated and ruined. At Novi Travnik in central Bosnia, Fr Alker found the Catholic church had not been attacked, and on the Feast of the Annunciation he surprised the worshippers by walking in combat gear down the aisle at the end of Mass to introduce himself to the priest. At Knin in northern Croatia, where the Catholic church had been desecrated, Fr Alker attended the Orthodox church on Christmas Day, 7 January, when Bishop Longin presided. The bishop spoke perfect English, having worked in England and Australia, and two of the monks had stayed for some time at the Benedictine Ampleforth Abbey in Yorkshire. At lunch, Bishop Longin told Fr Alker of the extreme nationalists who had taken over the town. The Catholic priest and many of his parishioners had fled at the onset of hostilities, but Bishop Longin promised that the Orthodox community would help to restore the damaged Catholic church.

British forces helped to rebuild shattered neighbourhoods and social amenities, and padres found that an important secondary element of their work was liaising with civilian communities of all religions and ethnicities. Many had lost everything. Fr Alker frequently gave Deutschmarks (as the local currency was worthless) to local groups so they could buy essential foodstuffs and, through one of the Catholic soldiers, the Union of Catholic Mothers in Glasgow sent three lorries filled with children's shoes. They were distributed to thankful recipients. On another occasion, surplus army scarves were given out to needy families. Parishes throughout the United Kingdom sent Fr Alker generous gifts of money that was distributed to all communities—Croat, Serb and Muslim.

Fr Martin Caddell was deployed to UNPROFOR in June 1993, replacing Fr Bernard Massey. After arriving at Split from BAOR, Fr Caddell took up his ministry to the troops and civilians. He travelled through Bosnia to celebrate Mass for soldiers in Gornji Vakuf and Vitez and witnessed the devastation and dislocation caused by war. Villages had been destroyed, and children were begging for sweets amidst the sound of shelling and gunfire. Working with Padre Bob Green, Anglican chaplain to the Coldstream Guards, Fr Caddell visited wounded soldiers at Nova Bila where a Franciscan church had been converted into a hospital. The soldiers' work within and for the community went alongside the padre's ministry to soldiers and civilians. British forces helped to decorate a hospital for disabled children and were involved in an Anglo-Croatian carol service, instigated by Fr Alker. The troops were there to complete a military and humanitarian operation, however, and much of their time was of necessity spent in dangerous and treacherous conditions. They appreciated the time the padre gave to them, as he shared their fears and listened to their anxieties about families and loved ones left at home.

Fr Francis Barber served with the UN Protection Force and for six months had been travelling throughout the British area of operations, holding services and "being a listening ear" for the soldiers. One of the most powerful moments for him was when he was setting up an observation post with a troop of the Household Cavalry. The site chosen was an isolated, burned-out hamlet with a few houses in a mountainous region. They set about sorting out their kit, and carrying the food ration, water and wood burner into one of the houses. A few of them went into the kitchen looking for somewhere to put their provisions. "Suddenly we all fell quiet", wrote Fr Barber, "and just looked around: it hit us all at the same moment; we had just moved into a building which, until 12 months or so ago, was somebody's home." It served as a good lesson to the soldiers that war "is about real people with real lives", but, he continued, "the real tragedy . . . is for the children".

> They are always the ones that take the rough end. They are the ones who always lose out. It is they who are brought up in the culture of hatred, distrust and violence. Around all the UN checkpoints and observation posts, the children gather like bees round a honeypot. Most reasonably friendly, many doing jobs for the boys like cutting firewood; all are on the scrounge. As I arrive, they are usually interested to see who I am and look in wonder at the pips on my shoulders. Then the eagle-eyed ones spot the dark crosses in the lapels of my combat jacket. In this situation, even I am forced to ask, 'How much longer, Lord?'

Fr Ian Evans recalled that, as in previous wars, church attendance did not have a high priority on the military agenda, but soldiers attended Mass and the Sacrament of Reconciliation where possible, on a voluntary basis and in varying numbers. The British were part of an international force and the padre celebrated Mass in Spanish for the Spanish contingent near Gornji Vakuf, recently captured from the Serbs. On the road to

Bugojno, he celebrated Mass for Catholics with the Light Dragoons and 1st Fusiliers, but trying to access Gornji Vakuf, other towns and isolated units was dangerous and stressful, especially along lines of confrontation. He recalled:

> I headed up the road to Maglaj school where 30 or so personnel maintain a presence in the town. Frequently shot at and once mortared, it is approached by entering sniper's alley, a 100 yards long stretch of road only passed when wearing helmets and body armour.

In such places, soldiers were in a constant state of readiness and in the presence of a Mobile Surgical Team. In some places, attacks by children, growing up in a culture of hatred, distrust, violence and ethnic cleansing, were almost as dangerous as being attacked or interrogated by the warring factions. In Muslim areas, Fr Evans suddenly realized that he was "one of the enemy" and the external signs of ministry on his uniform provoked demonstrations of in-built hatred: "For the first time in my life, I experience real antipathy to the thing I hold so dear. Their distrust of the sign of the Cross, has been bred so deep. The cycle is set."

Years later, Fr Evans recalled the massacre at Srebrenica in July 1995 when Bosniaks were fleeing the advancing Bosnian Serbs who were rampaging through neighbouring towns and villages. Thousands converged on Srebrenica in the vain hope that the UN enclave soldiered by the Dutch Battalion (DUTCHBAT) would be their hope of safety. Fr Evans wrote:

> How wrong could they be ... It was not long before the men and boys over a certain age were separated from their wives, mothers and sisters. With many placed on to buses with the tacit collaboration of the Dutch—who like the Muslims were told that the men were being relocated—they were taken away to areas in the vicinity of Srebrenica and murdered. Many women and sadly children, in full sight of the Dutch, were raped and sexually assaulted in the most appalling manner. The killing of the men lasted for days as they were hunted down in the fields

and forests. Mass graves attempted to hide the true extent of the carnage . . . news of the killings was communicated through the chain of command throughout the British Forces contingent (BRITFOR) . . . I recall quite vividly my feelings at the time. It was a profound sense of shame and anger that such a holocaust-like incident could be happening again in Europe. What had we learned from the experience of the almost annihilation of the Jews during World War II? I left Bosnia having served two tours, and I departed the country harbouring utter disdain towards all protagonists.

Catholic padres with SFOR

The Stabilization Force in Bosnia and Herzegovina (SFOR) was a multinational NATO peacekeeping force deployed to Bosnia and Herzegovina after the Bosnian War. It lasted from 1996 until 2007.

In August 1995, Fr Tony Paris was deployed with HQ 24 Air Mobile with UNPROFOR, and then in late 1995 and early January 1996 he was deployed with HQ 2 Signal Brigade and HQ 4 Armoured Brigade with SFOR.

Fr John Humphreys had prior military experience, having served as an officer in the Royal Engineers and also as Anglican chaplain in the RAChD. He left the Anglican Church in 1995, became a Catholic and was ordained as a Catholic priest in 1997. He maintained his contact with the army, serving as Catholic padre with the Territorial Army (subsequently termed the Army Reserve). He was mobilized for Kosovo in 1999 and deployed as Force Catholic Chaplain at the Multinational Brigade (Central) Headquarters in Pristina. His predecessor, Fr David Kelly, had already left the theatre, but Fr Mark O'Keefe, chaplain with Irish Guards, was able to show Fr Humphreys around before he returned with his battalion to the UK.

Fr Humphreys celebrated several Masses each weekend for different units, including the Field Hospital. His Mass at HQ KFOR (the NATO headquarters) was the best supported and had a usual congregation of between 20 and 50. Later in the tour, he was asked by the Catholic parish priest of Pristina to celebrate a Mass in English in his church. This was very well supported by UN workers and Albanians who wished to learn English! Every fortnight he went with the Anglican chaplain to 101 Logistic Brigade to visit a sub-unit in Skopje and celebrate a Mass there.

There was, recorded Fr Humphreys, high tension between Albanians and Serbs. Around Pristina, the Albanians were in the majority and Serbian monuments and churches had to be protected. If protection was withdrawn, they would quickly be destroyed. Sadly, Fr Humphreys witnessed a small Orthodox chapel outside Podujevo being guarded by a section of infantry. Close by, there were a number of Albanians. He wrote in his diary that if the guards went, the chapel would be destroyed. A few days later, this proved to be the case.

Fr Leonard Purcell of the Archdiocese of Glasgow had served as a Territorial Army Chaplain, an Officiating Chaplain and a Reserve Chaplain before joining the RAChD in 1990 and had completed tours of duty in Northern Ireland and with British Forces Germany. From 1999 to 2000, he ministered to troops in an area from Split in Croatia to Banja Luka in Bosnia, and from Sarajevo in Bosnia to Zagreb in Croatia. He covered the huge distances in his Land Rover, with an armed driver/bodyguard, and wore combat uniform unlike the clerical dress he had worn in Northern Ireland. Like all NATO personnel, he faced a dangerous and challenging task. He wrote:

> We were operating in a country traumatized by years of bloody conflict and atrocity in which there was still sporadic communal violence and huge tracts of countryside still festooned with live landmines. This made negotiating our way around the country's roads rather interesting, as the consequences of coming off road, or even off the designated, authorized routes, could have been devastating.

Although his primary role was the pastoral care of his soldiers, the padre could not but be moved by the villages and houses that were destroyed, the economy that was destroyed and most of all by the lives that were lost and shattered. Chaplains, wrote Fr Purcell, had "a duty to those in need caught up in the tragedy of conflict and war".

Fr John Nelson of the Diocese of Portsmouth was a Reserve Chaplain deployed to Kosovo. He joined the Territorial Army in 1990 and had experience with 308 Evacuation Hospital, which included specialists and trained medics. When TA personnel were mobilized for the Balkans War, Fr Nelson's unit became a Field Hospital. In 2001, he took over from Fr Donald Cumming as RC Brigade Chaplain based in Pristina. He stayed for eight months and on the day that he was due to return to the UK—11 September 2001—the World Trade Centre in New York was attacked. During his deployment, which followed the main conflict in Kosovo, Fr Nelson worked in a team of chaplains linked into a multinational group of chaplains and recalled that he learned much about how the army operates in the field and on operations. He had the freedom to travel across Kosovo and forged a good link with the Catholic bishop, who lived in Prizren, as well as local clergy. He came to understand how, on operations such as the one in Kosovo, the chaplain can be instrumental in linking with local religious figures. For example, Fr Nelson inherited from Fr Cumming the arrangement of celebrating a Saturday evening Mass in the town's Catholic church—attended by some locals but also many NGO and UN workers.

The impact of the padre's ministry

All padres were shocked at the ferocity of the fighting, the viciousness of the campaign and the genocide. Their task was to bring the sacraments to their military parishioners, of all nationalities, and offer as much support and counselling as possible to both military personnel and to civilians. Fr Stephen Alker recalled that alongside his spiritual ministry he acted as a surrogate father, an agony aunt, a lucky charm or talisman, and a court jester to soldiers who had a great sense of humour. Attendance at voluntary services may have been variable but visits by the chaplain were always appreciated. The padre's work was dangerous, challenging and tiring but also rewarding. And in addition to his primary role, he had somehow to act as a bridge between the British military and civilians and also between warring factions whose nationality was defined by faith.

Figure 27: Fr Stephen Alker CF (front right):
UNPROFOR-SFOR chaplain (Mgr Stephen Alker)

"A mission unlike anything we have seen": Army chaplains in Afghanistan

The war in Afghanistan

The campaign in Afghanistan lasted from 2001 to 2021. It began when the United States and its NATO allies invaded Afghanistan and toppled the so-called Islamic Emirate of the Taliban. The conflict ended with the Taliban regaining power after a twenty-year bitter struggle against an international alliance and Afghan armed forces. The United States' involvement was termed OPERATION ENDURING FREEDOM, and after 2014 OPERATION ENDURING FREEDOM'S SENTINEL, while the British contribution was called OPERATION HERRICK (Op HERRICK).

British forces played a major role, at first with the coalition ISAF (International Stabilization and Assistance Force) peacekeeping force and later, from 2004, in greatly extended coalition operations against Taliban insurgents. Britain's contribution grew considerably as the conflict progressed, with Op HERRICK going through 20 phases. Commanders were changed; troops were rotated, replaced and refreshed; and weapons and medical equipment were resupplied and replenished. Britain's combat mission in Afghanistan ended in 2014.

In 2014, Camp Bastion, British headquarters in Helmand Province, was the biggest British base in the world, housing 14,000 troops. It was also the most active with frequent ground and air operations. At one point, there were 600 aircraft sorties a day against Taliban positions. Over 150,000 British military personnel served in Afghanistan.

The war came at a terrible cost for the people of Afghanistan and for American, international and British forces. Of the British troops, 453 died and many were seriously wounded. The repatriation of 355 killed in Afghanistan became a familiar sight as they were brought home to RAF Lyneham, Wiltshire. Their corteges wound slowly and respectfully through the town of Royal Wootton Bassett, so-named after 2011 for its dignified reception of the dead and their grieving families. Help for Heroes, a charity devoted to the care of military veterans, was founded in 2007 and raised millions of pounds, while the Invictus Games was inaugurated to use the power of sport to inspire recovery, support and rehabilitation. Both charities generated a wider public understanding of the British military and respect for its casualties.

Chaplains in Afghanistan

Op HERRICK led to a significant reappraisal of British military attitudes and methods. It also had a profound impact on the concept and practice of military chaplaincy. Many service personnel were recruited from weaker religious backgrounds than in previous generations, and chaplains worked in a very different ecumenical environment and according to revised military command structures. Approximately 160 army chaplains served in Afghanistan.

In the light of such changes, historians of military chaplaincy have examined continuities and discontinuities between, for example, British army chaplaincy on the Western Front from 1914 to 1918 and in the war in Afghanistan. Michael Snape has explored the religious beliefs and practices of British soldiers caught up in the deadly and protracted struggles on the Western Front and in Helmand Province. While acknowledging differences in the operational contexts involved and shifts in British religious life over the course of the twentieth century, Snape identified striking degrees of continuity evident in the ministry of army chaplains and the religious attitude and behaviour of soldiers themselves.

Catholic chaplains in Afghanistan

Catholic padres deployed on Op HERRICK were not the first to experience warfare in Afghanistan. In 1879, Mill Hill Missionaries Frs Thomas Jackson and Thomas Prenger were chaplains in the Second Afghan War, but they were seen by the enemy as motivating agents rather than bringing religious consolation. In one engagement, Fr Jackson was wounded and carried in a "bullock wagon" to Kandahar—one of 700 out of the 2,000 who survived. In the following year, *The Tablet* reported that there "were five Mill Hill Missioners attending the spiritual wants of the troops".

Training for the modern conflict was thorough. In 2011, Fr Ian Stevenson of the Diocese of Paisley was Senior Chaplain to 20 Armoured Brigade based at Paderborn, Germany. Having joined the RAChD in 2001 he had already served one tour of Afghanistan in 2008 and he was given the task of preparing a team of nine chaplains for a six-month deployment in the theatre as part of Op HERRICK VIII. He became the first Catholic padre to lead chaplains of other denominations in the conflict. The padres came together in Paderborn and undertook ecumenical, cultural, recreational and military activities to form a team that would work together and support each other. The pastoral care of families remaining in Germany was regarded as highly important and Fr Tom Butler of the Diocese of Lancaster was posted from Catterick to cover Fr Stevenson's absence in Afghanistan. Another chaplain, Fr David Smith of the Diocese of East Anglia, came from Northern Ireland, and units from 19 Brigade joined 20 Armoured Brigade to become Task Force Helmand.

Padres underwent extensive military training with their units and also attended family briefings prior to deployment. As individuals and as a team, they prepared spiritually and were made aware of their pastoral and welfare role on operations. Their specific ministry to the wounded, the dead and the bereaved, their pastoral support to soldiers, and training for repatriation vigils and loading ceremonies was emphasized. Prior to departing for Afghanistan in September 2011, the team came together at the Jesuit Retreat Centre in Belgium. As Fr Stevenson said: "It was vital that each one of us was spiritually sustained in order to support those under our care." The team was to work together, train together, deploy together and, hopefully, return together.

Afghanistan—the front line

Twenty Catholic army chaplains served on Op HERRICK. Fr Daren Brown of the Diocese of Nottingham was commissioned in 2005 and completed training for Afghanistan with Joint Forces Medical Group in January 2006. On 16 April, he embarked for Kabul via Bahrain on Op HERRICK IV and on arrival found a huge base with military, medical, social and spiritual facilities. Padre Brown shared accommodation with international and inter-denominational chaplains and, in the next few days, the base was the target of enemy missile attacks. Fr Brown recalled that "this was my first taste of hostility, and it was an unsettling moment". The Medical Group then headed to Camp Bastion in Helmand, "a desert which can only be described as a complete wilderness", wrote Fr Brown. Camp Bastion held 2,000 military personnel; Fr Brown had pastoral care of the hospital and was also padre for 3 Para, which fought 500 "contacts" in the six-month tour.

Fr Brown eventually had pastoral care of three more units and, with other padres, set up a chaplaincy centre. Many service personnel had been away from home for longer than six months and the church and chaplaincy centre became a place "to remind soldiers of their humanity and the love of God for them". At Lashkar Gah, the capital of Helmand, Fr Brown met with the Senior Chaplain who showed him the camp and town, including a school run by UNESCO which catered for 7,000 students! In addition to saying Mass for the military, Fr Brown said Mass for a Filipino community of workers and visited soldiers in isolated Forward Operating Bases (FOBs).

As the war intensified, injuries to the military and civilians increased in number and severity. Soldiers and locals of all ages were brought to Camp Bastion for treatment and the Joint Forces Medical Group Chaplaincy provided spiritual and moral welfare for all. Casualties and fatalities among the military were frequent and memorial and repatriation services were held for the dead. During his six-month tour of duty, Fr

Brown conducted services for 17 deceased soldiers, and padres combined to provide moving and solemn repatriation ceremonies. "For those left behind", he wrote, "it is very important for them to say goodbye and to salute their comrade. It's not easy . . . every one was just as hard as the one before." Memorial services were frequently held in one of the cook houses and were always well attended.

On completion of his six-month tour, Fr Brown recalled that it had been "a shocking introduction to the realities of armed conflict and the consequences of what that entails". Some combatants dealt with the situation alone; others handled it with the help of others. As his soldiers prepared to leave, he said to them: "Six months ago nobody knew what would be ahead of us, and looking back a lot has happened. So, we come here today just to reflect on what we've seen, accomplished and experienced as the Joint Forces Med Group and as individuals." He told the soldiers to give themselves "a pat on the back" for a job well done but "to go home in peace". Finally, he exhorted them to pray for those who had died and had been seriously injured and to learn from their "amazing, emotional, and demanding time here in the Helmand Desert". In 2010, Fr Brown returned to Afghanistan on Op HERRICK XII.

In September 2007, Fr David Smith was Regimental Chaplain to 4 Regiment Royal Artillery, based in Osnabrück, Germany, and was deployed to Afghanistan, where he soon experienced the dangers of warfare. In November, he was flying in a Chinook helicopter to an isolated Forward Operating Base (FOB) in the Helmand Desert to visit his soldiers and to conduct a Remembrance Sunday church parade. They were coming in to land when suddenly the helicopter lurched upwards and off to the right. It shot sideways and the crew began manhandling machine guns at the side and rear of the helicopter in case of attack. Fortunately, the pilot was able to get them out of trouble and they flew back to Camp Bastion. Fr Smith recalled: "I am absolutely convinced that we were protected and saved by the prayers of Our Lady of Victories and St Michael—to whose prayers I had already commended us during the flight."

Fr Smith's units provided artillery support to various military operations aimed at defeating the Taliban and promoting the rebuilding of Afghanistan after many years of war. Most units were camped in the middle of the desert or in the FOBs and living was tough and without modern comforts. Mail was sporadic, and most locations did not have electricity or running water. And as for sanitary arrangements, "thunderboxes" and wet wipes were the order of the day. But food was plentiful and they survived for weeks on boil-in-the-bag rations. The occasional welfare parcel from home was a real boost for the soldiers, and the padre had a major role in their distribution. The chaplain shared life with soldiers, supporting them and praying for them. He lived with the soldiers, in the same conditions and sharing the same dangers.

The chaplain did what he could to support the soldiers with prayer and practical help—celebrating Holy Mass where possible, hearing confessions and anointing the sick and dying. He was there as a friend to soldiers, many of whom were frightened and homesick; he was also a friend and confidant to those in positions of command and responsibility, many of whom spoke of the troubling and difficult moral decisions that had to be made. Commanding troops in war, the padre felt, must be one of the loneliest jobs but somehow strength was given to those who needed it.

Frequent media reports of the deaths of British soldiers ensured that the British public was aware that violence and danger were a part of daily life in Afghanistan. At FOBs, British forces were attacked frequently and, sadly, repatriation ceremonies conducted by the padres became an all too frequent occurrence. Seriously wounded soldiers seldom made the news, even though their wounds were devastating and life-changing. This is the reality of what the country asks of its armed forces.

"One of the best things about being a Catholic padre", wrote Fr Smith, "was that when you get to mix with the locals, you always find the Catholic Church in some way." Not that there were many Afghan Christians, but there were Catholic migrant civilian workers, including Catholics from India, Sri Lanka, South America, the Philippines and even Pakistan working alongside the military, involved in the rebuilding work. Fr Smith said Mass for these "civvy-contractors" every week and was able to provide some small measure of pastoral care for them. The Filipinos, especially, were very devout and, just as important to a hungry army padre, excellent cooks. The padre didn't know where they got fresh chickens from in the middle of Helmand and did not dare to ask, but the "Filipino chicken noodles were out of this world!"

As Christmas 2007 approached, the chaplains and troops produced a pantomime. Fr Smith was unsure that amateur dramatics and the military went together, but he was amazed how much talent there was among the servicemen and servicewomen. The four chaplains held the auditions and eventually had a cast of about 40 with more helping backstage. Senior officers were involved and even Royal Marine Commandos needed little persuading to slip into tutus and fishnet tights for the performance! The panto was a huge boost for morale—for both the performers and the audiences. Christmas is hard enough for soldiers, being away from family and friends—and in a war zone it is even worse—so a little light relief was a real lift to keep them all going until the end of the tour. The panto was filmed and copies sent to troops in isolated locations who were unable to get back to camp to see live shows.

Many Afghans, wrote Fr Smith, had experienced only war and its effects: the Russians and then the Taliban had imposed violent regimes. Yet when the British troops got out among the locals and on patrol, they were told that they wanted peace and stability. Afghans wanted not fighting and despotic governance but schools and hospitals, good roads, and law and order. They wanted to make an honest living in their traditional rural-based ways. But one of the major problems in Afghanistan was the presence of the opium poppy crop. Nineteen per cent of the world's opium, used to make heroin, was grown in Afghanistan and then sold on to Western markets. The Taliban, for all their puritanical rhetoric, "taxed" the local farmers for growing poppies and then manipulated the lucrative narcotics industry flooding the West. The income funded Taliban weaponry. The problem for the Afghan government was trying to wean the locals off the lucrative poppy crop and on to more conventional but poorly paid subsistence farming crops. British and coalition forces were determined to help the people of Afghanistan decide their own future.

Fr Paschal Hanrahan, of Ennis, County Clare, was ordained in 1998 for the Diocese of Killaloe. He was commissioned into the RAChD in September 2005 and served as padre to the Queen's Royal Lancers, 1st Battalion the Princess of Wales's Royal Regiment, 7th and 16th Signal

Regiments, Third Regiment Royal Horse Artillery and the Irish Guards. During this time, Fr Hanrahan served in Iraq (Op TELIC IX and XIII) and was deployed on Op HERRICK XVII and XVIII.

In 2013, as Joint Force Support Senior Chaplain, Op HERRICK XVIII, Fr Michael Fava was required to function as the sole United Kingdom Catholic army chaplain in theatre. There he supervised a chaplaincy team of 12 chaplains of different denominations. While based at Camp Bastion in Helmand Province, these two roles required him to travel around theatre on a regular basis in order to visit chaplains and to offer worship for Catholic personnel. This took him to Kabul, Kandahar and Lashkar Gah, as well as FOBs such as FOB Price and FOB Shawqat on a regular basis. The challenges of functioning in a very hostile war zone were many and varied—not least when it came to travel (most of which was by helicopter) and in summer temperatures approaching 50 degrees Celsius.

In preparation for the later extraction of the British from Helmand, the responsibility for taking an active fighting role transitioned from British forces to personnel of the Afghan National Army during this tour. While sustaining some British fatalities early in the tour, it soon became the case that daily instances of death and injury to Afghan National soldiers brought a steady inflow to the Role 3 Hospital in Bastion as the transition took place. Fr Fava recalled that his experience of Op HERRICK XVIII was unique among his deployments in terms of the scale and complexity of the operation and in terms of finding himself under direct enemy fire. Pastorally, he regarded it as one of the most satisfying experiences of his ministry with the RAChD.

Death in Afghanistan

Ordained in 1999 for the Diocese of Galloway, Fr Stephen Sharkey joined the RAChD in 2008 and was deployed on Op HERRICK X from June to October 2009, and on Op HERRICK XIX from September 2013 until April 2014. Fr Sharkey's account of his duty in an FOB emphasized the padre's instinctive reaction in battle, the need for his moral and physical courage, and the importance of sustaining the morale of those he served.

The padre recalled how, on one tour, he went to a company at an FOB where the Platoon Sergeant had been seriously injured and a soldier killed by an Improvised Explosive Device (IED). The distance from his own FOB to where the incident had taken place was six kilometres. Fr Sharkey wrote: "It was a dangerous road often travelled by these soldiers, just off the route where the soldier had been killed earlier that day." The thirteen-hour journey to the FOB, in searing temperatures, was very risky, for there was the strong possibility of IEDs and attacks by insurgents, but the padre was more concerned at breaking the news of the soldier's death to his comrades. "The boys knew, but I just could not confirm it; it was not advantageous to break the news at that time and it would not have helped matters. The news would be better broken in the safety of the FOB." The mood in the FOB was a mixture of sadness and anger; "The heads were down . . . morale was very low. It was a scene of a morose lot." Instinctively, the padre offered prayers, spoke to each soldier and gave them a hug. He felt that his presence was appreciated and "just being there was worth more than words would ever explain". Next day he conducted an evening Memorial Service—a time of quiet, a period of prayer and remembrance, a show of solidarity except for sustained fire from insurgents. Fr Sharkey wrote:

> With the parade of around 150 from the battalion and attached personnel gathered around me on three sides, we stood quietly, the heat of the day was starting to reduce and the light was decreasing. The service started and the quiet reflectiveness was suddenly broken by the sound of a rocket propelled grenade landing next to one of our guard-posts. It was just at that point that all went mad and we came under steady streams of fire from the area outside the FOB. The gunfire could be heard as a pop in the distance but overhead the whizz of the bullets could be heard uncomfortably close. It felt as though we could almost jump up and catch the bullets.

The Officer in Charge and the Sergeant Major gave no signal to the padre to stop the service. A few soldiers peeled off to assist in repelling the insurgents, but the other soldiers stayed on parade.

> The service continued, and the most memorable point was to be during the minute's silence, the bugler sounded the Last Post, and all our soldiers stopped firing, the incoming rounds continued but we never retaliated, that is until after the minute's silence and Reveille sounded and our Mortar Line went into action.

At the end of the Memorial Service, everyone rushed to their allotted points to guard the FOB and go about their normal tasks, but the Service had been an "incredibly moving and . . . somewhat frightening" experience for the padre. His decision to go to the FOB and give succour to the troops was an instinctive reaction rather than a calculated or courageous response. To conduct the Memorial Service under such conditions was a determination not to mar the memory of a dead soldier but also, from a military point of view, a notice to the enemy that the British would not be deterred from fulfilling their mission.

Like many chaplains before him, Fr John Nelson was questioned about his own faith. At the end of a gruelling shift in Camp Bastion, where staff were working to save soldiers badly injured by IEDs, he was asked by a nurse: "Padre, how is it that you get to have faith and I don't?" On other occasions, soldiers, surrounded by carnage, questioned the padres about God's ways. The military worked hard to look after the various needs of its serving personnel and, as Fr Nelson and other padres testified, chaplaincy was a vital and unique part of that provision.

Figure 28: Fr Stephen Sharkey CF: Chaplain in Afghanistan

2 9

War and humanitarian assistance: Modern naval chaplaincy

Since 1982, the Royal Navy has been deployed in a number of conflicts, including the two Gulf Wars, a civil war in the former Yugoslavia and operations in Afghanistan. It has also provided the United Kingdom's nuclear deterrent as well as carrying out routine peacetime tasks such as counter-piracy, narcotics patrols and humanitarian missions.

Catholic naval chaplains in the Gulf Wars

The Royal Navy's contribution to OPERATION GRANBY (1990–91) saw the deployment of frigates, destroyers, minesweepers, and supply and hospital ships. Naval chaplains were deployed with surface ships, Royal Marine Commandos, hospital ships and Royal Fleet Auxiliaries. In 1991, there were twelve Catholic chaplains in the Royal Navy and Royal Marines, but Fr Richard Madders of the Diocese of Arundel and Brighton was the only one serving at sea during OPERATION GRANBY. Commissioned in September 1985, he had served on several shore bases. His previous sea time had been in HMS *Brilliant*, *Rothesay* and *Glasgow*.

Fr Madders deployed to the Gulf in January 1991, having been issued with combat kit and protection against anthrax and biological weapons. He left RAF Brize Norton by RAF air transport for Saudi Arabia and Bahrain to join HMS *Cardiff* at sea in the northern Gulf, having first transferred from RFA *Fort Grange* by Sea King helicopter. By then, operations had begun. The naval Task Group was under the constant threat of missile and mine attack and so *Cardiff* routinely went to action stations. During each alert, Fr Madders tried to get around the ship to see and steady as many people as possible. Hard to recognize in his action kit, he devised a lanyard with a cross on it. He provided daily Mass and Sunday church services and also spent time helping out in the galley.

On 30 January, a Lynx helicopter from *Cardiff* took out an armed Iraqi torpedo boat posing a serious threat to the Task Group. There was rejoicing in the wardroom, but Fr Madders later reflected on how a chaplain should react in such a situation. By 25 February, he had transferred to HMS *Gloucester*. Nearby, the veteran battleship USS *Missouri* and other coalition ships had come under Iraqi Silk Worm missile attack. *Gloucester* responded using its Sea Dart missile weapons system. It was a tense time for all.

On 28 February 1991, hostilities ceased. Fr Madders, still on *Gloucester*, sailed south, away from the by now liberated Kuwait, visiting Egypt, Cairo and the pyramids before returning to Portsmouth on 25 March 1991.

OPERATION TELIC was the name for the Second Gulf War (2003–09). There were 11 Catholic naval chaplains in 2003. Fr David Yates of the Diocese of Salford, commissioned in 1998, was in HMS *Liverpool*, a destroyer acting as escort to the aircraft carrier HMS *Ark Royal*. Fr David McLean, a Dominican, was commissioned in 1996. He served in HMS *Argyll*, deployed in 2008 to provide maritime protection for Iraq.

Catholic naval chaplains in the former Yugoslavia

OPERATION GRAPPLE was the UK's contribution to the UN's international peacekeeping force (IFOR) in the former Yugoslavia, particularly in Bosnia and Croatia, between 1992 and 1995. The IFOR mission transitioned into the Stabilization Force (SFOR).

In January 1993, Fr Richard Madders was Task Group Chaplain in HMS *Ark Royal*. Working alongside the ship's chaplain, the Revd Ted Edwards USN, he was responsible for chaplaincy support to a naval deployment as part of OPERATION GRAPPLE. *Ark Royal* sailed on 8 January, and for three months Fr Madders became a mobile chaplain, spending much time in the Fleet Auxiliaries *Olwen* and *Argus*, the latter carrying troops.

On 17 March, Fr Madders went into war-torn Split, where he joined Fr Stephen Alker, senior Catholic army chaplain. Staying at Dubrovnik Barracks, he visited Naval Air Squadron 845, which was undertaking dangerous missions often under fire. Fr Madders soon discovered that Split was within range of Serb artillery! With Fr Alker, he visited mess halls and was available for people who wanted to "unpack" their experiences of war. On 19 March, Fr Madders joined the Fleet Auxiliary *Resource* in Split where he was given a warm welcome and a cabin.

Fr Madders realized that returning to the Task Group could be a problem. A plan was devised and he was collected from *Resource* and taken to the airport. Unfortunately, he had no passport, having been sent ashore with little warning. However, two burly soldiers whisked him past Croat military officials and onto an RAF Hercules which took him to Ancona, Italy. He still had no passport, no local currency, was still in battle dress; and when he landed, there was no one to meet him. He changed into civilian clothes, got some money from an ATM, walked through a gap in the perimeter fence and at the local railway station caught a train to Bari. There a Royal Navy Liaison Officer directed him to the Sheraton Hotel for an overnight stay. The chaplain had hoped for a longer stay, but transport had been arranged for the next day. Arriving at the military section of the airport (no passport needed), he boarded a waiting Sea King. To his surprise, other passengers included Linda Lusardi (of *The Sun*'s Page 3 fame) and Admiral Michael Boyce. The helicopter flew directly to *Ark Royal*, and there was amazement when Fr Madders and Admiral Boyce returned with Linda Lusardi!

The remainder of the deployment was spent sailing up and down the Adriatic coast avoiding potentially hostile shore threats. Once relieved, *Ark Royal* visited Naples from where Fr Madders and Ted Edwards organized a visit to Rome. On 21 April 1993, 90 sailors attended a General Audience with Pope John Paul II in St Peter's Square. For the remainder of the deployment and on the way home, Fr Madders continued to visit ships of the Task Group.

The Royal Navy in Afghanistan

OPERATION HERRICK was far away from the Royal Navy's familiar surroundings yet the Senior Service played a major role in the war. It included missile strikes fired from submarines, Royal Marine sweeps through the mountains, extensive Commando patrols on the ground, helicopter missions, air strikes, medical services, training Afghan security forces and assuming the lead role in tri-service operations. The Royal Navy was present in the principal British base at Camp Bastion and in outposts and FOBs. Royal Marines served on 12 deployments and on three occasions led the British mission.

HMS *Fearless* and *Illustrious* were involved, as were the Fleet Air Arm's Sea King and Lynx helicopters, which carried troops and supplies, and Sea Harriers of the Naval Strike Wing. Other branches included surgeons and medics, engineers and technicians, air and ground crew, logisticians, Royal Marines musicians and chaplains.

Catholic naval chaplains in Afghanistan

The Royal Navy has traditionally fulfilled a worldwide role and chaplains are a part of that service. As ministry to the Royal Marines is also a part of the Royal Navy's chaplaincy service, naval chaplains accompany Marines on deployments.

Fr Michael Sharkey of the Archdiocese of Glasgow became a Royal Navy chaplain in 1990. He served at sea, in Cyprus and in Germany, and in 2001 was deployed to Kosovo with 45 Commando Royal Marines. He also undertook two tours of duty in Afghanistan, one as padre to 42 Commando Royal Marines (Op HERRICK V) and another as part of HQ joint forces support staff on Op HERRICK XIV. As Joint Force Senior Chaplain, he had responsibility for 15 chaplains of all denominations across the three services.

Service with the marines gave Fr Sharkey an insight into the conditions they experienced and he witnessed some of the toughest fighting that British forces have ever encountered. On his first tour, he went on patrol with the marines. "You'd never go out on a patrol if there wasn't a pastoral reason, but sometimes there was a reason ... if there was a team who'd lost a man, or who had been through a tough time, then I might go out with them. As a non-combatant I won't carry a weapon, though I might carry something useful—a radio, for example." Once, his patrol came under fire when a rocket-propelled grenade came over them. They threw themselves out of their vehicle, but over the radio the padre heard that there was a man down. Fr Sharkey went to him. "He was terribly shocked", he recalled. "Even though he was going to be ok. It's a terrifying thing, to be shot." The padre stayed with him and tried to help him stay calm while they were waiting for him to be evacuated. "It was near Christmas, and we talked about the carol concert."

Fr Sharkey maintained that shared experience of active service facilitated an appreciation of his ministry. He wore army fatigues in the hospital and crosses on his lapels signified that he was a padre, but otherwise he wore normal uniform. "It shows the men that I'm one of them ... when I tell them I've been out to Afghanistan, I've done a tour there, that makes a big difference—they know I genuinely understand what the conditions there are like." Most soldiers were young, a group not known for strong religious beliefs or outlooks, but, said the chaplain,

> when you're up against it in a war, no one doubts for a second the merit of having someone prepared to lead a prayer, or to talk about God. I've never once been in a situation where I've suggested saying a prayer, and anyone has turned it down. When you're in a life-and-death situation—and the men in Afghanistan are, every day—who wouldn't want to say a quick prayer?

Fr David Conroy, ordained in 1992 for the Diocese of Galloway, joined the Royal Navy Chaplaincy Service in September 2000 and ministered at sea and land bases. In 2011, he was appointed Joint Aviation Group Chaplain on Op HERRICK XIV. Later, in recognition of his ministry at Camp Bastion, he was awarded the Queen's Commendation for Valuable Service.

Other Royal Navy chaplains who served in Afghanistan were Frs Mark Cassidy and David McLean OP. Fr Cassidy of the Diocese of Dunkeld joined the Royal Navy in 2000 and served in HMS *Manchester*, HMS

Lancaster and the carrier HMS *Illustrious* before being deployed to Afghanistan with 3 Commando Brigade in 2011. The Brigade headed Op HERRICK 14 and with supporting units totalled over 6,000 British military personnel.

Fr McLean was also deployed on Op HERRICK 14 in 2011 as chaplain to Camp Bastion Hospital. At this time, the hospital was staffed by Royal Navy medics supported by US and army and RAF personnel. Many medics, especially reservists, normally worked in NHS Accident and Emergency departments, and Fr McLean naively commented that they would be familiar with horrific injuries, but he was soon corrected. Civilian medics deal with "momentum" injuries rather than blast injuries. An amputation emergency in the UK would be a rare event while in Bastion they took place daily. It was soon appreciated that the padres were to support staff as well as patients.

British TV bulletins were seen throughout the hospital, and it was a bugbear of the staff that it was only British fatalities that made the news. Every day, the dead and casualties came into the hospital from allied forces, the enemy, and Afghan civilians. A principle of international law on warfare was applied: injured, friendly or foe, are treated according to their medical needs. That principle applied also to spiritual needs.

In 2018, Fr McLean was posted to Permanent Joint Headquarters (PJHQ), based at Northwood, London. PJHQ runs the United Kingdom's overseas military operations, and all units and service personnel, irrespective of their service, belong to and are under the command of PJHQ while deployed on operations. Fr McLean contributed to the chaplaincy aspect of planning, the training of chaplains nominated for operations, and the management of them while deployed. It involved visiting operational locations, and Fr McLean went to most of the operational areas, including Afghanistan and the Gulf.

Afghanistan—the human cost

Returning from Afghanistan, Fr Sharkey became chaplain to the Royal Centre of Defence Medicine at Birmingham's Queen Elizabeth Hospital and was responsible for the pastoral care of injured service personnel, their families and the medical staff.

Those injured in Afghanistan were the "invisible victims of war", for in addition to well-publicized fatalities there were many more less well-known injuries. Work at the hospital was in a sense a battle zone, for the battle being waged was against lasting damage and compromised futures. Fr Sharkey said that for some this was the worst possible outcome of being a soldier: "Many men say they would rather die than end up without limbs, their lives utterly transformed from what they once were due to the explosive devices used by the Taliban. It's very tough for them, there's no doubt about it." Fr Sharkey was among the first that soldiers encountered after being airlifted out of Afghanistan. "These . . . are young men, at the peak of their fitness, doing a job they love and with their whole lives ahead of them . . . it's going to be difficult to accept that things are going to be very different from now on", he wrote. He had to help them realize that the very personality traits that made them good soldiers—tenacity, determination, hard work and a sense of humour—were the ones to help them to cope now and in the future. He said: "It's a question of helping them to realize that they can do it, that they can achieve things and have successful, fulfilled lives."

As the Centre's only padre, Fr Sharkey ministered to all patients. Nothing he did was exclusive or limited to Catholics. He served men and women of any faith and none—his job was to be with them, to listen, support, encourage and to pray with them if they wanted to do that. It was not only about solidarity and being alongside those receiving care, but also about reminding people of the spiritual dimension of life.

Piracy patrols, narcotics and evacuation

Fr Paul Donovan, of the Diocese of Northampton and commissioned in 1985, was chaplain to the Fleet Flagship HMS *Illustrious* in 2006, when she was in Mumbai as part of OPERATION AQUILA. There volunteers cleaned up a British military cemetery and distributed clothes and toys to local children. *Illustrious* had been part of a four-month anti-piracy patrol in the Arabian Sea and on the way home led a naval task group 2,300 miles from Gibraltar to evacuate British citizens from Lebanon. With HMS *Bulwark, Gloucester, York* and *St Albans*, HMS *Illustrious* welcomed evacuees airlifted by Chinook helicopters. At a church service, Fr Donovan had used the words, "Whatever you did to the least of these children, you did to me." The crews, he recalled, responded magnificently.

In 2017, while on OPERATION KIPION, Fr McLean ministered to sailors on Royal Navy ships in the Gulf and also served on HMS *Ocean* in anti-drug operations in the Caribbean.

OPERATION UNIFIED PROTECTOR

Fr Charles Bruzon, a Gibraltarian priest commissioned in 2010, had previously served as an Officiating Chaplain and a Reservist Chaplain to the Royal Gibraltar Regiment. In June 2011, he was chaplain in the destroyer HMS *Liverpool*, when it came under fire off the coast of Libya, then under the rule of Colonel Gaddafi. *Liverpool* had been in the Mediterranean since March 2011 to support NATO's OPERATION UNIFIED PROTECTOR and her tasks included enforcing the no-fly zone and conducting embargo operations to prevent arms from reaching pro-Gaddafi forces by sea.

Liverpool was providing cover for NATO vessels near the port of Misrata when it was attacked by shore-based heavy-calibre weapons. The destroyer took evasive action and returned fire before escorting several vessels to safety. Fr Bruzon recalled: "I undertook a roving role visiting personnel in all compartments until the alert state was reduced." *Liverpool's* captain reported that although the crew had been in danger, they had worked bravely and calmly under pressure.

Since the beginning of the deployment, the ship's company had spent 81 hours at action stations on 28 separate occasions, been fired at and returned fire ten times, and launched 211 rounds of illumination and high explosive shells from her 4.5-inch gun. Illumination or star shells were fired to light up pro-Gaddafi positions for NATO aircraft to identify and destroy. The ship's company witnessed the siege of Misrata and the fall of Tripoli and other towns. While enforcing the no-fly zone, *Liverpool*'s flight controllers spent 360 hours controlling fourteen different types of NATO aircraft.

Fr Bruzon exercised pastoral responsibility for four ships, including *Liverpool*. He divided his time between ships and had only recently completed a deployment on HMS *Iron Duke* in the Arabian Gulf when *Liverpool* came under fire. "I felt my ministry was very much brought to the fore at this time", he recalled, undertaking his rounds, and offering spiritual guidance and confidential support. Amid the general anxieties and uncertainties, he offered his own reassurance to the ship's company in his sermon at the Sunday service in the Junior Rates' dining hall. "Jesus, like the Royal Navy, does not say where He is taking us," he said, "but we trust Him." *Liverpool* returned to Portsmouth in November 2011.

Humanitarian missions

In October 2000, a British task force was deployed as part of OPERATION PALLISER to support United Nations troops in peacekeeping operations in Sierra Leone. HMS *Ocean*, HMS *Fearless*, Royal Fleet Auxiliary vessels and Royal Marines were diverted from the Mediterranean. Fr Andrew McFadden, ordained in 1989 and commissioned in 1998, was chaplain to HMS *Ocean*. Fr McFadden of the Diocese of Paisley had served at the Royal Naval Hospital, Haslar, and at Portsmouth Naval Base's Fourth Frigate Squadron. At sea, he served in HMS *Iron Duke* in the Adriatic and HMS *Marlborough* in the Gulf before joining HMS *Ocean*. The carrier's crew became involved in humanitarian work in Sierra Leone and rebuilt a hospital, church and school in the wake of the civil war.

In late 2013, Typhoon Haiyan hit the Philippines, and the Royal Navy was called upon to provide humanitarian assistance. Fr David Yates was serving in HMS *Daring* in the Pacific Ocean, when the destroyer was redirected to the Philippines. On reaching the disaster zone, the Royal Navy unloaded supplies, medical equipment and temporary accommodation facilities. The chaplain, in addition to his normal duties, found that in the wake of the disaster he had to help many people through the grieving process. He conducted burials, comforted bereaved relatives and assisted the homeless. The chaplain relied on his naval training, his previous experience as a hospital chaplain, and his faith to help him cope with a very difficult situation.

In November 2013, Fr David Conroy was in HMS *Illustrious* on counter-piracy operations off the African coast. The carrier had started its transit through the Gulf of Oman and was heading for Christmas leave, when it received instructions to sail for the Philippines, where Typhoon Haiyan was devastating the region. The crew watched television coverage of the scenes of devastation, and their disappointment at a vanished Christmas turned into a determination to help.

In Singapore, *Illustrious* loaded blankets, candles, food, shelters, jerry cans, water carriers, tents, wood, hammers, nails, wheelbarrows, nuts and bolts and tools into vacated hangars. On 25 November, *Illustrious* arrived in south-west Philippines and replaced HMS *Daring*. Fr Yates and Fr Conroy completed their handover by email. Helicopters were despatched to evaluate the situation—locating people in the greatest danger and assessing what type of materials were most needed.

The crew, Royal Marine, army and RAF detachments brought relief to the stricken areas and began rebuilding shattered communities. Over 22,000 people received emergency medical treatment from the carrier's crew, and news that the ship had a Catholic chaplain was a gamechanger for the crews' interaction with the people. There was no resident priest and Mass had not been celebrated for two years, so the chaplain's offer to celebrate Mass was greeted with joy. It was, Fr Conroy recalled, as if a papal visit were imminent. But there was still emergency work to do, so while the crew and Royal Marines lifted in supplies, the chaplain celebrated Mass for the traumatized islanders. The church building was badly damaged, but people flocked in and as Fr Conroy celebrated Mass, they could see, through holes in the roof, helicopters bringing in aid.

Over the next few weeks, he celebrated Mass, counselled the local people and prayed with them over their dead.

At the end of the operation, the overall feeling was one of satisfaction at a successful if sad undertaking. The Royal Navy had not fixed everything, but the people knew they were being cared for. The children were fascinated by the helicopters, by the Royal Marines who never seemed to get tired, and by many people who just wanted to help. When the Royal Navy completed its mission on 13 December, stones on a beach said "Thank You".

Figure 29: Fr David Conroy RN: Naval chaplain

From divided Germany to Afghanistan: Royal Air Force chaplains

The Royal Air Force in West Germany

British Forces Germany (BFG) was Britain's military presence in divided Germany after 1945. The RAF's component was the British Air Forces of Occupation (BAFO). The RAF made a huge contribution to the capability of the British Armed Forces and, through its high level of battle-readiness, helped ensure the survival of an independent, democratic West Germany.

Divided Berlin was the epicentre of potential conflict between the Allied occupying powers of Britain, France and the USA and their former ally, the Union of Soviet Socialist Republics (USSR). This relationship deteriorated in June 1948 when the Soviets closed land routes into the Allied sectors of Berlin. RAF Transport Command commenced OPERATION PLAINFARE, flying supplies from Wunstorf in West Germany to Gatow in the British sector of Berlin. Flights were along defined air corridors and the Berlin Blockade, as it became known, continued until August 1949 as RAF aircraft delivered foodstuffs, fuel and medicines. Uprisings against Soviet rule in East Germany (1953), Hungary (1956) and Czechoslovakia (1968) kept the RAF on constant alert and prepared for any military eventuality.

Political and military developments gradually reduced the RAF's presence in West Germany. In 1945, there were 20 stations comprising headquarters, airfields, hospitals and other facilities. In 1955, there were 19 stations, six in 1965, four in 1985, and two in 1995. German reunification in 1990 and the withdrawal of Soviet forces from Eastern and Central Europe lessened the need for a British presence in West

Germany and in 1993 BAOR and RAF Germany (formed in 1959) reverted to British Forces Germany (BFG).

Catholic RAF chaplains with BFG

After 30 years' service with the RFC and RAF, Mgr Henry Beauchamp retired and was succeeded in 1948 as Principal Catholic Chaplain by Fr John Lavin of the Archdiocese of Liverpool. In 1949, there were eight chaplains on establishment and 22 temporary chaplains. In 1950, there were 38 RAF chaplains in total, and by 1953 there were 47, but as the RAF's presence in BFG was reduced so was the number of chaplains. In BFG, they were subject to a non-Catholic Senior Chaplain in some administrative matters but were independent in appointments, routine administration and places of worship.

From post-war BFG, Fr Peter Blake SJ wrote: "I visited almost the whole of the British zone and saw the unforgettable sights and horrors of modern war." Chaplains adhered to the policy of non-fraternization but were conscious of the responsibilities of the German priesthood. In April 1945, Fr John MacSeumais SJ wrote that "the German clergy bear a terrific weight on their shoulders" having to restore religious life and minister to their own congregations, enlarged by displaced Catholics from all over Europe. By June 1945, his squadron had "disintegrated", but he continued with Moral Leadership courses, convinced that the abolition of the church parade "will not make any difference in the attendance of Catholics at Sunday Mass". By August 1946, he was in Schleswig-Holstein, where he buried a Catholic airman. Organizing welfare visits in Lübeck in December, he wrote that the "job requires great patience, and involves a great deal of discomfort". He had 60 Catholics in his congregation. In January 1947, he reported from Hamburg, with temperatures below freezing, there is "no light and very little fuel" and the Irish Guards "give some of their food every day for hungry children". By 1948, Germans were still clearing bombed cities and suffering great shortages. Fr MacSeumais distributed food parcels from the Vatican and Catholic organizations and, like chaplains who succeeded him, covered hundreds of miles visiting RAF facilities.

Chaplains were stationed at major bases at RAF Laarbruch, Wildenrath, Gütersloh and Brüggen and the RAF Hospital at Wegberg. Chaplains also ministered to English-speaking communities of West Germany long after the war. In 1987, Fr Ken McLaughlan, of the Diocese of Galloway and commissioned in 1967, Senior Catholic RAF Chaplain Germany, was pastor to English-speaking Catholics in the Düsseldorf area.

RAF Catholic chaplains, 1950s–90s

Fr Aidan White-Spunner OSB of Glenstal Abbey had been a wartime army chaplain but in 1947 became an RAF chaplain and served in the United Kingdom, Egypt, Iraq, Aden and Singapore before retiring in 1966. Fr Rudesind Brookes OSB, of Downside Abbey, also joined the RAF after being an army padre and became Senior Chaplain Malta in 1955. Other Benedictines with the post-war RAF included Dom Hugh Bowler OSB of Douai Abbey, who served from 1942 until 1958; Dom Leander Duffy OSB of Ampleforth Abbey, who was commissioned in 1961 and served in the United Kingdom and Cyprus; and Dom Laurence Beer OSB of Belmont Abbey, who served from 1966 in the United Kingdom, Germany and Cyprus. Fr Kevin Mulhearn of the Archdiocese of Liverpool, commissioned in 1961, served in the United Kingdom, Cyprus, Bahrain, Malaya, Hong Kong and at RAF Laarbruch. Fr Michael Cassidy of the Diocese of Lancaster was commissioned in 1968 and, after service in the United Kingdom, the Far East and RAF Brüggen, became Command Chaplain at Headquarters Germany in 1983. Fr Tony Harris, a Pallotine Father and commissioned in 1973, served in Germany, the United Kingdom, Cyprus and Ascension Island and became Principal Catholic Chaplain. Fr John Daly, of the Diocese of Salford and commissioned in 1985, was the first Catholic chaplain to RAF Lyneham from where the RAF supplied aid to Ethiopia and assistance to Cameroon and Mexico, and which was the air-bridge to the Falklands. After a posting to RAF Halton, his first overseas tour was to RAF Wildenrath. He was also chaplain to RAF Hospital, Wegberg, and during his tour of West Germany, the Berlin Wall, symbol of divided

Europe, was dismantled after 1989. Fr Daly became the first Catholic chaplain to be College Staff Chaplain at RAF Cranwell and also Principal Catholic Chaplain.

The RAF, the First Gulf War and OPERATION GRANBY

Jaguar squadrons from RAF Wattisham were based at Thumrait, Oman, when Iraqi forces invaded Kuwait. Tornado squadrons were temporarily based in Cyprus while Nimrods patrolled the seas and air transports ferried personnel, weapons and equipment. The RAF carried out 2,500 sorties during the war, and a thirty-eight-day bombing campaign preceded the ground invasion. This decimated Iraqi divisions in the open desert and prevented the Iraqis resupplying forward units. The Allied ground assault quickly overwhelmed Iraqi forces.

RAF units were scattered. Joint Headquarters, Air Headquarters and the War Hospital were in Riyadh, Saudi Arabia; Tornados were at Tabuk and Dhahran; Support Helicopters were based in the north Saudi desert near Al Khatim; a Nimrod detachment was at Seeb in Oman; and RAF Movers were in Kuwait. Personnel were housed in tents, hotels and portacabins.

RAF Catholic chaplains in OPERATION GRANBY

Mgr Michael Cassidy, Principal Catholic Chaplain, was aware of the view that chaplains condoned war. The caricature of padres "blessing bombs", common in anti-war circles, was erroneous, he wrote. The ministry of the chaplain was to bring Christ into situations where there was separation, tension and suffering.

RAF chaplains were rare in the Gulf despite over 6,000 RAF personnel being on active service. At the beginning of OPERATION GRANBY, Fr John Daly deployed with two Anglican chaplains, one Church of Scotland chaplain and one Free Church chaplain. Eventually, 17 RAF padres were deployed to air bases and with helicopter forces.

Fr Daly was based at RAF Wildenrath, when, in August 1990, Iraqi forces invaded Kuwait. He was flown by Hercules transport to Cyprus before travelling to Oman and on to Bahrain, where he was billeted in a hotel. He paid weekly visits to RAF personnel and army field hospitals, when established, in Saudi Arabia, attending to religious and welfare issues. At Christmas 1990, he preached at the Forces Christmas Services, which were broadcast from the Gulf, Germany and Britain to bases around the world via satellite link.

Fr Tom Devanney, of the Diocese of Salford and commissioned in 1982, and Fr Gordon Beattie OSB, of Ampleforth Abbey and commissioned in 1980, deployed to the Gulf in January 1991. Fr Beattie left RAF Cranwell in 1981 and served in the UK, on Ascension Island and in Germany. In January 1991, he was deployed from RAF Kinloss to the Gulf and flew to Oman. After a stopover at RAF Akrotiri, Cyprus, he landed at Seeb Air Base, Oman, and was billeted in the Intercontinental Hotel. Such luxury was short-lived and after two days he was transferred to a tent and given a car so he could fulfil his duties as "RC Chaplain Peripatetic". He was responsible for all RAF Catholics stationed in Bahrain, Saudi Arabia, Oman and Kuwait after its liberation.

Fr Beattie "clocked up" 8,000 miles flying to and from the Gulf and 5,800 miles in the theatre of war. He also drove over 9,000 miles through Saudi Arabia, Oman and Kuwait, which involved delays at border checkpoints, and visiting bases and hospitals. Occasionally he was accompanied by an armed escort.

The army had six Catholic chaplains while the Royal Navy had one. In contrast, the American military had 119 Catholic military chaplains in the Gulf. With the other chaplains, Fr Beattie undertook normal priestly duties and visited Field Hospitals and bases as part of his general duties. To avoid disturbing Muslim religious sensibilities, chaplains were styled "Morale Welfare Workers" on visas and passports.

Enemy Scud missile attacks were frequent. A missile warning came in Bahrain while Fr Beattie was celebrating Sunday Mass. Everyone, including Fr Beattie, was able to get to a shelter and put on chemical warfare suits. Mass continued after the "all clear". Fr Beattie was near missed or "scudded"– when under attack from Iraqi missiles—four times in two different countries within nine hours of each attack. Returning on a Royal Navy Sea King helicopter from the RAF Support Helicopters' base in the north Saudi desert, Fr Beattie touched down in Al Quisysumah minutes after an attack. He then travelled in a Hercules to Al Jubayl and from there to Bahrain where, two hours later, he was awakened by another Scud attack.

Flying into Kuwait after its liberation, wrote Fr Beattie, was "like seeing a sight worthy of Dante's inferno". A black oil cloud seemed to cover the whole country and the smell of burning oil pervaded the aircraft. They counted 40 burning oil wells, while on the ground there were scenes of devastation, abandoned cars, and the remains of burned-out aircraft.

RAF Catholic chaplains on OPERATION TELIC and OPERATION HERRICK

OPERATION TELIC was the United Kingdom's involvement in Iraq between March 2003 and April 2009 and is often referred to as the Second Gulf War.

Fr John Daly flew to Kuwait in October 2003 and ministered to Catholics in the RAF and in an American unit. The Augustinian Fr Chris Marsden, commissioned in 2001, deployed with an RAF Air Point of Departure in Turkey, and Fr Marcus Hodges OP, commissioned in 1997, deployed to Iraq. The war and its environment presented Fr Hodges with an opportunity to consider the nature of his ministry to the military. He found that among all the tasks facing him and "the all-pervasive fog of desert dust notwithstanding, there is a clear and powerful chaplaincy vision out here in the Iraqi desert". Military ministry, he wrote, was the same "for all who labour in the rich harvest of the Church's ministry", yet in Basra it was "in some senses simply more undiluted, more vital and more immediate".

Praying, preaching, explaining the faith and administering the sacraments, wrote Fr Hodges, were the essence of his ministry. Counselling and offering guidance, support, comfort and assurance through prayer and spiritual reading were all methods of helping others through difficulties. "Chaplains are iconic", he wrote, as Catholics have traditionally understood this in terms of their priests being *in persona*

Christi. This was not an arrogant boast but a source of humility and even dread for those who answered the call. "The chaplain is fallible and weak," wrote Fr Hodges, "seeing himself as one with those he serves in uniform, membership, loyalty and duty. Like them, he is at constant risk of injury or death." But the chaplain is "set apart from those he serves. For the religious and the sceptical alike, he represents a calling and mission; he makes visible his membership of a kingdom of values and hope which he hopes will transcend the dirt and confusion that characterize armed conflict." The padre was aware that as well as those who welcomed his presence there were others who rejected it and challenged his ministry. He was convinced, however, that many believed in a God and an afterlife, particularly when in a battle situation.

Fr James Caulfield of the Diocese of East Anglia was commissioned in 1997 and served in Iraq, where his duties included conducting the repatriation ceremonies of eight British personnel, two Americans and one Dane. A month after his return from Iraq, he was appointed Roman Catholic Chaplain to RAF Brize Norton, which hosted repatriation ceremonies and received medical teams bringing home the wounded. Fr Caulfield assisted the wounded, comforted grieving relatives, and supported service personnel involved in repatriation ceremonies.

RAF chaplains and Afghanistan

Operations in the Gulf and Afghanistan meant that in the late 1990s and early 2000s chaplains saw service at the front line as well as serving on RAF facilities far removed from hostilities. Included in this cohort were Fr Alan Wilson of the Diocese of Galloway, commissioned in 1989; Fr Paul Owens of the Diocese of Leeds, commissioned in 1990; Fr Chris Webb of the Archdiocese of Westminster, commissioned in 1992; Fr Bob Halshaw of the Diocese of Lancaster, commissioned in 1999; Fr Chris Marsden, an Augustinian and commissioned in 2001; and Fr Ivan Boyle, of the Diocese of Motherwell and commissioned in 2001. Fr Boyle supported bereaved families and the station community at RAF Kinloss when a Nimrod crashed in Afghanistan killing 14 airmen. Fr Boyle had previously served in the Gulf and was chaplain to a deployment of Harriers to Afghanistan.

Fr John Walsh of the Archdiocese of Liverpool was commissioned in April 2003. His first posting was to RAF Brize Norton from where he accompanied aircrews of the transport fleet across the world, notably to Exercise Red Flag in Nevada. Other postings included RAF Marham, a front-line station, and Fr Walsh was deployed twice to Al Udeid Air Base in Qatar in 2005 and 2006 as chaplain to the UK air contingent. Further postings included RAF Cranwell and RAF Halton where he helped deliver the Beliefs and Values programme. Fr Walsh also led the RAF detachment in the annual International Military Pilgrimage to Lourdes in 2006. His final posting was to RAF Halton as Principal Catholic Chaplain.

As the number of dead and wounded passing through Brize Norton increased, questions were asked about the morality of the conflict in Afghanistan. Fr Caulfield's immediate task, however, was with the wellbeing of those engaged in it. He prayed that those who made the decisions on the ground acted with honour and integrity, but it was not only the faith of service people he asked for. He also asked that his own faith was strong enough to help others carry their load. He was a chaplain, he wrote, "because the young men and women who have to fight should never find the tent empty". OPERATION HERRICK came at a terrible cost for British forces.

Fr Caulfield's career included service on operational and training bases throughout the United Kingdom and also postings and deployments to Belize, the Balkans, the Middle East, Italy (Libya), the Falkland Islands and Afghanistan. Fr Caulfield became Principal Catholic Chaplain and in 2014 welcomed the Revd David Skillen of the Diocese of Lancaster as the first Permanent Deacon to be commissioned as a Catholic Chaplain in the RAF. In 2019, upon Fr Caulfield's retirement, Padre Skillen was appointed Principal Catholic Chaplain.

Chaplain on OPERATION SHADER

Flight-Sergeant Neil Galloway had 25 years' service in the RAF Tactical Communications Wing, opening up airstrips and setting up radar, radio and communications systems. He had served in Iraq and on two tours of Afghanistan, including deployment in Kandahar, Camp Bastion and Lashkar Gah. On his last tour, he was with a patrol which narrowly escaped death. An Afghan police vehicle travelling behind detonated an explosive device meant for the British. Its occupants were killed.

In 2012, Neil was ordained Permanent Deacon for the Diocese of Middlesbrough and in 2015 rejoined the RAF as a chaplain. Instead of being devoted to the RAF, he now devoted himself to God and observed:

> From Soldier to Soldier of Christ, both are a vocation, a way of life, not merely a career path or job, both deserve serious consideration and place heavy demands upon their members. Both have an ordered and formal way of life, a hierarchical and regimented structure. Both are steeped in history and tradition, ceremonials and uniforms. But most importantly, at their heart both exist to serve. True they serve in what at first glance may be totally different ways but, at their core, is service for the greater good.

He returned to Iraq on OPERATION SHADER, the coalition committed to defeating the Islamic State through military action in Iraq and Syria.

Padre Galloway provided Eucharistic services and devotions for Catholics of all coalition nations, gave pastoral support to all personnel, and worked with Jewish, Muslim and Christian faith leaders to support and rebuild the Kurdish community. He saw combatants from a different perspective: "They may not be churched, they may even be a little rough round the edges, but they understand service, and they live sacrifice. They feed my faith and spirit as much as I feed theirs, that is why I am proud to serve with them and honoured to be their Chaplain."

Since the beginning of OPERATION SHADER, Padre Galloway, Padre Skillen and Fr James Mealy of the Archdiocese of Birmingham, commissioned in 2016, each served as Air Component Chaplain.

OPERATION TAILPIN

On 26 June 2015, 30 British holidaymakers were killed in a terror attack in Tunisia, and the RAF was tasked with their repatriation. This took place via the Repatriation Centre, RAF Brize Norton, where Padre David Skillen was part of the Chaplaincy Team.

OPERATION TAILPIN took place from 1 to 4 July 2015, and Padre Skillen and other chaplains welcomed bereaved families to Brize Norton and tried to make them as comfortable as possible prior to the arrival of the aircraft carrying their loved ones. The coffins were unloaded and carried into the Repatriation Centre by the Queen's Colour Squadron and placed in the chapels of rest. If required by the families, chaplains accompanied the coffins and over four days Padre Skillen consoled grieving families. This was a sorrowful but privileged experience for the chaplain as he sought to provide pastoral support and prayerful consolation to families who asked how God could allow such a tragedy to happen. The families were grateful for the chaplain's words of comfort and reassurance.

Padre Skillen received a Commanding Officer's commendation for his contribution to OPERATION TAILPIN and for his "exceptional pastoral support to the service community". In 2016, an anniversary service was held in Westminster Abbey, in the presence of HRH Prince Harry, Prime Minister David Cameron and other dignitaries, to commemorate the dead and support the families. Padre Skillen represented the RAF Chaplains' Branch.

Chaplains and training schools and churches

RAF training schools gave chaplains the opportunity to forge relationships with those entering the service and to lay the groundwork for future contacts. For some Catholics, it may have been their only contact with a Catholic chaplain because there were so few chaplains in the RAF. It was common for personnel to keep in contact with their chaplain from training and formation days. The training schools, therefore, were important for faith development.

RAF Cranwell opened in 1918, and the RAF College, Cranwell, was established in 1920. Since then, it has been responsible for selecting and training generations of RAF officers and it houses the Central Flying School, the Air Warfare School and the Tedder Leadership Academy. RAF Halton, originally the base of No 1 School of Technical Training, was home of the Halton Apprentices and the station where Fr Beauchamp welcomed so many new entrants into the RAF. It later became the school of initial training where chaplains delivered the RAF's Beliefs and Values Programme.

The church at RAF Halton became the RAF's Catholic church. Some stations had a purpose-built church; others had shared chapels. In Germany, each base had its own church. In Cyprus, a fund was made available for each faith to have one purpose-built church on the island and one shared church on each base. The Anglicans chose Dhekelia for their church; the Church of Scotland and Free Churches chose Akrotiri; the Catholics were given Episkopi. When the Catholic church at Akrotiri was condemned, a new church was created in the former Sergeant's Mess and opened in 1984. The cost was shared by the station and the RAF Roman Catholic Trustee Fund.

Figure 30: The Revd David Skillen RAF:
First Catholic deacon in the Forces

Cyprus, the Baltic and Africa: Chaplains with peacekeepers

Cyprus: United Nations Peacekeeping Force

Following Cypriot independence, Britain retained control of Sovereign Base Areas Akrotiri and Dhekelia. Episkopi is part of SBA and provided troops to a United Nations (UN) Peacekeeping Force. In July 1974, Greek-Cypriot extremists, backed by the Greek military junta, staged a coup in Cyprus and demanded union with Greece. This sparked a Turkish invasion which overran 40 per cent of the island. The Greek-Cypriot National Guard responded by attacking Turkish-Cypriot enclaves. UN forces were powerless to stop the invasion and Cyprus became two separate states with the UN policing a 180-mile buffer zone between them.

Catholic chaplains on Cyprus

A Catholic infrastructure had already developed and chaplains continued to minister to the military and their families in the Greek-Cypriot zone. Padres provided opportunities for worship and access to the sacraments and offered a welcome to those of every denomination and none. Catholic children attended Ministry of Defence schools, meanwhile, and their religious education was provided within the Catholic military community.

In September 2009, Fr Michael Fava of the Diocese of Portsmouth was based at Episkopi as Chaplain to British Forces and led a team of five army and RAF Christian chaplains. Fr John Nelson, also of the Diocese of Portsmouth, had served as a commissioned Reserve Chaplain with a medical unit in Kosovo, Iraq and Afghanistan before becoming a commissioned chaplain in 2018 when he was posted to Cyprus. He was on Cyprus for three years and wrote that there was a tendency among some service personnel to see it as "a sunshine posting" because of its climate and relaxed holiday atmosphere. But garrisons at Episkopi, Akrotiri and Dhekelia, and smaller contingents in Nicosia and Ayios Nikolaos, remain strategically vital to the British military, and the location that attracted the British to the island in the nineteenth century is still important. Guarding these bases is an essential part of the British military presence.

In April 2019, the Bishop of the Forces Paul Mason and the Deputy Chaplain-General Fr Michael Fava made a pastoral visit to British Forces Cyprus. RAF Padre David Skillen secured places on a Search and Rescue training flight with personnel of 84 Squadron, and Bishop Mason also visited British military establishments, forces chaplains and the contested demilitarized zone. The bishop was able to gain a deeper insight into this strategically important British overseas operating location.

Intervention in Sierra Leone

In May 2000, the United Kingdom began a military intervention in the civil war in Sierra Leone under the codename OPERATION PALLISER. There followed OPERATION BASILICA, OPERATION BARRAS, and OPERATION SILKMAN which lasted from October 2000 to July 2002. The United Nations' military mission (UNAMSIL) had been in Sierra Leone since 1999, and a small contingent of British personnel had already deployed to support the Sierra Leone Army (SLA). OPERATION PALLISER was to evacuate foreign citizens, and this was achieved within the first two days of the operation commencing. Increased British involvement came with OPERATION SILKMAN in January 2001, when 42 Commando on board HMS *Ocean* made an amphibious landing and 11 Squadron RAF Regiment parachuted into Sierra Leone. This demonstration of British force built on OPERATION BARRAS, a successful land mission, and brought hostilities to an end. The United

Kingdom deployed 4,500 personnel in the operation. During two years of intervention in one of Africa's bloodiest civil wars, there were two British fatalities, of which one was in action. OPERATION SILKMAN was a peacekeeping initiative that changed into retraining the SLA upon ethical and more professional lines, seen as essential to the rebuilding of a country ravaged by war and poverty.

Catholic padre in OPERATION SILKMAN

Fr Michael Fava was commissioned in 1997 and served in the United Kingdom with the Irish Guards, in Germany with HQ 20 Armoured Brigade, and on an operational tour of Bosnia. Between January and April 2001, he was deployed with HQ 1 Mechanised Brigade to Sierra Leone.

OPERATION SILKMAN was to re-establish the SLA and enforce stability. As the only chaplain in theatre, Fr Fava's task was to minister to the tri-service British and UN Forces present in various locations, conduct Moral Awareness Training for SLA soldiers being reintegrated into the "new" national army at Benguema Training Camp, and re-establish and stabilize the Chaplains' Department of the Sierra Leone army. The army chaplains, comprised of Christian and Muslim in almost equal measure, worked and co-operated very successfully together in a country of wide religious diversity, and the Chaplains' Department was selected as the "guinea pig" to test-run the very first Officer Commissioning Board to sit in Sierra Leone since before the Civil War. The process of identifying candidates to go forward for interview, and possible commissioning, was challenging due to the difficulties in establishing the credibility of academic credentials for both Christian and Muslim candidates, and the different progression towards becoming ministers and imams determined by different religious traditions. The process reached a successful outcome with the selection as officer candidates of a roughly equal number of Christian and Muslim chaplains. As the only British chaplain in theatre for the duration of this deployment, Fr Fava was required to offer pastoral support as well as regular worship for all personnel regardless of their religious affiliation. The success of the process meant that further promotions and commissioning boards could take place in order to create stability and viability for the new SLA. For Fr Fava, it was a testing and stressful experience, but the deployment was an emotional reconnection with Africa and his birthplace (Kampala, Uganda). He recalled with respect the valiant, enthusiastic and hopeful efforts made on all sides to normalize and maintain peace in a traumatized society—not least the work done to reintegrate former child soldiers towards acceptance once again by their families and communities.

OPERATION CABRIT: Catholic padres with NATO

OPERATION CABRIT was the British element of the Enhanced Forward Presence established in 2016 by the North Atlantic Treaty Organization (NATO) to protect Estonia, Latvia, Lithuania and Poland from threats posed by Russia.

In April 2017, Fr Philip Smith of the Archdiocese of Southwark was to deploy for nine months on OPERATION CABRIT in Estonia. This was his first formal deployment since joining the RAChD in 2015. Preparations for 5 Rifles Battle Group had begun a few months before and Fr Smith's chaplaincy preparations began in Portsmouth over fish and chips with Fr Aleksander, a senior Estonian Chaplain. Fr Aleksander's friendship and becoming familiar with the Estonian Defence Force (EDF) Chaplaincy Department were to be particular highlights of Fr Smith's deployment. As the only British chaplain deployed with the 900-strong Battle Group, Fr Smith found Fr Aleksander and other Estonian chaplains to be great sources of support, friendship and practical help. Estonia is one of the least religious countries in Europe and before his arrival Fr Smith was concerned that this would make the work of a chaplain harder. However, this was not the case. The padre was fortunate that the camp at which he was based contained the only chapel on any Estonian military establishment. Through the hospitality of the Estonian Chaplains' Department, it became a focus for NATO soldiers who worshipped there during the deployment. Along with EDF chaplains, Fr Smith also worked alongside the small Catholic community in Estonia, a devout community led by Bishop Phillippe Jourdan who occasionally celebrated the great feasts of the Church with the troops.

Fr Smith reflected on OPERATION CABRIT 1 as an amazing multi-national deployment. For him, a vivid memory was seeing soldiers of different nations sitting together in the back of a vehicle sharing a brew together during a break. It summed up NATO's motto: "By standing together we are strong."

Fr Patrick O'Driscoll of the Diocese of Cloyne joined the RAChD in September 2017. After training at the Royal Military Academy, Sandhurst, and at the Joint Forces' Chaplaincy Centre, Amport, his first regiment, 22 Signals, provided him with a firm foundation of army life. A subsequent attachment with 1 Royal Regiment of Fusiliers gave him infantry experience and a foreign deployment, for in March 2020 the regiment became the lead unit of the Battle Group for OPERATION CABRIT 6. On their arrival in Estonia, however, the soldiers experienced a situation different to previous deployments but not for any military reasons.

As Fr O'Driscoll arrived on 10 March, Estonia, along with the United Kingdom and other European countries, had gone into "lockdown" due to the Covid pandemic. This threw up new and different dynamics on how the Battle Group was going to work, not only because of health and safety and social distancing but also because of the anxieties that soldiers felt for their families back home.

Fr O'Driscoll worked on a day-to-day basis trying to keep up spirits and maintain morale. For the first two months, the acquisition of TVs, PlayStations, games and films was an essential part of the padre's activities. Due to the fact that the camp was gated, and Fr O'Driscoll was one of the very few who could get out for pastoral issues, he became, metaphorically speaking, the local shopkeeper, going to the cash-and-carry to buy provisions for soldiers. His journeys from the camp also gave the padre an opportunity for personal prayer and reflection. In camp, he offered the soldiers a safe and private place outside the chain of command where they could share their worries and anxieties. Most of the time the padre was just a listening ear or offered words of advice and support. Soldiers could also make a private phone call from the padre's office, so that they could have, even at a distance, contact with home.

For Fr O'Driscoll, celebrating Mass was a joyful break from the usual humdrum of daily base life. On weekdays, the padre would often say Mass by himself, but on Sunday, with up to ten worshippers, there was a great celebration of Mass, with prayer and music, and soldiers who attended came from many different parts of the UK and the Commonwealth. On such occasions, Fr O'Driscoll would frequently say, "I do the praying, you do the soldiering, and we look after each other in between." It was a dictum that he held on to as it gave him strength in his ministry. During the frequent military exercises, the padre's job was bringing a bit of happiness and laughter to the soldiers in many different ways. His Irish accent and his lack of military knowledge were both sources of amusement, but the real morale booster was the big bag of sweets which Fr O'Driscoll kept in his respirator bag—which made the soldiers wonder where the padre kept his gas mask. Due to the virus, the padre was unable to meet regularly with the Estonian chaplains or see much of the country, but from the middle of June 2020, as the country opened up much more, the soldiers got out and visited the places of interest. An advantage that the deployment brought Fr O'Driscoll was his personal fitness. He recalled: "The soldiers were still trying to work out, am I running away fast from hell or quickly to heaven, and that is where my prayer life comes in. I am still trying to work it out!"

The Covid pandemic was challenging and difficult for all people wherever they were. In Estonia, the soldiers, amidst the anxieties for their own families, were still willing to do their professional duty and the padre was always on hand to assist them.

OPERATION NEWCOMBE: United Nations Peacekeeping in Mali

Since 2020, the British army had stationed 350 soldiers in Mali, a former French West African colony with gold reserves, as part of a United Nations anti-jihadist peacekeeping mission. The British contribution was called OPERATION NEWCOMBE. Eleven thousand seven hundred troops from 65 countries made up the UN force and 250 UN peacekeepers have been killed in Mali since 2013. The state-condoned intervention of Russian-supported European mercenary groups caused a serious deterioration in relations between Mali and the UN members. France and the United Kingdom withdrew troops from Mali in 2022.

In 2020, when the coronavirus pandemic changed certainties into doubt for huge swathes of the world's population, robbing millions of all normality, spontaneity, celebrations and even life itself, the work of deploying a British Army Task Group continued.

Catholic army chaplain on OPERATION NEWCOMBE

Fr Paul McCourt of the Diocese of Hexham and Newcastle was chaplain to England's "northern cavalry"—the Light Dragoons—which traced its history back to four antecedent regiments—13th/18th Royal Hussars (Queen Mary's Own) and 15th/19th The King's Royal Hussars, all cavalry regiments. In modern times, they were still mounted but on all-terrain "Jackal" and "Coyote" armoured vehicles.

Fr McCourt had been a reservist chaplain and had completed a tour of duty in Afghanistan before joining the RAChD as a Regular Chaplain in 2014. Not every priest finds the military chaplain's life to his liking, but Fr McCourt saw it in many ways to be a "calling within a calling" and at the same time liberating, fulfilling and challenging. He moved to Colchester to the specialist Air Assault Brigade, before taking up the role of Catholic Chaplain to the Royal Military Academy, Sandhurst, in December 2016. In 2018, he returned to the infantry which preceded his appointment to the Light Dragoons and OPERATION NEWCOMBE in Mali.

In 2020, the Light Dragoons led a British Task Group including a company of 2nd Royal Anglian Regiment and other units in an operation in Mali as part of the longest established, but most dangerous, of the United Nation's Peacekeeping Missions. At the request of the UN, the British were primarily to protect the civilian population from the rise of instability and violence in the country, and to help implement the UN Peace Treaty by their presence. After a year of intense preparation, whilst the world grappled with Covid, its restrictions, consequences and lockdowns, the Task Group carefully and professionally trained for a six-month deployment in the sub-Saharan desert which began in

December 2020. On deployment, the Task Group settled into a newly constructed camp and began their work in earnest. The troops were engaged on various peacekeeping missions, brought protection to the local Malian population, and helped to stabilize an area of Africa which had experienced some challenging problems in recent years.

As chaplain to the Task Group, Fr McCourt's work was similar but also different to the work of any priest. In a clearly defined military role, he was responsible for the spiritual, pastoral and moral care of the deployed force. Soldiers are mostly young men and women who are full of questions and opinions, vitality, quick wit and a challenging outlook. Added to this, they are inspiring to live with, and they thrive within a culture built on the shoulders of the best in our society, men and women who unselfishly place themselves at the front of the defence of the realm and the establishment and maintenance of world peace.

At Christmas 2020, Fr McCourt offered Midnight Mass at a newly commissioned "flat-packed" altar under a starry desert sky with a cool breeze blowing—a far cry from Christmases past in draughty churches packed with excited joy. Christmas here was memorable, for in the simplicity of the outdoor makeshift church, the atmosphere of prayer was one the padre had never before encountered in 30 years of priesthood. Young people, recalled the padre, far from home and without their families, were now together as a new family, and they knelt before the newborn Christ, the Prince of Peace, with a great deal on their minds. Challenging times were ahead for the young soldiers and those who led them. Yet the stable presence of Fr McCourt's chaplaincy in a culture of uncertainty was highly valued and prized—even if not everyone would admit it.

Near the end of their six-month tour of duty, the soldiers were probably very different people as a result of it, wrote Fr McCourt. Without always being conscious of it, humanity is prone to alteration and change as a result of the circumstances it finds itself in, and never more so than when living without the familiar people, things and rituals that make their lives what they are. Living without the everyday comforts of home, which were now classed as luxuries, soldiers began to search deeper and rely less on "things" and "others", and more on a profound satisfaction which comes from the soul. The Desert Fathers of the early centuries were expert in matters spiritual because they developed a vibrant relationship with

God, unhindered by people and things. In no way, recalled Fr McCourt, could a direct comparison be made between the ancient Desert Fathers and a modern twenty-first-century British Army Task Group, but it was possible that the Saharan wilderness served to bring about a re-evaluation of who and what was most important.

Members of the Task Group deployed from the main camp much deeper into the desert on a number of specific operations and directly under the UN Peacekeeping banner. Sometimes they operated solely as a British Task Group and at other times with UN colleagues—German, Swedish, Jordanian and Malian forces. Each mission was designed to build up a detailed picture of the pattern of life in the local civilian community and the threats which disturbed its peace. Working "at reach" (military speak for long-distance), the Task Group operated from a self-reliance posture and without easy access to the main camp. They were seen as a force for good and a stabilizing energy in areas and villages often overpowered by terrorist armed groups. They attempted to establish a ring of confidence around the most vulnerable in the local society, riven by complex issues.

As padre to a Long Range Recce Group (LRRG), Fr McCourt travelled in armoured convoys, experienced searing heat clad in body armour, helmet and gloves, lived alongside the soldiers in makeshift overnight camps, and offered Mass. If anything had altered him during his time with the Task Group, he recalled, it was the tangible reliance on faith in adversity. "When Easter followed the most austere Lent I have ever lived," he wrote, "the message of Our Lord's resurrection from death could not have been more palpable. The sunrise over the desert horizon on Easter Sunday morning before 6am was a breathtaking accompaniment to a mystery we cannot ever exhaust." Joining him were a handful of hardy soldiers, who, with others in the previous days of the Sacred Triduum, had faithfully stayed close to the liturgy of Easter at the Mass of the Lord's Supper, the Passion of St John and Stations of the Cross on Good Friday, and the joy of the Easter Vigil Mass shared with German and Swedish colleagues. On Easter morning, after the sunrise, they celebrated the Baptism of an officer and later the confirmation of him and another soldier. Fr McCourt saw the fruits of faith in the desert, aided a little bit by priestly chaplaincy.

Ukraine

The Revd John Power of the Archdiocese of Liverpool was commissioned in 2021 and became the first Catholic Deacon to serve as an army chaplain. On 24 February 2023, as chaplain to the Royal Lancers, he led a multinational service to mark the first anniversary of Russia's invasion of Ukraine. Padre Power led members of British, Canadian and Lithuanian armed forces in a service including bidding prayers and the recitation of the Lord's Prayer in both English and Ukrainian.

NATO troops had been training the Ukrainians for several weeks, but the service allowed time out of their arduous and rigorous training to remember those lost in the conflict. and reflect on what was happening in their country. During the service, Padre Power said: "We gather together in strength and hope of a brighter tomorrow for Ukraine and its armed forces. In this time of crisis, may we all speak words of truth and justice." A minute's silence was held for all those who had lost their lives and, after the final blessing, the Ukrainians sang their national anthem, "*Slave Ukraini*"—"glory to Ukraine". During the week prior to the service, Padre Power had distributed miraculous medals to the Ukrainian soldiers. These the soldiers brought to the service and venerated them during the final blessing.

Padre Power said that the atmosphere was sombre, but he maintained that such services brought hope for a brighter tomorrow for the people of Ukraine. In the British army, he continued, troops often pause in the middle of a training exercise to gather for a field service, relief and reflection. When training was over, the padre, through Google Translate, tried to speak alone with the Ukrainian troops. It was, he felt, a privilege to minister in this way as a chaplain with such an important group of people for such a vital exercise.

Ukrainian military chaplains, Catholic and Orthodox, visited the Armed Forces Chaplaincy Centre, where British chaplains shared their experiences of chaplaincy on active service in Afghanistan and elsewhere. John Power's regiment was deployed to Poland and I believe this service took place in Poland.

Figure 31: Fr Paul McCourt CF: Peacekeeper chaplain

Catholic chaplains in the British Armed Forces: Authority, control, convergence

Early authority, control and supervision

The *missio castrensis* derived authority from ecclesiastical and temporal sources. Although chaplains were appointed by papal and Spanish authority in Counter-Reformation Europe, no comparable infrastructures existed in the British Isles. The army was dominated by Protestantism, and Catholic clergy ministering to Catholic soldiers did so at the behest of a Catholic officer. Catholic chaplaincy in the British navy was similarly limited.

Catholics in the army were denied chaplains until the mid-nineteenth century, and when the British government began to rectify this injustice, after 1858, the locus and nature of authority and issues of control and supervision of chaplains came to the fore. Ecclesiastical responsibility lay with a Catholic prelate while military authority lay with the War Office. Catholic sailors had to wait longer for their religious needs to be satisfied.

Bishops and chaplains

From 1853, Bishop Grant was the British hierarchies' intermediary with the government regarding military chaplains. His first tasks included recruiting volunteer army chaplains for the Crimean War and the Indian Mutiny and nominating the first commissioned Catholic army chaplains.

Grant's quiet, workmanlike approach proved more acceptable to the government establishment than the triumphalism of Cardinal Wiseman.

Government consulted Wiseman on policy but turned to Grant with details of ecclesiastical–military administration. Grant's diocese, stretching from London, south of the River Thames, to the Channel Islands, included all the major military establishments in the south of England, and he had much to do with the military beyond his huge diocesan commitments.

Relations between Wiseman, Grant and the Vatican were complex. England and Wales, still missionary territory, came under the control of Propaganda Fide, the Vatican department responsible for the missions. Propaganda Fide failed to appoint a *Cappellano Maggiore*, or Superior of Chaplains, for British forces, and exclusive control of chaplains and jurisdiction over their priestly faculties was reserved to the Vatican. As Archbishop Cullen of Dublin pointed out to Bishop Grant in 1858, there would be ecclesiastical and political difficulties associated with such a post in Protestant England. Grant's brother bishops, meanwhile, were ill-disposed to allow their priests to be at the disposal of another prelate, while Irish bishops were sensitive to their episcopal jurisdiction and reluctant to allow their priests to serve the British military. Irish bishops were also opposed to Mass being celebrated on army property, which was used for purposes such as the flogging of soldiers.

The restructuring of army chaplaincy after the Crimean War, including the commissioning of other Christian clergy, was not a popular innovation. Anti-Catholic bigotry remained strong, Catholics in the military suffered discrimination, and public opinion of the military was low. Army padres experienced a clash of cultures. In 1859, Bishop Grant told Fr John Vertue he was dismayed at chaplains wearing uniform lest their priestly role be subordinated to their military rank. Fr Vertue did not share Grant's misgivings.

Bishop Grant's achievements regarding chaplaincy were enormous. On his death in 1870, Bishop Ullathorne of Birmingham wrote: "All our really successful negotiations with the Government for military chaplains, for mitigation of aggressive laws, for the navy, for workhouses, etc, etc, have been directly, or indirectly, accomplished through him."

Administrative responsibility for military chaplains remained with the Bishop of Southwark until 1882, when Bishop Vertue of Portsmouth, a former army chaplain, took charge of Royal Navy chaplains, although they were not commissioned and did not serve in fighting ships. In 1900, on Bishop Vertue's death and at the government's request, Bishop Bourne of Southwark took control of naval chaplains, and once again the Bishop of Southwark was responsible for all Catholic military chaplains. Bourne, unimpressed by military and ecclesiastical arrangements for Catholic chaplains in the Boer War, was in a stronger position to introduce, as he saw it, more order and discipline into the ecclesiastical organization of all chaplains. When he became Archbishop of Westminster in 1903, he lobbied the Vatican to transfer control and supervision of army and navy chaplains to Westminster, and in 1906 he was appointed Ecclesiastical Superior of Catholic chaplains and Delegate of the Holy See to the British army with the exclusive right to grant priestly faculties to chaplains.

Bourne appointed priest-secretaries to liaise with serving and aspiring chaplains and also with military departments. He negotiated new terms of service for chaplains and proposed that army chaplains should not have rank or uniform. This was anathema to padres in an organization so dependent on rank and dress.

An *Episcopus Castrensis* for the British army

The growth of the Army Chaplains' Department during the Great War, when over 800 priests were granted temporary commissions, challenged Bourne's inadequate administration. Such was the scale of episcopal criticism and Catholic unrest at Bourne's control that the Vatican divested him of authority for army chaplains in 1917 and appointed the Principal Chaplain to the Army in Salonika Mgr William Keatinge as Bishop of the Army and Royal Flying Corps. Royal Navy chaplains, however, remained under the ecclesiastical jurisdiction of the Archbishop of Westminster.

Bishop Keatinge, the first British *Episcopus Castrensis*, was given the title Bishop of Metellepolis, but confusion over his ecclesiastical role and responsibilities was immediately evident. He was termed "Bishop of the Army", "Army Bishop", "Bishop of the Army and Air Force", *Episcopus Castrensis* and *Episcopus Militaris*. His pastoral jurisdiction had no geographical boundaries and consisted of army and, after December 1918, RAF padres, military personnel and their dependants.

Ecclesiastical jurisdiction was a major problem for bishops with military establishments within their dioceses. Chaplains were incardinated to the Army Bishopric for their military service and the Army Bishop had papal authority to dispense faculties to chaplains. However, because he was not a diocesan bishop, Keatinge was not a member of the national hierarchies. From the beginning of his episcopate, relations between Bourne and Keatinge were strained and Keatinge was only allowed into Hierarchy meetings when military matters were (very rarely) discussed. The centenary history of the English and Welsh Hierarchy, published in 1950, made no mention of army chaplaincy beyond Grant's involvement.

In 1925, Bishop Keatinge retired from the army but remained as *Episcopus Castrensis*. The War Office and the RAF allowed him to keep his rank and salary and funded his military expenses. His successor, from 1935, was Mgr James Dey, a chaplain who had served on the Western Front and in East Africa during the Great War. Dey, the first Catholic Staff Chaplain to the Royal Air Force and later Rector of Oscott College, Birmingham, became titular Bishop of Sebastopolis. Archbishop Hinsley, who succeeded Cardinal Bourne as Archbishop of Westminster in April 1935, was forewarned of the lax administration of Catholic naval chaplains and quickly improved matters. With Vatican and Admiralty approval, he allowed Dey to assume delegated responsibility for Royal Navy chaplains, and in effect Dey became Bishop of the Forces. During the Second World War, he had responsibility for hundreds of temporary military chaplains but, like Keatinge before him, was dependent upon diocesan bishops and heads of male religious orders to provide chaplains.

On the death of Bishop Dey in 1946, his see was left vacant and Principal Roman Catholic Chaplain (Army) Mgr John Clarke of the Archdiocese of Westminster was appointed Apostolic Administrator of the Forces Bishopric. In 1947, the Apostolic Delegate to Great Britain Archbishop William Godfrey requested the Holy See to appoint "a special Bishop in Ordinary for the Forces" to succeed Bishop Dey. In 1951, the Vatican regularized military chaplaincies and issued the Instruction *Solemne semper* regarding Military Vicariates, and in 1953, by the Decree *Inexhausta Caritate*, the Military Vicariate to Her Majesty's Forces was erected. In 1954, Archbishop David Mathew, a priest of the Archdiocese of Cardiff who had been appointed Auxiliary Bishop of Westminster in

1938 and Apostolic Delegate in Africa in 1946, was named as Bishop in Ordinary to Her Majesty's Forces with ecclesiastical jurisdiction derived directly from the Holy See. In 1963, he was succeeded by Mgr Gerard Tickle of Shrewsbury Diocese, an army chaplain of the Second World War. Bishop Tickle was given the titular See of Bela. The Vicariate lasted from 1954 until 1986, when the Apostolic Constitution *Spirituali militum curae* raised the status of Military Vicariates to that of a diocesan bishopric with authority vested in a bishop appointed by the Pope.

The Military Ordinariate

In 1975, Fr Francis Walmsley of the Archdiocese of Southwark, who had served in the Mercantile Marine in the Second World War and from 1960 as a chaplain in the Royal Navy, was appointed Principal Catholic Chaplain (Royal Navy) and Vicar-General to Bishop Tickle. Mgr Walmsley was appointed Military Vicar in succession to Bishop Tickle in 1979 with the titular see of Tamalluma. In 1986, he became the first Bishop of the Military Ordinariate of Great Britain by virtue of the decree *Pro Solicitudine Omnium Ecclesiarum*. In 1987, he became a member of Bishops' Conference of England and Wales.

Following the rebuilding of Aldershot Garrison in the 1960s, the Anglican church of St George was transferred into the care of the Roman Catholic Church. Catholic soldiers in the South Camp had continued to worship in the old wooden church of St Michael and St Sebastian, while in the North Camp the church of St Patrick had been opened in 1913. Both churches were closed, and their congregations moved into the church of St George. The church was named the Garrison Church of St Michael and St George, Aldershot, and became the Cathedral of the Catholic Bishop of the Forces and the only Catholic church whose foundation stone was laid by Queen Victoria. The statue of St Patrick was taken from the church in the North Camp and placed in the new cathedral.

Fr Tom Burns, a Marist Father, succeeded Bishop Walmsley as Bishop of the Forces in 2002. Ordained in 1971 and commissioned as a Royal Navy chaplain in 1986, Fr Burns held land and sea appointments and as bishop carried out official and pastoral visits to military establishments throughout the United Kingdom and overseas, including Iraq in Holy Week 2005. At this time, there were over 40 full-time Catholic military chaplains, Reserve and Officiating Chaplains.

Bishop Richard Moth, who succeeded Bishop Burns in 2008, was ordained to the priesthood for the Archdiocese of Southwark in November 1987 and had served as a Territorial Army chaplain. He was consecrated Bishop of the Forces on 29 September 2009. In 2015, Bishop Moth was appointed as Bishop of Arundel and Brighton and following his translation, Fr Michael Fava, a priest of the Portsmouth Diocese, Principal Roman Catholic Chaplain (Army) and Deputy Chaplain-General, served as Apostolic Administrator until the appointment of Bishop Paul Mason as Bishop of the Forces in 2018. Bishop Mason, ordained in 1998, had previously been an Auxiliary Bishop in his own Archdiocese of Southwark with the title of Bishop of Skálholt (See Appendix II).

Commissioned Catholic chaplains to the British Armed Forces, 1950–2020

As Britain's international political and military commitments have reduced since the end of the Second World War and as the nature of warfare has changed, the size of the nation's armed forces has been scaled down. This reduction in the armed forces is reflected in the decline in the number of Catholic military chaplains. Military campaigns involving the United Kingdom since 1945, however, have meant that Catholic chaplains have always been needed.

Table 2: Commissioned Catholic Chaplains to the British Armed Forces, 1950–2020

	1950	1973	1990	2003	2020
Royal Navy	15	14	12	11	5
Army	41	38	24	25	12

	1950	1973	1990	2003	2020
Royal Air Force	38	22	12	9	3
	94	74	48	45	20

Catholic chaplains: Command structure and Convergence

Changes to the command structure of military chaplaincy involve the government, the military and the churches, and economic, military and religious considerations are always major factors. After the Great War, it was recommended that all chaplains work under a Head of Chaplaincy Services, but in 1927 a committee appointed to review the establishment of the Royal Army Chaplains' Department reported that Catholic chaplains continued to be administered separately. In 1930, Bishop Keatinge agreed to a unified field command for army chaplains, but this was scrapped after the Dunkirk evacuation in 1940. In 1946, a Ministry of Defence committee recommended the amalgamation of all military chaplaincies in a unified department, but the recommendations were not brought to fruition. In 1945, the Senior Catholic army chaplains and Senior Catholic RAF chaplains were termed Principal Roman Catholic Chaplains and remained responsible for posting and deploying Catholic chaplains within military parameters. The Senior Catholic Chaplain to the Royal Navy became the Principal Roman Catholic Chaplain (Navy) in 1958.

Another attempt to merge chaplaincies in the 1960s failed, but since then modifications in command structures have affected the practice and delivery of chaplaincy in all three services. This "convergence" has meant a more ecumenical chaplaincy with which Royal Navy and RAF chaplains, but not army chaplains, are traditionally more familiar. It has also broken the traditional hold of higher ranks by Anglican chaplains. Senior posts are now open to chaplains of any denomination on merit.

Royal Navy chaplains remain under the authority of Chaplain of the Fleet for their professional duties but report to their Principal

Denominational Chaplain for ecclesiastical matters. The Chaplain of the Fleet manages all matters relating to chaplains and the Deputy-Chaplain of the Fleet (a post revived in 2011) is responsible for operational delivery, recruitment and training. Chaplains are appointed by the Deputy-Chaplain of the Fleet to ship and shore establishments and Royal Marine units. The career management of chaplains is undertaken on behalf of the Chaplain of the Fleet by an Executive Assistant and the denominational groupings (Anglican, Roman Catholic, Church of Scotland and Free Churches) are each headed by a Principal Denominational Chaplain appointed by their Sending Church or Group.

On active service, chaplains minister to all personnel and "the bish" is "friend and adviser to all". When Fr David Conroy was chaplain to HMS *Illustrious*, he was chaplain to 1,300 servicemen and servicewomen regardless of faith. In 2018, Fr Conroy was promoted to Principal Roman Catholic Chaplain (Navy) and in 2021 he became the first Catholic chaplain to be appointed Deputy-Chaplain of the Fleet with an input into all matters relating to policy, ecclesiastical issues, delivery and discipline.

In 2001, a Ministry of Defence review of army chaplaincy recommended that all denominational elements should converge into a single command structure, a model already followed by the Royal Navy and the RAF. In 2005, RAChD departmental structures and army chaplains now came under the command of the Chaplain-General and any chaplain, irrespective of denomination, was eligible for senior rank. Army chaplains now ministered in an "All Souls Ministry" and provided pastoral support to all unless there were specific denominational needs. As before, Catholic chaplains were not subject to any other ecclesiastical authority. Some Catholic chaplains claimed that Convergence took away their exclusive denominational identity and religious integrity. However, the army would have ceased to pay for Catholic chaplains if Catholic authorities had rejected Convergence. Dioceses and religious orders would not have had the resources to fund army chaplains.

Whereas Catholic chaplains had been formerly recruited, assigned and served as chaplains for Catholic personnel covering garrison-wide areas of responsibility, they henceforth became unit chaplains. With chaplains of other denominations, they now minister to all personnel and dependants (of any faith or none) in addition to providing for Catholic servicemen and servicewomen and their families. Catholic chaplains may now be called upon to serve as Senior Chaplains with responsibility for chaplains of other denominations and in turn Catholic padres may serve under the leadership of other denominational chaplains. Catholic service personnel may also turn for spiritual counselling, and in others matters where they feel comfortable, to non-Catholic padres. As one Catholic chaplain wrote: "While denomination has not disappeared it has been placed in a modern and practical perspective, unity in diversity."

Since Convergence, Catholic army chaplains have experienced unit chaplaincy, and shared training, exercises and deployments, allowing for stronger bonds of trust and camaraderie. At many levels this has made for a more satisfying experience of ministry with Catholic chaplains reaching across the denominations and attaining higher ranks. In 2013, Fr Ian Evans became Corps Colonel of the Royal Army Chaplains' Department, a new designation introduced by the Chaplain-General. As Assistant Chaplain-General, Fr Evans attended the monthly Army Corps Colonels' Forum at Army HQ and was the first chaplain of any denomination to hold that post. A Catholic padre now contributed directly to policymaking.

Another significant change in Catholic army chaplaincy came in 2018 when Fr Michael Fava became the first Catholic padre to hold the post of Deputy Chaplain-General to Her Majesty's Land Forces. The Deputy Chaplain-General represents the Chaplain-General and the RAChD at ceremonial, religious and social events. His responsibilities also included liaison with Assistant Chaplain-Generals on personnel and promotion issues, including the selection of padres for advanced non-chaplain courses designed for success on operations and leadership in defence. The Deputy Chaplain-General attends a tri-service forum with Royal Navy and RAF Principal Chaplains which informs the Chiefs of Chaplaincy on tri-service matters of shared relevance.

Convergence has led to frustration among Catholic army padres now having to prioritize their ministry to Catholics. Small numbers of Catholic chaplains have meant that Catholic spiritual and pastoral cover has been patchy or lacking in some locations. There has been an effort to maintain a Catholic "footprint" to minimize the impact of fewer chaplains, but this becomes more challenging as numbers of chaplains are reduced in line with defence requirements and as it becomes harder to recruit Catholic priests to military chaplaincy.

In 1918, the RAF had four denominational Staff Chaplains with the rank of Group Captain and an Advisory Board to provide a link between the churches and the service. The RAF had no structures comparable with a regiment or a ship but had Commands, large training establishments and scattered stations at home and abroad. This has influenced the development and uniqueness of the service's chaplaincy.

The RAF Chaplains' Handbook (2008) made it clear that padres in Chaplaincy Teams should work closely with colleagues of denominations other than their own. However, the denominational integrity of an individual chaplain was not to be compromised and the Principal Catholic Chaplain had to ensure that this was the lived reality. As ever, for Catholic padres the challenge lay in balancing priorities; station duties to all versus Catholic duties to a small number of Catholics.

RAF padres remain under the authority of a Chaplain-in-Chief for professional duties but to their own Principal Denominational Chaplain for ecclesiastical matters. The Chaplain-in-Chief manages all matters relating to chaplains while the Deputy Chaplain-in-Chief (Personnel) is responsible for matters including postings in the United Kingdom and overseas. The career management of chaplains is also undertaken by the Deputy Chaplain-in-Chief (Personnel) and a non-chaplaincy senior officer. The major Christian groupings (Anglican, Roman Catholic, Church of Scotland and Free Churches) are each headed by a Principal Denominational Chaplain appointed by their Sending Church, or religious group, in consultation with the Chaplain-in-Chief. Principal Chaplains are responsible for specific denominational issues and ecclesiastical discipline. The recruitment of Catholic chaplains is achieved through collaboration between the Catholic Bishop of the Forces, the Deputy Chaplain-in-Chief (Personnel), the Principal Roman Catholic Chaplain and the Chaplaincy Recruiter chaplain. The Deputy Chaplain-in-Chief (Operations) is responsible for the training and deployment of chaplains on military operations and exercises overseas and also for padres who are training personnel on topics pertaining to the "Core Values and Ethics of War—the Moral Component of Fighting Power".

Like Royal Navy and army chaplains, RAF padres are central to their service community and are responsible for the pastoral and spiritual care of all personnel and their dependants, irrespective of religious belief or rank. When Deacon David Skillen became chaplain to the British Forces South Atlantic in 2015, he was the only deployed chaplain to 1,800 servicemen and servicewomen regardless of faith background. In 2014, signifying another major change in Catholic military chaplaincy, Padre Skillen became the first permanent deacon to be recruited and commissioned to full-time regular service in the British Armed Forces. In July 2019, he was appointed Principal Roman Catholic Chaplain (RAF).

In moving to Convergence, all three services retained a Principal Roman Catholic Chaplain to be the vital link between the Catholic Bishop of the Forces and each of the single service Heads of Chaplaincy. The Principal Catholic Chaplain is tasked with overseeing Catholic provision in their own service (RN, Army, RAF). This would include offering spiritual leadership by advising the single service Heads of Chaplaincy on denominational matters, supporting Catholic Chaplains in their own ministry in the services, enabling Catholic initiatives, being a strong advocate for ecumenical collaboration, and ensuring pastoral and sacramental care for Catholic service personnel and their dependants.

Each service has its own traditions, culture, ethos and mindset. These have inevitably influenced how Convergence was originally implemented, how it has developed and how it continues to be practised.

3 3

Catholic chaplains in the British Armed Forces: Entry, induction, training and assimilation

Since Commissioned Chaplains were introduced into the British army, methods of entry, induction, training and assimilation of clergy into all branches of the armed services have changed considerably.

The entry of priests into the military has changed from being the prerogative of the sponsoring religious authority to being the responsibility of the armed forces, and the recruitment of chaplains has become closely attuned to that of officer entry. The induction of padres into the armed forces and introductory and in-service training have become more professional and the increasingly technological nature of warfare has compelled chaplains to learn how to conduct their ministry in modern battle situations. Chaplains have become familiar with ministering across service boundaries as integrated structures of command have evolved. The dominance of Church of England clergy in service chaplaincy and the exclusivity of Catholic chaplains has also given way to more ecumenical approaches to chaplaincy. Christianity is no longer the dominant creed of the armed services and military chaplaincy is no longer a male preserve.

The methods employed by the Church to provide chaplains, the induction of priests and deacons into the military and their training and assimilation into the services have been influenced by military, religious and social factors. The development of a Catholic culture in the armed services has also been subject to secular and religious influences over which padres have little or no control but which impinge heavily on their ministry.

The chaplain's role has remained essentially the same but has developed. Priests and deacons have to be physically and mentally strong, be able to work unsupervised, comprehend and absorb the military culture, and display personal piety.

Royal Navy

Before and during the Second World War, Catholic naval chaplains were so few and so scattered in deployment that induction, training and assimilation were of lesser importance than the number of chaplains. Serving chaplains struggled to minister to the fleet, acquire places of worship, administer the sacraments and generate a Catholic atmosphere among sailors.

When Fr Francis Walmsley joined the Royal Navy in 1960, he was one of 14 Catholic naval chaplains. His method of entry was typical of the time. He was informed by his diocesan bishop that he had been selected for naval chaplaincy, was interviewed by the Principal Chaplain, had a medical and was welcomed by Fr Tom McDonagh, an Irish priest of the Diocese of Leeds, at the Royal Naval Barracks, Portsmouth. He then embarked on a two-week Officer Acquaintance Course, learning about service traditions, drill and the meaning of naval terms. Fr McDonagh, a veteran chaplain, told him of the navy's expectations of chaplains and stressed the need to get to know the men and engage with chaplains of other denominations. As Fr Walmsley recalled: "I now found myself living cheek by jowl with my non-Catholic brethren, and this was literally true on board ships."

Fr Simon Bradbury's entry and induction into the Royal Navy Chaplaincy Service was very different. In 1996, Fr Bradbury of the Diocese of Leeds participated with other Catholic and Anglican priests in one of the first Admiralty Interview Boards (AIB) for chaplains. Formerly, chaplains had been commissioned with the approval of the Principal Chaplain, but now potential chaplains had to undergo an AIB like other candidates wishing to enter the Royal Navy as an officer. The AIB consisted of interviews, exams, discussions and team exercises, with assessors watching for evidence of leadership qualities.

A Short Introductory Course (SIC) for chaplains, doctors, dentists and nurses was held at Britannia Royal Naval College. Applicants wore no badge of rank and were treated like other cadets, enduring aptitude tests, physical exercises and cabin inspections. An Assessed Command Exercise followed on Dartmoor, where cadets were tested for stamina and leadership skills. Sleep deprivation was normal, and applicants stumbled over moorlands at all hours carrying bergens and with ration packs for sustenance. Challenging exercises took place involving rivers, gulleys, cliff edges and abandoned tin mines. After passing out at Dartmouth, chaplains went on a listening skills course, a divisional officer's course, the helicopter dunker at Royal Naval Air Service, Yeovilton, and two weeks initial sea training involving survival and firefighting. Endurance exercises and psychological, social and leadership challenges prepared new chaplains for military service. They also prepared them to be full members of a ship's company, ready to be of use and able to help others in battle.

Chaplains were trained and competent but, as Fr Bradbury commented, little of the training related to his priestly vocation. His first appointment was to a squadron of minesweepers, fishery protection vessels and minor war vessels. In later years, chaplains underwent Initial Sea Training and shadowed an experienced chaplain in a warship for several weeks.

In 2021, Fr Philip Carroll, ordained in 2015 in the Diocese of Portsmouth, experienced a different form of entry into the Royal Navy. After completing the officer entry course at Dartmouth, he was sent to the Royal Marines at Lympstone, where he worked alongside two other chaplains and ministered to trained ranks and new recruits, visiting them in the field, helping them to adjust to Marine life and offering weekly Sunday worship. In May 2021, Fr Carroll was chosen to undertake the Commando Course, a unique privilege for a chaplain, being the only example of someone over the maximum age of entry (32 years) entering into mainstream training. It is considered the longest and hardest initial military training in the world.

The course was fast-paced, relentless and gruelling but, despite its challenges, training gave the chaplain an opportunity to get to know the recruits and understand what they were experiencing. This enabled him to establish trust and enter into conversations about faith and, recruits, initially perplexed by an "old" chaplain being with them, began to talk about his role. In revealing that a padre was there to pray for them and with them, there was interest, but when asked if they would like a blessing, there was reluctance. However, when beginning and ending the final Commando Tests and Endurance course, recruits came for a blessing! Fr Carroll passed and became the proud owner of a Green Beret. The "green lid" would be of great advantage, presenting huge opportunities for evangelization. In a predominantly secular institution, the role of the chaplain was still held in high esteem.

Army

Victorian army chaplains received no induction or training save an introduction to a regiment and its Catholic officers, soldiers and their families. On campaign, chaplains experienced the same conditions as the men. In the Crimea, the Egyptian campaigns and the Boer War, chaplains conducted their ministry usually without military hindrance but frequently with help and admiration.

During the Great War, the number of volunteer chaplains from Christian denominations grew exponentially, but they received little induction beyond a perfunctory introduction to the service and an outline of the chaplain's role. As the Revd Fraser McCluskey wrote, "In the first great war Army chaplains were left to sink or swim, and 3,475 chaplains received no preliminary training for their new job." Such was the shortage of chaplains on the Western Front that the War Office had no option but to immediately deploy inexperienced priests.

Senior Catholic chaplains were aware that new chaplains, unclear about their role, were called upon to minister in difficult and unforeseen circumstances while maintaining their own spiritual discipline and supporting the faith and morale of others. Devoid of regular contact with other clergy, many chaplains experienced loneliness, suffered the same privations as the men and witnessed varying degrees of personal faith, outstanding courage and much carnage. Their vocation was fulfilled in a dangerous milieu, in unexpected ways and with little direction. Fr

Michael Mullins wrote: "There was no public policy, no one to train us, no one to lead. Each had to learn his own work by the experiences of his own failures." Mgr Francis Bickerstaffe-Drew, a Chaplain, 1st Class with experience of the Western Front, alerted Cardinal Bourne and the War Office to the need for training chaplains. His offer to brief new chaplains in military discipline, manning levels and deployments was turned down as he was needed in France.

Training, however, was introduced and after 1916 chaplains in France and Flanders received instruction in military matters. Chaplains without previous military experience attended training courses at Tidworth and Catterick with the syllabus including the chaplain's work, medical advice, topography, anti-gas, cooking, riding and cycling.

In the Second World War, all new chaplains, except Catholics, attended the Chaplains' Training Centre at Tidworth on Salisbury Plain. But for specialist training, such as parachute padres, chaplains trained at the Depot and School Airborne Forces, Harwick Hall Camp, Chesterfield. They functioned as padres only on the church parade and "the Padre's Hour", but it was noted by Fraser McCluskey that some of the men were "impatient with narrow denominationalism". When forces were massing for D-Day, padres trained with the units they were to accompany. The Second Army's Chaplains Battle School at Stowe included training in camouflage, care of wounded, direction finding and building up stamina.

Chaplains had to immerse themselves in army life but not to the detriment of their priesthood. In 1942, Fr Michael Pelly SJ attended days of recollection in York, and Fr Tyndal-Atkinson OP, Senior Chaplain in Scotland, inducted new chaplains and provided retreat facilities. Fr Conal Murphy SJ was able to make a personal retreat at the Redemptorist Monastery, Kinnoull, but in the Middle East his spiritual life became enmeshed with military responsibilities. He found himself Divisional Chaplain and "the authority for all matters of RC administration". In 1940, Mgr Coghlan issued a *Memorandum for Catholic Army Chaplains and Officiating Chaplains to the Forces* and in 1942 he introduced a revised and enlarged version "to help Chaplains in the discharge of their onerous responsibilities and duties". Chaplaincy, he wrote, "was a field for real apostolic work", and the *Memorandum* contained information and advice of benefit to chaplains including reference to their responsibilities to the troops, the need for personal spiritual renewal, and acquiring senior rank and administrative duties. It encouraged co-operation with chaplains of other denominations "based on goodwill and mutual respect".

From 1946, the RAChD's Headquarters, Depot and Training Centre were at Bagshot Park, Surrey, and later at Netheravon House, Wiltshire. In 1996, the Armed Forces' Chaplaincy Centre moved to Amport House near Andover, the former RAF Chaplains' School. Since 2020, the Tri-Service Chaplaincy Centre, part of the Defence Academy of the United Kingdom, has been based at Shrivenham, and chaplains of all services attend courses offered at national and international locations. Entry and training are based on officer entry courses at the Royal Military Academy, Sandhurst, and a chaplaincy-focussed course at the Tri-Service Chaplaincy Centre. New and experienced padres are expected to respond to the intellectual, spiritual and physical demands of their role, and intake and refresher courses help to strengthen a clear sense of purpose, identity and direction of chaplaincy.

Since 2004, aspiring candidates have to pass an AOSB (Army Officer Selection Board) comprising intensive interviews, academic assessments, personality profiling, leadership and fitness tests. Several weeks at the Armed Forces' Chaplaincy Training Centre focus on understanding the construct of the army and the chaplain's role within it. A formal Service of Commissioning—and the Oath of Allegiance—conclude the course and chaplains then report to their unit of first assignment. They then embark on the Professionally Qualified Officer Training Course at the RMA Sandhurst, a twelve-week course ending with the traditional Passing Out Parade on Old College Square officially marking chaplains as graduates of the RMA Sandhurst, together with all those who carry the sovereign's commission.

Since the late 1990s, more testing academic training has evolved, designed to broaden chaplains' skillsets and identify chaplains for longer-term managerial roles in the RAChD. These advanced courses, in some cases degree bearing, have also been augmented by an increasing number of developmental courses for all chaplains at various stages of their rank and seniority progression. Army chaplaincy has become more professional, largely driven by the increased operational tempo of the army's duties during this period. The RAChD has had to maintain its validity and credibility in an increasingly testing military culture.

Royal Air Force

After its formation in 1918, the Royal Air Force developed its own chaplaincy service. Naval chaplains served on board ships and army chaplains ministered to regiments, but RAF chaplains worked on stations where personnel lived, worked, socialized and worshipped. Some RAF stations had over 15,000 personnel. A major feature of the RAF was that not all personnel, including chaplains, took part in flying operations.

The RAF stipulated that training in peace must be carried out in accordance with the policy adopted for war. The *War Manual* of 1939 included instructions for RAF officers including chaplains. Deployment of chaplains was the responsibility of the Principal Chaplain, and chaplains were to care for the spiritual and moral welfare of all personnel in the field, to attend the wounded and the dead, and liaise with the graves commission and medical services.

In 1940, Mgr Henry Beauchamp, RAF Catholic Staff Chaplain, issued Catholic chaplains with *Catholic Commissioned and Officiating Chaplains, RAF, Guide*, which included everything they should know about their role. He was especially anxious that although chaplains should be proud of the RAF and integrate themselves in the service community, their sacerdotal duties were paramount.

Alongside RAF officers and other padres, Catholic chaplains drilled, acquainted themselves with *King's Regulations* and were instructed in Catholic matters by the resident Catholic padre. Once this was completed and the chaplain had received the black bag with Mass kit, he was posted to a station. There, at home and abroad, he would have to contend with religious, administrative and logistical challenges. Like chaplains in other services, the RAF chaplain met spiritual, personal and physical challenges he had not foreseen when he was a seminarian, or in a parish or monastery.

Gradually, methods of entry have been modified. Potential RAF chaplains now go through a rigorous recruitment process that begins by examining issues of vocation before attending the Officer and Air Crew Selection Centre at RAF Cranwell, which tests physical, intellectual and temperamental suitability for RAF service. Successful applicants attend a thirteen-week military training course followed by specialist chaplaincy training.

Throughout their ministry to the RAF, chaplains follow a programme of training and personal development with opportunities for further study. The RAF is committed to the training and education of the service community through its Beliefs and Values Programme, which is integral to the whole training system and is part of understanding the Moral Component of Air Power. Chaplains are also regularly involved in offering courses on RAF stations, including Listening Skills, Bereavement and Loss, and Christian Basics.

Catholic communities in the Forces

Apart from the Jesuit *missio castrensis*, prohibitions on the practice of their religion and the transient nature of their calling prevented Catholics in the military from developing stable faith communities. Before the late nineteenth century, it was not easy for Catholics in the British military to develop a sense of religious community, but commissioned army chaplains eventually provided liturgical facilities, encouraged religious rites of passage, inspired evangelization and fostered and supported the emergence of a Catholic identity. Chaplains established schools, sodalities and societies and helped to create and sustain the development of a Catholic culture. The establishment of prayer groups, reading clubs, study groups, pilgrimages, family events and social facilities at various periods in history and in different locations contributed to the confident assimilation of Catholic service personnel and their chaplains into the military.

For the Catholic military stationed in the British Isles during the early and mid-nineteenth century, the proximity of other Catholic communities was an obvious link with their co-religionists, but civil–military relations were not always harmonious. Before the building of garrison chapels, soldiers attended urban chapels and their presence often caused difficulties. In 1859, army chaplain Fr James Carey appealed to the War Office for funds to pay for extra labour for "mopping and cleaning" the church at Portsea after military services. In 1860, Bishop Grant was informed by Archbishop Cullen of Dublin that soldiers from nine different barracks were using civilian chapels. At home and abroad, and in later periods, dedicated places of worship for the military were always scarce. Churches were built at the Aldershot camps in 1855 for ecumenical use, and in 1910 for Catholic use, but the provision of chapels was a problem during the First World War. In the 1930s, army chaplain Fr Francis Carless built and furnished a chapel in Singapore, and in the 1970s Fr Francis Walmsley used a Second World War Nissen hut as his chapel in HMS *Haslar*.

In wartime, contemporary Catholic newspapers printed appeals for magazines, Bibles, books, rosaries and scapulas for the military. Catholic charities provided clubs for the Royal Navy before and during the Great War and the Catholic Women's League (CWL) provided recreational facilities on the Western Front. In the Second World War, the CWL arranged for social facilities, reading matter and devotional objects while the Catholic Libraries for H.M. Forces, founded in 1939, supplied books to the services, merchant marines and prisoners of war. The CWL still supports the modern military through grants to veterans and to serving Catholics, while the Catholic Truth Society and Apostleship of the Sea have long traditions of providing prayer books, devotional objects and social facilities for serving Catholics.

Catholic societies were formed within the military to strengthen the faith of all ranks, protect Catholic interests, establish a Catholic social life and develop a religious identity. The Catholic Soldiers' Association (CSA), established in 1902, was based on the Confraternity founded by former padre Bishop John Butt of Southwark in 1887. The CSA was strong in the late nineteenth and first half of the twentieth century, and garrison churches built with its financial support are testimony to the memory of its members killed in battle. The United Services' Catholic Association (USCA), formed in 1939, replaced the CSA and included all Catholics in the forces, sponsoring handbooks for chaplains and combatants in wartime. In 1941, it funded *A Catholic Prayer Book for the Use of Catholics Serving in the Royal Air Force in the Time of War* and petitioned the hierarchies for more chaplains and spiritual facilities for the army and RAF.

The Catholic Military Association (CMA), established in 2018, has episcopal approval and officially represents Catholics in the British military at the *Apostolat Militaire International* (*AMI*). The CMA offers young recruits pastoral and prayerful support during long and often difficult training periods, and encouragement and understanding as their service careers and personal lives develop. It recognizes the challenges that Catholics face in the military, offers support on deployment, exercises and operations, and understands the dangers faced by all in arduous environments and in stressful combat conditions.

The *AMI* is a lay organization, endorsed by the Vatican. Its purposes, based on its Non-Governmental Organization status, are to promote at the national and international levels the affirmation of a Christian vision of military life and of the values that characterize this vision, to promote and support international understanding and co-operation, as a contribution to strengthening peace, and to study, in the light of the gospel and the teachings of the Church, the spiritual, moral and social problems peculiar to the military sphere.

Over the years, Catholic military and religious magazines have helped padres and service personnel maintain contact with their clerical brethren and with each other. The *Catholic Forces News* is the latest of a long line of publications that includes the *Forces Catholic Gazette* and the RAF's *Flarepath*. Religious orders kept contact with their chaplains, especially in wartime, through regular editions of their in-house magazines. The Roman Catholic Bishopric of the Forces now provides diocesan news, items of tri-service interest and links with other dioceses and Catholic communities via electronic means.

The role of the chaplain has always been, and continues to be, paramount in developing the faith of Catholics in the military. Animating, encouraging and strengthening the faith through pastoral advisory groups, prayer and rosary meetings, reading clubs, retreats and pilgrimages, schools and social facilities are critical for the development of the faith in difficult circumstances. In the Second World War, prisoners of war benefitted from chaplains who acted as community leaders in appalling conditions. Those with the British liberation forces in war-torn

Europe had the opportunity to make retreats and make sense of their experiences. The RAF Sword of the Spirit movement driven forward by Mgr Beauchamp in the Second World War was instrumental in developing a strong and thoughtful Christianity and applying its principles through the Moral Leadership Course.

Until recently, Catholics in the armed services were noticeably separate from non-Catholics in the practice of their religion, but ecumenical developments since the Second Vatican Council and developments in military command structures have moved major Christian denominations in the military closer to each other in many external manifestations of their beliefs.

APPENDIX I

Commissioned Catholic chaplains
in the British army, March 1859

Numbers 1 to 15 were all commissioned 4th Class in 1859.

1. Fr John Francis Browne   Seniority date: 1 April 1859. 3rd
    Class 15 September 1857; 2nd Class 15 September
    1872. India (1859), Gosport (1860), Aldershot (1869,
    1875), Egypt (1887). Diocese of Salford, then Diocese of
    Portsmouth priest.

2. Fr Edward Butler   Seniority date: 1 April 1859. 3rd Class 1
    April 1869; 2nd Class 1 April 1874. Nova Scotia (1860),
    Devonport (1875).

3. Fr James Carey   Seniority date: 1 April 1859. Portsmouth
    (1860). Archdiocese of Westminster priest.

4. Fr Thomas Lloyd Coghlan   Seniority date: 1 April 1859. 3rd
    Class 1 April 1869; 2nd Class 1 April 1874; 1st Class 1
    April 1879. Plymouth (1860), Netley (1874), Shorncliffe
    (1880). Diocese of Plymouth priest.

5. Fr Michael Cuffe   Seniority date: 1 April 1859. 3rd Class 7
    September 1868; 2nd Class 7 September 1873. Crimea
    (1855–56), India (1859), Dublin (1859), Chatham
    (1869). Retired 1884. Irish-born Diocese of Portsmouth
    priest.

6. Fr James Hamilton   Seniority date: 1 April 1859. 3rd Class 1
    April 1868. Curragh Camp (1859), Woolwich, Bermuda,
    Aldershot (1869). Originally a Diocese of Kildare and
    Leighlin priest, later a Diocese of Southwark priest.

7. Fr Michael Hogan   Seniority date: 1 April 1859. Dover (1859). Diocese of Southwark priest.

8. Fr Thomas Molony   Seniority date: 1 April 1859. 3rd Class 7 September 1868; 2nd Class 7 September 1873. Crimea (1855–56), India (1859), Portsmouth (1860), Curragh Camp (1864). Retired 1879. Irish-born priest.

9. Fr William Morley   Seniority date: 1 April 1859. Chatham (1859). Diocese of Southwark priest.

10. Fr Charles Morgan   Seniority date: 1 April 1859. Woolwich (1860). Not affiliated to a diocese.

11. Fr Joseph O'Dwyer   Seniority date: 1 April 1859. Crimea (1854–55), India (1859), Aldershot (1869). Irish-born Diocese of Plymouth priest.

12. Fr John O'Flaherty   Seniority date: 1 April 1859. 3rd Class 1 April 1869; 2nd Class 1 April 1874; 1st Class 1 April 1879. Gibraltar (1860), Aldershot (1869, 1875), Chatham (1880).

13. Fr Joseph McSweeney Seniority date: 1 April 1859. 3rd Class 1 April 1859. Crimea (1855), Shorncliffe (1859), New Zealand. Archdiocese of Westminster priest.

14. Fr Robert Shepherd   Seniority date: 1 April 1859. 3rd Class 1 April 1869. Colchester (1860). Transferred to Reserve 23 April 1871. Archdiocese of Westminster priest.

15. Fr R. Blake   Seniority date: 1 April 1859. Cork (1860).

The following chaplains were also appointed with commission/seniority apparently ante-dated.

They were not included on the War Office list transmitted to Bishop Grant on 25 March 1859.

1. Fr Laurence Parsley   Seniority date: 1 April 1847. 3rd Class 1 April 1861; 2nd Class 1 April 1862; 1st Class 1 April 1867. Royal Military Hospital, Phoenix Park, Dublin (1846), New Zealand (1866), Plymouth (1868). Archdiocese of Dublin priest.

2. Mgr John Vertue   Seniority date: 24 June 1855. 3rd Class
18 May 1865; 2nd Class 2 February 1870; 1st Class
2 February 1875. Crimea (1855), Chatham (1855),
Aldershot (1856), Bermuda (1861), Colchester (1869),
Portsmouth (1875), Malta (1880). Bishop of Portsmouth,
1882. Diocese of Southwark priest.

3. Fr Thomas Unsworth   Seniority date: 10 July 1855. Crimea
(1855–56), Portsmouth (1859). Retired 14 November
1863. Diocese of Salford priest.

4. Fr Joseph J. Mahé   Seniority date: 19 September 1855. 3rd
Class 5 December 1861. Crimea (1855–56), Hong Kong
(1859), Shorncliffe (1860). Retired 4 February 1866.
Archdiocese of Westminster priest.

APPENDIX 2

Catholic Chaplains to the British Armed Forces: Ecclesiastical authority and control

1851–70 Thomas Grant, Bishop of Southwark: Army and Royal Navy chaplains

1871–81 James Danell, Bishop of Southwark: Army and Royal Navy chaplains

1882–85 Robert Coffin CSSR, Bishop of Southwark: Army chaplains

1882–1900 John Vertue, Bishop of Portsmouth: Royal Navy chaplains

1885–97 John Butt, Bishop of Southwark: Army chaplains

1897–1903 Francis Bourne, Bishop of Southwark: Army and (from 1900) Royal Navy chaplains

1903–17 Francis Bourne, Archbishop of Westminster: Army and Royal Navy chaplains

1917–35 Francis Bourne, Archbishop of Westminster: Royal Navy chaplains

1917–34 William Keatinge, Bishop of Metellopolis: Military Bishopric, Army, RFC, RAF chaplains

1935–46 James Dey, Bishop of Sebastopolis: Military Bishopric, Army and RAF chaplains

1935–43 Arthur Hinsley, Archbishop of Westminster: Royal Navy chaplains

1943–46 Bernard Griffin, Archbishop of Westminster: Royal Navy chaplains

1946–53 Mgr John Clarke OBE: Apostolic Administrator of the Forces

1953–54	Mgr Patrick O'Connell CBE CSA: RAF, Apostolic Administrator of the Forces
1954–63	David Mathew, Archbishop of Apamea: Bishop of the Forces, Military Vicariate
1963–78	Gerard Tickle, Bishop of Bela: Bishop of the Forces, Military Vicariate
1979–2002	Francis Walmsley CBE, Bishop of Tamalluma: Bishop of the Forces, Military Vicariate, Military Ordinariate (1986)
2002–08	Thomas Burns SM: Bishop of the Forces, Military Ordinariate
2008–15	Richard Moth: Bishop of the Forces, Military Ordinariate
2015–18	Michael Fava CBE: Apostolic Administrator of the Forces
2018–	Paul Mason: Bishop of the Forces, Military Ordinariate

Select Bibliography

Books

Anson, P. F., *The Church and the Sailor* (London: John Gifford Ltd, 1948).

Anstruther, G., *The Seminary Priests, Volume II: Early Stuarts 1603–1659* (Great Wakering: Mayhew-McCrimmon, 1975).

Anstruther, G., *The Seminary Priests, Volume III: 1660–1715* (Great Wakering: Mayhew-McCrimmon, 1976).

Arthur, M. *Above All Courage: Personal Stories from the Falklands War* (London: Cassell Military Paperback, 2002).

Barnett, C., *Britain and Her Army* (London: Allen Lane, 1970).

Bartlett, T. and Jeffery, K. (eds), *A Military History of Ireland* (Cambridge: Cambridge University Press, 1996).

Bergen, D. L. (ed.), *The Sword of the Lord: Military Chaplains from the First to the Twenty-First Century* (Notre Dame, IN: University of Notre Dame Press, 2004).

Betts, J., *Blessed Peter Wright SJ (1603–1651): His Life and Times—The Last Northamptonshire Martyr* (Leeds: Beckett Press, 1998).

Billings, A., *The Dove, the Fig Leaf and the Sword: Why Christianity Changes its Mind about War* (London: SPCK, 2014).

Bishop, P., *Air Force Blue: The RAF in World War Two* (London: William Collins, 2017).

Caraman, H., *Henry Morse: Priest of the Plague* (London: Longmans, Green & Co., 1957).

Catholic Commissioned and Officiating Chaplains, R.A.F. Guide (London: United Services Catholic Association: Air Ministry, 1942).

Challoner, R., *Memoirs of Missionary Priests* (London: Burns Oates & Washbourne, 1924).

Clifford, H., *Henry Clifford VC: His Letters and Sketches from the Crimea* (London: Michael Joseph, 1956).

Clifton, M., *The Quiet Negotiator: Bishop Grant, Bishop of Southwark* (Liverpool: Sandfield Press, 1990).

Cormack, A. (ed.), *A Long, Long Trail A-Winding: Centenary Perspectives on the Great War* (London: The Society for Army Historical Research, 2018).

Corrigan, G., *Mud, Blood and Poppycock* (London: Cassell, 2003).

Dannatt, R., *Boots on the Ground: Britain and Her Army Since 1945* (London: Profile Books, 2016).

Dempsey, M. (ed.), *The Priest among the Soldiers* (London: Burns & Oates, 1947).

Dow, A. C., *Ministers to the Soldiers of Scotland: A History of the Military Chaplains of Scotland prior to the War in the Crimea* (Edinburgh: Oliver & Boyd, 1962).

Dungan, M., *They Shall Grow Not Old: Irish Soldiers and the Great War* (Dublin: Four Courts Press, 1997).

Ede-Borrett, S., *The Army of James II, 1685–1688: The Birth of the British Army* (Solihull: Helion & Co., 2017).

Edgerton, R. B., *Death or Glory: The Legacy of the Crimean War* (Boulder, CO: Westview Press, 1999).

Foley, H., *Records of the English Province of the Society of Jesus: Historical facts illustrative of the labours and sufferings of its members in the sixteenth and seventeenth centuries* (eight volumes) (London: Burns & Oates, 1875–83).

Foster, S., *The Deceased Clergy of the Diocese of Brentwood: Biographical Summaries* (Brentwood: Brentwood Diocesan Archives, 2013).

Gale, H. P., *Uganda and the Mill Hill Fathers* (London: Macmillan & Co. Ltd., 1959).

Gooch, J. (ed.), *The Boer War: Direction, Experience and Image* (London: Frank Cass, 2001).

Hagerty, J. and Parsons, S., *Monks in the Military: Benedictine Chaplains in the British Armed Forces during the Twentieth Century* (Stratton-on-the-Fosse: Downside Abbey Press, 2017).

Hagerty, J., *Priests in Uniform: Catholic Chaplains to the British Forces in the First World War* (Leominster: Gracewing, 2017).

Hagerty, J., *No Ordinary Shepherds: Catholic Chaplains to the British Forces in the Second World War* (Leominster: Gracewing, 2020).

Harvey, D., *A Bloody Dawn: The Irish at D-Day* (Newbridge: Merrion Press, 2019).

Hastings, M., *The Korean War* (London: Pan Books, 1987).

Heenan, J. C., *A Crown of Thorns: An Autobiography 1951–1963* (London: Hodder & Stoughton, 1974).

Henry, G., *The Irish Military Community in Spanish Flanders, 1586–1621* (Dublin: Irish Academic Press, 1992).

Hird, N., *Our Fathers in Faith*, four volumes (Leeds: Diocese of Leeds, 2008 and 2019).

Holland, T., *For Better and for Worse: Memoirs of Bishop Thomas Holland* (Salford: Salford Diocesan Catholic Children's Rescue Society, 1989).

Holmes, R., *Sahib: The British Soldier in India* (London: HarperCollins, 2005).

Howson, P., *Muddling Through: The Organisation of British Army Chaplaincy in World War One* (Solihull: Helion & Company Limited, 2013).

Jackson, A., *Distant Drums: The Role of the Colonies in British Imperial Warfare* (Eastbourne: Sussex Academic Press, 2010).

James, W. M., *The Royal Navy Officer's Jutland Pocket Manual 1916* (London: The Pool of London Press, 2016).

Johnstone, T. and Hagerty, J., *The Cross on the Sword: Catholic Chaplains in the Forces* (London: Geoffrey Chapman, 1996).

Keegan, J., *The Face of Battle* (London: Jonathan Cape, 1976).

Knight, I., *Go to your God like a Soldier: The British Soldier Fighting for Empire, 1837–1902* (London: Greenhill Books, 1996).

Laurence, A., *Parliamentary Army Chaplains, 1642–1651* (Woodbridge: Boydell Press, 1990).

Louden, S. H., *Chaplains in Conflict: The Role of Army Chaplains since 1914* (London: Avon Books, 1996).

MacDonnell, J. A., *A Sketch of the Life of the Honourable and Right Reverend Alexander MacDonell* (Alexandria: The Glengarrian Press, 1890).

Mallinson, A., *The Making of the British Army from the English Civil War to the War on Terror* (London: Bantam Press, 2009).

Miller, R. W. H., *One Firm Anchor: The Church and the Merchant Seafarer* (Cambridge: The Lutterworth Press, 2012).

Paice, E., *Tip & Run: The Untold Story of the Great War in Africa* (London: Weidenfeld & Nicolson, 2007).

Plumb, B., *Arundel to Zabi, A Biographical Dictionary of the Catholic Bishops of England and Wales 1623–1987* (Warrington: Harwyn, 1987).

Plumb, B., *"Found Worthy": A Biographical Dictionary of the Secular Clergy of the Archdiocese of Liverpool (Deceased), 1850–2000* (Wigan: North West Catholic History Society, 2005).

Pollock, P. H., *Wings on the Cross: A Padre with the RAF* (Dublin: Clonmore and Reynolds Ltd., 1954).

Purcell, L. A., *Chaplaincy in the British Army: A Personal Guide* (Whittlesey: Edgehill Enterprises, 2020).

Rasor, E. L., *Reform in the Royal Navy: A Social History of the Lower Deck 1850–1880* (Hampden, CT: Archon, 1975).

Reynolds, A., *To War without Arms: The D-Day Diary of an Army Chaplain* (Devizes: Sabrestorm Publishing, 2019).

Reynolds, C., *Redemptorist Forces Chaplains: The Redeemer Abroad* (Amazon Kindle Direct Publishing, 2019).

Riding, J., *Jacobites: A New History of the '45 Rebellion* (London: Bloomsbury, 2015).

Royle, T., *Crimea: The Great Crimean War 1854–1856* (London: Abacus, 2000).

Smyth, J., *In This Sign Conquer: The Story of the Army Chaplains* (London: A. R. Mowbray & Co. Ltd., 1968).

Snape, M., *The Redcoat and Religion: The Forgotten History of the British Soldier from the Age of Marlborough to the Eve of the First World War* (London: Routledge, 2005).

Snape, M., *The Royal Army Chaplains' Department: Clergy Under Fire* (Woodbridge: The Boydell Press, 2008).

Snape, M. and Madigan, E. (eds), *The Clergy in Khaki: New Perspectives on British Army Chaplaincy in the First World War* (Abingdon: Routledge, 2013).

Steel, N. and Hart, P., *Jutland: Death in the Grey Wastes* (London: Cassell, 2003).

Stewart, R., *Broken Lives* (London: HarperCollins, 1993).

Strachan, A., *Precious Blood Remembered—St Joan of Arc Catholic Memorial Church, Catterick Garrison, 1929–2019* (Catterick: Privately printed, 2019).

Stradling, R. A., *The Spanish Monarchy and Irish Mercenaries: The Wild Geese in Spain, 1618–1648* (Dublin: Irish Academic Press, 1994).

Taylor, G., *The Sea Chaplains: A History of the Chaplains of The Royal Navy* (Oxford: Oxford Illustrated Press, 1978).

The Catholic Encyclopedia (New York: The Encyclopedia Press, 1908).

Toomey, K., *Alexander Macdonell: The Scottish Years, 1762–1804* (Toronto: Canadian Catholic Historical Association, 1985).

Walmsley, F. J., *From Sea to See: The Extraordinary Voyage of a Very Ordinary Priest*, three volumes (Guilford: The Wonersh Press, 2014).

Watkins, O. S., *With Kitchener's Army* (London: S. W. Partridge, 1899).

Watson, G. and Rinaldi, R. A., *The British Army in Germany—BAOR and after: An Organizational History, 1947–2004* (Milton Keynes: Tiger Lily Publications, 2005).

Articles

Griffin, M., "The Foundation of the Chaplaincy Corps", *Journal of the Society for Army Historical Research* 80 (2002), pp. 287–95.

Hombres, R., "The Pastoral Care of the Armed Forces in Canon Law", *Priests and People* 6:2 (July/August 1988).

Lunn, M., "Chaplains to the English Regiment in Spanish Flanders 1605–1606", *Recusant History* 11:3 (October 1971), pp. 133–55.

Mulvihill, M., "'Peculiar Circumstances': Catholic Chaplains of the Victorian British Army in India", *The Electronic British Library Journal*, 2008.

Seligmann, M. S, "'Mass Anywhere on Sea or Land': Catholicism and the Royal Navy, 1901–1906", *War in History* 29:4 (2022), pp. 763–81.

Snape, M. and Henshaw, V., "From Flanders to Helmand: Chaplaincy, Faith and Religious Change in the British Army, 1914–2014", *Journal of Beliefs and Values* 38:2 (2017), p. 199–214.

Wynne, T., "The Conversion of Alexander Cameron", *The Innes Review* 45:2 (Autumn 1994), pp. 178–87.

Newspapers, magazines and journals

Forces Catholic News
Priests and People
Royal Air Force Chaplains' Branch: Annual Review
Royal Army Chaplains' Department Journal
The Catholic Herald
The Roman Catholic Church in Today's RAF
The Tablet
The Times
The Universe
The Ushaw Magazine

Memoirs

Fr George Forbes OSB, "War Diary" (Ampleforth Abbey archives).

Fr Gervase Hobson-Mathews OSB, "War Diary" (Downside Abbey archives).

Fr Thomas Hourigan, "The Odyssey of a Chaplain in the RAF" (*St Kieran's College Record*).

Mgr Phelim Rowland, "Military Career" (in private possession).

Fr Denys Rutledge OSB, "War Diary of an Unknown Army Chaplain" (Ampleforth Abbey archives).

Fr Herbert Welchman, "War Diary" and "Welchman Papers" (Archives of the Military Ordinariate).

Index